CUBA

Marxist Regimes Series

Series editor: Bogdan Szajkowski,
Department of Sociology, University College,
Cardiff

Further Titles

CUBA

Politics, Economics and Society

Max Azicri

With the editorial assistance of
Elsie Deal

 Pinter Publishers
London and New York

© Max Azicri, 1988

First published in Great Britain in 1988 by
Pinter Publishers Limited
25 Floral Street, London WC2E 9DS

British Library Cataloguing in Publication Data
A CIP catalogue record for this book is available from the British Library

Library of Congress Cataloging-in-Publication Data
Azicri, Max.
    Cuba: politics, economics, and society/Max Azicri: with the
editorial assistance of Elsie Deal.
    p.   cm.—(Marxist regimes)
    Bibliography: p.
    Includes index.
    ISBN 0-86187-407-2: $12.50.   ISBN 0-86187-406-4: $35.00
    1. Cuba—Politics and government—1959-   2. Cuba—Constitutional
history. 3. Communism—Cuba—History. 4. Cuba—Economic
conditions—1959-   5. Cuba—Social conditions—1959-   I. Title.
II. Series: Marxist regimes series.
JL1002   1988
972.91′064—dc 19   87-29149
                                                              CIP

Typeset by Joshua Associates Limited, Oxford
Printed in Great Britain by SRP Ltd, Exeter

Editor's Preface

This timely, comprehensive and penetrating study of Cuba's politics, economics and society provides the reader with an in-depth analysis of the background to, current state of and prospects for success of the country's economic, social and political life. In 1959 Cuba had a revolution without Soviet help, a revolution which subsequently became to many political elites in the Third World not only an inspiration but a clear military, political and ideological example to follow. Apart from its romantic appeal, to many nationalist movements the Cuban revolution also demonstrated a novel way of conducting and winning a nationalist, anti-imperialist war and accepting Marxism as the state ideology without a vanguard communist party. The Cuban precedent was subsequently followed in one respect or another by scores of Third World regimes, which used the adoption of 'scientific socialism' tied to the tradition of Marxist thought as a form of mobilization, legitimation or association with the prestigious symbols and powerful high-status regimes such as the Soviet Union, China, Cuba and Vietnam.

So this monograph is a particularly important contribution to the overall analysis of contemporary Marxist regimes. The study of Marxist regimes has commonly been equated with the study of communist political systems. There were several historical and methodological reasons for this. For many years it was not difficult to distinguish the eight regimes in Eastern Europe and four in Asia which resoundingly claimed adherence to the tenets of Marxism and more particularly to their Soviet interpretation—Marxism-Leninism. These regimes, variously called 'People's Republic', 'People's Democratic Republic', or 'Democratic Republic', claimed to have derived their inspiration from the Soviet Union to which, indeed, in the over-whelming number of cases they owed their establishment.

To many scholars and analysts these regimes represented a multiplication of and geographical extension of the 'Soviet model' and consequently of the Soviet sphere of influence. Although there were clearly substantial similarities between the Soviet Union and the people's democracies, especially in the initial phases of their development, these were often overstressed at the expense of noticing the differences between these political systems.

It took a few years for scholars to realize that generalizing the particular, i.e., applying the Soviet experience to other states ruled by elites which claimed to be guided by 'scientific socialism', was not good enough. The relative simplicity of the assumption of a cohesive communist bloc was questioned after the expulsion of Yugoslavia from the Communist Information Bureau in 1948 and in particular after the workers' riots in Poznań in 1956 and the Hungarian revolution of the same year. By the mid-1960s, the totalitarian model of communist politics, which until then had been very much in force, began to crumble. As some of these regimes articulated demands for a distinctive path of socialist development, many specialists studying these systems began to notice that the cohesiveness of the communist bloc was less apparent than had been claimed before.

Also by the mid-1960s, in the newly independent African states 'democratic' multi-party states were turning into one-party states or military dictatorships, thus questioning the inherent superiority of liberal democracy, capitalism and the values that went with it. Scholars now began to ponder on the simple contrast between multi-party democracy and a one-party totalitarian rule that had satisfied an earlier generation.

Despite all these changes the study of Marxist regimes remains in its infancy and continues to be hampered by constant and not always pertinent comparison with the Soviet Union, thus somewhat blurring the important underlying common theme—the 'scientific theory' of the laws of development of human society and human history. This doctrine is claimed by the leadership of these regimes to consist of the discovery of objective causal relationships; it is used to analyse the contradictions which arise between goals and actuality in the pursuit of a common destiny. Thus the political elites of these countries have been and continue to be influenced in both their ideology and their political practice by Marxism more than any other current of social thought and political practice.

The growth in the number and global significance, as well as the ideological, political and economic impact, of Marxist regimes has presented scholars and students with an increasing challenge. In meeting this challenge, social scientists on both sides of the political divide have put forward a dazzling profusion of terms, models, programmes and varieties of interpretation. It is against the background of this profusion that the present comprehensive series on Marxist regimes is offered.

This collection of monographs is envisaged as a series of multi-disciplinary textbooks on the governments, politics, economics and society of these countries. Each of the monographs was prepared by a specialist on the country concerned. Thus, over fifty scholars from all over the world have contributed monographs which were based on first-hand knowledge. The geographical diversity of the authors, combined with the fact that as a group they represent many disciplines of social science, gives their individual analyses and the series as a whole an additional dimension.

Each of the scholars who contributed to this series was asked to analyse such topics as the political culture, the governmental structure, the ruling party, other mass organizations, party–state relations, the policy process, the economy, domestic and foreign relations together with any features peculiar to the country under discussion.

This series does not aim at assigning authenticity or authority to any single one of the political systems included in it. It shows that, depending on a variety of historical, cultural, ethnic and political factors, the pursuit of goals derived from the tenets of Marxism has produced different political forms at different times and in different places. It also illustrates the rich diversity among these societies, where attempts to achieve a synthesis between goals derived from Marxism on the one hand, and national realities on the other, have often meant distinctive approaches and solutions to the problems of social, political and economic development.

University College   *Bogdan Szajkowski*
Cardiff

To the Cuban people, who are struggling, against all odds, building a socialist society in José Martí's fatherland

Contents

List of Illustrations and Tables

Map

Figures

Tables

Preface

I have been preparing myself for this book practically during my entire life. I was born in Cuba, lived there until my mid-twenties, was educated in Havana University and Havana School of Journalism, worked on several of Havana's newspapers, in the family business, and for the Revolutionary Government, and traveled as a journalist to the United States, Trinidad, Argentina, Uruguay, and Brazil with Fidel Castro in 1959. After leaving Cuba in November 1960, I had the opportunity of seeing the anti-Castro movement in the United States and South America from within, and pursued a graduate school education in the United States. Part of the latter, including my doctoral dissertation, was dedicated to studying Cuba. In the almost twenty years I have been a member of the Edinboro University faculty, a good part of the time has been dedicated to teaching courses on Latin America and the Third World, in which Cuba occupies a central position.

After eighteen years, I returned to Cuba in 1978 as part of a delegation of Cuban-Americans that traveled to Havana to participate in the Dialogue Conference with the Cuban government. I have been back many times since. Also, I have been closely involved with a group of Cuban-Americans who support the re-establishment of relations between the United States and Cuba because we consider it is in the best interest of both countries.

I am responsible for everything that is said in this book. I am very grateful, however, to many good friends who have given me advice and helped me throughout these years. Without their support I would not have been able to write this book. My thanks go to my good friends Elsie Deal and Thomas E. Gay, Jr. (Edinboro University). Thanks to the close friendship and advice of Roger H. Harrell (California State University, Northridge), and his wife Margaret, I was able to finish my doctoral dissertation at the University of Southern California. Many of the ideas used in this book were initially developed while working on my dissertation. Two faculty from the University of Southern California have my gratitude for the knowledge and advice they gave me: Paul E. Hadley and Joseph Nyomarkay. While Professor Hadley made me aware of the vitality of Latin American studies in the United States, Professor Nyomarkay was my mentor in my area of political science specialization, comparative politics. Also, my doctoral dissertation was written under their guidance.

Other good friends, who helped me during the last years with advice and research materials, are Daniel Trainer (Edinboro University), Marifeli Pérez-Stable (SUNY, Old Westbury), and Jenny Lincoln (Mershon Center, Ohio State University).

I am grateful to good friends in Cuba for their friendship, and honesty in our conversations and relationships; to Eugenio R. Balari, director of ICIODI at the time when I made several trips to Havana, and to the staff of the Institute who worked with me in a research project on the internal demand in Cuba; to Rafael Hernández and Juan Valdés Paz of the Centro de Estudios Sobre América (the Americas Study Center); to two old friends from Havana University, Raúl Comín, attorney, and Alberto Adato, public accountant; to schoolmates from Havana School of Journalism, Gabriel Molina, Reinaldo Peñalver, and Alfredo Viñas; and to Esteban Morales, José Luis Rodríguez, Hernán Yanes, Miguel Alfonso, Lisandro Otero, Alfredo Guevara, José Massip, Roberto Fernández Retamar, and Tomás Gutiérrez Alea; and to so many others, perhaps too many to mention here—my gratitude to all of them.

And to my wife, Nicolette, I know that these last years have been difficult for her. My being so involved in a research project like this, in addition to all the demands on my time that an institution like Edinboro University places on me, created difficult situations at home, Fortunately, we managed to survive this difficult period; she took upon herself the care of many of my household responsibilities that would have been neglected for a while otherwise.

Finally, to Bodgan Szajkowski, Marxist Regimes Series Editor, Heather Bliss, Managing Editor, and Frances Pinter, the publisher, my gratitude for their helpful advice while working on this book. And, especially, for their graceful patience when several deadlines passed without me having finished the manuscript.

Max Azicri
Edinboro University
of Pennsylvania

Basic Data

Official name	Republic of Cuba
Population	10,221,000 (1986E)
Age distribution	0–29 (55.9%); 30–59 (32.8%)l 60+ (11.3%)
Population density	238 per sq. m.
Population growth (% p.a.)	0.81% (1984). The period of fastest growth was 1960–6 (from 7 to 8 million)
Urban population	70% (1986)
Total labor force	3,058,945 (1986)
Life expectancy	72.5 (1980–5); men, 70.9; women, 74.2
Infant death rate (per 1,000)	One year old or less, 19.3 (1979)
Ethnic groups	Caucasian or European ancestry, 66%; black or African ancestry, 12%; mulatto (mixed Caucasian and black), 22%; of Asian origin, 0.1%
Capital	Havana
Land area	105,007 sq. km.; Isle of Youth, 2,200 sq. km.; small islands and keys, 3,715 sq. km.
Official language	Spanish
Other main languages	None
Administrative division	14 provinces
Membership of international organizations	United Nations (FAO, IAEA, ICAO, IFAD, ILO, IMO, ITU, UNESCO, UNIDO, UPU, WHO, WIPO, WMO); GATT; Council for Mutual Economic Assistance (CMEA/COMECON); International Bank of Economic Cooperation (IBEC); International Investment Bank (IIB); Latin American Economic System (SELA); Non-Aligned Movement (NAM); Permanent Court of Arbitration (PCA)
Foreign relations	Formal member of the socialist bloc; founder and member of the Non-Aligned Movement; trade and diplomatic relations with market economy countries, including Canada and Latin American countries
Political structure	
Constitution	24 February 1976

Highest legislative body	National Assembly of the Organs of People's Power
Prime Minister	None
President	Fidel Castro
Ruling Party	Cuban Communist Party (PCC)
Party membership	511,050 (1988E)
Economy	
GNP	(US 1974 dollars) $14.9 billion (1982E); annual average growth rate, 1.4% (1982E). (Cuba's economic performance is measured by global social product (GSP), and gross material product (GMP).) (GSP) $27.410 billion (1985E); average growth, 7.3% (1981–5)
GNP per capita	(US 1974 dollars) $1,490 (1982E); $1,590 (1983E)
State budget	

Expenditures (% p.a.)	1978	1979	1980	1981
Health, education, culture	29.2	31.1	32.7	29.3
Housing and community services	3.6	4.2	3.8	3.7
Public administration	5.9	5.5	5.1	6.0
Financing of the economy	43.9	41.3	41.7	41.7

Expenditure on defense and internal order, % of state budget	8.6 (1978); 8.9 (1979); 8.9 (1980); 7.5 (1981); 18 (1988) (projected)
Monetary unit	Peso (Dec. 1986 1 peso — US$1.20); before the revolution the peso was rated equal to the dollar, but now the rate fluctuates with the peso up to 35% above the dollar

Growth indicators (% p.a.)

	1977–82	1984
National income	6.9% (GDP)	7.4% (GSP)
Industry		7.2% (GSP)
Heavy (1978–80)		
Mining and iron metalurgic	7.28%	
Mining and non-iron metalurgic	9.84%	
Construction materials	2.53%	

Non-electric machinery	5.27%	
Electronic and electrotechnology	2.83%	
Forests and lumber	−12.98%	
Consumer (1978–82)		
Foodstuff	4.77%	
Textile	−1.09%	
Liquor and tobacco	−0.76%	
Agriculture	7.0% (1977);	4.0% (1980)

Trade and Balance of Payments

Exports	$4.162 billion (June 1987): socialist countries $3.900 billion; market economy countries $261.7 billion
Imports	$3.627 billion (June 1987): socialist countries $3.198 billion; market economy countries $429 billion
Exports as % of GNP	33.3 (1982E)
Main exports (%)	Sugar, and sugar derivatives, 83.4; minerals, 6.5; tobacco, 2.3; cattle and agriculture, 1.9; other products, 3.6 (including rum, fish, and shellfish) (1977)
Main imports (%)	Industrial and capital goods, 24.2; petroleum and lubricants, 19.5; foodstuffs, 19.1; others, 37.2 including consumer goods other than foodstuffs, and intermediate goods (1975)
Destination of exports (%)	Soviet Union and other socialist countries, 86 (1984); European Economic Community (EEC) and European Free Trade Association (EFTA) member nations, and some African, Asian, and Latin American countries, 22 (1977–80), and 13 (1982–4)
Main trading partners	Soviet Union and other socialist countries, $3,394 million; capitalist Western European nations, $1,278 million; Asia and Australia, $871 million; Latin America, $175 million; Canada, $161 million; Africa and the Middle East, $115 million (1975)
Foreign debt	With market economies $3.87 billion (1986E); with socialist countries $6 billion (1986E)

Foreign aid	From the USSR $10 billion (1977); development loans $459 million (1960–4), $402 million (1973–6). Total credits from socialist countries $5.178 billion (1976); loans and credits from Western countries $3.722 million (1973–9); Eurocurrency loans $519.3 million (1973–6)
Foreign investment	Joint commercial ventures with the USSR and other socialist nations; a joint oil drilling project was signed with Mexico's state oil enterprise (PEMEX), and, in compliance with Legislative Decree No. 50 15 February 1982, other ventures are considered with market economies
Main natural resources	Agriculture; minerals (cobalt, nickel, iron, copper, manganese); cattle (6.5 million), pigs (2.4 million) (1985); fish catch 221,000 metric tons (1985); industries (textiles, wood products, cement, chemicals, cigars)
Main crops	Sugar, tobacco, coffee, rice, pineapples, bananas, citrus fruits, coconuts
Land tenure (%)	Government property, 80; cooperative property, 12; individual private property, 8. Cooperatives represent 61.3 of the total land owned by private farmers. Producer cooperatives number 1,378 (1985). Private farmers with up to 67 hectares of land were grouped in May 1961 in the National Association of Small Farmers (ANAP), according to the Agrarian Reform Law of May 1959
Food self-sufficiency	Food production increment (1959–82): noodles, 5.5 times; children's food, over 7 times; fish, 16.8 times; eggs, 7.2 times; ice cream, 14.6 times; wheat processing, 5.5 times; beer and malt, 2.1 times; fruits and produce, doubles; milk, 5 times; poultry, doubles; rice, doubles (satisfies half of actual consumption)
Armed forces	227,000 (2.32% of the population) (1982)
Education	
School system	(1) *circulos infantiles* (day-care centers); (2) elementary school; (3) secondary

	school basic, and general; (4) preuniversity institutes; (5) technical and vocational schools; (6) university level
Primary school enrollment	3,223,400 (1982) (92% of those between ages 6–14 attend school)
Secondary school enrollment	610,100 (1982)
Higher education	preuniversity 506,700 (1982); university 173,400 (1982)
Adult literacy	97% (1988)
Health	
Population per hospital bed	168.17 (1982E); total beds 58,271 (1982)
Population per physician	1,121 (1973); 722 (1979); 578 (1982)
Main religions	Roman Catholic; Protestant, different denominations; a small Jewish community
Rail network	13,361 km. (1981)
Road network	11,746 km. (fully paved roads) (1982)

Population Forecasting

The following data are projections produced by Poptran, University College Cardiff Population Centre, from United Nations Assessment Data published in 1980, and are reproduced here to provide some basis of comparison with other countries covered by the Marxist Regimes Series.

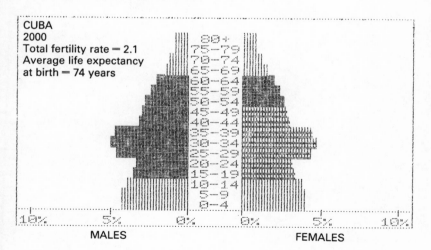

CUBA
2000
Total fertility rate = 2.1
Average life expectancy at birth = 74 years

MALES   FEMALES

Projected Data for Cuba 2000

Total population ('000)	11,717
Males ('000)	5,935
Females ('000)	5,782
Total fertility rate	2.10
Life expectancy (male)	72.7 years
Life expectancy (female)	76.7 years
Crude birth rate	17.1
Crude death rate	7.2
Annual growth rate	0.99%
Under 15s	24.12%
Over 65s	8.95%
Women aged 15–49	25.85%
Doubling time	71 years
Population density	102 per sq. km.
Urban population	75.2%

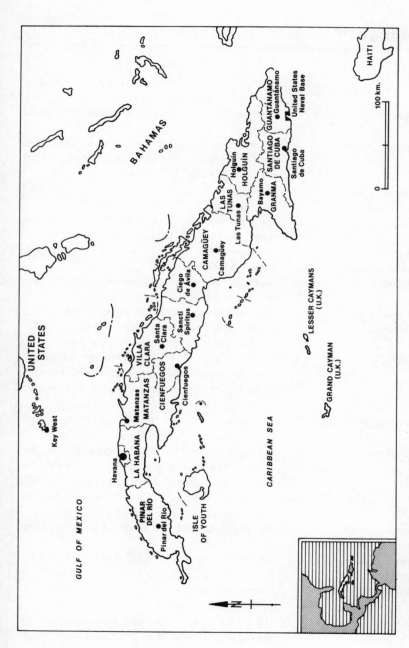

Cuba: provincial boundaries and capitals

Glossary

acopio	a private farmer's officially assigned production quota
bufetes colectivos	government regulated attorneys' offices. The legal fees are officially determined, and paid by the citizens using their services
cafetales	coffee plantations
casas de cultura	cultural centers
caudillismo	the personalized and authoritarian exercise of power by a *caudillo* (strongman)
cimarrón(es)	a maroon slave
círculos infantiles	Infant day-care centers
conciencia	indicates an attitude of active support and commitment for the revolution
conquistadores	(Spanish) conquerors of the New World
cooperantes	name given to participants in the overseas workers program undertaken in the 1980s
criollo(s)	(1) (in Cuba): a person of mixed parentage (usually Spanish and black) who identifies with Cuba; (2) (in Latin America): a person of Spanish parentage born in a Spanish colony
encomendero	a Spanish colonist who had received an *encomienda*
encomienda	the right, granted by Madrid, to use Indians for labor by Spanish colonists in the New World; in return, the colonists were responsible for the well being of the Indians and their conversion to Christianity
ennegrecimiento	the predominance of black culture, or black persons
escuelas básicas en el campo	Basic boarding countryside schools
guateque	a dance party
hacienda comunal	communal ranch (or *finca*)
institutos preuniversitarios	pre-university institute
ladino	(1) a black slave who had been in Spain or Portugal for two or more years, and could speak

Spanish; (2) old Castilian (Spanish) spoken by Sephardic Jews (i.e., Jews of Spanish ancestry)

latifundio(s) — a large farm or landholding

macheteros — manual cane-cutters; *macheteros* did their work by hand until cane-cutting became mechanized under the revolution

machismo — social male dominance signified in cultural attitudes and behavioral patterns in Cuba, and Latin America

mambí(ses) — word used first by Spaniards to refer to Cuban patriots rebelling against Spain's colonial rule, and later used by the Cuban rebels to name themselves

mutualista — the member of a private mutual assistance association that provides medical, educational, and social benefits

ñáñigo(s) — a member of the African Abakuá cult

palenque(s) — (1) a fenced area in which a public celebration is held; (2) a place of great confusion and noise

peninsular — a person of Spanish blood born in Spain

polacos — Jewish migrants of Polish or Eastern European ancestry

puros, habanos — Cuban cigars; also, cigars made using high quality tobacco from the Pinar del Río province *vegas*

sitio(s) — (1) the siege of a city or garrison; (2) a particular place or location

tiempo muerto — off-season (after the sugar harvest)

turcos — Jewish migrants of Turkish, or Eastern Mediterranean ancestry

regalía — (1) a royal privilege, exception, or right; (2) a bonus collected at the end of the year in addition to the worker's regular salary

vegas — tobacco plantations

zafra — harvest time for the canes

List of Abbreviations

AJR	Association of Rebel Youth
ANAP	National Association of Small (Private) Farmers
CARICOM	Caribbean Community
CEM	Military Study Centers
CELAM	Latin American Conference of Bishops
CIA	Central Intelligence Agency
CIEC	Cuban Council of Evangelical Churches
CDR	Committees for the Defense of the Revolution
CTC	Cuban Confederation of Workers
COMECON	Council for Mutual Economic Assistance
DR	(Havana University students') Revolutionary Directorate
ECLAC	United Nations Economic Commission for Latin America and the Caribbean
EJT	Youth Labor Army
FAR	Revolutionary Armed Forces
FEU	University Students Federation
FELA	Artistic and Literary Economic Fund
FLN	(Algerian) National Liberation Front
FMC	Federation of Cuban Women
FNLA	National Front for the Liberation of Angola
FSLN	Sandinista National Liberation Front
GDP	Gross Domestic Product
GMP	Gross Material Product
GNP	Gross National Product
GSP	Global Social Product
ICAP	Cuban Peoples' Friendship Institute
ICAIC	Cuban Institute of Cinema Art and Industry
ICIODI	Cuban Institute of Research and Direction of Internal Demand
IMF	International Monetary Fund
INRA	National Institute of Agrarian Reform
JUCEPLAN	Central Planning Board
M–26–7	26 July Movement
MINFAR	Ministry of Revolutionary Armed Forces
MININT	Ministry of the Interior

MINREX	Ministry of External Relations
MPLA	Popular Movement for the Liberation of Angola
OAS	Organization of American States
OECS	Organization of Eastern Caribbean States
ORI	Integrated Revolutionary Organizations
OPPs	Organs of People's Power
PCC	Cuban Communist Party
PEMEX	Mexican Petroleum (Mexico's state oil enterprise)
PRG	(Grenada's) People's Revolutionary Government
PSP	Popular Socialist Party (pre-revolutionary Communist party)
PURS	United Party of the Socialist Revolution
SDPE	System of Economic Management and Planning
SWAPO	(Namibian) South West African People's Organization
UJC	Communist Youth Union
UMAP	Military Units of Aid to Production
UNEAC	National Union of Cuban Writers and Artists
UNITA	National Union for the Total Independence of Angola

1 History and Political Traditions

Cuba was founded as an independent republic on 20 May 1902. This historic event crowned a long struggle for her independence that included three successive wars in the second half of the nineteenth century, culminating with direct US military intervention provoked by the last one, the Spanish–Cuban–American War of 1898. Earlier in the nineteenth century conspiracies of various kinds sought to sever colonial relations with Spain. Altogether, the long years of struggle and the asymmetrical distribution of military forces between Cubans and Spaniards led Fidel Castro to say that Cuba had been the nineteenth-century Vietnam of Latin America.[1]

It was in this context—struggling relentlessly for its independence, one revolutionary attempt after another in pursuit of freedom—that the history of Cuba followed a pattern which became characterized as politically violent and revolutionary-prone. (Spain, however, liked to refer to it as 'the ever-faithful Island of Cuba,' apparently oblivious to Cuba's numerous but frustrated attempts to gain her independence.) That political independence was finally achieved as a result of United States' intervention added new controversial elements that further complicated its political development in the twentieth century. The dominating influence, exercised by the United States in Cuban life for approximately six decades, aggravated considerably what might have been, without such foreign interference, a less frustrating and perhaps somewhat orderly process towards achieving more mature stages of nationhood and effective independence. Historically, a major factor contributing to the 1959 revolution, as well as to the events that preceded it, was US interventionism in Cuban affairs.

Geographic Characteristics

With an area of 110,922 sq. km. (69,326.25 sq. m.), the Cuban archipelago is the largest, and also the most populous and westernmost island-nation of the West Indies, making up part of the Greater Antilles in the Caribbean (nearly as large as the state of Pennsylvania of the United States). Its strategic location allows Cuba to control the approaches from the Atlantic to the Gulf of Mexico, the Caribbean Sea, and the Panama Canal. Its neighbors are the Bahamas and the United States to the north, Mexico to the west, Jamaica to the south, and Haiti to the east. To the north lie the Gulf of Mexico and the Straits of Florida. The Atlantic Ocean is northeast of the Island; while the Caribbean Sea is to the south, the Strait of Yucatan to the west, and the Windward Passage to the east. Key West, Florida, and Haiti are only 180 and 77 km. away (112.5 and 48.12 m.), respectively, and Yucatan, Mexico, is 210 km. (131.25 m.) west (*Atlas de Cuba*, 1978, *passim*).

Cuba covers 1,250 km. (781.25 m.), from Point de Quemado in the east to Cape San Antonio in the west, with a total land area of 105,007 sq. km. (65,629.37 sq. m.). Its coastline is approximately 5,746 km. (3,591.25 m.), extending 3,209 km. (2,005.62 m.) along the northern coast, and 2,537 km. (1,585.62 m.) along the southern coast. The coastal topography of the north is steep and rocky whereas that of the south is low and marshy containing some major swamp areas. Making up the Cuban archipelago are numerous smaller islands and keys covering 3,715 sq. km. (2,321.87 sq. m.), plus the largest and furthermost of the outer islands, the Isle of Youth, formerly known as the Isle of Pines, covering 2,200 sq. km. (1,375 sq. m.) and located 130 km. (81.25 m.) south of Havana. Two of the largest keys are off the northern coast: Romano Key, Ciego de Avila province, and Coco Key, Camagüey province, with 926 sq. km. (578.75 sq. m.) and 370 sq. km. (231.25 sq. m.), respectively. Cuba averages 80 km. (50 m.) in width. The island's widest point extends from Tarracos Beach, north of Camagüey province, to Camaron Grande, south of Granma province, a total of 191 km. (119.37 m.). Its narrowest point is only 31 km. (19.37 m.), extending from Mariel Bay to Majana Cove, in Havana province.

Known as the Pearl of the Antilles, Cuba is blessed with a benign semitropical (not tropical) climate. The average annual temperature is 25.2° C (77.3° F). The temperature usually drops to 22.1° C (71.7° F) during February, the coldest month of the year, rising in the warmest months, July and August, to 27.6° C (81.68° F). Its warmest recorded temperature from 1966 to 1977 reached 38.6° C (101.4° F); while its coldest temperature from 1966 to 1973 dropped to 1.0° C (33.8° F).

Cuba's average yearly rainfall is 1,375 mm. (55 in.), which includes the average of 1,059 mm. (42.36 in.) the rainy season (May–October), and 316 mm. (12.64 in.) the dry season (November–April). Its annual relative humidity is 80 percent, changing mildly in the rainy season to 81 percent, 79 percent in the dry season. It also has a fertile soil supporting approximately 8,000 different species of plants and trees. Low hills and valleys cover most of the country, with approximately 3,500,000 acres of dense forest (1,400,000 ha). In 1812, 90 percent of the national territory was covered by forests. It dwindled to 14 percent by 1959, increasing slightly to 18 percent by 1975.

The mountainous regions are concentrated in Pinar del Río province in the west; in the central provinces of Villa Clara and Sancti Spíritus provinces; and in the eastern provinces of Granma, Santiago de Cuba, and Guantánamo (which was formerly part of what used to be Oriente province).[2] The historic Sierra Maestra is the highest of three mountain ranges. It is located in the southeastern part of the island, not far from the Guantánamo Base of the US Navy. Its highest point is Pico Turquino, with an altitude of 1,972 m. (6,507.6 ft), followed by Pico Cuba with 1,872 m. (6,177.6 ft).

Cuba's main harbor is located in the City of Havana province—considered one of the finest and safest in the world. Other excellent harbors along the northern coast are Bahía Honda, Mariel, Cabañas, Matanzas, Nuevitas, Puerto Padre, Gibara, Banes, and Nipe. On the southern coast the major harbors are Cienfuegos, Guantánamo, and Santiago de Cuba.

The largest river is the Cauto, which flows for 343 km. (214.37 m.) through the eastern provinces of Holguín, Granma, and Santiago de Cuba. Its basin extends for 8,969 sq. km. (5,605.6 sq. m.). The second largest river is the Sagua La Grande, located in the central province of Villa Clara. It flows for 144 km. (90 m.), with a basin of 2,188 sq. km. (1,367.5 sq. m.).

Colonial History

The Founding Period

Cuba was discovered by Christopher Columbus on 27 October 1492, during the first of four voyages to the New World. He would later visit the island on his second trip. Columbus named the island Juana, after the daughter of Ferdinand V of Aragon and Isabella I of Castile. Historically known as Spain's Catholic King and Queen, they sponsored Columbus's voyages and explorations. The name was changed later to Fernandina, after the Spanish monarch. The name Cuba was initially used only for Santiago de Cuba—one of the seven initial settlements founded by the Spanish. However, as time progressed, the name Cuba prevailed. The conquest of the island was not undertaken until 1511 by Diego Velazquez (1465–1524). He was acting under military and administrative orders of Diego Columbus (the son of the 'discoverer'), at the time the Viceroy of Hispaniola (today Haiti and the Dominican Republic). Velazquez became Cuba's first Spanish Governor, after having established a reputation for mistreating the Indians of Hispaniola. The first settlement he founded, Baracoa, on the northern coast of Guantánamo province, was followed by others along the island's southern coast. Cuba's development, however, was postponed, due largely to the fact that gold and other precious metals were not readily available in the amount the Spaniards preferred—such as the quantities found elsewhere in the New World (Le Riverend, 1967, 1978; Masó, 1976).

A combination of mistreatment at the hands of the *conquistadores* and the diseases that they brought with them decimated the existent Indian population of approximately 100,000 very early during the colonial period—hard labor and inhumane working conditions drove many to commit suicide rather than endure such hardships. The Indian Hatuey was burned alive in 1512, and there were several massive killings of aborigines similar to the one in Caonao in 1513. Many rebelled without success against this inhumane treatment (as took place in the eastern region in 1527 and 1533), and during the uprising led by the Indian Guamá that lasted almost a decade. Under the laws of the Crown, the Indians were assigned to a *peninsular* (a native of Spain) along with the land (a *regalía*), both as a concession from the Spanish monarch under the *encomienda* system. Meanwhile the recipient, an *encomendero*, was responsible for the welfare of the Indians under his care (those working for him), and particularly for their conversion to Christianity. The enslaved Indians found a champion in Friar Bartolomé de Las Casas (1474–1566), who pleaded their case before the Spanish Crown with little success.

There were three groups of aborigines when the Spaniards arrived in Cuba—the Taínos, who inhabited the area which is now the eastern provinces, were the most advanced. They were sedentary, practicing primitive agriculture and manufacturing utensils out of clay; and they had developed patterns of social differentiation and organization. A second group, known as the sub-Taínos, was less developed and lived scattered throughout the island. They were dedicated to fishing and hunting. The most backward group, the Guanahatabeyes, lived in the western region.

In 1519, the village of Havana (San Cristóbal de La Habana) was established on its present site (it was initially founded on the southern coast). It developed rapidly soon becoming a key commercial center in the Caribbean, notwithstanding the trade restrictions imposed by the Crown. This monopolistic policy was not lifted until the British captured Havana in 1762.

Although the population remained loyal to Spain and fought against British occupation, the fact that Havana could trade freely for a year under British rule had a positive effect upon commerce and the welfare of the population. This was manifested later as discontent grew again after Spain regained control of Havana and re-established its old trade policy. Demands for the elimination of the trading monopoly became a bone of contention between Cubans and the colonial authorities. In defiance many Colonials engaged actively in contraband trade. Realizing the importance of Havana for its own trade with its colonies, the Crown took steps toward general freedom of trade and sent governors with better administrative skills to organize public finances, improve the judicial system, and initiate some public works. In 1765 Havana was authorized to trade with several Spanish ports, and in 1778 it was allowed to trade with foreign vessels entering its port (Le Riverend, 1967; Thomas, 1971).

During the early colonial period Cuba was also plagued by pirates and corsairs. As a rule they were Europeans, mostly French and British, although there also was a Cuban pirate among them named Diego Grillo. These incursions represented a serious threat to coastline cities. Paradoxically, however, it increased the strategic value of Havana's harbor. In order to protect the vessels from such attacks, the Crown organized fleets to sail to and from Spain. Thus Spain turned Havana into a gathering place for its fleet travelling to and from other Spanish colonial ports.

The Colonial Socioeconomic System

The Crown established in Cuba a rigidly stratified society reflecting a hierarchy based on place of birth, race, and political, social, and economic status, not unlike the societies of the other Spanish colonies. The Spaniards occupied the highest echelon of an inegalitarian social pyramid whose elite was made up of colonial officers (controlling the administration of government), the clergy (controlling the educational system and exercising an influence on behalf of the Church that pervaded society as a whole), and the military (exercising military and political control over the governmental structure, and social life in general).

Beneath this top social layer were the children of the Spaniards born in Cuba, or Creoles (*criollos*). Under them, were those of mixed race (mulattoes, black and white), followed by blacks (born free blacks and former slaves first, and last actual slaves). A spirit of unabashedly amassing riches as rapidly as possible prevailed among the Spaniards, setting the tone for life in the colony. In Madrid the colonies were seen along similar lines: mostly a source of income for Spain, initially ideologically justified by the evangelical drive directed at the Indian population. As in the rest of Spanish America, this type of social order, combined with Spain's controlled trade and business practices and centralized governmental structures, produced societies ill-suited for change and modernization. Furthermore, Cuba's geographical isolation from the Spanish mainland colonies made it even more difficult later to achieve independence, and to modernize.

The emerging Cuban propertied class—owners of sugarmills, tobacco and coffee plantations, and other commercial assets—found in the late eighteenth century an articulate and intelligent advocate of their economic interests and aspirations in Francisco Arango Parreño (1765–1837). Arango Parreño argued in favor of introducing technical advances in agriculture and in the sugar industry as a means of increasing production, as well as expanding trade with the United States. Also, he supported a more rational and effective use of slave labor, not so much in order to improve their living conditions but to increase their productivity. Arango Parreño, and those Cuban entrepreneurs who supported his reformist ideas, also sought regulations simplifying governmental requirements for the selling and buying of real estate—farms and *latifundia* (large land holdings)—and cattle raising, and other economic activities.

As part of the emerging cultural life in Cuba, there was the scientific work of Tomás Romay (1764–1849). As a medical doctor he was instrumental in improving the state of medical science as well as the standards for teaching science. One of his major contributions was introducing the vaccine to combat what at the time was a mortal disease, chicken pox. The work of Father José Agustín Caballero (1762–1835) in education made possible the adoption of new teaching methods contributing to the decline of the traditional scholastic philosophy.

Early in the colonial period Cuba became an important producer of sugar, adding coffee and tobacco to its agricultural and industrial output by the eighteenth century. Its plantation economy was rooted in monoculture, and a system of large-scale production, linked to and servicing metropolitan markets, was established. The foundation of the island's economic welfare was largely based on sugar supplemented by a few agricultural and industrial products. The uncertainties of international trade and pricing were established rather early. At the time, however, the success of producing and marketing sugar, and also tobacco and coffee, made the economy look rather promising. Eventually private wealth was accumulated in significant amounts. But the prevailing mercantilist and utilitarian ethics made the economy look better than it really was.[3]

Importing African Slaves

As early as 1515 the authorities petitioned the Crown for permission to bring slaves to Cuba from Hispaniola. With the decline of the Indian population, efforts were redoubled after 1520 to import the labor supply. The importation of black slaves from Africa supplied the labor needed to construct a successful plantation system and satisfy the principle of mercantilism. The slaves were exploited and mistreated, although their treatment was somewhat better than the Indians' because of the monetary investment the slaves represented, and the economic system based on slavery that evolved. The first shipment of slaves arrived in 1526, a group of 145 from Cape Verde. In 1527 the Crown approved the importation of 1,000 slaves. Their number continued to increase as the development of the economy of the Cuban colony became dependent on slave labor:

> The process of growth of the slave population was intimately linked to the organization of a cane *plantation* economy. Cane cultivation and sugar production demanded hundreds of slaves, and, as the exports of this product increased, the intensification of labor brought about a greater number of deaths among Africans . . . and forced a speedier replacement of the exterminated ones. No less significant was the employment of numerous slaves in the El Cobre mines . . . [Le Riverend, 1967, p. 83]

Slavery was not restricted to sugar plantations, agriculture, and mining. Many slaves in the urban areas worked on the construction of buildings and forts, in artisan industries, as stevedores and domestic servants, and on other jobs. It is estimated that by 1763 the number of imported slaves totaled between 52,000 to 60,000 slaves, with an increase of up to 40,000 by 1789. By the mid-1800s 527,828 slaves had been imported.

Race relations created a colonial society that by the nineteenth century had placed race as its central social value. Its economic foundation was a stratified socioeconomic system based on slave labor supporting white Spanish-born racial supremacy:

> The basic line of cleavage dividing Cuban nineteenth-century society was race, to the extent that legislation was passed regulating and restricting interracial marriage . . . Racial perception was a direct consequence of the degree to which slavery and its exigencies had affected the total social stucture. Slavery appears as a system of forced labour but also of social organization, and of class and racial discipline. At every point the coloured person, whether slave or free, was forced to shape his behaviour in accordance with the actions and expectations of the dominant white sector, who, in turn, also had to adjust to the presence of the non-whites . . . [Martínez-Alier, 1974, p. 2]

The white population needed black slaves but they also feared them. By the beginning of the seventeenth century they suspected that African slaves had aided Spain's enemies, such as the Dutch. More important, however, they feared runaway slaves, or *cimarrones*, as they were called. It became customary to organize searching parties to hunt for *cimarrones*, who would hide alone or in their own settlements, known as *palenques*. Often runaway slaves were apprehended and severely punished. Slavery was finally abolished in Cuba in November 1879, but the law was not applied until 29 July 1880. An extended patronage system was established then for all newly freed slaves in lieu of compensation for slave owners, although a large number of unregistered slaves were set free. In reality, slavery was not abolished until eight years later, in 1888 (Knight, 1970).

The Independence Movement

Several conspiracies and frustrated revolutionary actions attempting to liberate Cuba from Spain took place in the first half of the nineteenth century, starting as early as 1810. A free black man, José Aponte, was executed in 1812 for leading a slave conspiracy in an attempt to seek freedom while promoting rebellion.

Narciso López led two expeditions, landing first in Cardenas on 19 May 1850 and later in northern Pinar del Río province on 11 August 1851. Born in Venezuela, he left his native land after fighting against his country's liberators, during the Wars of Independence. After settling in Cuba and marrying the sister of the wealthy Count of Pozos Dulces, López became actively involved in the separatist and annexationist movement (in support of the annexation of Cuba to the United States), paying in the end with his own life. Several earlier conspiracies included the 'Gran Legión del Aquila Negra' (Great Black Eagle's Legion) and the 'Rayos y Soles de Bolívar' (Bolivar's Rays and Suns), which were supported by the newly liberated Spanish colonies, and the one led by Andrés Manuel Sánchez and Francisco Agüero, which provided the first two martyrs of Cuban independence. Sánchez and Agüero were executed after landing with eight revolutionaries on the southern coast of Camagüey province in January 1826.

The annexationist expeditions led by López were related to a movement among Southern US plantation owners, who supported the annexation of Cuba. They believed Cuba could be Africanized and therefore could threaten their own socioeconomic system. Spain's acceptance of British demands to stop the importation of slaves to Cuba increased their fear that in the end the island could become another Haiti—a country ruled by blacks. In spite of its commitment to England, Spain allowed the traffic of slaves to continue. If anything, the treatment afforded the slaves worsened. A prominent intellectual of the period, José Antonio Saco (1797–1855), opposed the annexationist movement, and advocated ending the traffic of slaves to the island. Saco wrote a historical indictment of slavery, *History of Slavery*, after he had been expatriated by order of the Spanish Governor, Miguel Tacón, because of his political and social ideas.

The Southerners' annexationist movement, supported by López and some wealthy Cubans, was not the first in the United States. As early as 1823, John Quincy Adams, then US Secretary of State, firmly believed that the 'island was one of the most vital elements in the economic and strategic future of the United States.' In a letter to Hugh Nelson, US Ambassador to Spain, Quincy wrote that 'the annexation of Cuba to our federal republic will be indispensable to the continuance and integrity of the Union itself' (Freeman Smith, 1966, p. 5). This spirit of American manifest destiny would emerge again and again in the history of United States–Cuban relations. Moreover, this interest in Cuba by the major powers was largely based on the island's strategic geographic location; much more so than on any economic consideration. Spain first, then France, England, and particularly the United States, and more recently the Soviet Union, demonstrated similar interest and motivations.

The nineteenth century witnessed a cultural movement that contributed to the development of a national identity. There were significant literary works, such as the important novel *Cecilia Valdés* by Cirilo Villaverde (1812–94), and the poetry of José María Heredia (1803–39), Juan Clemente Zenea (1832–71), and Rafael María Mendive (1821–86). There were several publications of certain value, even if short-lived, such as *El Americano Libre*, *Revista Bimestre Cubana*, and *La Moda*, among others. The reformist philosophical influence exerted by Friar Félix Varela (1787–1853) was of great significance. He was followed by his disciple, José de la Luz y Caballero (1800–62), who also excelled as an educator. Havana University was reformed in 1852, after being under the guidance of the Dominican Order since it was founded in 1782.

In the earlier part of the century, however, most Cubans were not ready to support separatist movements openly. The idea of Cuba's separation from Spain, and particularly its complete independence, seemed too radical. The will and desire for political independence would not flourish until later. The American revolution, and the wars for Latin American independence during the first part of the nineteenth century, had an impact among educated creoles, but most wealthy Cubans, still economically satisfied with the colonial status quo, were not ready to support Cuba's separation from Spain.

Instead of complete independence, other political options were initially more widely considered besides annexation to the United States. Reformism and autonomism would alter the existing colonial status, but they would not result in separation from Spain. Cuba would remain under Spanish hegemony (Padrón Larrazábal, 1975, pp. 18–23; Le Riverend, 1978, pp. 43–62).

On 10 October 1868, after freeing his slaves working in his sugarmill La Demajagua, Carlos Manuel de Céspedes (1819–74) started the Ten Year War (1868–78). In his call for Cuba's independence, Céspedes had the support of Francisco Vicente Aguilera (1821–77), Ignacio Agramonte (1841–72), Pedro Figueredo (1819–70), and many others. On 10 April 1869 the Guaimaro Assembly was convened. The Cuban Republic in Arms and the country's first (revolutionary; *de facto*) Constitution were proclaimed and Céspedes was declared President. The difficult war years that followed were fought mostly in Cienfuegos, Villa Clara, Sancti Spíritus, Ciego de Ávila, Camagüey, Las Tunas, Granma, Holguín, Santiago de Cuba, and Guantánamo provinces. However, the effects of the war were felt across the island. The uncompromising spirit and desire for revenge of the ruling class was manifested in the extreme actions of the volunteers who joined such groups as the (Spanish) Volunteer Force of Havana's Commerce. On 27 November 1871 eight medical school students were shot under false charges of having desecrated the graveyard of a prominent Spaniard, who in the eyes of the volunteers represented the Spanish cause.

During the Ten Year War many wealthy creoles witnessed their economic ruin, especially those who supported the revolution and carried out Céspedes' decree to set fire to the canefields. As the war dragged on Spain continued its economic control, while the United States increased its investments, particularly in the sugar industry. The so-called Little War (Guerra Chiquita) 1879–80, followed. This second war was started by several of the revolutionary leaders of the Ten Year War—Antonio Maceo, and his brother José; Calixto García; Guillermo Moncada, and others. They had refused in their historic Baraguá Protest to accept the terms of the peace agreement signed by the belligerent forces and the Spanish authorities in the Zanjón Pact, which put an end to the Ten Year War.

José Martí

After these two disappointing and costly experiences in both human lives and economic resources, a new, fresh leadership was needed. New leadership would come in José Martí (1853–95), perhaps the most remarkable man in nineteenth-century Cuba, and probably in the nation's history (Foner, 1975; Kirk, 1983; Mañach, 1975). In his struggle for Cuban independence, Martí would be joined by several heroes of the long years of struggle against the superior Spanish forces. They included Antonio Maceo, a leading revolutionary figure and military strategist known in Cuban history as the 'Bronze Titan'—whose ten brothers fought for Cuban independence—and Máximo Gómez, the principal military strategist of the Ten Year War. Gómez was born in Santo Domingo, known today as the Dominican Republic.

In 1869, when he was only 16 years old, Martí was arrested and subsequently condemned by a Spanish Military Tribunal to six years of forced labor in prison. At that early age he had been accused of subversive activities supporting the revolution. The charges were based on a letter critical of Spain that had been intercepted by the police. Martí claimed sole responsibility, although he was only one of the co-authors. He was already publishing an underground newspaper, *Patria Libre* (Free Fatherland), which included his drama *Abdala*. After being sentenced to exile in 1871, Martí was deported to Spain where he wrote a sensitive account denouncing the prevailing inhuman political prison conditions under Spanish rule, *El Presidio Político en Cuba* (*Political Prison in Cuba*).

While living in Spain, Martí alternated between being a political exile and a university student. In May 1871, he enrolled at Madrid University, and two years later authored another political essay condemning Spanish rule in Cuba, *La Republica Española Ante La Revolución Cubana* (*The Spanish Republic and the Cuban Revolution*). A year after transfering to Zaragoza University in 1873, Martí received first the degree of *bachiller*, which was followed in a few days by the *licenciatura* in civil and canonic law. Five months later, he received the *licenciatura* in philosophy and letters.

After leaving Spain for Paris in December 1874, he quickly moved to Mexico, where he worked as a journalist contributing to several publications. Two years later, he visited Cuba briefly using his second Christian name and surname, Julian Pérez. After teaching at Guatemala's Central School of modern languages and philosophy for approximately a year, he resigned his position in protest against the unjust dismissal of the school director. He returned then to Cuba, where his request for permission to practice law was denied. A few months later, September 1879, he was arrested, accused of subversive activities, and deported for a second time to Spain.

In January 1880 Martí arrived in New York City where his political work for Cuban independence gained a new momentum. In May he presided over the formation of the Revolutionary Committee of New York, which celebrated the arrival in Cuba of revolutionary forces led by Calixto García to fight in the Little War. After a brief stay in Venezuela, he returned again to New York City in 1881. In the following years Martí made a living by writing for newspapers of Argentina, Uruguay, Venezuela, and the United States. He was also named Consul of Uruguay in New York, and later of Argentina and Paraguay. His important contribution to Latin American letters continued with works like *Ismaelillo*, *Versos Sencillos*, and *Versos Libres* (published posthumously), which became the bedrock of the *modernista* school of poetry (Martí, 1953). In July 1889, Martí published the first edition of a children's magazine founded by him, *La Edad de Oro* (*The Golden Age*).

But above all, Martí became the new force for Cuban independence. His outstanding oratorical skills aroused the communities of Cuban exiles in New York City, Tampa, Key West, Jacksonville, and other US cities into revolutionary action. His work took him also to Jamaica, Haiti, and Santo Domingo. In 1892, he organized and wrote the statutes of the Partido Revolucionario Cubano (Cuban Revolutionary Party), which he visualized as the political arm of the revolution. He met twice with Máximo Gómez in Santo Domingo, coordinating the common struggle in order to include the old revolutionary in his plans. Thus a new era was launched. The struggle for Cuban independence went into high gear, in spite of all of the obstacles the Cuban patriots had faced in the past and those that would follow. The ensuing events would lead to the War of Independence of 1895 and to the direct United States military intervention in 1898.

After months of preparation the expedition that would have started the revolution in Cuba on 10 Janaury 1895, the Fernandina Plan, was aborted by American authorities on the grounds that it violated United States neutrality laws. By then, however, events began to take shape very rapidly. After the representatives of the exile groups signed in New York the order authorizing the beginning of the revolution, Martí joined Gómez in Santo Domingo, where both signed the Montecristi Manifesto. On 11 April 1895 Martí set foot once again on Cuban soil, joining the revolutionary forces that had already initiated the War of Independence on 24 February, following the uprising at Baire. Gómez proclaimed Martí as Major-General (many were already calling him President). On 5 May Martí met at La Mejorana with Maceo and Gómez to plan for the war. By then, the three men symbolized the revolution and Cuba's long struggle for independence. Tragically, however, two weeks later, on 19 May Martí was killed in action in Dos Ríos. A day before, in a letter to his Mexican friend Manuel Mercado, in what is considered to be his political testament, Martí wrote:

It is my duty—inasmuch as I realize it and have the spirit to fulfill it—to prevent, by the independence of Cuba, the United States from spreading over the West Indies and falling, with that added weight, upon other lands of our America. All I have done up to now, and shall do hereafter, is to that end . . . I have lived inside the monster and know its entrails—and my weapon is only the slingshot of David . . . [Foner, 1975, p. 3]

At the very moment his presence was so needed, Martí was gone forever. The war continued, although his death was such a blow to the revolutionary cause that its implications went beyond the war itself, reaching into Cuban history then and today. Thereafter, the meaning of Martí's life and ultimate sacrifice would guide, intrigue, and inspire future generations of Cubans. The independence of his beloved island, however, finally was achieved in the way he feared most, and wanted to avoid above all: by the United States replacing Spain as the new power controlling Cuban affairs.[4]

The Spanish-Cuban-American War

After Martí's death, the war continued under the leadership of Maceo and Gómez. Unlike what happened in 1873-4 when the invasion from east to west reached only the central provinces, this time it was accomplished—'*la invasión de Oriente a Occidente*.' The Cuban revolutionary forces (the *mambises*, as they were called), started their march from Baraguá, the site of their historic protest in 1878 against the Zanjón Pact. This time the outcome of the war was on the Cuban side, even if momentarily. Moving west, Maceo and Gómez forced the Spaniards to retreat, while more and more disaffected Cubans joined them. By 1 January 1896 they had reached the province of Havana, a bastion of Spanish military might.

Maceo moved on to Pinar del Río Province, the western end of the island. After he had joined Gómez again in Havana, they moved eastward and fought together against Spanish forces in Matanzas. Maceo and Gómez parted again. They would see each other for the last time in the village of Bolondrón in western Matanzas. Following an intense campaign in Pinar del Río, Maceo returned to Havana en route to Oriente. In the Punta Brava zone of Havana his temporary encampment was surprised by a Spanish column. Maceo was mortally wounded while reorganizing a counterattack, and died on 7 December 1896. The two great native heroes of the Cuban revolution, Martí and Maceo, had died in the first two years of the War of Independence. They were slain at opposite ends of their beloved island, both far distant from the places where they were born.

But the war went on, and Spain responded harshly. A tough and vindictive disciplinarian, General Valeriano Weyler, was appointed Governor to replace Marshal Arsenio Martínez Campos, who had been somewhat conciliatory toward Cuban grievances. A period of repressive measures against civilians followed: the rural population was concentrated in restricted areas across the island fortified with troops, while Spanish reinforcements turned the war against the rebel forces. Uncompromising in spite of all odds, Gómez continued fighting. Supporting him were determined men like Calixto García, Quintín Banderas, and many others. Gómez rejected out of hand a belated Spanish attempt for autonomism in 1898, when Madrid offered to grant Cuba self-governing status under continued Spanish rule.

The Cubans had been fighting alone since 1895 with little international support. On 6 April 1896, however, both houses of the US Congress passed a concurrent resolution recognizing the belligerency of Cuban revolutionaries, and Cuba's right to be independent from Spain. The resolution went unheeded by President Grover Cleveland, who refused to recognize the state of belligerency of Cuban insurgents. Finally, in 1898, the United States intervened in the conflict.

The United States intervened militarily for important reasons, but not necessarily with the best Cuban interests at heart. There already were considerable American investments in Cuba and more would be forthcoming. These investments were being adversely affected by the ongoing conflict. Besides, the United States wanted Spain out of the Caribbean area. The British had already recognized the potential dominance of the region by the United States and vacated it—but they retained such possessions as British Honduras, several Eastern Caribbean islands, and some settlements along the Atlantic coast of Nicaragua. With Spain out, the United States could redirect its Manifest Destiny from the western part of the nation into the Caribbean and Central America. The era of American imperialism and hegemonic control of the region was about to unfold in full force. The Central American isthmus and the maritime routes surrounding it were already American interests and, as such, they would be protected. Thus regional harbors for US naval bases were needed and the forthcoming Panama Canal would simply reinforce the interventionist state of mind already in place.

Two related events facilitated the decision made by the then President of the United States, William McKinley, to enter the war in Cuba. First, American public opinion had been agitated for years by 'yellow journalism,' which depicted Spanish cruelty and mistreatment of Cubans in the worst possible terms. Such journalism fed the existent stereotypes of Latin American inferiority and promoted the Americans' 'white man's burden' role to be played out in the region. The second event was the sinking of the United States battleship *Maine* in Havana's harbor on 15 February 1898, which killed 260 men. On the other hand, the war was short (April–December 1898), an easy military success for an ascendant United States against a declining Spain. In the words of John Hay, US Ambassador to England at the time and later Secretary of State, '[It was] . . . a splendid little war' (Thomas, 1971, p. 404). Puerto Rico, the Philippines, and Guam, in addition to Cuba, fell into American hands, no small prize indeed.

Besides the sugar and other United States' economic interests in Cuba, which were always capable of wielding significant influence on the decisions of the US government, other corporate and individual figures best symbolized the ambivalent attitude of the United States towards Cuba during this historic period. William Randolph Hearst (1863–1951), the champion of American 'new journalism,' was one. He used the war in Cuba to gain not only wealth, notoriety, and unheard of circulation for his newspapers, but also to exercise his own personal credo: 'newspapers form and express public opinion. They suggest and control legislation. They declare wars' (Thomas, 1971, p. 313). Thus Hearst's historic exchange with his correspondent in Havana in 1897, who complained to him that contrary to their expectations 'There will be no war,' and who wanted to return to the United States. Hearst's response epitomized the character of the man and his time: 'Please remain. You furnish the pictures and I'll furnish the war.'

But above all, there was Theodore Roosevelt (1858–1919), whose political career was greatly aided by the war. After being appointed Assistant Secretary of the Navy by a reluctant President McKinley, he became then the new force behind the interventionism and expansionism of the United States in the region. After commanding the American Rough-Riders to victory at San Juan Hill and other sites, he would comment with joy that, 'The Spaniards shot well but they did not stand when we rushed. It was a good fight.' More than anyone else, he had captured the spirit of the awakening giant that the United States had already become, ready to capture an easy prey: the small nations located in the Caribbean Basin. Thus he would move on to become Governor of New York (1899–1900), Vice President (1900–1), and finally President (1901–9). The era of American 'Gunboat Diplomacy' and the 'Big Stick' in the Caribbean and the Central American isthmus would soon arrive.

The consequences of the new order created by the intervention of the United States in the Cuban War of independence were dramatized by the treatment of General Calixto García and his men. They were not allowed by the US forces to participate in the victory celebrations and the military parade held in Santiago de Cuba, and were also excluded from the cities by the American army. This was after American military commanders had used García's war plans for the battle of Santiago de Cuba, and had accepted his critical and decisive military support during the war. (García was not allowed to visit Santiago until later, when a 'Cuban victory celebration' was finally held.) Moreover, the attitude of American newspaper reports about the Cuban rebels and their leaders shifted significantly. In one story after another, they were vilified and ridiculed for their lack of a proper martial appearance. Their dirty clothes and makeshift equipment were held against them. American racist perceptions also played a significant role in this attitude. An American observer, Irene Wright, stated that the 'decadence and depravity in Cuba are due, largely, to the too free commingling of black blood and white.'

Serious questions were also raised regarding whether the Cubans were fit or not to become truly independent. A US Army officer, General Young, characterized Calixto García's army as 'a lot of degenerates, absolutely devoid of honour or gratitude. They are no more capable of self government than the savages.' In spite of all the years they had struggled for their freedom, the Cubans played no part in the Treaty of Paris (1898) ending the war between the United States and Spain. It was played as an affair that pertained only to the two big powers.

The future of the island was now in American hands. When the last Spanish Captain-General, Lieutenant-General Adolfo Jiménez Castellanos, handed the keys of Havana to a senior American officer, General John Rutter Brooke (1838–1926), almost four centuries of Spanish rule ended. However, the future status of Cuba was rather unclear at the time. The island was ruled by a US military government between 1 January 1899 and 20 May 1902. General Brooke was replaced as Military Governor by General Leonard Wood (1860–1927) on 20 December 1899. Wood was helpful in the eradication of yellow fever in Cuba, although the work done by the Cuban scientist Carlos J. Finlay—who discovered the mosquito vector of yellow fever—was largely ignored at the time in the United States, and still is today. Wood believed that Cubans desired annexation to the United States, and he made such decisions as reorganizing the schools so they would adapt 'as far as practicable to the public school system of the US.' Meanwhile, the Cuban Army that fought against Spain, the Ejercito Libertador, was dissolved and some of its men were incorporated into a rural guard organized by General Wood.

The birth of the Cuban Republic was problematic indeed. Determined to gain their independence, the Cuban patriots suffered a difficult period in their relations with United States' military authorities. On 25 February 1901, prior to the Cuban Constitutional Convention held later that year, the US Congress approved Senator Orville H. Platt's amendment to a bill. It defined the future relations between the United States and Cuba, disregarding any plans for the latter's future independence. In its third provision the Platt Amendment established that,

the government of Cuba consents that the United States may exercise *the right to intervene for the presevation of life, property, and individual liberty, and for discharging the obligations with respect to Cuba imposed by the Treaty of Paris on the United States, now to be assumed and undertaken by the government of Cuba*. [Suchlicki, 1974, pp. 96-7; emphasis added]

Cuba had no say, as had happened with the Paris Treaty, in Washington's legislative process deciding its future which the US Congress now made its own responsibility.

On 12 June 1901, three months after the bill became law in the United States, the Constitutional Convention convening in Havana approved the Platt Amendment by a one vote majority, but only after a rather bitter debate that remained deadlocked for a long time. The US government had made it clear, in no uncertain terms, that without the Platt Amendment being added to the Cuban Constitution there would be no Cuban Republic. Juan Gualberto Gómez, a black revolutionary and journalist who had been a close friend of Martí, expressing the generalized frustration created by it, stated, 'The Platt Amendment has reduced the independence and sovereignty of the Cuban republic to a myth.' The Platt Amendment remained attached to the 1901 Constitution, giving birth to charges of *plattismo* as a symbol of US control of Cuban affairs. It was finally abrogated on 29 May 1934 during President Franklin D. Roosevelt's first administration.

Cuba and the United States signed a Commercial Treaty of Reciprocity in 1903. It opened the American market for some Cuban products. The treaty provided Cuban sugar entering the United States with a 20 percent tariff preference, but it also opened the Cuban market for many American products. The main effect of this commercial agreement was to turn Cuba into a single-crop (sugar) economy largely dependent on the American market. In 1895 American investment totaled approximately $50 million. Fourteen years later, in 1909, it had reached over $200 million. Twenty years later, in 1929-30, it was estimated at somewhere between $1.15 and 1.5 billion. (After a decreasing or contracting period, it was close to $1 billion by 1958; although it was estimated by some at around $1.5 billion.) Americans were buying sugarmills, land, railroads, and other commercial enterprises. Politically, economically, commercially, and militarily the new Cuban Republic was very much under Washington's grip. Its post-independence years started contrary to Martí's vision of a politically and economically independent nation.[5]

Article VI of the Platt Amendment prescribed that the Isle of Pines 'shall be omitted from the proposed constitutional boundaries of Cuba, the title thereto being left to adjustment by treaty.' A sizable American community had settled in the small island, and worked as a pressure group to keep it as part of the United States. Spain had always treated the Isle of Pines as Cuban territory, so there was no legal basis for treating it differently in 1901–2. The first of two treaties on this subject was signed by both countries in 1903, but the US Senate failed to ratify it. A second treaty signed in 1904 had no ratification deadline, and was finally ratified by the Senate in 1925. The US Supreme Court in 1907 had recognized, however, that the Isle of Pines was *de facto* Cuban territory.

Another provision established by the Platt Amendment (Article VII) was not solved in a favorable way for the Cubans, and it turned into a source of further irritation for them. It was the establishment of a US naval base in Cuban territory. Initially the United States wanted to establish bases on four different sites. The Cubans reduced the list to two in 1912 (Guantánamo and Bahía Honda), but only one, Guantánamo Bay, was finally agreed upon. In exchange, the size of the lease was increased, the rent paid for a 45 square-mile naval base was set at only $2,000 a year, and no terminal date was stipulated for it. Therefore, the US Naval Base at Guantánamo still exists.

The Cuban Republic (1902–58)

Political analysts have subdivided the post-colonial, republican period extending from 1902 to 1958 into two distinct phases of political development—even as two differentiated political systems, notwithstanding elements of continuity present in both. (The following republican period, from 1959 to the present, under the Castro regime, is considered then as the third political system. In this last period more radical changes have been taking place, with less continuity from the earlier periods.) The first phase of political development, or first political system, extends from 1902 to 1933. On 12 August 1933 a revolution overthrew the tyrannical Machado regime and gave birth to several short-lived, *de facto* governments. The second phase of political development, or second political system, extends from 1934 until the fall of the Fulgencio Batista dictatorial regime on 31 December 1958 (Domínguez, 1978).

The first phase, 1902–33, was characterized by an incipient pluralization of the polity. It included the development of political, economic, and social power centers as the unintended outcome of direct American influence on, or control of, the political system. The power Washington had over Havana precluded the formation of a stronger and more capable central government.

In the second phase, from 1934 to 1958 (after the Platt Amendment had been abrogated), American control of Cuban affairs seemed to decrease—it became less obvious or direct, but remained equally effective. The period was characterized, nevertheless, by increasing regulation and distribution of available resources by the central government. This second phase witnessed a steady growth of political institutions, the economy, and the state at large. In both phases, however, existent social and economic cleavages were not strong enough to determine political behavior collectively or nationally. Political office holders, largely insulated from pressure groups, were capable of governing. None the less, there was an incremental growth of governmental power upon society and the economy from one phase of political development or political system to the next, a trend that increased substantially after 1959 under the Castro regime.

The First Political System (1902-33)

The Cuban Republic was inaugurated on 20 May 1902 with Tomás Estrada Palma as its first President. He had been chairman of the Cuban Revolutionary Party in New York City. He had not lived in Cuba for years. After living in New York City for so long, Estrada Palma was seen by American authorities as a good friend of the United States. The people's choice, however, was General Bartolomé Masó, a hero of the revolution since the Ten Year War. The American government's opposition to his candidacy, including the opposition of President McKinley and General Wood, as well as that of the Cuban propertied and wealthy classes, forced him to withdraw from the race. When General Gómez oddly enough came out publicly in support of Estrada Palma, the internal and international opposition Masó faced made it practically impossible for him to continue running for the presidency.

In 1906, Estrada Palma's attempt to get re-elected, provoked a rebellion led by the Liberal party. It all ended with a second American intervention, 1906-9. This time the American Governor was a civilian judge, Charles Magoon (1861-1920). Magoon left the country deeply in debt after squandering each year's public income as well as $12 million left in the nation's treasury by the Estrada Palma Administration. He was charged with profoundly corrupting the political process, and was characterized as 'gross in character, rude of manner, of a profound ambition, [and] greedy for despoilment.' Also, it was charged that his 'government opened its hands and let loose the purse strings without any regard,' and that his 'kindness in granting botellas—i.e. sinecures—became a public scandal . . . the administration in general returned to the corrupt practices of colonial times.' Magoon's rationalization for his ill-advised actions was that he simply did what the Cuban politicians wanted and asked him to do (Thomas, 1971, pp. 482-3).

Finally, a leader of the Liberal party, General José Miguel Gómez, was elected President and inaugurated on 28 January 1909, ending the second American intervention. An uprising by the Independent Color party in 1912 provoked a massacre of blacks by the Rural Guard—3,000 blacks or more that joined the revolt were killed. In 1912, 1917–20, and 1933–4 American troops and/or battleships were sent to Cuba for the purpose of intervening directly in, or influencing indirectly, its internal affairs.

Continuing the four-year presidential cycle, Gómez was succeeded by another general in 1913, General Mario García Menocal, who served two consecutive periods. His re-election ignited wide opposition, and his Administration became effective mainly because of the support it received from Washington. The United States refused to recognize the popularly supported liberal revolt opposing Menocal's re-election, known as the 'Chambelona' uprising of 1917, and sent its troops again. Historically called the years of *vacas flacas* (of famine and scarcity) due to the sharp decline in the price of sugar, his second term was economically disastrous. In spite of the relative prosperity enjoyed earlier, from 1915 to 1920, he left a national debt totalling $164 million. Menocal was followed by a civilian president, Alfredo Zayas, 1921–5.

The control exercised by Washington during this period was dramatized by General Enoch H. Crowder's special mission, undertaken in January 1921 at the request of President Woodrow Wilson. After having drawn a new electoral law and having posted observers to watch the voting in the 1921 Presidential election without being able to curb violence and fraud, Crowder turned his attention to the pressing economic and financial problems the country faced. In 1920 the Menocal Administration had proclaimed a moratorium that had paralyzed businesses. Crowder recommended that it should be gradually lifted in order to revive economic activity. Also, he listed the conditions the government should meet, so Cuba could receive a $50 million emergency loan from the United States. Crowder's conditions included such items as budget reductions, cancellations of contracts, and the reorganization of the national lottery. Finally, President Zayas had to appoint a new Cabinet that would give credibility to his decision of making good the proposed changes, and that would convince Washington to grant the loan. It was finally approved in November 1922. After his Presidential mission ended, Crowder remained in Cuba as US Ambassador.

Then came the presidency of General Gerardo Machado, 1925–33. Machado's rule was characterized by harsh repression. His dictatorial methods worsened after his re-election, and he tried to reform the Constitution so his presidential term could be extended. The popular discontent of the late 1920s culminated in open revolution by the 1930s. Machado had to flee the country on 12 August 1933 after being forced to resign by a general strike and by the Army. These events marked a historic transition for the young republic. It entered an era of increasing political conflict, civil unrest, and, paradoxically, modernization.

The severe socioeconomic crisis suffered during this period was almost unavoidable for a country as underdeveloped as Cuba. It was caught in the world economic crisis while undergoing a delayed nation- and state-building process. Also, it had suffered from endemically weak political institutions and *caudillismo* since its inauguration as a republic. Direct control of Cuban affairs by the United States under the Platt Amendment contributed to a delay in the growth of its political institutions and in the state altogether. However, university students, trade unions, and the middle sectors were now among the political forces that had to be considered. Increasing politicization was taking place among heretofore non-politically active social groups. In 1925 the Cuban Communist Party had been founded by Carlos Baliño, José Antonio Mella, and others. Founder of the Anti-Imperialist League and revolutionary student leader, Mella was assassinated in Mexico in 1929, allegedly ordered by Machado. Another member of the Communist Party, the poet Rubén Martínez Villena, was a prominent revolutionary leader until his untimely death in 1934.

In the post-Platt Amendment period, the relationship between the United States and Cuba was mostly based on the latter's political and economic dependency upon the former. In keeping with Cuba's subordinate status, US hegemonic power over it was a daily, unavoidable fact of life affecting the island's national and international politics. A myriad of political leaders had learned to live with the situation, and individually each had profited from Cuba's lack of effective sovereignty. A major factor compounding this oppressive relationship was the economy. Cuba's single main commodity, sugar, had rather unstable prices in the international market. Consequently the existent bilateral trade relations served to bind Cuba even closer to the United States. A new Commercial Reciprocity Treaty was signed in 1934 replacing the earlier one of 1903. After the Treaty was amended later, a total of 487 different American commodities entering the Cuban market received preferential tariff concessions, ranging from 20 to 60 percent below the established rate.

Meanwhile, American capital in the island increased and became more diversified. US financial investment continued moving into Cuba from 1914 to 1925 and beyond, increasing the rate of the earlier period from 1898 to 1913. In 1926 a US Department of Commerce Report estimated a total of

$1,360 million. It included sugar, railroads, tobacco, mining, banking, commerce, manufacturing, public services, financing of Cuba's public debt, real estate, and port facilities and warehouses. Some of these were controlled by American capitalists as virtual monopolies; i.e., power (electricity and gas), telephone, and the perfume and soap industry. (However, between 1946 and 1953 the American investment rate in Cuba decreased in comparison to previous years, and also in comparison to US investment in Latin America for the same period: 24.1 percent for Cuba, and 98.2 per cent for the latter (Pino-Santos, 1973, pp. 65, 213; *Monopolios Norteamericanos en Cuba*, 1973, *passim*).)

The Second Political System (1934-58)

The main political actors for this second phase of political development emerged from the events of the 1930s, particularly those directly involved in overthrowing the Machado regime. Similarly, in the first phase, the political leaders had emerged from the struggle against Spanish colonial rule. After 1959, the revolutionary leaders were among those at the forefront of the struggle against the Batista dictatorship. They included Ramón Grau San Martín (civilian leader, and provisional and elected president), Fulgencio Batista (military leader, the country's new strongman, and elected president), the leaders of the University Student Directorate, and trade unions, and political activists, and many others.

All of them represented different political and ideological tendencies, as well as financial and commercial interests. The student movement included revolutionary non-Marxist, and Marxist groups like (University) Students' Left Wing and International Workers Defense. Grau San Martín was a middle-class university professor who became provisional president after the uprising of 4 September 1933. His government lasted almost five months (10 September 1933-15 January 1934). It fell due to US pressure and lack of diplomatic recognition. On 4 September the non-commissioned Army officers led by Batista and supported by the University Student Directorate, rebelled against the provisional conservative government of Carlos Manuel de Céspedes Quesada. He had replaced Machado three weeks earlier and was the son of Carlos Manuel de Céspedes, who had initiated the nineteenth-century Ten Year War (Aguilar, 1971; Suchlicki, 1969).

Grau San Martín's short-lived government initiated important social and nationalist legislation. It was mostly the work of a revolutionary cabinet minister, Antonio Guiteras, who truly cared for the people's needs and expectations. Guiteras was assassinated later, allegedly by Batista. A series of workers' protests and strikes, land confiscation by peasants, and the takeover of sugarmills by sugar workers—some of them turned into provisional Soviets—led to the formation of a strong opposition front by the wealthy and propertied class and supported by the American Ambassador, Sumner Welles (1892–1962), who was acting more as 'a Proconsul than an ambassador, a politician than a civil servant.' They were joined then by Batista, who readily double-crossed Grau San Martín. Batista had been promoted from Sergeant to Colonel, and later to General, and appointed head of the Army during the 4 September uprising. In this capacity he was able to come into close contact with Ambassador Welles, and they planned together the undoing of the nationalist Grau San Martín provisional government. Batista became Cuba's new strongman. He exercised full power from his military post while several appointed and elected Presidents were in office, a total of five. One President lasted only twenty-four hours. Batista was finally elected President in 1940.

Prior to Batista's election, the 1940 Constitution was promulgated. It was a rather progressive and democratic charter. Like Mexico's 1917 Constitution, it was oriented towards social security and affirmative action rights. In the second elections held under the new Constitution, Grau San Martín was elected President in 1944. He ran successfully in the Cuban Revolutionary Party (Auténtico) ticket. The party was an outgrowth of the revolutionary university student groups of the 1930s, and selected Grau San Martín as its leader. He had been living in exile in Miami and returned to Cuba only after being elected President. A second Auténtico President, Carlos Prío Socarrás, a student revolutionary leader of the 1930s, followed in 1948. By the end of his term, when the country was preparing for another presidential election, Batista launched a military coup on 10 March 1952.

The Auténticos had been in power by then for eight consecutive years. Their government was marked by extraordinary corruption and civil unrest. Although the second Auténtico Administration, Prío Socarrás', was highly respectful of civil rights and promulgated substantive legislation complementing the 1940 Constitution, popular discontent on account of continuous political scandals and civil unrest had eroded its legitimacy. The protest movement founded by a former Auténtico leader, Eduardo Chibás, became organized as the Cuban People's Party (Ortodoxo) in the late 1940s. It was the fastest growing political party at the time, and it seemed the most likely victor in the June 1952 elections—even though its founder, Chibás, had committed suicide a year earlier. Fidel Castro was a member of the Ortodoxo party and a candidate from Havana province for the House of Representatives. But the elections were never held, because of Batista's coup. After having initiated a constitutional process twelve years earlier, Batista put an end to it after three elected administrations. Cuba was launched again into military rule and violent opposition. A new revolutionary era was about to begin.

The 1952–58 Insurrection.   The Batista regime lasted almost seven years. It ended when Castro came down from the Sierra Maestra mountains as both chief of the revolution, and architect of a new Cuba. However, the seven-year insurrection against Batista was bloody. The anti-Batista forces faced cruel repression, even by Cuban standards. An estimated 20,000 Cubans died during this period. They were victims of the repressive measures applied by Batista primarily against the revolutionaries, but also against the civilian population. Victims also included members of the armed forces, many of whom died defending the regime. In the last years of the insurrection close to a civil war plagued the country, especially in the central and eastern provinces (Bonachea & San Martín, 1974).

On 26 July 1953 Fidel Castro and his brother Raúl, together with more than a hundred men, attacked the Santiago de Cuba Moncada Barracks and the Bayamo Barracks, both in Oriente province. After months of preparation, at a cost of $16,480 paid with their own savings, their bold action served to alert the country to events to come. Militarily, it had been a failure; politically, it put Castro at the forefront of the anti-Batista struggle. On 21 September 1953, the survivors of the 26 July actions went on trial. After being removed from the courtroom by the authorities alleging that he was 'suddenly ill,' Castro was able to defend his own actions on 16 October in a speech known as *History Will Absolve Me* (Castro, n.d., pp. 1–67). Although it was initially repressed by the regime, Castro's underground network circulated the speech (or parts of it) clandestinely. It became an important political weapon in the struggle against Batista. Castro's *History Will Absolve Me* speech was regarded by many as an invaluable manifesto expressing his political ideas and future plans for Cuba.

Many more actions against the Batista regime followed, even from the armed forces. Army and navy officers, non-commissioned officers, and privates sought unsuccessfully to overthrow Batista. On 13 March 1957 members of Havana University (Students') Revolutionary Directorate attacked Havana's Presidential Palace, home of President Batista. While many of the attackers and palace guards were killed, Batista escaped unharmed. The attack was followed, however, by a massive police hunt for revolutionaries in the city underground, and many were killed on sight. Castro was already fighting in the Sierra Maestra, after landing in Cuba on 2 December 1956. He and his men had sailed from Mexico in the yacht *Granma*. During the last two years of the regime, 1957 and 1958, the warfare increased. The fighting involved the underground in Havana and other cities across the island and the guerrillas in the Sierra Maestra and Sierra del Escambray mountains, and other areas of the central and eastern provinces. The regime responded by escalating repressive measures.[6]

Finally, in the early hours of New Year's Day, 1 January 1959, Batista and his family and members of his regime fled the country. The revolution was now in power. Uncertainty about its meaning and direction loomed in Cuba's future. The people, however, joined in a massive celebration of Batista's fall, welcoming Castro and his fellow guerrillas as true liberators. Unknowingly, Cuba was about to embark on a new, uncharted path. That path would soon lead Cuba to start building a socialist regime, the first one ever in the western hemisphere.

2 The Cuban Republic

The revolutionary government has been in office for almost three decades. The extent and effect of revolutionary state power is meant to be different from the exercise of political power under conventional circumstances. Cuba has exemplified this beyond any previous experience in Latin America. The transformation of its polity has been radical, in many areas as total as it could possibly be. Cuban analysts have argued whether it was meant to take the direction it finally did: setting up the first Marxist–Leninist state in the western hemisphere. According to some critics, what was supposed to be and what was needed was just a reformist government that would bring about the necessary structural changes for an effective liberal democratic system. This is more than an academic debate. It is central to an understanding of the nature and dynamics of Cuba throughout the entire period, and especially today. In addition to some of the major events that took place during these years, the reasons behind the course followed by the Cuban revolution will be examined in this chapter.

The Third Political System (1959 to the Present)

The trend toward the formation of a stronger, more centralized government that had started earlier continued during the third phase of political development, or third political system, under the revolutionary regime. Castro's thinking and personality have been major factors determining the nature and direction of the revolution. His charismatic leadership has also been a major source for its legitimacy. All of this created a system whereby the regime's authority has always been highly centralized in and around Castro. Notwithstanding these facts, there seemed to be room for institutional behavioral differentiation within the system. Political analysts have interpreted differently the degree of semi-autonomous life (or lack thereof) enjoyed by such political bodies as the mass organizations. During the 1960s the mass organizations were instrumental in bringing about the high level of massive national mobilization achieved by the regime.[1] A systematic study of the regime's policies, methods of eliciting compliance from the population, and implementation of national programs among different population groups and the mass organizations during this period, indicates an observable degree of individualized (differentiated) behavior among the several actors involved. On a broader and institutionalized basis, this was also true after the institutionalization of the revolution was undertaken in the 1970s (Azicri, 1977).[2]

The revolutionary government followed drastic policy changes that were understood as the sign of an erratic leadership. These changes were also seen, however, as the sign of the difficult process of growth and maturation of the revolution. In growing and maturing, the revolution could not follow any clearly direct path. Nevertheless, some have regretted the lost reformist character of Castro's 26 July Movement (named after the date of the Moncada Barracks attack in 1953):

> [Castro,] after achieving power in Cuba, aligned his country with the Communist nations of the world and ... abandoned the concepts of nationalism and of democractic action that are basic characteristics of all the reform movements which his own originally resembled ... [Wilkerson, 1965, p. 1][3]

This critical radicalization process could be examined according to a sequential time-period: (1) from January 1959 to the fall of 1960 (the bourgeois-democratic stage, which lasted until the means of production were nationalized by the revolutionary government, including 166 enterprises some of which were wholly or partly US-owned); (2) from 24 October 1960 (the nationalization of the means of production) to 16 April 1961 (Castro's proclamation of the socialist character of the revolution on the eve of the Bay of Pigs invasion); and (3) from 16 April 1961 to today (including the moment in which Castro further defined the revolution as being Marxist-Leninist, 2 December 1961).

What started as a national liberation revolutionary process with patriotic, popular, and bourgeois-democratic components turned rapidly into a socialist, and then a Marxist-Leninist system. Although done under revolutionary state power, it was accomplished without a revolutionary communist party leading the radicalization process. Also, contrary to Marxist theory, the transition towards Marxism-Leninism was not done on behalf of 'the dictatorship of the proletariat.' Nevertheless, in only twenty-two months of revolutionary government, from January 1959 to October 1960, Cuba had moved away from its initial 'semicolonial' status into a country on its way to 'building socialism.'

The revolutionary leadership was made of Castro first, followed by his close associates from the Sierra Maestra, including his brother Raúl. Under this radical vanguard lay the institutionally weak political infrastructure of the regime: Castro's 26 July Movement (M-26-7), the [Havana University] students' Revolutionary Directorate (DR), and the old Communist Party, Popular Socialist Party (PSP). The difficult, at times agonizing, process of building a revolutionary political party started in 1961. First, the three revolutionary structures were unified into the Integrated Revolutionary Organizations party (ORI). Secondly, in 1963, ORI was transformed into the United Party of the Socialist Revolution (PURS). Finally, in 1965 PURS gave way to the present Cuban Communist Party (PCC).

The process of creating a unified political structure from three different revolutionary organizations proved to be rather conflictive. Some major crises, like the 1962 Anibal Escalante, and 1967 Escalante's 'microfaction' affairs arose. The main problem for some members of the PSP (who belonged to by far the best organized and institutionally strongest of the three organizations) was accepting Castro and his Sierra Maestra guerrillas (who lacked training and experience as communist cadres) as the leaders of a new communist party and Marxist-Leninist regime. Additionally, they seemed to forget, it was Castro's revolution and not theirs.

Domestic and international political dynamics, pressures, threats, and attacks against the revolution—as well as massive support for it by the majority of the Cuban population—provided both the context and the forces pitted against each other throughout this difficult period. A fundamental change in the locus of political and economic power had taken place. The regime has usually explained its policies as a continuation of Cuba's tradition in its struggle for independence since the 1860s. None the less, the goal of destroying the old social order created a situation whereby the revolution could find no basis in Cuban history, culture, and political traditions for a model of what the new society should be and look like.

The native bourgeoisie did have, however, an initial role in the revolution's developmental blueprint. But internal and external anti-revolutionary aggression in conjunction with internal and external support for it, served to demonstrate the uncompromising posture of those whose economic interests had been negatively affected by the revolution. This fact sheds some light on the ensuing socioeconomically based, ideological counterrevolutionary struggle that characterized those first years.

The revolution's social and economic policies were aimed at transforming the existent land tenure and banking, industrial, housing, and trade (internal and external) systems. They sought to improve educational, public health, and utilities services, and employment opportunities for low-income groups. Those policies finally eliminated the so-called *tiempo muerto* ('dead season') between sugar harvests, when most of the sugar workers were always unemployed.

The early politics of the revolution were mainly oriented toward a two-fold goal: (1) creating newly differentiated social roles and structures in order to meet the dual challenge of government stability and survival (based on revolutionary principles and objectives); and (2) unfolding its own blueprint for the development of a new revolutionary society. Numerous egalitarian policies sought new allegiances and wide support for the revolution. In addition to redistributing wealth, initiating finally a thorough agrarian reform, and nationalizing private enterprises (national and foreign), the revolution sought to eliminate social privilege, inequity, and prejudice (i.e., racism) as they existed under the *ancien régime*. Mobilization campaigns were used then as suitable means to generate political activism among the population, as well as to increase popular support for the revolutionary regime.

The regime did not ignore the political cultural aspects of the country's development. The erosion of the old political culture and the development of a new one based on revolutionary social and political values became a central concern for the regime. It led to an ideologically based cultural policy that could help generate as well as reinforce the emerging revolutionary political culture (Hart, 1978).

The First Decade: the 1960s

Cuban President Manuel Urrutia's resignation on 17 July 1959, after being less than seven months in office, caused a major political and ideological crisis within the revolutionary government. (He was replaced by Osvaldo Dorticós Torrado, who remained President until 1975.) On 16 February 1959, Fidel Castro had become the Prime Minister of the revolutionary government, succeeding José Miró Cardona.[4] Serious tensions had been growing between Urrutia and Castro for months. The tensions exceeded whatever personality problems could have been expected from two very different individuals having to make momentous decisions for a whole nation. While Urrutia was making public statements about the menace communism could represent for the people's welfare and the revolution, the real leaders of the revolution including Castro, his brother Raúl, Ernesto Che Guevara, and others, were thinking and planning quite differently. As indicated earlier, during the revolution's radicalization process, their problem was not Marxist ideology, the PSP, or the Soviet Union.

For the revolutionary leadership the dangers were coming from the privileged classes affected by the revolutionary laws and from the equally affected American interests in Cuba. Also, and more importantly, they saw an increasingly suspicious President Dwight Eisenhower looking with alarm at the direction the Cuban revolution was taking. Finally, on 3 January 1961, his Administration terminated US diplomatic and consular relations with Cuba, and on 31 March President John F. Kennedy reduced the Cuban sugar quota in the US market to zero. (Twenty-nine years later diplomatic relations have not been restored, and the economic embargo on all trade with Cuba imposed by President Kennedy on 3 February 1962 continues. Under the Administration of President Jimmy Carter, however, (diplomatic/consular) interest sections were opened in each nation's capital in 1977. They are housed in an established embassy; i.e., the US Interest Section in the Swiss Embassy in Havana, and Cuba's in the Czech Embassy in Washington.)

The Bay of Pigs and the Missile Crisis

On 17 April 1961 a force of approximately 1,500 Cuban exiles attempted the abortive Bay of Pigs invasion of Cuba. In two days the invasion had been defeated, and Castro had captured approximately 1,113 rebels. The members of the 2506 Brigade, as the exile force was called, had been 'recruited, trained, equipped, and transported by agents of the CIA. Their battle plan had been drawn by the CIA and approved by the US Joint Chiefs of Staff.' Upon leaving from Puerto Cabezas, Nicaragua—with the late Nicaraguan dictator Anastasio Somoza in attendance wishing them well—en route to Cuba, they were told by their CIA officers 'to fight their way inland to the main road and then turn left to Havana.'[5] (Pointedly, tourist shops in Cuba sell today small plastic bags filled with sand from Giron Beach—as the 2506 Brigade battle place is called in Cuba—with a printed legend that reads: 'Sand from Giron Beach—Bay of Pigs.' And on the other side: 'Giron—[the site of] the first defeat of [US] imperialism in Latin America.')

On 18 April an emergency session of the United Nations Security Council heard Cuban Foreign Minister Raúl Roa charging that Cuba was being invaded by mercenaries trained by the CIA in bases located in Florida and Guatemala. US Secretary of State Dean Rusk denied publicly any direct American intervention, but had also made known his sympathy for the rebels' cause. The aftermath of the invasion was manifold. For the Kennedy Administration it meant a loss of national and international prestige. For Cuba it meant a victorious moment for the revolution which now could boast of proven popular national support. For the CIA it meant a loss of bureaucratic prestige and an administrative overhaul that culminated in the replacement of its director, Allen Dulles. For the exile forces it meant almost two years in Cuban prisons until they were released and flown to Miami, Florida, on 24 December 1962. After long negotiations they were exchanged by Castro for some $54 million in drugs, medicines, and baby food supplied by American companies.

Regardless of how regrettable (and unlawful) the Bay of Pigs episode was, the CIA-sponsored anti-revolutionary actions did not start or end with it. In a way it culminated countless efforts at undermining and sabotaging the Cuban regime, and continuing the counterrevolution. But it was followed by numerous new attempts, including assassination plots against Castro.

The American-Soviet-Cuban crisis of 22 October 1962—the 'thirteen-day missile crisis'—was of a very different nature. It was the most serious ever involving the possibility of a nuclear war between the United States and the Soviet Union. The crisis was created by the Soviet Union's attempt that summer to install intermediate range ballistic missiles (IRBMs) in Cuba. As a defensive measure for Cuba, it was rooted in the Bay of Pigs and countless CIA sponsored anti-revolutionary actions. For the Soviet Union, it could have been an attempt to provide Cuba with a defensive nuclear umbrella barring further US attacks, and/or the desire to match American missiles in Turkey and Italy pointed at the Soviet Union. Also, it could have been just a bargaining card to exact a promise from the United States not to sponsor another invasion of Cuba.

For President Kennedy, this action, seen by many as a major threat to the security of the United States and other countries in the hemisphere, demanded some kind of comparable response. As Kennedy succinctly put it, '[Otherwise] I would have been impeached.' Nevertheless, some close advisors to President Kennedy did not see the Soviet missiles in Cuba as a major threat: 'a missile is a missile, regardless of whether it is in Cuba or in Europe; promixity to the American continent should not be such a major factor.' Psychologically, however, there was a great difference: the American public would hardly endure the anxiety that a generalized feeling of immediate national danger would create.

When Soviet Premier Nikita S. Khrushchev finally agreed to Kennedy's request to dismantle the missile sites and return all offensive weapons to the Soviet Union, after a US 'maritime quarantine' had been set up around Cuba, Castro (who was opposed to agreeing to any US proposal) felt bitterly betrayed by his Soviet allies. He refused to accept on-site inspection and verification that the missiles had been removed. Despite the US pledge not to invade Cuba, a small Soviet military detachment remained behind—a symbol of the Soviet commitment to Cuba's defense. Paradoxically, although the missile crisis led to a relatively safer military situation for Cuba, it was a moment that neither Castro nor his compatriots relished.

Later Castro seemed to have changed his mind. Asked if he had been disappointed with the Soviet Union and the way the final decision was reached, he said:

Well, we were not totally satisfied and we were enormously irritated. But if we are realistic, and we go back in history, we realize that ours was not the correct posture ... The Russian opinion was that two objectives would be gained from those negotiations: the promise not to invade Cuba ... and ... to eliminate the danger of nuclear war ... [These] [t]wo important political objectives were satisfied. [Mankiewicz & Jones, 1975, p. 151]

The most significant aspect of these remarks is not so much the change that usually comes from the benefit of hindsight, but the political maturity and statemanship that it signifies. Also, it could be seen as an expression of later periods of Castro's leadership in contrast to earlier ones.

Mobilization Campaigns

The revolution's initial sociopolitical policies and programs were pursued through the mobilization campaigns of the 1960s. Notwithstanding their social significance, these policies were mostly of a populist nature. They were not sufficient by themselves to build a socialist socioeconomic and political system. None the less, they provided the necessary foundation for later stages of socialist development. As the bedrock for revolutionary change, the policies needed massive popular support. Additionally, by supporting them and participating in the different ongoing mobilization campaigns, the people became actors in the revolutionary process. They were acquiring and acting out their *conciencia* (revolutionary consciousness), a major sign of being fully integrated into the revolution.

Based upon the 1953 census, with a population under seven million, the regime estimated Cuba still would have over one million illiterate persons in 1960-1. Although 15,000 new classrooms had been built in one year, and the student population was over one million, lack of education of the under-privileged was still a major problem. Hence the Literacy Campaign of 1961. Hundreds of volunteers taught peasants and other traditionally dispossessed population groups how to read and write. On 5 November 1961 a municipality in Havana province was declared the first one ever free of analphabetism. Others followed soon. By the end of 1961 an illiteracy rate close to 20 percent of the population—according to some estimates over

25 percent—had been reduced to 3.9 percent. That year's literacy census confirmed the literacy campaign estimates as the new national rates (*Cuba: Territorio Libre de Analfabetismo*, 1981).

Other innovative educational programs like La Escuela al Campo (Schools in the Countryside) allowed students the dual experience of receiving an education while doing agricultural work. Education developed as one of the successes of revolutionary social policy and its most widely recognized achievement next to public health.[6]

The founding of the Committees for the Defense of the Revolution (CDRs) in 1960, as a response to the intensive sabotage by the counter-revolutionaries, provided nationwide political participation through a single mass organization. (They were organized throughout the entire country, on a block by block basis.) Years later, as counterrevolutionary activism receded, the CDRs changed as well. Rather than watching for the enemies of the revolution, its goals became social, political, and ideological. It became the vehicle for all kinds of national campaigns ranging from educational to public health—i.e., massive vaccination programs. The CDRs effectiveness in these new tasks was proved frequently. When a national epidemic of dengue fever plagued the country in 1980, it was controlled and finally eliminated after a few months of intense campaigning and hard work. This would have been practically impossible without the organizational structure the CDRs provided. On the negative side, the CDRs have been charged with working as a spy network covering the entire nation for the revolutionary regime.

Socially and politically the mobilization campaigns had a common goal: to create a social interaction that would destroy the distinctive class differentiation of the pre-revolutionary society, while building an egalitarian one. Hence, by bringing urban dwellers to the countryside in a way unseen before, the traditional social dichotomy separating life in the cities from the rural areas was partly overcome. The urban population was exposed to the miseries of rural Cuba, creating an awareness and a level of consciousness that would lead to a better integrated polity. The mass organizations mirrored new and old social cleavages in their make-up, including current social differentiations. Thus institutional membership by workers, peasants, women, youth, and other population groups in the militias, armed forces, CDRs, FMC, and trade unions was representative of the emerging society. Equally representative was membership in such a youth organization as the Union of Communist Youth (UJC), which was organized in 1960 to replace the Association of Rebel Youth (AJR), and to a lesser extent in the Cuban Communist Party.

The mobilization campaigns demanded personal dedication and even sacrifice. Nevertheless, the combined effect of all these political undertakings had a liberating impact upon many Cubans, tapping unused human resources and releasing sources of constructive energy that could be channeled in specific directions. They exemplified the revolution's social engineering capability for transforming Cuban society.

A more critical way of looking at this sociopolitical process is to recognize that the regime at least induced, if not forced, the population to participate in revolutionary political life through its mobilization campaigns. Strong pressure was exerted upon the population to show 'oneness' with the revolution not just in words but in action. From the government's side it was particularly urgent to enlist the population in the works of the revolution, creating a close identification between the leaders and the masses.

A negative byproduct of this situation was that the government considered those who were not bona fide participants as disaffected and capable of harming the revolution either by action or omission. The perception of this dilemma by Cubans opposing Castro was clearly stated in these terms:

> in effect the authorities asked 'Are you with us or against us?' If the answer was 'With you,' then the citizen was required to demonstrate his 'withness' or integration through participation in revolutionary activities. Failure to do so was taken to indicate not just lethargy or lack of interest, but counterrevolutionary tendencies...
> [Fagen, 1968, p. 83]

This state of affairs did not make things easier for those who chose not to integrate themselves into the revolutionary process and still remain in Cuba. It reinforced their sociopolitical anomie, alienating them further from the newly emerging value system. For some, it provided an additional reason to emigrate to the United States, or elsewhere.[7]

The Social Cost of Revolutionary Policy

The initial societal changes undertaken by the revolution, which generated support for, and allegiance to, the regime, have been classified in three developmental stages. This classification is based on three conceptual assumptions seemingly present in Cuba in the 1960s: the revolutionary leadership was committed to rapid economic development; the regime faced a scarcity of resources; and the population was mobilized in order to maximize the regime's resources. On the basis of their social costs, the three developmental stages were classified as: (1) generating support through means of demand-satisfaction (1959–61); (2) reducing demand-satisfaction and increasing social regimentation (1962–5); and (3) advocating moral incentives while regimenting the society (1966-70s) (Malloy, 1971, pp. 23-42).

During the first stage, consumptionist and developmental policies ran simultaneously, with an emphasis on the former over the latter. This reinforced the already existent high level of popular support for the revolution. The social costs were allocated mostly to foreign investors and national upper and middle sectors. By 1962, however, a second phase marked the emphasis on developmental policies over consumption. Individualized demand-satisfaction decreased, becoming increasingly egalitarian through collectivistic programs. Free and universal social services became the trademark of a revolutionary egalitarian consumer society. Social costs, however, were transferred to the population at large, especially the urban sectors. The regime increased its reliance on mobilization and regimentation as its means for transforming society.

Finally, during the third stage, the developmental goals became paramount for the regime. Individualized consumption was reduced further. Collectivistic modality increased. The rural sector became a bearer of social costs, too. Moral incentives became the rationale for the 'new socialist man' and the eventual attainment of a communist society. Using the armed forces for civilian and economic tasks ameliorated the need for further mobilization of the population. Hence the revolutionary army became a multifunctional entity with new social, political, as well as military significance. Its status increased to a point where its subordinate position *vis-à-vis* the party was not as clear as it is expected to be in a Marxist-Leninist regime (Malloy, 1971).

The radicalization of the revolution and its incremental rate of social transformation brought rapid changes to Cuban society. Consequently, these changes affected various population groups differently at successive moments. The population was both the beneficiary of social policy and the bearer of social costs. In keeping with revolutionary ethics, the regime favored the system of moral over material incentives (the system was modified later, blending material and moral incentives into a unified policy). Ideologically, it moved the population further away from capitalist notions and closer to socialist values. From a material standpoint, the regime's capabilities were limited. Therefore, a policy of unrestrained individualized consumerism was neither feasible nor advisable on ideological, political, or economic grounds. The developmental dilemmas the revolutionary regime confronted were a mix of uniquely Cuban problems, and the general distressed conditions faced by developing nations. Cuba, however, was finally attempting to solve these problems.

Transforming the Economy

The pre-1959 Cuban economy has been characterized by such indicators as: (1) one-crop sugar concentration; (2) agricultural *latifundia* (large land holdings) tenure system; (3) weakness of the national industry; and (4) extreme economic dependence on the United States. Revolutionary policy was a radical response to the problems this economic system created, as well as to the system itself. However, by the 1950s Cuba had advanced more in its economically dependent model than other countries in the region. Aproximately 40 percent of the population lived in urban centres of 20,000 inhabitants or more. Also, Cuba had a population growth rate of only 2 percent (the result of lower mortality and lower birth rates cancelling each other out), while the region's was 2.8 percent. Life expectancy at birth had reached 62 years in the 1955-60 period, and the per capita income oscillated between $400 and $500—higher than that of most Latin American countries except Argentina and Venezuela (CEPAL, 1980, pp. 13–35).

And yet, Cuba's economy was plagued by 'marginality, unemployment and underemployment, the vulnerability of its external sector and the lack of economic dynamism.' Moreover, production, national income, and the level of social services had been frozen since the 1920s. They had recovered minimally from the economic disaster of the 1930s, when the price of sugar was only a tenth of what it had been a decade earlier. From 1952 to 1956 Cuba's purchasing power was the same as it had been thirty years earlier.

The major socioeconomic problems facing Cuba in 1957-8 were: (1) a low rate of economic growth; (2) sugar's excessive role in generating national income and exports; (3) an extreme dependence on the United States for capital investment and trade; (4) rather high rates of unemployment and underemployment; and (5) a wide gap in the standard of living between the urban and rural sectors (Mesa-Lago, 1971, pp. 277–338).

While other Latin American countries' economies improved in the 1940s and 1950s, Cuba's potential economic growth was structurally constrained by the relative security of a preferential quota in the American sugar market. The United States exercised a major influence on the Cuban economy as American products profited from a preferential access to its limited domestic market. Also, trade unions supported existent wages and social legislation made capital investment unattractive for the private sector. In spite of having a better economic infrastructure and better qualified human resources than other countries in the region, it did not profit from an import substitution and/or diversification industrial policy. Instead, it invested disproportionately in expensive urban housing, major hotels and gambling casinos catering to American tourism, while it suffered from generalized political and cultural corruption characterized by rampant prostitution and crime, especially in Havana. Discussing this complex phenomenon, Boorstein states in his first-hand account of revolutionary economic policy: 'Until the Revolution, the central fact about the Cuban economy was its domination by American monopolies ... It was from imperialist domination that the specific characteristics flowed. Unless this is recognized, the Cuban revolution cannot be understood' (Boorstein, 1968, pp. 1, *passim*).

The initial economic transformation policy covered three major inter-related areas: structural economic changes; improvements in socioeconomic and living conditions; and changes in the external trade system. The first included agricultural diversification, industrial development, reducing the historical dependence on sugar, and increasing the rate of economic growth. The second was primarily concerned with attaining full employment and improving living conditions for the rural population and low-income urban workers. The third area sought to achieve economic independence from the United States.

During the 1959–69 period, this broad range of goals was modified to include both the means used for policy implementation and the goals themselves. There were conflicting views concerning: (1) whether a developmental policy based on diversification and non-sugar agriculture or one based on sugar and primary activities should be pursued; (2) whether to favor distribution and consumption, or to accumulate needed capital for development; and, finally, (3) whether to organize economic production based on decentralized planning, economic incentives and self-financed enterprises, or to rely instead on centralization, budgeted enterprises, and moral incentives. Throughout the decade, policy shifted from the first to the second choice in all three categories (Mesa-Lago, 1971, p. 281).

The reasons provoking policy changes were manifold. They included shifting preferences in developmental strategies and organizational models, chosen according to their usefulness in the transition to socialism. Also, there was some interplay between the regime's policy objectives and domestic and international economic reality. The revolutionary leadership had to reassess and adapt its goals to the newly found constraints imposed by its limited capability and resources. Washington's anti-Cuba policy, Havana's response of seeking closer relations with the Soviet Union, and the regime's internal ideological transformation towards Marxism-Leninism were developments related to the economic problems examined here—if not caused by them.

The revolution had to agree on something more transcendental than a developmental model, notwithstanding its importance. It had to substitute a new partnership offering comparable resources, and badly needed aid, trade, credits, and other types of assistance on more satisfying terms—i.e., its close relations and association with the Soviet Union, and other socialist countries—for Cuba's traditional trade and economic relations with the United States. Whether it simply substituted one set of dependent relations for another is a controversial matter among Cuba watchers. For the revolutionary leaders, as long as Cuba's transition towards socialism was a logical and necessary development, its decision to join the socialist camp was a foregone conclusion.[8] Its new status is not comparable to the dependent relationship that it had with the United States in the pre-1959 period.[9]

Economic difficulties began to emerge in the early 1960s, however. There were shortages of all kinds of commodities. Rationing had to be instituted to assure equal access of staples in short supply to the entire population. The regime decided in 1963 to increase sugar production in order to pay for the industrialization program. Later, industrialization had to be postponed, and the traditional dependency on sugar as the nation's main export was renewed. Its economic growth during the years 1963–5 averaged 3.8 percent gross material product (GMP), but it declined to 0.4 percent in 1967–70 (Mesa-Lago, 1978, p. 57). Nevertheless, the national unemployment rate was consistently reduced throughout the entire decade. It was as high as 9 percent in 1962, but it was cut in half by 1968, to 4.3 percent, and reduced further by 1970 to 1.3 percent. By then the problem was 'no longer eradication of open unemployment so much as getting enough skilled people to do a particular job at a particular time' (Brundenius, 1985, pp. 194–5). The late 1960s is identified as a period of moral incentives and 'severe austerity to the entire Cuban population.' Also, in spite of insurmountable difficulties, it was a period characterized as having an 'attitude of aggressive optimism' that expected 'extraordinary rapid gains' (Edelstein, 1985, pp. 187–9).

A big push to increase economic growth was devised in the late 1960s. It sought to provide the regime with the needed capital for industrialization and enough financial capacity to pay its growing external debt with the Soviet Union and market economy countries. It was Castro's brainchild: the 1970 Ten Million Tons campaign, a drive to increase sugar production to this level. It became by far the most change-oriented revolutionary policy ever, but for reasons other than those originally intended. The ten million tons were never produced—output fell short by 1.465 million tons. Among its many costly results were the inordinate amount of resources put into this national effort, and the serious neglect of other sectors of the economy because of it. In the end it pressured the regime to move on with state institutionalization, including the Communist Party and the revolution as a whole. This made the change from a centralized political structure and decision-making practices to more decentralization possible.

The Second Decade: the 1970s

The changes of the 1970s did not come easily. The state-building phase of this period was credited to the failed Ten Million Tons campaign. In reality, failing to reach the sugar production goal helped to trigger it, but it was not responsible for the institutionalization as such. In his speech during the 26 July 1970 celebration, Castro offered his resignation for having failed in such a major national effort. But the crowd gathered for the occasion rejected his offer, asking him to stay on. The fact that the Ten Million Tons policy proved to be mistaken in both concept and implementation did not seem to affect their loyalty and support.

None the less, major changes were needed. The time for decentralizing decision-making had arrived. The changes included substituting new political structures to provide rational, stable, and continuous channels of decision-making for the existing centralized bureaucratic decision-making model and the charismatic dominance of the revolution by Castro's leadership. The latter made possible agreement on national policy without channels for critical and/or evaluative input in the decision-making process.

The campaign for institutionalizing the revolution was finally unleashed during the regime's second decade. As far back as 1966, however, Castro had explained why it had not been done before: 'We have not rushed into setting them up [the new legal and political institutions] because we would like them to conform to [social] reality, and not the other way around.' Adding that, 'There are many things . . . which demand definitions, concepts, and ideas, which should come from our revolutionary ideology and our Marxist view of society' (Cañizares, 1979, p. 303).

A proper conceptualization of the Cuban state was in order, as well as a new structure. The 1976 socialist Constitution provided a new political and legal framework. It was organized according to existing Marxist-Leninist modalities, i.e., the Soviet Union and other socialist countries. However, it also included Cuban traditions combining innovation and continuity into a single model. It safeguarded the changes of the 1960s, while devising the mechanisms for future change in a socialist polity.

The Matanzas Experiment and Beyond

A pilot project was held in Matanzas province in 1974 and 1975. It was an experimental test at the municipal and provincial level of the new Organs of

People's Power (OPPs). The positive result of this test led to the establishment of national, provincial, and municipal deliberative and administrative OPP assemblies throughout the nation. They were established in agreement with the 1976 Constitution, which recognized the OPP assemblies as the nation's new political and legislative structure. This put an end in December 1976 to the centralization of executive, legislative, and judicial functions in the Cabinet of Ministers practiced by the revolutionary regime since 1959.

Nevertheless, the Matanzas experiment ran into some serious problems. It served to alert the regime to what to expect once the OPPs were established on a national basis. Mostly, it had to do with the transition from sixteen years of centralized revolutionary decision-making into a new modality in which grass-roots participation was not only expected, but necessary.

As noted in Matanzas, a clear deficiency of administrative experience and expertise among the party and OPP cadres existed. This explains the ensuing backlash when people failed to participate in the decision-making opportunities made available to them through People's Power. The regime confronted this reality during the deliberations of the First Congress of the PCC, in December 1975. The proper utilization of manpower demanded further synchronization and planning of needed personnel in post-1975 OPP operations. In spite of these warnings, a 1979 official report realistically stated, 'The delegates of Popular Power . . . that work in those organs did not have any previous experience . . . it would only be with time . . . that they [would] learn the full extent of their responsibilities' (*Sobre las Dificultades Objetivas de la Revolución*, 1979, pp. 5, 11). As had happened before under the revolution, the OPPs became a major school for all involved, including the leadership and the population at large.

A national referendum seeking the approval of the new charter was held on 24 February 1976. This followed the party congress in December, in which the new Constitution and the institutionalization of the state had been approved. The PCC institutionalized itself first. Basically, this meant recognizing that the practice of having the party perform administrative functions in addition to providing political leadership had to stop. Administrative functions had to be left to the new political-administrative organs, the OPPs, and as the only political party and main political organ in the system, the party would be limited to its political guidance and leadership function. The administration of the state was left then to the OPPs (elected representative body), and the national administrative structure (appointed personnel) functioning under the Council of Ministers.

The first national elections since 1959 were held in October 1976. The delegates to the 169 political-administrative OPPs Municipal Assemblies were elected by direct and secret ballot by the people, who voted in their electoral circumscriptions. The municipal delegates proceeded then to elect by secret (indirect) ballot the delegates to the fourteen provincial OPPs (one assembly for each of the fourteen provinces), and the 481 deputies to the single National Assembly. The latter is the legislative body and highest political–administrative organ of the state. When the National Assembly met for the first time on 2 December 1976, the political and constitutional process of institutionalizing the Cuban state was completed. Finally, the revolutionary regime was entering its new political phase, the post-institutionalization period.

The Economy and Society

As a decade of change, achievements, ingenuity, improvization, and great sacrifice by the population at large, the 1960s were characterized by moral incentives, voluntary work, bureaucratic bungling of the economy, and centralized planning and administration, followed by high absenteeism and low productivity. In response to these problems and others, the 1970s brought their share of changes and new economic policies, modifying some of the modalities used before. Rather than relying on moral motivation as much as before, material rewards were also used as incentives.

The new economic policy was based on more pragmatic notions: (1) more attention was paid to consumption, with material incentives used to stimulate work performance (i.e., material and moral incentives were mixed together under a collectively oriented approach);[10] (2) greater efficiency in the economy was pursued and the labor force was rationalized, causing less social security and some unemployment (i.e., avoiding waste and reducing personnel); and (3) a reduction of the social wage system enjoyed so massively and universally by workers was enforced (i.e., limiting the expansion of the free goods sector, and the full-pay pensions awarded to vanguard workers).

Political opportunities for equal participation and grass-roots input into decision-making made available through the newly instituted political structure generally offset the emphasis on economic efficiency, workers' productivity, material/moral collectively pursued incentives, and the recognition and acceptance that some social inequality, and even unemployment, might come out of the new economic policy. The new economic policies were applied in time to profit from the bonanza the price of sugar enjoyed in the international market in the early 1970s. From 1971 to 1975 the GMP rose by a record 14.7 percent in absolute terms, and 13 percent per capita. The rate of economic growth for 1971 to 1975 averaged 6.3 percent total, and 14.5 percent per capita. From 1976 to 1980 the new rate was 4.1 percent total, and 3.1 percent per capita. The first half of the decade, then, was a time of economic recovery and growth (Mesa-Lago, 1978, p. 57; Mesa-Lago, 1981, pp. 33–5).

In the mid-1970s a new System of Economic Management and Planning (SDPE) was introduced and expected to be in full operation in the early 1980s. The rate of collectivization of the means of production established in 1961 was increased. The living conditions improved. Total education enrollment from 1970 to 1982 increased by 38.7 percent. The population grew 13.2 percent in eleven years, from 8,569,121 (1970) to 9,706,369 (1981). Improvements in public health included both the availability and quality of medical services. Life expectancy was extended from 69.3 (1970) to 70.2 years (1980) for men, and from 72.6 (1970) to 73.5 years (1980) for women. The mortality rate per 10,000 babies born alive decreased from 38.7 (1970) to 19.6 (1980); and the mothers' mortality for every 10,000 babies delivered alive decreased from 7 (1970) to 5.3 (1980).

Life expectancy in Cuba was comparable to life expectancy in highly industrialized countries in the mid-1970s, but it slightly surpassed the United States and Western Europe after reaching 72.5 years in the 1980s (70.9 for men, and 74.2 for women)—it was on average 71.7 years in the United States (although women's life expectancy reached 77 in 1982, and men's 69), and 71.9 in Europe. Life expectancy in Latin America was 63.5 years of age in 1975–80, and 54.6 among other developing countries (MINSAP, 1975, p. 106, as cited in Behm, 1980; United Nations, 1983, pp. 18, 79).

The 1970s ended with a major international event held in Havana that symbolized Cuba's new prominent standing in the international community. It was the Sixth Summit Conference of Nonaligned Nations held on 3–9 September 1979. Attending were ninety-two representatives of the ninety-five nation-members, including three kings, thirty-one heads of state, fourteen prime ministers, seven vice-presidents or deputy prime ministers, two vice-chancellors, nine ambassadors (to different countries, or to the United Nations), and one state minister. Castro presided over the conference and served as the leader of the nonaligned movement, until the next summit meeting in India more than three years later. He brought a new militancy to nonalignment, which was not always welcomed by all the country-members.

The Third Decade: the 1980s

The 1980 Mariel boatlift marked the transition from the 1970s to the 1980s. From 21 April to 26 September, 125,262 disaffected Cubans arrived in the United States, while others fled to Costa Rica, Peru, and other countries. Two other important events in that year of great international and domestic significance for Cuba were the election of a militant conservative American President, Ronald Reagan, and the Second Communist Party Congress held in Havana in December. However, the events preceding, during, and after the Mariel boatlift had internal and external repercussions such as had not been seen since the 1960s.

For some it meant a rejection of Cuba's socialism after more than two decades of revolutionary government. It was argued that by seeking refuge in Havana's Peruvian Embassy, many Cubans were expressing their opposition to the revolution as well as looking for a way out of the country. Here again, critics said, Cubans are 'voting with their feet.' But for the majority of the population it was a moment of crisis demanding support and militancy. Massive popular demonstrations were held in front of the Peruvian Embassy in April, in Havana's Revolution Square on May Day, and in front of the US Interest Section in Havana, as well as in other major cities throughout the country, on 17 May 1980. Mariel had reawakened the populace's revolutionary consciousness. The people realized that after more than two decades, the revolution could not be taken for granted, and expressed their feelings with fervor. Nevertheless, some inside, and many outside, the island were still questioning the regime's legitimacy. Mariel was too controversial internally and externally to be settled easily. Opposing interpretations were given as to its causes, meaning, and consequences for Cuba, as well as for the Cuban-American community in Miami and other US cities.[11]

The Routinization of Cuban Life

One characteristic of political life in the 1960s was the intense regime-led mobilization campaigns the population experienced at the same time as the government suffered from a noticeable institutional weakness. The latter was mostly due to the systematic undoing of the institutions of the pre-revolutionary regime while the new structure was still in the offing. But the regime's institutional weakness was also caused by many developmental policies that proved to be wrong. The official neglect the workers' confederation (CTC) suffered, which had rather negative consequences for the labor movement, and the people's poor compliance with the socialist legal system were some of the problems the regime faced later in the 1970s and 1980s. The routinization of daily life during and after the institutionalization period sought to rectify some of these problems. Under the new structural setting, many of the organizations and formalities weakened by official design and/or neglect were purposefully strengthened.

The workers' vanguard movement (approximately 10 percent of the labor force) had received undue attention, while the labor movement as a whole had been neglected. As a consequence of this, the CTC had been institutionally weakened. In the face of mounting labor problems including absenteeism, failing production goals, and the need for an overall improvement in efficiency, quality, and productivity, it was obvious that such a policy had been a costly mistake. Restoring the labor movement to its leading role in Cuban society included creating CTC chapters in 40,000 enterprises, electing approximately 280,000 grass-roots leaders, and establishing some new national trade unions. CTC congresses were held in 1973, 1978, and 1984 with a representation of 68 percent of rank-and-file workers. The trade unions were institutionalized, with their leading mass organization role in the socialist polity constitutionally recognized (Pérez-Stable, 1985, pp. 292–6).

A different problem developed when the populace publicly demonstrated a general disregard for the regime's legal system. The government found it was confronting a low level of compliance with revolutionary law, related to the overall societal changes of the 1960s. This unexpectedly provoked a social by-product of poor compliance with the emerging legal system. The population was acting on the belief that past and present laws and institutions were minimally important, that what really mattered was to be a revolutionary in thought and action. If a discrepancy (whether real or imagined) between the law and what was regarded as being truly revolutionary values and behavior ever existed, the latter would prevail. According to a Cuban jurist, the situation represented a serious danger for the revolution: 'Revolutionary [socialist] legality had become so relative, and respect for the law so lax, that it had been subordinated to "revolutionary usefulness" (i.e., expediency), which many regarded as a primary and overriding consideration' (Cañizarez, 1979, p. 398).

In keeping with the newly established political order, elections followed the $2\frac{1}{2}$-year cycle initiated in October 1976. After the first national elections, there were others in April 1979, October 1981, April 1984, and October 1986. In three consecutive elections (for three five-year terms), the National Assembly elected Castro as head of the Council of State (of the National

Assembly) and of the Executive Committee of the Council of Ministers. This has made him the country's President for the last decade.

After 1976 the mobilization campaigns that characterized early revolutionary political life gave way to the new political practices established by the regime. Political participation was now centered in the political space provided by the Organs of People's Power. Although mobilization campaigns continued, they ceased to have the meaning and urgency they had had before. The preservation of the new system, rather than the elimination of the old regime, which was by now practically completed, were the new goals of the revolutionary government. The Communist Party continued its own institutionalized practices. Following the five-year cycle between party congresses, the Third Congress was held in February and November–December 1986.

An era of reckoning with economic and production problems seemed to prevail in the second half of the 1980s. After having decentralized in the 1970s the personalized political modalities of the 1960s, Cuba was preparing itself in the mid-1980s to heed the demand for more self-reliance in a period of economic austerity. Moral incentives should serve as both an expression of revolutionary consciousness and as the proper motivation for higher productivity and efficiency. Material incentives would reward those who overfulfill their production quotas (*la norma*) maintaining a high quality level, but would not provide the actual motivation for excellence. Even if substantively modified, critics of the regime found serious built-in dangers with Castro's decision to return in the 1980s to the controversial moral incentives model of the 1960s—at a time when the Soviet Union was introducing some of the material incentive mechanisms rejected by Cuba (Lewis, 1987).

None the less, Castro was steering the revolution toward further economic development, industrialization, and even more integration with the socialist common market, COMECON. Still, according to him, Cuba's future must be based on its own labor and productivity, achieving the best use of its human and natural resources. The groundwork was being laid by Castro and his fellow revolutionaries for the second generation of leaders that would carry the revolution into the twenty-first century and beyond.

3 The Social System

Pre-1959 Cuban Society

Pre-revolutionary Cuban society had similar features to other Latin American societies, although its own peculiar characteristics set it apart in some respects. While Cuba was characteristically divided by a small wealthy elite positioned at the top of society and the largely deprived masses at the bottom, it had, nevertheless, a fluid social stratification system. Its society was more modern; no social class was based upon nor operating according to the traditional and patrimonial Latin American social structure. (This section draws on Manitzas 1973a, and 1973b; Black, *et al*., 1976; and *Las Clases y la Lucha de Clases en la Sociedad Neocolonial Cubana*, 1981).

Historical forces had conditioned Cuba's social matrix. While most Latin American countries gained their independence in the earlier part of the nineteenth century, Cuba had continued until the end of the century under Spanish rule. This was followed by four years of US military government first, and years of economic and political control by Washington after the Republic was proclaimed in 1902. Cuba's dependence on the United States was terminated after 1959, when the revolution came to power. Since then, however, United States–Cuban relations (or lack thereof) were turned into mutual hostility underlined by the former's covert operations seeking to subvert the latter's militant revolutionary government.

Throughout the first six decades of the Cuban republic its social order was affected by such events as the post-1902 domestic political processes, which, due to the lateness of the island's independence, had to undergo in a short period of time the kind of development that took other Latin American countries most of the nineteenth century. As a consequence of the war and final independence, the downfall of the Spanish oligarchy was followed by the access to power of the politically and economically active *criollo* elite. Equally relevant were the international conditions that prevailed at the time of Cuba's inauguration as an independent nation: the emergence of the United States as an international power, and the hegemonic control it exercised over Cuba. This practice became institutionalized by having the Platt Amendment added to the 1901 Cuban Constitution, which made Washington's direct intervention in the island's internal and external affairs legal. Full national sovereignty was not attained until the Platt Amendment

was abrogated in 1934. Thereafter, the nature and style of US interventionism changed. While still playing a central role in its economic life,
Washington remained the final arbiter of Cuban politics until 1959.

Social Stratification System

No *criollo* aristocracy emerged after 1902. In a conventional sense, the island
was left without a traditional upper class. The social vacuum left by the
Spanish landed aristocracy was not filled by a *criollo* counterpart as happened
elsewhere. While its social stratification system was fluid, the social order
lacked legitimacy in the eyes of the population. The existent fourfold social
class structure (the upper, middle, and working classes, and a lower class
made up mostly of rural dwellers) was not perceived with any sense of finality
or moral justification. There was no tradition of social responsibility that
would justify the many privileges awarded to the wealthy and propertied
class. The main, even unique, requirement for social class status was the
acquisition of wealth based on a secular and modern, but not ethical,
rationale. Thus upper-class status was not inherited according to an
aristocratic social order but as a result of secularized upward mobility, which
could be attained within the limited social, political, and economic order.

The Upper Class. The traditional Latin American patrimonial agrarian
order based on a peasantry working for and serving a landed elite was not
fully replicated in Cuba, mostly because of the sugar industry. The latter
followed a capitalistic mold, even if highly dominated by foreign corporate
interests. Cuba's propertied class was dependent on powerful US corpora-
tions and capital. By not being able to attain effective political and economic
independence, the national bourgeoisie did not perform effectively the kind
of nation-building role that was expected of it. This contributed to the
creation of a general sense of frustrated nationalism that was built into the
country's ethos and collective identity.

Rather than pursuing cultural nationalism, the Cuban bourgeoisie
acquired the life-style and values of a dominating foreign power. The US
upper class provided a role model that was imitated by its Cuban counterpart.
American elite life-style was transmitted to Cuba in a demonstration-effect
fashion. While the national bourgeoisie's children were educated in
American schools, conspicuous and superfluous consumption of expensive
US goods became common practice. For many, this practice was a tangible
and observable confirmation of their own social status. Under the revolutionary regime, however, the old social system's days were numbered. This

was true not only because the revolution rapidly ended it by seeking a better distribution of wealth and an improvement in the living conditions of low income groups,[1] but also because of the ensuing estrangement between Havana and Washington. Once common ties and communication broke down after 1959, the United States could not continue providing the upper-class role model that it had provided before.

Other Social Classes.   Conditioning factors were also at work, making the working and lower classes atypical. No entrenched social system was keeping labor unorganized and peasants living a marginal subsistence to the degree that it did in other Latin American countries. No patrimonial socioeconomic system was established in the brief period between 1898 and 1902—the four years of US military occupation following the American-Cuban-Spanish War, and prior to the inauguration of the Cuban Republic.

The arrival of modern social and political doctrines like anarcho-syndicalism allowed for incipient forms of labor organization early in the republican period. Although labor suffered many serious setbacks at different times, the number of unionized workers was remarkably high, reaching close to 1.2 million by 1955—about 20 percent of the entire population.[2] The downfall of the repressive Machado government and of the short-lived Ramón Grau San Martín revolutionary government in 1933-4 brought new opportunities to trade unions, which gained in political power. The sugar industry made trade unionism an urban as well as a rural phenomenon. In the late 1930s and early 1940s the labor leadership was in the hands of the Communist Party. Later, during the Grau San Martín and Carlos Prío Socarrás' Auténtico administrations, 1944-52, a concerted drive to take away trade-union control from communist leaders was undertaken. As Labor Minister first, and President later, Prío Socarrás made a political career precisely by ousting trade-union communist leaders from office. After returning to power in the 10 March 1952 coup, Batista followed a similar policy: keeping the trade unions away from communist control, while establishing a labor leadership politically responsive to the regime.

Similarly to the upper class, members of the middle and working classes had a modern, urban orientation toward life. They shared to varying degrees political and economic power, and had assimilated North American cultural traits that had been blended into their Hispanic culture. The lower class, made largely of rural dwellers, exhibited more African traits in its Hispanic culture. This prevented it from becoming fully integrated into the main cultural system. The lower-class subcultural status was conveniently used by the upper and middle classes as a justification for perpetuating its inferior standing in the social stratification system. Because most economic, educational, and cultural opportunities were available only in the larger cities, lower-class access to upward mobility was limited to rural–urban migration.

This practice led to the formation of a ring of shanty-towns surrounding major cities, particularly Havana. No urban center had the capacity to absorb that kind of migration. No services were provided to the new arrivals. A culture of poverty and deprivation marked their existence (Black, *et al*., 1976, pp. 106–9). Meanwhile, rural areas remained backward, sparsely settled, and deprived of the most basic goods and services.

Social Class and Racial Cleavages

A recurring question among political analysts has been what role the revolutionaries' social class origin played in the revolution. In this sense, the revolution has been characterized as being originally middle-class with an initial democratic-bourgeois stage. Once in power, the revolutionaries departed from this phase by turning against their class origin while moving rapidly into a socialist phase. Also, the revolution has been socially characterized as a peasant rebellion, with Castro and fellow guerrillas as the (leading/intellectual) vanguard. Some Cuba watchers have questioned whether the revolution had a specific social class composition at all, drawing instead from across class boundaries for both support and membership. This includes its 1952–8 period (the anti-Batista struggle stage), and after its coming to power in 1959 (Manitzas, 1973b, pp. M261 1–8).The problems defining the revolution's social origin in part stem from the complexity of the class composition of the Cuban nation itself.

Pre-1959 Cuban society was characterized more by segmental, group identification than by a cohesive supra-class national unity. Loyalty to one's wealth and interests, more than to national goals and aspirations, was characteristic of upper-class behavior. In this sense, the upper and middle classes did not contribute effectively to the formation of a modern polity. Social aggregates, as the rural lower class, were excluded from the mainstream of national life. There were, however, cleavages within classes as much as there were lines differentiating social classes. While trade-union inspired social legislation protected workers by insulating them from job insecurity and major deprivation, the urban and rural unemployed found no social protection. No protective social net ameliorated the plight of the poor and needy. For the latter, organized labor, with its relatively competitive wages and fringe benefits, was as much elite as the upper class was for the nation at large. The overall effect was that intra-class cleavages and class differences prevailed, resulting in a social mix of poorly coalesced social strata. A coherent, well-integrated, national community could not emerge out of such a socially fragmented body.

Racial cleavages were also a major rationale for social stratification.. A contradictory pattern of racial relations had existed since the colonial period, when a racially stratified society was erected. However, contrary to the officially sanctioned social ethics advocating racial segregation, members of the white and black races engaged in sexual relations, resulting in racially mixed offspring. Nevertheless, during the republican period, racially based social and cultural practices became institutionalized.

Society and Revolution

Transforming the Matrix of Socially Sanctioned Values

A myriad of new policies and programs enforced by the revolution transformed the existent patterns of social stratification and relations. The pre-1959 social order was institutionalized according to ideological and cultural values that sanctioned social inequalities—rewarding some individuals and groups while penalizing others. This social system was based on such values as hierarchical elitism and individualism. The revolutionary regime sought to replace this type of society, and the values that supported it, through change-oriented social policies aimed at creating a new polity based on egalitarian and collective values. The societal transition to egalitarianism from hierarchical elitism under the revolutionary regime transformed established social relations that traditionally pitted some social groups against others. This included poor and rich, rural and urban, female and male, blacks and whites, and manual and white-collar workers. Social conditions for the first of each pair of social aggregates improved under revolutionary rule (Moreno, 1971, pp. 471–5; Azicri & Moreno, 1981, pp. 1245–70).

The social and cultural transition to collectivism from individualism included the transformation of a parallel set of social relations and their supporting values. The revolution's cultural system sanctioned the rejection of private ownership, selfishness, and indifference, while supporting collectivization, unselfishness, and mass mobilization (Moreno, 1971, pp. 474–5). The latter kinds of values reinforced the system of social relations that emerged under the revolution. The mark of being fully integrated into the revolutionary process was to acquire *conciencia* (to internalize these values), and to act them out regularly (to live according to revolutionary praxis). This became the regime's cultural and behavioral objective for the newly transformed society as a whole.

Culturally based traditions of cooperation and participation in prerevolutionary Cuba among some social groups eased the transition to revolutionary values. In those historical instances in which elections were free and competitive, Cubans demonstrated their belief in political participation by voting in high numbers. In the 1944 and 1948 presidential elections, 80.7 percent and 79.5 percent of those eligible voted, respectively. As impressive as they seem, these figures do not represent entirely the fact that voters went to the polls as a result of their own sense of political participation. The practices of buying the votes of the needy and coercing others to go to the polls were well established.

Although voters stayed away from the polls under different electoral conditions, as in 1954 when Batista ran unopposed, 52.6 percent still voted. However, much more so than in other cases, this election was tainted by fraud and intimidation, especially for government employees. Voting was mandatory in order to become eligible for work in, or to continue to hold, a government job.

At both ends of the social ladder were instances of formal attempts of group cooperation independent of government and political parties. Both the followers of the secret Abakuá society, and the practitioners of its Afro-Cuban religion (which originated among the Yoruba in Africa), practiced solidarity for both political and economic goals. By the 1950s, after the harshness and brutality of its initiation rites had been discarded, its membership flourished not only among blacks but among whites as well. The socioeconomic background of its membership was diversified to include middle- and upper-class members, and, according to some accounts, even Cabinet Ministers and Congressmen (Domínguez, 1978, pp. 466–8).

Spanish immigrants in Cuba had organized themselves into several charitable (*mutualistas*) societies that provided social services for their members including employment bureaux, night schools, social centers, and comprehensive medical care for a relatively inexpensive monthly fee. Organized according to the Spanish provinces from which they had emigrated, two of the largest regional associations were the Centro Gallego and Centro Asturiano, founded by Spanish Galicians and Asturians, respectively. Their membership was restricted, however. Although Cubans with non-Spanish background were admitted, blacks and Orientals were excluded. This discriminatory policy was accepted by both society's and government's values and practices at the time. Even with their limited membership policy based on a racist rationale, these regional *mutualista* associations with their comprehensive health-care systems, according to a Cuba watcher, 'paved the way for the new socialist system by creating a tradition of corporate rather than individual responsibility for the sick and needy' (Moreno, 1971, pp. 467–8; Black, *et al.*, 1976, pp. 96–7).

Eliminating Institutionalized Racism

Racial attitudes and relations were not as strained or openly hostile since the 1930s and 1940s as they had been in the early years of the Cuban Republic. However, the pathology and pervasiveness of racism in pre-1959 Cuban society was real. It was economically as well as culturally based. Whites and blacks lived according to values which assumed the superiority of the white race. Race was a major factor determining an individual's economic and social status. A white-looking person enjoyed a higher social standing by the mere fact of belonging, or appearing to belong, to the white race. Ethnic and cultural whiteness was favored; it provided better opportunities for upward mobility. Not infrequently, mulatto parents would prevent their children from marrying black people. Protecting their offspring from 'marrying down' racially—as this kind of union was regarded by some—was a way of trying to improve their social and economic opportunities. White social mores and culture were generally accepted as the model to be emulated by all, including blacks. Blackness, culturally and otherwise, was devalued by whites and nonwhites. The racially motivated social, political, and economic stratification system reflected such institutionalized values, which had been inherited from the colonial period.

The revolution's socioeconomic policies addressing the needs of marginal and traditionally dispossessed groups had the direct effect of improving the living conditions of black Cubans. They had lived in poverty in colonial and republican times, so blacks made substantive gains under the new egalitarianism. By opening to all citizens what had been the citadel of white social elitism—such as private clubs, beaches, nightclubs, and other segregated places—the regime had effectively enforced racial social equality. Other elements in racial relations existed in addition to economic deprivation and social segregation, however. Racism by the 1940s and 1950s was more an actual (*de facto*) than a legal (*de jure*) social problem. The sociocultural pervasiveness of racism had become institutionalized in Cuban society.

To eradicate such an ingrained practice and the ethnic hierarchy that it had created would take more than official condemnation and egalitarian policies. The people had to become acquainted with the revolution's political and social values. Moreover, the belief in, and practice of, racial equality had to be accepted by both whites and blacks. The people's attitudes and behavior could then reflect the ongoing cultural change process that was occurring.

Paradoxically, after having been subjected to such conditions for so long, some blacks had come to accept the notion of racial inferiority. They even felt embarrassed that the government had addressed the issue publicly. Although blacks in general welcomed a policy of racial equality, some would rather have dealt with such a thorny question less publicly. The centrality of racism in Cuban culture had affected whites as well as blacks, embracing society as a whole while determining its mores and behavior (Fox, 1971, pp. 21-30).

The revolutionary policy of racial equality was criticized by some black nationalists as concealing a policy of white cultural supremacy. According to them, the regime was combating racism while depriving blacks of their own cultural values and heritage. The ultimate objective of revolutionary policy was understood as trying to absorb blacks into the white culture (cultural *ennegrecimiento* in reverse). Under the revolution, black culture received serious support in the arts, and religious practices derived from African ancestry enjoyed a degree of freedom and official support not experienced before. However, according to militant Afro-Cuban nationalist Carlos More, the end result for blacks still was their absorption into the mainstream of white Cuban culture (Black, *et al.*, 1976, p. 103).[3]

Defending the regime's approach to actual racial equality, revolutionary leaders contended that given the long history of racial intermingling in Cuban society, the ethnic distinction between whites and blacks was by and large an artificial one. Moreover, they contended that rather than having a single major racial ethnic and cultural component, the country's makeup represented an amalgamation of different ingredients of whom black (African) and white (Spanish) were predominant components, but not the only ones. Cuban ethnic mix included Orientals (mostly Chinese, but also Japanese), European Jews (Eastern European and Mediterranean), Haitian French, Irish Catholics, Jamaicans, and others.[4]

By the second revolutionary decade, the mid-1970s, it was generally understood that 'the government [had] been successful in its campaign to provide equality of opportunity through legislation' (Black, *et al.*, 1976, p. 103). Racial equality and integration at all social levels are a reality. And yet, how much the ethic of racial separation has actually been entirely eliminated is difficult to determine. Traditionally cultural attitudes usually tend to linger in spite of official efforts to overcome them, particularly among the elderly. The regime's position, after years of conscientiously seeking an end to racial discrimination, is that the socioeconomic support for racial discrimination has been eliminated under socialism. Therefore, while racist cultural remnants might still linger among some individuals, without an economic foundation supporting it, racism has already disappeared as a social reality. For critics of the revolution, this attitude conceals a reality of somewhat subtle discriminatory practices. The limited number of blacks (and women) in the highest echelons of the revolutionary leadership is a fact mentioned in this regard.

Membership in the revolutionary hierarchy, however, has been based more on a leader's historic background (revolutionary merits) than on any other consideration. The highest positions in the Communist Party and the government have been occupied, and still are to a large degree, according to this practice. This has had the unintended outcome of preventing blacks (as well as women) from having a proportionate representation at the highest level of revolutionary officialdom. Although regrettable, and even counter-productive, this cannot be construed by itself as a deliberately racist (or male chauvinist) leadership recruitment policy.

Transforming the Traditional Family

The prerevolutionary family played a central role in Cuban society, fostering its unification and integration. The family structure reinforced the existent social stratification system, and supported such values as class status and ethnic heritage differences. It transmitted to new generations culturally defined male and female, and white and black social roles. The family transmitted such values while performing a political socialization function. The female role ideally exemplified virtue, subservience, domesticity, and religious dedication. And males were expected to be dominating and aggressive both in their private and professional lives, according to the values of *machismo*. The double standard of sex-stereotyping was socially accepted, and regarded as an unavoidable fact-of-life. Women were expected to endure this double standard passively, while men were expected to live by it and demonstrate it in their own actions. Likewise, values supporting social privileges and opportunities based on racial discrimination were supported by the social system and the family. They were communicated to whites and blacks alike as another unavoidable fact. Their racist rationale was institutionalized in the social stratification and cultural system. As an ancillary social institution, the family was expected to abide by and perpetuate these values.

The middle-class family emulated the upper social stratum, trying to imitate its values and life-style. (Whether this was a viable option or not, depended on the middle-class family financial capability.) The downward demonstration effect coming from the upper class reinforced middle-class social mobility aspirations but, also, eroded its group cohesiveness. Meanwhile, the upper-class close social integration remained intact. Customarily, the upper class sent its children to study abroad, while the middle sector had its own educated at home for financial reasons.

The patriarchical upper- and middle-class family enjoyed structural and financial stability. The matriarchal lower-class family lacked those attributes. Women in the lower-class family usually were both family head and breadwinners. Male family roles were peripheral to the sustenance of the family and the upbringing of the children. Altogether, lower-class families faced severe economic deprivation, unemployment, and social insecurity. They had a distinct Hispanic and African cultural mix, with common law unions, rather than marriage, prevailing. Educational opportunities were limited, and the children were encouraged, and expected, to work at an early age to help the family financially (Black, *et al*., 1976, Chapter Five).

The New Family

As experienced by other social institutions, the revolution's radical transformation of Cuban society provoked similar changes in the family. Regarding it the bedrock of socialist Cuba, however, the regime moved to reinforce and protect the emerging new family. The Family Code, Law No. 1289 of 14 February 1975, is a law enacted in pursuit of such a policy objective. It became effective during a special ceremony attended by the president of the Federation of Cuban Women (FMC), Vilma Espín, on 14 February 1975, International Women's Day of the International Women's Year. Customarily, new laws are openly evaluated and criticized nationwide by the people in work centers and other places before they are finally approved. The FMC favored the new Code's emphasis on women's equality and had given it wide support during the public discussions.

The Family Code unified all previous legislation regarding marriage, and parent-children, family, parental, and quasi-parental relationships into a single code. It superseded the often modified 1888 Spanish Civil Code (applied to Cuba in July 1889), as well as prerevolutionary legislation like the 1934 Divorce Law; and Law 9 of 1950, which had advanced women's rights in marital and family relations.

Niurka Pérez Rojas, a Cuban social scientist, noted some of the differences between the old Civil Code and the new Family Code: (1) the Civil Code defended the family on the basis of private property and bourgeois relations of production; the Family Code defends the family on the basis of public ownership of the means of production and socialist production relations; (2) the Civil Code promoted women's inferiority with a subordinate status to their fathers or husbands; the Family Code establishes legal equality between man and wife, including economic and personal relations between them, and with their children and society; (3) the Civil Code discriminated between out of wedlock and legally born children, establishing different categories for them; the Family Code establishes legal equality for all descendants, regardless of whether their parents were legally married at the time of their birth; and (4) the Civil Code ignored the need for governmental legal responsibility for the home environment of minors; the Family Code establishes government's legal responsibility for the proper home environment for the upbringing of minors (Pérez Rojas, 1979, pp. 57–8).

The Family Code has been carefully examined by other analysts, who arrived at opposite, even contradictory conclusions. They characterized the Code 'as being revolutionary, as well as conservative; as being innovative, as well as traditional; and as being under the influence of socialist (particularly Soviet) legal experience; as well as being a continuation of the latest modifications in prerevolutionary Cuban civil law' (Azicri, 1980a, p. 183). While elements of these different attributes are present in the Code, their weight and emphases vary. The concern with safeguarding the family as a central institution in a socialist polity was and is paramount to the regime as evidenced in the Family Code.

A Havana University law professor defines the Cuban family today as:

a group of persons related by an economic and social nexus stemming from a lasting sexual union and relationship, which satisfies the need for the propagation, development, and conservation of the human species; and which supports, educates, and forms the children according to *mutual, socialist understanding and cooperation, while sharing life and common social interests together* ... [Peral Collado, 1980, p. 4, emphasis added.]

This definition includes traditional and revolutionary social concerns. It gives a current definition to the family, however, by placing it in a social context imbued with socialist values. It defines family solidarity as the expression of such values, mutually held by man and wife. As envisioned by the Code, the family would then operate as a social institution concerned with the formation of future socialist generations. It would be in charge of the critical first steps in the formation of the new 'socialist man,' who is expected to emerge from the revolutionary socialization process. (The socialization process includes the family, schools, youth organizations, and other social structures.)[5]

According to Peral Collado, in the prerevolutionary 'bourgeois' family private property was the decisive influence in family life. (Such major components of family life as love and sexual relations between man and wife were determined by socioeconomic considerations.) By contrast, he argues, the 'socialist' family expresses the 'proper features of a socialist society, in which private property and man's exploitation by man have been abolished.' (Love and sexual relations regained their original humanity under socialism by eliminating any ulterior socioeconomic motives.)

Moreover, Peral Collado asserts that as long as individual and social economic interests were the determining factor in the formation of the nuclear family, its subsequent characteristics were conditioned by this initial concern. For him, the socialist family is born under different conditions. Protected by the state and society, human relations find in family life a proper conduit for harmonizing 'personal and social objectives.' This includes protecting women and children in addition to the general welfare of the family (Peral Collado, 1980, pp. 21-8).

Today, family roles and relations have lost many of their traditional social characteristics. Women are socially and politically integrated into the revolutionary process, and in growing numbers into the labor force. Children are educated under a highly politicized culture, in anticipation of the participatory life awaiting them in a highly mobilized society. Moving away from *machismo* as the rationale for their family role, men are expected to help actively in the upkeep of the home with a good share of household chores. In safeguarding these newly defined family roles, the family as a social institution receives more attention from society than it did before. Under the Family Code, the responsibility for overseeing that future generations will adjust successfully to a socialist society has initially been entrusted to the family.

The Family Code has been complemented by the Code on Children and Youth of 30 June 1978. I have stated elsewhere that,

The family orientation pursued by ... [the Family Code] was more specifically spelled out in relation to the social position, the expectations for advancement and mobility, as well as social obligations and roles to be played by Cuban youth in the 1978 Code on Children and Youth ... The need to build the proper infrastructure that would permit younger generations to achieve their highest level of development is [its] subject ... It complements and moves forward in the areas covered by the Family Code—in the sense of giving a direction to the regime's policies, not only regarding the family in general, and more specifically women's equality, but in relation to the national expectations regarding Cuban youth as well ... [Azicri, 1980a, p. 189]

Nevertheless, revolutionary family policy had to come to terms with existent tensions stemming from the interplay of opposing social and economic realities. First, conditions of economic underdevelopment still present (material infrastructure) imposed major limitations in determining policies affecting family life, including such social issues as women's working opportunities. Second, the regime's commitment to accomplishing the socialist vision of an egalitarian 'open family' (ideological superstructure), with all the changes in family relations that it implies, is a matter of public record as well as a generalized expectation—albeit, not universally supported (remnants of *machismo* still linger on, particularly among older men).

The family is expected to be politically mobilized, highly participatory, and fully integrated into the revolutionary process. Man and wife are socially and politically equal with the same socioeconomic and legal rights and obligations, and the children's socialization process prepares them to play similar roles as they grow up. In spite of existent limitations, the regime confronts the family policy dilemma by moving toward these social and political goals. The creation of the new socialist family is necessary for the creation of a socialist polity. The regime cannot ignore that 'the elementary cell of society' (as the Family Code characterizes the Cuban family), is the bedrock upon which the emerging socialist system is built.

New Marriage and Divorce Rates

The marriage and divorce rate increased sharply after 1959. From 1960 to the mid-1970s, the number of marriages doubled while divorces increased eightfold. Revolutionary social change in general, and women's new social roles (as well as men's and even children's), affected family life decisively. The traditional family cohesiveness was replaced by a less stable family structure, which caused a higher divorce rate. Also, the newly found ease of entering into marriage contributed to an increase in the divorce rate—one of every two marriages was estimated to end in divorce (Black, *et al.*, 1976, p. 120). The government has established 'Palaces of Marriages' throughout the country in which civil (secular) ceremonies are held, while the Family Code's *Rights and Duties Between Husband and Wife* (Articles 24–8) are read by the person officiating at the marriage ceremony.

Cuba's adolescent and adult divorced population (15 years old and older) increased 6.9 times in the twenty-two years between 1931 and 1953—a total of 6,168 and 43,030, respectively. The total divorced population in the following seventeen-year period, between 1953 and 1970, increased 4.2 times—it reached then 182,323 divorced men and women from a population of 5,354,712. The total divorce rate in four consecutive censuses marked a steady growth: 0.25 percent in 1931; 0.75 percent in 1943; 1.16 percent in 1953; and 3.40 percent in 1970. Between 1931 and 1953 the divorce rate grew annually by 0.04 percent, and from 1953 to 1970 to a higher annual rate, 0.13 percent—eleven of the seventeen years were under revolutionary rule. Women's divorce rate increased from 0.33 percent of the total female population in 1931 to 4.83 percent in 1970, and men's from 0.18 to 2.07 percent of the male population—women's divorce rate was consistently higher than men's throughout the thirty-nine years (*Características de la Divorcialidad Cubana*, 1976, pp. 23–5).

The age group between 30 and 39 years old had the highest divorce rate in the first three censuses (1931, 1943, and 1953): 33.4 percent, 34.9 percent, and 36.4 percent, respectively. But in the 1970 census this age group only had a 23.5 percent divorce rate, while a somewhat younger group, from 20 to 29 years of age, received the highest rate, 26.5 percent.

Growth and fluctuations in the divorce rate during this period should not be examined as an isolated social phenomenon. Such social factors as demographic growth and the overall modernization experienced in Cuba after the 1930s must be considered. This process was accelerated under the revolutionary government, which applied a radically different and comprehensive developmental model to change the social fabric. Divorces in one-year marriages rose from 2,250 in 1977 to 2,925 in 1981—a 23 percent increase. A similar incremental curve occurred in divorces in two-year, three-year, and four-year marriages in the same period; however, divorces in five-year marriages totalled 2,171 in 1977, decreasing to 1,786 in 1981—a 17.7 percent reduction. In the intervening years between 1977 and 1981 there were instances in which the total rate for different years-of-marriage categories decreased, just to rise again in most cases. In the ten-to-fourteen year marriage category the divorce rate grew steadily: 2,390 in 1977; 2,715 in 1978; 2,871 in 1979; 3,411 in 1980; and 4,487 in 1981—an annual growth of 9.3 percent, for a total 46 percent in the five-year period (*Anuario Estadístico de Cuba 1982*, n.d., p. 83, Table II.21).

The last category seems to indicate that approximately a tenth of the married couples from the 1960s had difficulties adjusting to the social changes still occurring at the end of the second and beginning of the third decade of revolutionary government. Years of social pressure and demands on the family weakened their stability and in some cases ended in divorce. Of 62,113 marriages in 1977, 22.8 percent of the men and 17.6 percent of the women had already been married previously. By 1981, five years later, the ratio and proportion were still similar: of a total of 72,824 marriages,

23.3 percent of the men and 17.8 percent of the women had been married before (*Anuario Estadístico de Cuba 1982*, n.d., p. 83, Table II.20).

Increasing the Marriage Ratio

Before 1959 there were five marriages for every one thousand people. The number of marriages increased markedly in 1960–1, with a short decrease in 1962, followed by an increase in 1963, when it leveled off at a rate of six marriages in every one thousand people. Between 1965 and 1968 the marriage rate increased again to eight and nine, climbing in 1970–1 to thirteen, but declining by 1972 to nine (*20 Años de Matrimonios en Cuba*, 1977, pp. 17–20).

In 1953, 12.6 percent males and 24.6 percent females of every hundred men and women between 15 and 29 years old were married. The marriage rate increased for both in 1970, with a higher increment for male than female: 22.6 percent and 34.8 per cent, respectively. In the 15 to 49 years old category, married males increased from 30.8 in 1953 to 36 percent in 1970, while married females increased from 38 percent to 43 percent in 1970. From 1953 to 1970, the increment for those living together out of wedlock in both population groups was almost nil (Table 3.1).

The reasons for these changes in the Cuban family include political, socioeconomic, and legal factors. New employment opportunities, coupled with the lowering of rents and the positive economic impact that the agrarian reform had in the countryside, increased the population's purchase power. This improvement in economic conditions allowed for some of the changes in lifestyle. Also, women's advancement in education, and their integration into the labor force and full participation in revolutionary mobilization programs, made it more difficult for the old family structure to survive.

As they gained financial independence, women less frequently experienced economic dependency. They did not have to stay married so they would be supported by their husbands. Also, as part of the secularization of values experienced under the revolution, such beliefs as Roman Catholic sanctions opposing divorce lost influence among the populace.

The marriage rate increase under the revolution was caused by similar and new factors. Legislation facilitating the legalization of cohabitation was reinforced by public campaigns inviting those living out of wedlock to get married. The breakdown of long-held social patterns among those traditionally deprived of education and social opportunities offered new possibilities, including marriage as a viable lifestyle. Many people could afford legal services, which were made more accessible through the newly established

Table 3.1 Civil status of male and female population by age groups*

Civil Status	Male		Female	
	1953	*1970*	*1953*	*1970*
15–29 Years Old Group				
Single	76.2	64.0	52.5	39.5
Married	12.6	22.6	24.6	34.8
Consensual union	11.0	12.2	21.8	21.4
Divorced	0.2	1.2	0.8	4.0
Widower/widow	0.0	0.0	0.3	0.3
15–49 Years Old Group				
Single	49.5	41.6	34.7	25.9
Married	30.8	36.0	38.0	43.0
Consensual union	19.0	20.3	23.7	25.1
Divorced	0.5	1.8	1.6	4.8
Widower/widow	0.2	0.3	2.0	1.2

* In percentages for every hundred men and women.
Source: *20 Años de Matrimonios en Cuba* (Havana, Cuba: Editorial de Ciencias Sociales, 1977), p. 9.

bufetes colectivos (government regulated attorneys' offices) (Azicri, 1985b, pp. 57–9).

What might seem an apparent contradiction—an increase of both marriages and divorces after 1959—is really part of the erosion of social institutions that followed the revolutionary social transformation. Social institutions, such as the family, based on traditional values were more sensitive to ongoing social and cultural changes. People began to feel that it was no longer necessary (nor expected) to continue a marriage with one whom they might regard as an undesirable partner. Hence these and other motivations might have encouraged people to divorce when they might not have otherwise. But people also felt that they could choose partners and marry more freely than before 1959, when more traditional values prevailed. As a sign of revolutionary modernity, this contributed to increase both the marriage and divorce rate, but not stability in marital and family life.

The Demographic Curve

In 1959 the Cuban population was 6,900,888. In 1988 it was estimated at 10,221,000. In a twenty-nine year period, it grew by 3,320,112 (48.1 percent; an annual growth of 1.65 percent) (*Anuario Demográfico de Cuba 1979*, 1981, pp. 9–62; *Comunicado—La Población de Cuba Alcanza los 10 Millones de Habitantes*, 1984, pp. 1–16; 'Cuba,' 1986, pp. 127–31; and author's computation. For a discussion of Cuban demographic studies available in the United States, see Pérez, 1983, pp. 69–76.)[6] The official estimate is that by 1990 it will be 12,309,200, and 14,758,200 by the end of the century. This means a growth of 2,449,000, 1.98 percent annually in 1990–2000. But it seems unlikely that the current 1.65 percent annual average rate will rise by 0.33 percentage points in the next decade. It is estimated that the population will be 50.46 percent male and 49.53 percent female, 32.1 percent will be under 14 years of age, 61.1 percent between 15 and 64 years old, and 6.8 percent 65 years and older by the year 2000 (*La Población de Cuba*, 1976, p. 198, Table 50).[7]

Since the 1970s, however, the most important demographic development in Cuba has been the decline of its fertility ratio, which has been reported to be below the replacement level (annual deaths could exceed the annual number of births). It is estimated that it has been in this stage since 1978 (Díaz-Briquets, 1983, pp. 78–9). In 1959 the population growth rate was 21.1 percent for one thousand people. Twenty years later, by 1979, it had declined to 7.4 percent. The decreasing rate of population growth reached 1.41 percent in 1975–80—decreasing further to 1.23 in 1980–5. The low new births trend, 2.03 percent (1.88 in 1980–5), was tempered by an equally low mortality rate, 0.63 percent.

This type of demographic trend is rare among developing nations. Normally, it is found among highly industrialized market economy and/or socialist countries. Cuba's declining demographic growth in large measure is related to the social modernization experienced under the revolution.

The increase in women's educational level and incorporation into the labor force, coupled with a significant decrease in infant mortality, seems to have persuaded many Cuban women to delay having children—or simply to reject this possibility altogether. The generalized practice of family planning, including contraceptives and even abortion, allows the women to determine their attitudes and actual decisions on whether to have children or not. Medical services available at no cost to the entire population have had an incremental effect on women and men's capacity to control the size of their families. Among married women (or those living in a consensual union) between the ages of 20 and 29, approximately 30 percent do not want children. For younger women, below 20 years old or slightly over, the percentage is even higher (Díaz-Briquets, 1983). The size of the nuclear family was reduced from 4.46 in 1970 to 4.10 in 1981, continuing a steady decline from the 1931 peak of 5.24 members per family.

A possible reason for the demographic problematic is the disincentive role played by the economy. If not a decisive factor, it has at least contributed to this phenomenon. The state of the economy has reinforced some women and men's decision not to have children, and/or against large nuclear families. Precisely, the years of fertility decline seem to coincide with a period of severe international economic problems. The 1981-3 economic recession suffered by industrialized Western countries affected the world economy badly, including Cuba's.

Another disincentive contributing to the fertility decline is the serious housing shortage affecting Cuba. It has forced the children on many occasions to continue living with their parents, even after being married. By sharing the same dwelling, the nuclear family has become a newly extended family. The predominant population nucleus in the 1953 census was three people living together in one single house (16 percent), while one, two, three, and four-person nucleuses combined totaled 54 percent. By 1970, the predominant nucleus had increased to four people living in a single house (18.3 percent), while the total for the same nucleuses was 57.7 percent. This problem was more serious in the cities than in rural areas. In urban areas four-person families living in single houses totalled 17.7 percent in 1953 and 19.1 percent in 1970; in rural areas was 13.85 percent and 16.6 percent, respectively. From 1953 to 1970 both the cities and the countryside had increased the frequency of the three- and four-person nucleuses, and above, living in a single house (Pérez-Rojas, 1979, p. 23, Table 3).

In spite of recent legislation the housing problem continues to be serious. The housing law of December 1984 was approved after widespread public discussion of the draft-legislation. The debates in the National Assembly were broadcast live to the entire country. The law would turn 460,000 rent-paying families, representing approximately one-fifth of households, into actual owners. They will pay for the 'price of their dwellings with their regular monthly rents'.

The new law converts householders in government-owned housing into home-owners; permits limited short term private rentals; fosters self-built housing construction by individuals and cooperatives; and updates existing legislation regulating housing management, maintenance and repair, evictions, and the buying and selling of land and housing. The law applies to all housing not just those in urban areas . . . [Hamberg, 1986, pp. 21, 18–23]

New government-built housing is also included in this policy. High-rise structures will be sold in twenty-year periods, and all other types of housing in fifteen-year periods. Low-interest loans will be made available to 'high priority families,' which will be selected according to guidelines set forth by the National Housing Institute (Hamberg, 1986, p. 21). While making many new house owners, the law switched the responsibility for the upkeep of the property from the government to the new owner. However, the owners will have access to needed materials to take care of their newly acquired property. It is unlikely that this significant social policy will reverse the demographic trend all by itself. Nevertheless, it could reduce some of the pressure created by years of severe housing shortage.

A review of both positive and negative factors affecting Cuba's declining fertility rate underscores the fact that rather than being trapped in an uncontrolled population growth, the country has reached a point in which a decision on family size is feasible, and it is actually made at the family level. Moreover, the social conditions that make this possible are objectively available to the population at large. As a matter of public policy, however, the declining fertility rate would have to be reversed by providing young families with additional incentives that would induce them to have more children.

The Impact of Internal and External Migration

The arrival of permanent settlers has historically been a source of Cuba's demographic growth. Since the 1950s, however, the direction of migration changed. Arriving migrants ceased to be relevant for demographic growth, while a significant increase in external migration started—Cubans leaving for other countries, particularly the United States. This process intensified during the 1960s in response to the radicalization of the revolution. It lost strength in the 1970s, but regained momentum in 1980 with the Mariel boatlift (*Estadísticas de Migraciones Externas y Turismo*, 1982).

The colonial period, from the sixteenth to the nineteenth century, was a time of heavy migration. In addition to Spaniards and other Europeans, African slaves were imported in large numbers and, also, Orientals (particularly Chinese)—all destined for forced labor. Migration by those three ethnic groups provided most of the population growth in the nineteenth century. Starting with approximately 400,000 in 1800, the population grew rapidly in the next seventy years with the arrival of 900,000 African slaves and

125,000 Chinese. During that period 100,000 Europeans arrived, followed by more than twice that number—210,000—in the next thirty years, 1871–1900. The Cuban population totalled 1,572,797 in 1899. The foreign-born population grew steadily in total numbers and as a percentage of the total population in the first three decades of the twentieth century. In 1931, however, the foreign-born share of the total population reversed back to what it was in 1899. According to four censuses conducted over thirty years, the foreign-born population amounted to 172,535 (11 percent) in 1899; 228,741 (11.2 percent) in 1907; 339,082 (11.7 percent) in 1919; and 436,897 (11 percent) in 1931. Between 1902 and 1931 1,285,011 migrants arrived in Cuba. In 1931 the population reached the 3,962,344 mark—a 60.3 percent growth from 1899, at an annual rate of 1.88 percent (*Estadísticas de Migraciones Externas y Turismo*, 1982, p. 37, Table 9).

The steady flow of entrants early in the twentieth century coincided with an expansion of the sugar industry. From 1899 to 1907 sugar production increased by 114.6 percent while 180,000 migrants arrived. From 1907 to 1919 sugar production increased by 270.2 percent and migrants totalled 506,000. In the 1919–31 period migration continued unabated—599,000—but sugar production declined by 92.8 percent. This economic reversal was followed by a declining migration trend that led to the 1950s, when it finally dwindled to almost no demographic import (*Estadísticas de Migraciones Externas y Turismo*, 1982, p. 39, Table 11).

Migration Under the Revolution.   The migration flow in the 1959–77 period was heavily oriented in the outward direction. It continued until the end of the decade, although the number of those leaving decreased. According to official estimates, while 207,027 migrants arrived in the 1959–72 period, 768,591 departed. It was a net migration loss of 561,564 in fourteen years. The number of departing migrants dropped from 20,153 in 1972 to 8,806 in 1973. In the five years from 1973 to 1977, 12,688 migrants arrived and 30,384 left—17,716 more departures than arrivals. The grand total for the nineteen-year period, 1959–77, was 219,695 arrivals and 798,975 departures—a net migration loss of 579,280. The peak years for arrivals were 1959–61: 1959, 86,069; 1960, 56,557; and 1961, 19,137. It totalled 161,763 arrivals. The strongest years for departures were 1959–62: 1959, 73,724; 1960, 118,936; 1961, 86,605; and 1962, 75,698. It totalled 354,963 departures. The lowest negative balance in the nineteen-year period was in 1977, when only 968 more people migrated from the country than to it (*Estadísticas de Migraciones Externas y Turismo*, 1982, Annex, Table 3).

There were important changes in the country of origin of immigants after 1959, and in their motivation for moving to Cuba. In the 1950s, most immigrants came from market economy countries, particularly the United States. The migrants' objective was usually some kind of economic gain. In the first years of the revolutionary regime, 1959-61, many entrants were still coming from the United States. However, this time they were mostly Cubans returning to their homeland after having been away for political and economic reasons. This trend came to a halt by 1965. By then the entrants' motivation and country of origin had shifted. Many of them were professionals and technicians (from a fourth to half of the entrants) from socialist countries that came to work in Cuba in some advisory capacity. In 1963-5 52.7 percent of all immigrants were already from the Soviet Union, followed by Czechoslovakia (18.5 percent), German Democratic Republic (8.4 percent), and Bulgaria (6.6 percent). Immigrants from capitalist countries in 1963-5 were from such countries as Mexico (11.6 percent), Spain (11.3 percent), France (9.5 percent), and England (8.2 percent) (*Estadísticas de Migraciones Externas y Turismo*, 1982, pp. 51-3, Tables 17 and 18). None the less, regardless of their country of origin, from 1960 to 1975 most immigrants were male in a three-to-one ratio—some years there was even a four-to-one male ratio.

The Cuban Exodus.   Before 1959 small Cuban colonies existed in several United States cities (New York City, Tampa, Miami, and others), as well as in Mexico, Spain, and other countries. After the radicalization of the revolution in the early 1960s, however, a massive exodus of disaffected Cubans started. They migrated to different nations depending on the Cuban government's facilities (sometimes helpful) and restrictions (sometimes harmful), and the prospective exile's admissibility to his/her chosen destination (being able to obtain a visa), as well as the availability of transportation and other factors. Whenever possible, Cubans went to the United States. Sizable Cuban-American communities developed, particularly in southern Florida (in the Miami area), and in Union City and other parts of the Bergen County area, New Jersey, and in New York City, Los Angeles, and in other cities (Azicri, 1982a, 1982b; also, see Meyer Rogg, 1980; *Memorias*, 1984; Pedraza-Bailey, 1985; and Pérez, 1986).

In a twenty-one year period, from 1959 to 1980, approximately 611,339 Cubans entered the United States, by legal and other means. The actual number is estimated to be over 750,000. This massive exodus corresponds to six migration stages. Some years had numerous arrivals, there were fewer in others:

First Stage (January 1959 until missile crisis, 22 October 1962; 153,534 arrivals). Former Batista associates and upper class Cubans left using available commercial flights; also, middle-class businessmen, professionals, managers, and technocrats. Their socioeconomic interests were mostly affected by revoultionary policies redistributing wealth.

Second Stage (23 October 1962 through 30 November 1965; 29,692 arrivals). Regular flights between Cuba and the United States were suspended; only indirect, and unconventional means of transportation were available. The period ended with the Camarioca boatlift (the first of its kind), when Florida-based Cubans sailed to that port to pick up their relatives.

Third Stage (1 December 1965 to April 1973; 268,040 arrivals). An airlift was instituted from Varadero Beach to Miami. It operated under two American Presidents, Lyndon Johnson and Richard Nixon, as a result of a Memorandum of Understanding between Cuba and the United States (1965). Approximately half of all Cuban migrants in the United States arrived during this period.

Fourth Stage (April 1973 through 19 September 1978; 17,899 arrivals). Migration was substantively reduced without the airlift. Most arrivals came via Spain, where they had to wait for a long time for their visas. An executive order signed by Henry Kissinger, then Secretary of State, in October 1973, allowed Cubans to enter the United States as parolees, without visas.

Fifth Stage (October 1978 to March 1980; 16,642 arrivals). This period is related to a conference held in Havana in November–December 1978 between the Cuban government and representatives of Cuban communities overseas, mostly from the United States. The Dialogue Conference, as it was called, was followed by an uninterrupted monthly flow to the United States of political prisoners released during 1979 for a total of approximately 3,600. At a much lower rate, this practice continued the following years.

Sixth Stage (April 21 through 26 September 1980; 125,262 arrivals). This is the Mariel boatlift period. It was preceded by political dislocations in Cuba. The events started the night and day of 4 and 5 April at the Peruvian Embassy in Havana, and street-fighting started among would-be-immigrants and revolutionary bystanders in front of the United States Interest Section in Havana. Later, these arrivals created disturbing political and socioeconomic problems for both the Cuban-American community and the host country as a whole. Similarly to the Camarioca boatlift, Florida-based Cubans sailed to the port of Mariel to pick up their relatives.

After months of negotiations, the United States and Cuba signed an immigration agreement in December 1984 establishing orderly channels for the arrival of Cubans—mostly those who already had relatives living in the United States. The repatriation of nearly 3,000 Cuban refugees who arrived during the Mariel boatlift and were still detained in US federal prisons was also approved. (They had been termed unacceptable by US officials because of their past criminal record.) However, after 20 May 1985, when the US government started broadcasting to Cuba from the newly established Radio Martí station, Havana cancelled the new immigration agreement. It was done on the grounds that the radio station represented a hostile US policy and an intrusion in Cuban internal affairs. Washington responded to Havana's action by 'temporarily' suspending issue of visas to Cubans to visit the United States. Many cultural and other types of events held under the sponsorship of universities and private associations that invited Cubans to participate in their proceedings were affected by this decision. In most cases Washington refused to issue the visas, or they were granted after the event had already taken place (Shaw, 1986, p. F2).

In very low numbers, Cubans continued arriving to the United States after the Mariel boatlift using unconventional and non-legal means. The number of Cuban-Americans (Cuban born and of Cuban parentage) reached the one million mark in the early 1980s. In 1985 the city of Miami elected a Cuban-born mayor. Under the Reagan Administration, conservative Cuban-American political groups received more than usual attention and support from Washington. Cuban-Americans openly supported Reagan's controversial Central American policy in exchange. They disrupted political and cultural events that were perceived as being left-leaning, or contrary to their political agenda. Programs in the Miami-area had to be cancelled for fear of bomb threats. Community leaders characterized this behavior as non-democratic and the expression of a minority that did not believe in pluralistic political practices.[8]

A bomb threat forced ... [cancellation of] a comedy by Cuban-born playwright Dolores Prida.... Having worked in the 1970s for closer relations between Cuba and the US, [she] ... was apparently considered a pro-Castro leftist ... That controversy came on the heels of violent rival public rallies over the issue of US aid to the ... Contra[s] ... Members of the pro-Contra rally turned against the anti-Contra group, pelting them with eggs, rocks and an occasional glass bottle. The police brought in a riot squad to control the mostly Cuban-American pro-Contra crowd ... [Nazario, 1986][9]

By the mid-1980s the earlier migration crisis atmosphere had receded. Cuban-Americans continued supporting Reagan and his controversial policies. The people in Cuba paid close attention to the disclosures Castro made during the 1986 Third Communist Party Congress and to the economic problems affecting them. Apart as ever, both sides had turned inward, seemingly falling into introspective moods. None the less, they followed closely the Central American upheaval. Actively supporting opposite sides, Cubans and Cuban-Americans regard Central America as a close, personal issue.

4 The Ruling Political Party

Cuba's present political system is based upon Marxist-Leninist principles, institutions, and practices. Radical social transformation under the revolution made possible the creation of such a system, the first of its kind in the western hemisphere. The existent order serves to perpetuate the major sociopolitical and economic changes that took place in the 1960s and early 1970s. It also permits future change and growth within the parameters of the system itself. But dismantling of the newly created Marxist-Leninist polity is not permissible. The 1976 socialist charter established a new constitutional framework for the state and government, and sanctioned the institutionalization of the political system undertaken in the mid-1970s (Azicri, 1985a, p. 307).

The institutionalization process expanded the revolutionary government's legitimacy. The source of its legitimacy somewhat shifted from Castro's original charismatic leadership and the core of revolutionary values to the newly created socialist institutions. However, Castro's centrality continues as the main source of the revolution's traditional legitimacy, and he is the leader towering above all individuals, and institutions. Thus the polity is still ruled by a uniquely qualified charismatic leader, who is also the system's founder and major architect. The complex nature of Cuban politics in the 1980s lies, precisely, in the supportive reinforcement and dysfunctional tension that coexist within the system's leadership and institutional setting. Although by and large they support one another, they also create internal structural tension. The current exercise of revolutionary power exemplifies both the capability and limitations of an institutionalized socialist polity that is still developing politically and socioeconomically.

The Ruling Political Party

Since its foundation in 1965, the Cuban Communist Party (PCC) has held three congresses: 1975, 1980, and 1986. Although it took ten years for the First Congress to be held, the Second and Third Congresses followed closely the prescribed five-year cycle between them. (Among other reasons, the Third Congress was delayed for two months from its initial December 1985 date due to such factors as the time-consuming international debt conference held in Havana in the summer of that year.) It was a difficult, even traumatic, Party Congress, departing from the more positive note of the first two. It was also held in two separate sessions: the first on 4–7 February, and a final session on 30 November–3 December 1986. Its common theme became the new campaign for correcting the significant mistakes made during the late 1970s but especially the 1980s, the second and third decades of revolutionary government.

Given the centrality of the Communist Party in Cuba's political system, the Party Congress was the proper occasion to reflect upon, and to plan how to overcome, such mounting problems. Domestic and international audiences were rather surprised at the extent of Castro's negative evaluation of the government's performance in almost all areas. Those attending discussed and approved important changes in top governmental and party positions and new policies. The political system demonstrated significant resilience while enduring Castro's direct and frank acknowledgement of past mistakes and the rather difficult times facing the country. Castro (and perhaps his brother Raúl too, and Che Guevara back in the 1960s) is probably the only individual in today's Cuba who could have discussed publicly mistakes of such a magnitude.[1]

Whether sound and feasible policies were agreed upon and how they were received by the populace are questions worth examining. Only time will answer them satisfactorily, however. Although Cuba's record in this area is mixed, past experience still provides some ground for conjecture. Understandably, in almost thirty years of revolutionary government, many costly mistakes have been made. On what have become historical occasions, Castro has recognized serious mistakes publicly while seeking corrective measures, as he did at the Third Party Congress—i.e., the 1970 Ten Million Tons campaign, which led to the institutionalization movement, and the decentralization of the political system and policy-making for the economy.

Some mistakes have been righted, others not. The latter seem to defy whatever solutions are available to the regime at its present stage of development. A recent example is the free farmers' markets (*mercado libre campesino*), and the numerous problems encountered during their short existence. The May 1986 decision to close them was hardly popular among consumers. Some feared that it could signal a return to past practices of economic, and even political centralization. However, according to Castro, the free farmers' market had become 'a source of enrichment for neo-capitalists and neo-bourgeois.' Recognizing the negative influence that such practices could exert on a socialist society, the regime decided to close them. None the less, the consumer is surely missing the more generous supply of staples available during the six years of the free farmers' markets existence (*New York Times*, 20 May 1986, p. A5).

Anatomy of the PCC

The first Cuban communist party was founded in 1925 by labor leader Carlos Baliño, student leader Julio Antonio Mella, and Polish-born political activist Fabio Grobart (who is today in his 80s and President of the (Cuban) Institute of the History of the Communist Movement and the Socialist Revolution), and others. Later, the party changed its name to Popular Socialist Party (PSP). It played an important political role in the 1930s and 1940s, but after 1947 its importance declined due to the isolation it suffered during the Auténtico Administrations. After 1952 Batista banned the PSP and persecuted its members, forgetting past alliances when PSP leaders had joined his first Administration as Cabinet members, 1940–4. In 1961 Castro's 26 July Movement, the PSP, and the (Havana University) Student's Revolutionary Directorate formed the first political party under the revolutionary government: the Integrated Revolutionary Organizations (ORI). In 1963 it became the United Party of the Socialist Revolution (PURS). Finally, in 1965, the present Cuban Communist Party (PCC) was inaugurated, replacing PURS.

The unification of different communist forces did not happen easily. Friction and strain developed between some old and new communist leaders (members of the PSP and the new communists led by Castro) caused by mutual mistrust. Some rather serious incidents happened: (1) the 1962 Escalante affair when some old communists were accused of 'sectarianism' in their handling of personnel appointments for the first revolutionary party, the ORI; (2) the March 1964 trial of Marcos Rodríguez, who was sentenced to death (he was a student member of the PSP who in 1957 had betrayed four Havana University leaders of the Student's Revolutionary Dictorate to the Batista police, all of whom were assassinated in their hideout in what became known as the 'Humboldt Street Crime'); (3) the arrest in 1964 of PSP leaders Joaquín Ordoqui, and his wife Edith García Buchaca, who had been involved in the 1962 Escalante affair and in the Rodríguez trial; and (4) the 1967 'micro-faction' affair when thirty-seven hard-liners, including Anibal Escalante and other PSP members purged in 1962, were arrested, put on trial, and sentenced to prison terms. (Escalante and fellow conspirators were charged with conspiring to undermine Soviet support for the Castro regime, and seeking to put in its place a government faithful to communist orthodoxy, and more 'loyal' to Moscow.)

However, members of the pre-revolutionary communist party (PSP) became members of the new Communist Party, coming to occupy important positions. Most notable are Carlos Rafael Rodríguez, a member of the PCC's Politburo and Central Committee;[2] and Blas Roca, also a member of the Politburo and the Central Committee. The 1986 Third Party Congress agreed to Roca's request for retirement from the former due to his age (nearly 80) but continued his membership in the latter. In the 1970s Roca, a well known old communist leader, presided over the party's judicial committee in charge of drafting the 1976 Constitution. He died on 25 April 1987.

Also, old communist leaders like Juan Marinello, Isidoro Malmierca, Severo Aguirre, Arnaldo Milián, Leonel Soto, Clementina Serra, and others, became prominent figures in the PCC hierarchy. When the PCC was inaugurated in 1965, twenty-three of the hundred members of the party's Central Committee were old communists (23 percent). Their number was reduced to twenty by the time of the First Party Congress in 1975 (19.6 percent of the Central Committee membership which had been expanded to 112 members) (Black, *et al.*, 1976, p. 299; Domínguez, 1978, pp. 533–4).

The PCC is the only political party in Cuba. Its structure, role, and position in the political system are different from those of Western political parties, but similar to Communist parties in other Marxist-Leninist regimes. Among the latter, the Communist party—alone or in alliance with other parties—plays a dominant, hegemonic role, and is situated at the center of an organically integrated social and political system. This makes the PCC the most important political institution in the country. From its central position it provides comprehensive leadership and guidance to the national polity and all its subsystems.

Article 1 of the 1976 Constitution states that Cuba is 'a socialist state of workers and peasants, and all other manual and intellectual workers.' The charter also institutionalizes the PCC position and role in the socialist state and society (Article 5):

The Communist Party of Cuba, the organized Marxist-Leninist vanguard of the working class, is the highest leading force of society and of the state, which organizes and guides the common effort toward the goals of the construction of socialism and progress toward a communist society. [Simons, 1980, p. 102]

The question of the Communist Party's central role in exercising leadership and guiding the political system is a source of possible tension (of confusion for outsiders) between the party and such politico-administrative institutions as the Organs of People's Power, and the different offices and agencies forming the government's administrative structure, and the mass organizations, if not properly handled. Party decisions are made according to the Marxist-Leninist practice of democratic centralism, which prescribes free discussion of issues but which also makes decisions binding once they have been approved. These decisions are only binding for party members, however, and not for the rest of society.

Thus relevant questions could be raised here, like how could the PCC safeguard its hegemonic leadership role in a political system and society that legally (constitutionally) is not under its control? (Notwithstanding, however, is the fact that its role as the 'leading force of society and of the state' is also constitutionally established.) Also, would the party exercise its expected political influence by convincing others of the correctness of its position (a desirable choice, which would also place significant pressure on the party to take proper stands and sound policies so the populace would gladly agree with its policy choices)? Or, instead, would the party exercise its influence by intimidation or sheer force (undesirable choices, which would be not only illegal—unconstitutional—but politically costly, even self-defeating in the long run)?

Among other political leaders, Raúl Castro has provided important guidance on this matter to both members and nonmembers of the PCC. Regarding the position of the Communist Party in relation to the political system's political and governmental (administrative) institutions, and the mass organizations, he stated that even though 'the Party *directs*, the state *directs*, and the mass organizations *direct*,' the level of importance in these directives is not always the same. According to him, the party directives stand above those from other political, governmental, and social institutions throughout the system, even though each and all of them have their own jurisdiction (Castro & Castro, 1975, p. 85).

Moreover, the political *directionship* exercised by the party is qualitatively different from the state organs'. Again, according to Raúl Castro: 'the methods and means of *directing* are very different. While those of the state organs are mainly administrative, the party's methods and the mass organizations' are basically those of persuasion, and of being able to convince others on the basis of a higher political authority' (Castro & Castro, 1975, p. 85). In relation to the possible or actual control of the political system exercised by the party, he states: '*To control*. This term could be used in the sense of governing, managing, reigning, dominating, or in the sense of *confirming, revising, examining, inspecting*. It is the last meaning the one used in this case' (Castro & Castro, 1975, p. 85).

Parenthetically, preventing the PCC from intruding in the government's domain has been a difficult problem to solve in actual practice. One of the major issues faced during the 1975 institutionalization of the PCC and the state was to prevent the party from continuing intruding in the different administrative tasks. An effort was made to prevent the PCC from actually running the government administratively, as it did in the 1960s and early 1970s. While the party still performs its constitutionally established guiding and supervisory role over the government (guaranteeing that PCC policies are actually carried out), the administration of the state is no longer the direct responsibility of PCC bureaucrats. Today, this is supposed to be in the hands of government officials, and of the Organs of People's Power in some administrative areas as well.

The PCC's Structure. The institutionalization of the state in the mid-1970s was preceded by a similar process in the PCC. This included internal relations among different organizations within the party, as well as the role to be played by the party in its relations with the government's bureaucracy. The PCC and the government have parallel representation throughout the society from the national, to provincial, and local levels. The same individuals have held party and government posts simultaneously, contributing to blur the distinction between one and the other. Party–government relations were more clearly defined. Although still unsatisfactory according to some accounts, the demarcation of functions separating the party from the bureaucracy was more firmly established than ever before. Also, relations between the PCC and the mass organizations, always more clearly defined, were regulated further. The PCC's internal structural processes were formalized, including determining the function of the Central Committee and agreeing on holding meeetings regularly.

The PCC is organized according to territorial divisions, including work centers throughout the country. The Secretariat, Politburo, and Central Committee are located at the top of the party pyramidal structure. Under the party's national umbrella, its territorial division follows the country's politico-administrative subdivision in fourteen provinces and 169 municipalities. The party's structure starts at the base, climbing up to the municipal, provincial, and national levels. Lower party bodies are subordinated to the party organization in charge of the territory (jurisdiction) in which they are located. As a rule, municipal committees are in charge of those organizations within their jurisdiction. Also, the party work center committees are in charge of the nuclei and lower committees located in their jurisdiction.

The supreme PCC organ is the Party Congress, which elects the party's Central Committee. (The party's decision-making power is concentrated, however, in the Secretariat and Politburo, particularly in the party's First

Secretary, a position held by President Castro since 1965, followed by Raúl Castro as the Second Secretary.) Below this echelon, the party assembly at any given level becomes the ruling body in charge of electing the committees and base organizations under its jurisdiction. The Party Congress and all assemblies are formed with delegates elected by their respective assemblies by secret and direct vote according to elections procedures established by the Central Committee. The Central Committee's election procedures are established by its own Plenum.

The Central Committee and lower committee's auxiliary bodies are organized by sections and/or departments. The lower committees' auxiliary bodies are subordinated to a higher authority, the party's Executive Committee. The Central Committee auxiliary body is then subordinated to the party's highest authority, the Politburo and Secretariat, under the immediate supervision of the latter. Additionally, committees and bureaus at all levels would see that party members engage in voluntary work in different party tasks while continuing working in their regular jobs. (The party uses its members for voluntary work in addition to having a regular full-time staff.)

Decisions made at a higher level are binding for party members at lower levels. The party's interlocking levels of authority are purposely structured so the central and operational principle of democratic centralism function effectively. The party's organization provides avenues for discussion and participation at the different structural levels. But it also seeks to guarantee that the line of command throughout the party's hierarchical structure is followed, and that discipline among party members is properly enforced (*Estatutos del Partido Comunista de Cuba*, 1981, pp. 20–4). See Figure 4.1.

The PCC's Membership. Articles 1 through 27 of Chapter One of the Statutes of the Communist Party deal with regulations for membership and admission to the party. In order to belong to the PCC it is necessary to be a Cuban citizen, accept its programmatic platform and statutes, belong to one of its nuclei, be active in it or in one of its organisms, and accept the decisions and agreements of the party. Admission to party membership follows an established procedure. The applicant must be at least 18 years of age and remain as a candidate for no less than a year under the systematic attention of a nucleus. Another alternative is to have been a member of the Communist Youth Union (UJC) for a period of no less than three years. (Young people under 25 years of age enter the party through the UJC; once admitted to the party their membership in the UJC ends.) In addition to submitting the candidate to 'consultation with the masses,' the supervising nucleus has to agree by at least a two–third majority to grant admission, and its decision has

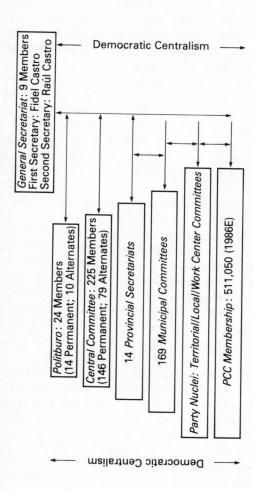

Figure 4.1 The Cuban Communist Party (PCC) Structure and Membership (1988)

Notes: Article 28. The Communist Party of Cuba is organically structured and functions according to the principles of democratic centralism.

Article 29. The Party is structured on a territorial and work center basis and has ground, municipal, provincial and national levels. All those that direct part of a given territory and exercise their functions and authority within the jurisdiction that their names indicate are subordinated to the organism of the Party that directs the territory. All the nuclei functioning at a work center are subordinated to the Party Committee at that center.

Article 30. The Supreme Party Organ is the Congress, which elects the Central Committee. At each intermediate level the highest organ is the corresponding assembly, which elects its Committee, and in ground-level organizations, the General Assembly, which elects its corresponding Committees or Secretariats.

Source: Statutes of the Communist Party of Cuba. Department of Revolutionary Orientation of the Central Committee of the Communist Party of Cuba, Havana, Cuba, pp. 34–5.

to be ratified by the next higher level (*Estatutos del Partido Comunista de Cuba*, 1981, pp. 7–8, 17–20).

When the PCC was inaugurated in 1965 it had 45,000 members, and 5,000 aspirants (applicants for party membership). By 1975 its membership had increased to 211,642 members and aspirants. With an annual growth rate of 42.3 percent, it totalled almost a 423 percent growth in a decade. In five years, growing at an annual average of 21 percent, the membership totalled 434,143–almost a 105 percent increment between 1975 and 1980. If the same 21 percent annual growth rate would continue throughout the 1980s, party membership could reach over a million members and aspirants by 1990. However, it has declined instead, slowing down significantly what was a phenomenal membership growth rate in the first ten-year period, and a respectable one in the following five years. In 1981 the party membership totalled 443,148. With an annual growth rate of 2.22 percent, by 1986 it had increased to 492,500–for a total of 11.13 percent growth in a five-year period.

In 1986, with an estimated population of 10,221,000 and the party membership estimated at 492,500, the latter numbered 4.81 percent of Cuba's population. At the 2.22 percent annual growth rate of the 1980s, the PPC's membership will be close to only 530,790 by 1990 (instead of the calculated mark of over a million members according to the 1970s rate of growth), for a yearly increment of 9,572 members, a total of 47,862 in a five-year period. Hence, the party's membership will represent 4.31 percent of an estimated population of 12,309,200 by 1990–a loss of approximately half a point in the party–population ratio in a four-year period, from 1986 to 1990 (Grobart, 1981, pp. 85–6; Cavallini, 1986, p. 43; *Anuario Demográfico de Cuba*, 1979, Chapter 1). (See Table 4.1.)

With a 6.05 percent annual rate of growth, party nuclei increased 30.25 percent in a five-year period, from 20,344 in 1975 to over 265,000 in 1980. The share of production (construction, agriculture, and industry) and service workers' membership also grew in the five-year period: from over a third in 1975 (36.3 percent) to almost half (47.3 percent) in 1980 (Grobart, 1981, p. 85; Cavallini, 1986, p. 43).

Most PCC members have joined the party recently; seniority is significantly low in the membership ranks. In 1985 the number of founding members (twenty years or more of seniority) represented only 5 percent of the total. Between sixteen and twenty years of seniority included 11 percent, and from eleven to fifteen years 16 percent. Over two-thirds of all party members had ten years or less of seniority (68 percent of the membership). Members with six to ten years of seniority totalled 29 percent (the second

Table 4.1 Cuban   Communist   Party
(PCC) Membership (1965–88)

Year	Membership
1965	45,000
1969	55,000
1971	101,000
1972	122,000
1973	153,000
1974	186,995
1975	211,642
1980	434,143
1981	443,148
1984	454,545E
1986	492,500E
1988	511,050E

Source: F. Castro, 'Main Report Presented to the 1st
Congress of the Communist Party of Cuba,' *Granma
Weekly Review*, 4 January 1976, p. 2; F. Castro, *Main
Report Presented to the 2nd Congress of the Communist
Party of Cuba*. Havana, Cuba, Political Publishers,
1980, pp. 71–8; M. Cavallini, 'La Revolución es una
Obra de Arte que Debe Perfeccionarse,' *Pensamiento
Propio*, vol. 4, no. 33 (1986), pp. 43–5; Gianni Beretta,
'III Congreso del PCC: Firmeza Revolucionaria
Frente a Crisis Económica,' *Pensamiento Propio*, vol. 5,
no. 39 (1987), pp. 49–51; and estimates computed by
the author.

largest group), while those with less than five years numbered 39 percent, the
largest group. The low rate of party seniority seems to reflect the periods of
growth in party membership throughout the 1970s, and to a lesser degree in
the 1980s, as well as a possible higher turnover of party members than
previously appraised. Article 19 of the party's Statutes states that if a

Party member has breached the Statutes or committed other faults, the following
sanctions may be applied, according to the case: (a) Admonition; (b) Suspension from
the Party post; (c) Temporary ineligibility to hold Party posts; (d) Suspension of
member's rights up to a year; (e) Suspension from Party ranks; and (f) Expulsion. The
maximum sanction that the Party takes is expulsion. This should be carefully
weighed. [*Estatutos del Partido Comunista de Cuba*, 1981, pp. 17–18]

Two-thirds of the total party membership is middle-aged or younger. While those 27 years old or younger represent only 0.8 percent of the members, and between ages 28 and 35 a fourth (25.1 percent), those from 36 to 45 total two-fifths of the membership (40.8 percent), the largest age group in the party. Those aged 46 to 55 total slightly over a fifth of the membership (21.1 percent), while those 55 years old or older are over a tenth (12.2 percent). By any political party standards the PCC membership is relatively young, a positive indicator of the stability and continuity of the system in the next decade and beyond (Cavallini, 1986, p. 43).

In the mid-1980s party members included over a third of production workers (37.3 percent), more than a tenth of administrative and service workers (5.9 and 7.2 percent, respectively), and a small number of peasants (2 percent). Professionals, technicians, and educators numbered 16.5 percent, while administrative leaders and political leaders were 20.7 percent and 3 percent of the total membership, respectively. Other occupations totalled 7.4 percent.

Another significant change in the party's membership composition was the improvement in the level of education among party members: from almost two-thirds of all members (60.3 percent) having completed an elementary education (or more) in 1975, it had increased to slightly over four-fifths (80.7 percent) in the early 1980s. The increment at the secondary level was equally important. From less than a fifth of party members with a secondary education (16 percent) in 1975, it increased to slightly over three-fourths (75.5 percent) by 1980.

The educational advancement of party members continued at the more advanced party schools. In a five-year period (1975–80), 24,512 party members graduated receiving social science degrees. Marxist-Leninist theory in the party curriculum received special attention: 81,324 members and aspirants took courses on this subject. Consistent with its central political role, the party moved to increase the share of labor membership (particularly production workers), as well as improving its members' qualifications through educational programs on an ongoing basis. Recognizing Cuba's present political modalities, these were steps in the right direction. The party needs to improve itself qualitatively (particularly the level of education of its membership) if it is going to perform its assigned leadership function ably.

Women's Low Membership Rate.   At the time of the First Party Congress (1975) women constituted only 13.23 percent of the party's membership. Their membership grew slowly but steadily for the next eleven years, totalling a little over a fifth by 1986, 21.9 percent. This modest annual growth rate of 0.78 percent hardly would bring parity to women's membership in the near future. Although limited, women's membership growth continued in the first half of the 1980s: from 85,970 members in 1981 (19.4 percent), 91,622 in 1982 (19.7 percent), 98,496 in 1983 (20.5 percent), 105,947 in 1984 (21 percent), to 112,762 in 1985 (21.5 percent). In the same five-year period men's membership dropped from 80.6 percent to 78.5 percent. However, in total numbers men's recruitment into the party ranks was slightly more than a two-to-one ratio over women: in the five-year period 54,537 men joined the party for 26,792 women (Espín, 1986, pp. 27–68, at p. 55).

'On the Full Exercise of Women's Equality,' is a well-known thesis discussed at the First Party Congress. It meant to provide an estimate of the state of women's political representation in the party, and political participation in general, as well as a guideline for future action to remedy an unsatisfactory situation. Women's leadership positions increased steadily from the municipal to the provincial level, to decrease again at the national level, from 1974 to 1984. At the municipal level, the most dramatic increment, it grew from 2.9 percent (1974) to 18.9 percent (1984); provincial, the second largest increment, from 6.3 percent (1974) to 16.9 percent (1984); and national from 5.5 percent (1974) to 12.8 percent (1984)—there was a loss of 0.8 percent from the provincial to the national level in 1974, and 4.1 percent in 1984. Women occupied almost a fourth of the leadership positions (23.5 percent) in the party's nuclei, less than a fifth in the work center committees (16.6 percent), and over a tenth (13.1 percent) in the committees at the party base.

Women's leadership rate in the Union of Communist Youth (UJC) is much better than in the PCC. Their municipal leadership posts increased from 22 percent (1974) to 32.1 percent (1984); provincial (the largest increment), from 7 percent (1974) to 28.9 percent (1984); and national (the second largest increment), from 10 percent (1974) to 27.1 percent (1984).

The Central Committee has had women members all along, but in small numbers. It was not until the 1986 Third Party Congress, however, that a woman was appointed to the party's Politburo as a full member: Vilma Espín, President of the Cuban Federation of Women (FMC) and the wife of Raúl Castro. Even the late Celia Sánchez, regarded today as the heroine of the revolution *par excellence*, and for years a member of the government's Cabinet, did not go higher than the party's Central Committee. In reality the problem is more complex than just party membership, or leadership positions in its top ranks. It has to do with women being also discriminated against by the voter when electing delegates and deputies for the Organs of People's Power, where they also find themselves underrepresented. In comparison with membership in mass organizations, women have a high level of national leadership in the Committees for the Defense of the Revolution (CDRs).

The possible generational nature of this problem is suggested by the fact that in youth organizations female members find a more positive context (less prejudicial) for their political activism. Women constitute 40 percent of the University Students Federation's National Council. The Secondary Students Federation's National Council is 61.1 percent female (the highest of any organization other than the FMC itself, an all-woman mass organization); and the Pioneers (Children) Organization's Guides are 55.5 percent girls (the second largest female representation in the country) (Espín, 1986, p. 55).

In Castro's estimation, women's poor political representation is the result of subjective and objective factors which demand further socioeconomic and cultural changes. These include freeing women from the 'double shift,' when they face full responsibility for housework after a full day working outside the home. Although the Family Code and a myriad of educational campaigns, launched with the FMC's support, have had a beneficial effect by having men increasingly sharing in house chores with their wives, the political problem still remains. Traditional values linger in spite of radical revolutionary change. It seems that accepting women in political roles as equals to men is a notion some Cuban males still find difficult to accept. At the Fourth Congress of the Federation of Cuban Women held in Havana in March 1985, Castro addressed the problem stating that, 'it is the duty of our society, our Revolution, our Party, and our state, to wage a resolute struggle in order to gradually overcome such difficulties' (*Granma Weekly Review*, 24 March 1985, pp. 4, 2–11). The solution to the problems facing women's equal political representation has so far eluded the revolution, notwithstanding the impressive gains accomplished by women since 1959.

The Three Party Congresses

The political significance of the PCC in its first ten-year period (1965–75) was relative at best. Throughout the decade its organizational structure, decision-making process, and leadership were not sanctioned by a legitimizing congress. The party appointed a preparatory commission made up of members of the Politburo and Secretariat to organize for the forthcoming congress. Since the celebration of the First Party Congress on 17–22 December 1975, the party has played an important role, in agreement with the central political functions assigned to it in a Marxist–Leninist state. These functions do not include the actual administration of government. A clearer line differentiating political and administrative functions was then established in 1975, preventing the party from intruding in the latter, as had happened before when it actually made most administrative decisions.

The three party congresses celebrated so far (1975, 1980, and 1986) provide a historical sequence to Cuba's performance in the economic, social, and political arenas, as well as in international relations. The record, a product of internal and external factors, has been uneven. Some of the events were under Cuba's control (with positive and negative results), while others were beyond its capacity to affect them. Under these conditions, the most Cuba could do was to cope with adversity in the best possible terms, so it would not be seriously harmed. This critical situation is developing all over again. Developing nations (socialist or not) were plagued by economic problems both during and after the 1981–3 recession suffered by advanced industrialized market economies. While the latter emerged relatively unscathed by an economic crisis of their own doing, the effect on developing nations was socially and economically devastating.

The First Party Congress.   Probably, the First Congress was one of the highest points in the life of the PCC. After waiting for so long, without statutes and a written program, the party was finally allowed to perform its proper role in Cuban political life. This happened at a time when the entire political system was being institutionalized, and when the political structure of the Cuban state was defined under a new socialist Constitution. A main event at the Congress was to endorse the new charter, which was submitted later for the people's approval in a national referendum.

The First Congress was inaugurated with an opening speech by Raúl Castro, followed by a major report by Fidel Castro (a 248-page document including such subjects as a summary of the country's history and the revolutionary movement, the transformation to socialism, the first ten years of the party, the achievements of the revolution, and the struggle against US imperialism and in support of 'liberation movements'). Messages from fraternal parties, governments, and visiting dignitaries were received. The attending delegates examined and approved important theses and resolutions. The party's preparatory commission had previously approved them after numerous assemblies throughout the country, starting in April 1975, discussed draft resolutions and the work of the party, and elected or reelected leaders and delegates to the party's central organizations. The party congress also approved the statutes and the programmatic platform of the PCC. They were needed components in the institutionalization of the party.

Approved theses and resolutions included such policies as the internal organization of the party; the social and economic five-year program (1976–80); the Organs of People's Power; the new System of Economic Management and Planning (SDPE); the party's relationship with organized religion, the church, and believers; the mass media; the educational, scientific, cultural, and artistic policy; the development of children and youth; the full exercise of equality by women; and the agrarian problems, including official relations with the peasantry.

The congress elected the party's leadership. Castro continued heading the PCC as First Secretary, followed by Raúl Castro as the Second Secretary. Castro also headed the Politburo, and therefore presided over the two main power centers in the party: the Secretariat and Politburo. The party's Secretariat had had twelve members since 1973 (when five new members were added), but it was reduced to nine members in 1975, then increased to ten in 1976, and finally to eleven members in 1977. The Politburo increased its membership by five, from eight (1965) to thirteen (1975). The secretaries-general of three large provinces and individuals of recognized merit were added. The Central Committee's membership was expanded to 112 full members (from a hundred in 1965). While thirteen members of the 1965 Central Committee were dropped, thirty-five full members and twelve alternate members were added.

The First Congress formalized party procedures, set up deadlines for decision-making, reinforced its relations with the international Communist movement, and had an overall salutary symbolic and legitimizing effect for the party and the regime. Moreover, it institutionalized the PCC while setting the stage for the institutionalization of the state. It approved the new socialist charter that gave a united legal and juridical framework to the organization of the polity under the revolution. Cuba completed the institutionalization process a year after the First Congress. The inauguration of the National Assembly of the Organs of People's Power in December 1976 climaxed the process initiated at the party Congress. By then, Cuba was embarked on its post-institutionalization period.

Critics of the regime noted, however, that the party congress (as well as the overall institutionalization process) was far from representing an effective decentralization of decision-making and of the exercise of revolutionary power in general. They also noted that, as before, political power was localized in Fidel Castro, and his close collaborators—mostly those who fought alongside him in the Sierra Maestra, and some old communist leaders, like Carlos Rafael Rodríguez.

The Second Party Congress.   The Second Congress was held in December 1980 under the shadow of the declining sugar prices of the late 1970s, the 1980 Mariel boatlift, and the election of a militantly conservative President of the United States, Ronald Reagan. Castro responded to mounting internal problems with new policies. The parallel price system was instituted in stores and food markets to service the neglected Cuban consumer. By allowing prices to float freely (*liberados*), next to the subsidized lower prices of rationed items, the regime made it possible to purchase consumer goods at higher prices without the limitations imposed by the rationing system (which was established in the 1960s to guarantee lower prices and equal access to the entire population of scarce consumer goods). Also, the free farmers' markets were approved. Functioning next to state food markets, which had subsidized lower prices, the supply-and-demand price-based new markets managed to attract customers with the diversity and quantities of available staples in spite of higher prices.

Characteristically, changes occurred in the upper hierarchy of the party during the Second Congress. Two senior members left the Secretariat but retained their membership in the Politburo (Blas Roca and Carlos Rafael Rodríguez). Isidoro Malmierca left the Secretariat to become Minister of Foreign Affairs. One member was demoted, but retained his membership in the Central Committee. With the addition of four new members the Secretariat retained its eleven membership as before.

The Politburo had its share of changes. Three new members were added (all belonged at that time to the Central Committee) for a total of sixteen. The Politburo alternate member position was created and a total of eleven were appointed. The new alternate members were three Division Generals, and the presidents of the four main mass organizations. Thus the armed forces and the mass organizations received a higher level of party representation. The other alternate members were two members of the Secretariat, a provincial party first secretary, and the President of the Central Planning Board (JUCEPLAN), Humberto Pérez, who represented highly technical and managerial personnel before the party.

The Central Committee increased its members to 148 (from a hundred in 1965, and 112 in 1975). The number of alternate positions grew from twelve in 1975 to seventy-seven in 1980. The majority of the Central Committee's membership was reelected to this important post: 78.8 percent of the members who were still alive in 1980. Six of the twelve alternate members appointed in 1975 were promoted to full members, while one was dropped altogether. The mass organizations gained in their membership—from 7 percent in 1965 to 18.9 percent in 1980. Following a trend initiated earlier, the military representation declined proportionately (but its total of thirty-six members remained the same)—from 58 percent in 1965 to 24.3 percent in 1980. However, after some who were on military duty in 1975 were moved to civilian posts by 1980, the Central Committee was opened to new military members. The bureaucracy share of posts declined slightly, from 17 percent in 1965 to 16.9 percent in 1980. Meanwhile, the share of educators, scientists, and those in cultural activities increased from 4 percent in 1965 to 6.8 percent in 1980. Foreign affairs representatives more than doubled between 1965 (3 percent) and 1980 (7.4 percent). Political leaders doubled from their initial 10 percent in 1965 to 20.3 percent in 1980 (Domínguez, 1982, pp. 22–5). The most relevant changes in the composition of the Central Committee in 1980 seemed to be the increase of mass organizations' representation and the steady decline of the percentage of those in military duty.

A central event of the Second Congress was Castro's main report. It examined socioeconomic developments during the 1976–80 period, and the state of the military, government, social and mass organizations, PCC, ideological struggle, world economic situation, and Cuba's foreign policy. The 1980 congress approved a total of nineteen resolutions. They regulated internal party life, Marxist–Leninist studies, the training, selection, placement, promotion, and advancement of political cadres, relations with the Church and believers, and the education of children and young people. Also, the resolutions included how to improve the work of the Organs of People's Power, and agricultural, educational, international, artistic, and scientific policy. They also included mass media, women's equality, and sports policy, the economic planning and management system, and the socioeconomic guidelines for 1981–5.

Continuing the institutionalized practices started in 1975, the Second Congress provided a forum assessing the party's and the polity's performance. The record was mixed, including achievements and shortcomings. However, the congress had a positive sense of purpose and direction that was badly needed in the face of recent events. (The Mariel boatlift episode seemed to have had a sobering effect on everyone.) The people seemed to appreciate Castro's and the party's leadership. With renewed dedication, Cubans appeared to be ready for the five-year period ahead of them.

The Third Party Congress.   The Third Congress was the most difficult of the three party congresses. This was evidenced, among other developments, by the fact that the conclusion of the congress was deferred for nine months (a final comprehensive plan remedying the rather serious problems confronted by the country's economy was still in the offing). The first session took place 4–7 February, but did not conclude until a second meeting was held 30 November–2 December 1986, with 1,723 delegates attending.

Castro's main report, delivered during the first session, was particularly relevant. After the customary listing of accomplishments, he moved on to a rather negative evaluation. His intense criticism of the economy and of the government's performance surprised almost everyone. His critical comments spared hardly any sphere of national life, not even education and public health, which are regarded by most Cuba watchers as the regime's major domestic achievements.

In his closing speech on 2 December to the Third Congress, Castro acknowledged the numerous ongoing nationwide debates discussing how to rectify existent mistakes and negative tendencies, which had been prompted by his February report.

In addition to gaining support for the new policies and the major administrative and political personnel changes approved by the party congress, one of the main objectives of denouncing production and administrative errors and shortcomings in such a highly public manner seems to have been to focus the nation's attention on these problems and the urgent need of overcoming them.

According to Castro, during 1981–5 the economy achieved a rate of growth in global social product (GSP) of 7.3 percent, and 8.8 percent in industrial production. (The global social product (GSP) used by socialist nations is conceptually and operationally different from the gross national product (GNP) used by Western market economies to measure economic productivity and growth.)[3] Moreover, labor productivity increased at an annual rate of 5.2 percent, which accounted for 74 percent of the total increment in production. Personal consumption grew at an annual rate of 2.8 percent, and social consumption by 7.1 percent. Average monthly salaries increased by 26.4 percent for the entire period (Castro, 1986, pp. 2–21).

Paradoxically, these impressive figures seemed to indicate a healthy growing economy. According to an American economist, twenty years of economic history indicate that 'Cuba['s] [rate of] industrial growth during 1965–84 was 6.3 percent. This is a very healthy, if not impressive rate of growth and stands out in sharp relief when compared to the growth experienced in the rest of Latin America.' Moreover, 'the reasons for this favorable industrial performance' are not yet understood. 'Some will attribute it to high investment ratios, propitious structural change, heavy human capital investments, full resource employment or central planning, others will argue that Soviet aid is responsible and yet others will seek more complex explanations' (Zimbalist, 1987, p. 24).

Nevertheless, as Castro rightly discerned, the problem with the economy was not just growth as such, but growth in those areas where it mattered most: in exports of goods and services and import substitution. At the heart of Castro's report were such problems as the failure to increase production of exporting goods to, and reduction of imports from, capitalist market economies. Apparently, Cuba's low productivity in these sectors was caused, at least partly, by poor coordination in economic planning. Rather than keeping an overall, panoramic vision of the economy, planners were responding to the compartmentalized concerns, pressures, and interests of state enterprise administrators. As Castro surmised, in order to make itself commercially competitive, Cuba had to increase labor productivity, and improve the quality of manufactured goods.

Major personnel changes at the highest levels of the PCC and government occurred at the Third Congress (see Table 4.2). Demotions of high ranking officials started in 1984, however. Institutionally, the Central Planning Board (JUCEPLAN) seemed to suffer a significant loss of prestige and influence as a major economic agency. Its director, Humberto Pérez, who had ministerial ranking and was Vice President of the Council of State, had been replaced prior to the party congress and became an economic advisor to Castro's brother, Raúl. Although other JUCEPLAN high level administrators and technicians reportedly stayed in their posts, more changes followed in high economic management posts in 1985 (approximately eleven), and in 1986.

As had happened in earlier congresses, the higher party echelons changed. More competent professionals were brought to the Politburo, while trusted comrades left, including an aging communist leader, the late Blas Roca (then nearly 80 years old), and three other members who also had lost their Cabinet posts. First, Ramiro Valdés, former minister of the interior and a veteran of Moncada, Granma, and the Sierra Maestra with the ranking of 'Commander of the Revolution' (he was replaced as interior minister by Division General José Abrantes, who is not a Politburo member). Second, the former transportation minister, Guillermo García Frías, who was one of the earliest supporters of the Sierra Maestra struggle coming from among the peasants and also holds the title of 'Commander of the Revolution.' (Besides Valdés, García Frías, and Fidel and Raúl Castro, the only other person holding such a title is Juan Almeida.) And third, the former minister of health, Sergio del Valle. García Frías and del Valle's demotions were seemingly caused by their poor administrative performance. In the case of Valdés, unconfirmed rumors suggested that he had abused some of his posts' perquisites. However, all four retained their seats in the Central Committee. Roca, García, and Valdés lost their Council of the State Vice Presidential posts when the National Assembly's Third Legislature was inaugurated in December 1986 (García and Valdés remained members), and del Valle lost his membership.

The Politburo was reduced in size from sixteen to fourteen full members, but alternate members increased by one, from nine to ten. Two vacancies had remained after the earlier deaths of two permanent members in 1983, Osvaldo Dorticós and Arnaldo Milián Castro, and the four 1986 demotions. Voicing an affirmative action concern in his report, Castro indicated the need to bring women, blacks, and youth to the highest party posts. Vilma Espín, president of the FMC, became the first female Politburo full member. Also appointed as full members were Division General Abelardo Colomé Ibarra, representing the new generation of military officers, and Roberto Veiga, representing labor as Secretary General of the National Trade Union of Cuban Workers (CTC). Esteban Lazo, a black man who was party secretary of Santiago de Cuba province, but not a full member of the Central Committee at the time, was also appointed to the Politburo. In another personnel change, an alternate member of the Politburo, Division General Senén Casas Regueiro, was transferred to the Secretariat while remaining as head of the Military Department of the Central Committee, a position he had held since 1984.

Reduced from eleven to nine members, the major personnel changes in the party's Secretariat preceded the Congress' demotions and promotions. Antonio Pérez Herrero, responsible for PCC's ideology and propaganda, was removed from the Secretariat in 1985. His diverse areas of responsibility, including culture, education, and science, were distributed among others. Pérez Herrero had been a major party organizer seeking to apply systematically Marxist-Leninist principles to the PCC and the country. Reportedly, however, he had also opposed two major policy developments in the 1980s: the new opening to the Catholic Church in Cuba, Latin America, and elsewhere, and the short-lived opening toward the United States. Nevertheless, he was appointed ambassador to Ethiopia. Another major change was that of Jesús Montané, who headed the Central Committee's Foreign Relations Department and had always been close to Castro since his participation in the attack to the Moncada Barracks in 1953. Still, Montané lost his Politburo and Secretariat posts. He now works directly with Castro as Assistant to the First Secretary of the Party.

The Central Committee had half of its alternate members dropped—its full members were reduced by two, to 146, and alternate members increased by two, to seventy-nine. Its military membership became the lowest ever in

Table 4.2 Cuban party, state, and government leadership in 1987 (including changes made in 1985 and 1986)

Name	Politburo*	Secretariat†	Central Committee‡	Council of State/ National Assembly§	Council of Ministers; Other Posts and Titles¶
Castro Ruz, Fidel	Member	First Secretary	Member	President (Head of State)	President (Head of Govt); 'Commander of the Revolution'
Castro Ruz, Raúl	Member	Second Secretary	Member	First Vice President	First Vice President; Minister, MINFAR; 'Commander of the Revolution'
Almeida Bosque, Juan	Member		Member	Vice President	President, Party's National Control and Review Commission; 'Commander of the Revolution'
Camacho Aguilera, Julio	Member		Member		Ambassador to the Soviet Union
Cienfuegos Gorriarán, Osmani	Member		Member	Vice President	Vice President; Min. Secretary; Head of Central (Planning) Group
Colomé Ibarra, Abelardo	Member		Member	Member	Division General, FAR
Espín Guillois, Vilma	Member		Member	Member	President, FMC
Hart Dávalos, Armando	Member		Member	Member	Minister of Culture

Name				
Lazo Hernández, Esteban	Member		Member	PCC Secretary, Santiago de Cuba Province
Machado Ventura, José R.	Member	Member	Vice President	Pres., National Electoral Commission
Miret Prieto, Pedro	Member		Vice President	Vice Pres., Basic Industries
Risquet Valdés, Jorge	Member	Member	Member	
Rodríguez Rodríguez, Carlos Rafael	Member		Vice President	Vice Pres., Foreign Relations and Trade
Veiga Menéndez, Roberto	Member		Member	General Secretary, CTC
Casas Regueiro, Senén	Alternate		Member	Division General, FAR
Fernández Alvarez, José Ramón	Alternate		Member	Vice President; Min. Education
Ramírez Cruz, José	Alternate		Member	President, ANAP
Alvarez de la Nuez, Luis	Alternate		Member	
Ferrer Gómez, Yolanda	Alternate		Member	Director Ideology Dept, FMC
Michel Vargas, Raúl	Alternate		Member	
Rizo Alvarez, Julián	Alternate		Member	
Rosales del Toro, Ulises	Alternate	Member	Member	Division General, FAR
Simeón Negrín, Rosa Elena	Alternate		Member	President, Academy of Science
Vázquez García, Lazaro	Alternate		Member	

Table 4.2 *(Cont.)*

Name	Politburo*	Secretariat†	Central Committee‡	Council of State/ National Assembly§	Council of Ministers; Other Posts and Titles¶
Balaguer Cabrera, José Ramón		Member	Member	Member	
Batista Santana, Sixto*†		Member	Member		Head of the Central Committee Military Dept.; Division General, FAR
Crombet Hernández-Baquero, Jaime		Member	Member		
Soto Prieto, Lionel		Member	Member		
Bravo Pardo, Flavio			Member	Member; President, National Assembly	
García Frías, Guillermo*§			Member	Member	'Commander of the Revolution'
Valdes Menéndez, Ramiro*§			Member	Member	'Commander of the Revolution'
Acosta Cordero, Armando*			Member	Member	National Coordinator, CDRs
Aguirre del Cristo, Severo			Member	Member	
Abrantes Fernández, José			Member		Minister, MININT; Division General, FAR
Domenech Benítez, Joel			Member		Vice President, No Portfolio

Name	Status	Position
Escalona Reguera, Juan	Member	Min. Justice
Esquivel Yedra, Antonio	Member	Vice. Pres., Min. Light Industries
López Moreno, José	Member	Vice President; Min. Pres. Central Planning Board
Malmierca Peoli, Isidoro	Member	Minister, MINREX
Torralba González, Diocles	Member	Vice President; Min. Transportation
Portal León, Marcos J.	Member	Min. Basic Industry
Teja Pérez, Julio	Member	Min. Public Health
Vecino Alegret, Fernando	Member	Minister, Higher Education
Linares Calvo, Francisco	Member	Min. Pres. State Committee Labor Social Security
Rodríguez Llompart, Hector	Member	Min. Pres. Central Planning Board
Naranjo Morales, José Alberto	Member	Minister Without Portfolio
Díaz Suárez, Adolfo A.	Alternate	Min. Agriculture
Roca Iglesias, Francisco A.	Alternate	Min. Food Industry
Robaina González, Roberto	Member	President, UJC
Montané Oropesa, Jesús*†	Member	Assistant to the First Secretary of the Party

Table 4.2 (*Cont.*)

Name	Politburo*	Secretariat†	Central Committee‡	Council of State/ National Assembly§	Council of Ministers; Other Posts and Titles¶
Pérez González, Humberto*			Member		Economic Advisor to the Second Secretary of the Party
Pérez Herrero, Antonio*†			Member		Ambassador to Ethiopia
Valdés Vivó, Raúl			Member		Rector, PCC's School of High Learning 'Nico Lopez', President, ICAP
Rodríguez Cruz, René			Member		
del Valle Jiménez, Sergio*§			Member		
Roca Calderío, Blas*§			Member		Vice Pres.; Min. Construction
Cabrera Núñez, Raúl					
Cabrisas Ruiz, Ricardo					Min. Foreign Trade
Castillo Rabasa, Manuel					Min. Communications
Fernández Cuervo Jorge A.					Minister Fishing Industry; Ship Captain
Herrera Machado, Juan					Min. Sugar Industry
Lage Coello, Marcos					Min. Steelworking
Vila Sosa, Manuel					Min. Domestic Trade
Meléndez Bachs, Ernesto					Min. Pres., State Com. Economic Cooperation

* *Changes in Politburo membership at the Third Party Congress* (it was reduced from sixteen to fourteen permanent members, but four new members were appointed: Division General Abelardo Colomé Ibarra, Vilma Espín, Esteban Lazo Hernández, and Roberto Veiga Menéndez).

Ousted Permanent Members: Blas Roca Calderío (for health reasons, upon his own request); Guillermo García Frías; Ramiro Valdés Menéndez; and Sergio del Valle. Blas Roca died 25 April 1987.

Ousted Alternate Member: Armando Acosta Cordero; Division General Sixto Batista Santana; Miguel Cano Blanco; Jesús Montané Oropesa; Humberto Pérez González; and Antonio Pérez Herrero (in 1985).

† *Changes in Secretariat membership at the Third Party Congress* (it was reduced from eleven to nine members). (José Ramón Balaguer was appointed to the Secretariat in 1985, while Division General Sixto Batista Santana was appointed in 1986, after his removal from the Politburo as an alternate member).

Ousted Secretariat Members: Jesús Montané Oropesa, and Antonio Pérez Herrero (in 1985).

‡ *Changes in Central Committee membership at the Third Party Congress* (it was reduced from 148 to 146 members, and increased from seventy seven to seventy nine alternates). (Fifty five new members were appointed, representing 38 per cent of current members.)

Ousted Central Committee Members and Alternates (according to their affiliations): eight from the PCC; twenty three from MINFAR; nine from MININT; eleven from CTC; twenty seven from different ministries and government agencies; and thirteen from mass organizations.

§ *Changes in the Council of State/National Assembly in 1986.* On 27 December 1986, the Third Legislature of the National Assembly was inaugurated. It reelected Fidel Castro President of the Council of State, Raúl Castro First Vice President, and Flavio Bravo President of the National Assembly (who was then elected member of the Council of State). Blas Roca, Guillermo García, and Ramiro Valdés lost their Council of State Vice Presidential posts. However, García and Valdés were elected members. Sergio del Valle lost his membership. The Council of State membership totals thirty one, including a President, five Vice Presidents, a Secretary, and twenty three members.

¶ *The Council of Minister membership.* It totaled forty six in 1985. It includes a President, eleven Vice Presidents, a Minister-Secretary, a Deputy Secretary, nine Minister Presidents (heads of different agencies), twenty Ministers (with Portfolio), and two Ministers Without Portfolio, and an Assistant (in charge of overseas construction).

Sources: Government of the United States, Directorate of Intelligence, *Directory of Officials of the Government of Cuba*, CR 85-13573, Washington, DC, November 1985, *passim*; *Gramma Weekly Review*, 16 February 1986, pp. 23-4, and 1 January 1987, pp. 1-5; US Department of State, *Republic of Cuba—NDE*, Washington, DC, July 1986.

both the total number and percentage of its members (no naval officer is currently a full member of the Central Committee). Civilian party leadership was clearly asserted; 28 percent of the Central Committee's membership was black or mulatto, and women's permanent members increased slightly from 1980, to 13 percent. More importantly, the changes at all party levels were conducted using competence and efficiency as guidelines, while those who had occupied major posts retained their membership in the Central Committee. According to a Cuban watcher, 'This was not, however, a bloody or vicious purge . . . No faction was crushed, no overarching policy dispute surfaced. Recruitment was also rational. Promotion to the top organs rewarded good performance and followed appropriate hierarchical channels' (Domínguez, 1986, p. 121). As the Third Party Congress clearly indicates, complacency leading to poor performance and inefficiency is a luxury that no one could afford in Cuba in the mid-1980s, particularly among those in leading governmental and party posts.

At the December session a draft resolution on the PCC's new program was approved. It had been presented earlier at the February meeting, and was publicly discussed nationwide by party and non-party members in the intervening months. Out of 8,336 proposed amendments, 574 were accepted and incorporated into the final draft, modifying the original text. At the December session eight more amendments were recommended for approval. Expressing a concern similar to what he said earlier when the free farmers' markets were closed, Castro told the party congress delegates,

I have seen the example of what was happening to us: the blind belief—or it began to be blind—that the construction of socialism is basically a question of mechanisms. As I pointed out [at a recent meeting with Cuban journalists] . . ., I think that the construction of socialism and communism is essentially a political task and a revolutionary task. It must be fundamentally the fruit of the development of an awareness and educating people for socialism and communism [*Granma Weekly Review*, 14 December 1986, p. 12]

As he had done time and time again, Castro was placing revolutionary consciousness above any other consideration, particularly institutional structures. For critics of the regime this was another example that he was not ready to live with decentralized channels that would take major decision-making away from him. For Castro, however, at the center of any system was man, and at the center of man's behavior was his own consciousness. Evidently, he wanted to be sure that the party would not allow the earlier revolutionary fervor (*conciencia*) to fade slowly away.

5 The Political Structure

The 1976 Constitution

The revolutionary government functioned under a provisional constitutional setting from 1959 to 1976. Rather than restoring the 1940 Constitution as some had expected, the regime enacted in 1959 the Fundamental Law (of the Republic) as its constitutional foundation. The law was rapidly amended, however. As societal transformation under the revolution became increasingly radical, the provisional charter became less representative of the new political reality. From 1959 to 1963, over a hundred new statutes were enacted, covering almost every aspect of society. In the period between 7 May 1959 and 31 December 1962, the 1959 Fundamental Law was modified nineteen times, affecting in the process thirty-five of its 233 articles, including on one occasion an entire section of this law.

Changes in the Fundamental Law were needed to provide a legal foundation for the approved revolutionary legislation. The changes were facilitated by the concentration of legislative and executive powers centered in the Council of Ministers. This kind of decision-making practice lasted until the politico-administrative and legislative bodies established by the 1976 Constitution, the National Assembly and the provincial and municipal assemblies of the Organs of People's Power, were inaugurated in late 1976.

As with other Latin American constitutions, the 1901 Cuban Constitution was influenced by US liberal democratic political institutions and pragmatic philosophy. More progressive than Cuba's first charter, the 1940 Constitution was oriented toward mild, evolutionary social transformation. It was influenced by the reformist type of constitutionalism initiated in Latin America by Mexico's 1917 Constitution. While socially oriented, and rather progressive in many aspects, the 1940 Constitution was nevertheless a liberal democratic (bourgeois) charter that could not embrace the profound social transformation that had taken place after 1959.

Thus Cuba had to adopt a new constitutional model; i.e., the Soviet Union's and other Marxist–Leninist states' socialist constitutions. Following a legal change process that was started in the early 1960s, the regime had replaced Cuba's Roman (civil) law with a socialist law system. The legal transformation process was completed with the new constitution, which safeguards the social, political, and economic changes accomplished in over two decades of revolutionary government, while creating new political and judicial institutions. Mainly, it provides a socialist constitutional framework to the new Cuban polity: the first Marxist–Leninist state in the western hemisphere.

The new socialist charter was initially approved at the PCC's First Congress in December 1975, followed by a national referendum held on 24 February 1976. A draft constitution had been circulated nationwide earlier seeking jurists and attorneys' and laymen's recommendations for possible modifications. It is not publicly known, however, how many of the suggested changes were actually heeded and included in the final text.

The 1976 charter breaks new grounds in Cuban constitutional history. However, it also includes some degree of continuity. On occasions, it departs from other socialist countries' structures. It allows a single person (who would become President of the nation's main political organ, the Council of State, and of the governmental/administrative body, the Council of Ministers) to head both the state and the government, according to the Latin American tradition of a strong executive.

Also, the possible change in the name of the country provoked a debate on the value of safeguarding some of the country's traditions. When the draft constitution was being examined, it was proposed that, in view of the new socialist charter, the country's name be changed to 'Socialist Republic of Cuba.' The new name would have been stated then in Article 1 of the 1976 Constitution, which acknowledges the socialist character of the Cuban state. But, according to a Cuban jurist, the late Fernando Álvarez Tabío, the proposed name change was finally discarded, among other reasons, 'because the name of Republic of Cuba had its roots in the progressive and patriotic traditions of our people, and it is not contradictory to our current social system' (Álvarez Tabío, 1981, p. 29). As in previous cases, the revolution's strong identity with Cuba's history prevailed. The new political system based on the 1976 Constitution is meant to convey elements of nationalism to the socialist system, expecting that the former would reinforce the latter.

The 1976 Constitution has 141 articles and twelve chapters. It recognizes Marxism–Leninism as the state ideology (Preamble of the Constitution), and the Communist Party as the only political party in the country (Article 5). It regulates relations between the different state organs based on the principle of democratic centralism (Article 66). It defines state political power according to the dictatorship of the proletariat: the working people wield political power through legislative and politico-administrative assemblies, Organs of People's Power, in alliance with the peasants and the 'remaining strata of urban and rural workers' (Article 4). It also eliminates 'the exploitation of man by man' by establishing a socialist economic system with the public ownership of the means of production (although there are instances in which private property is allowed, as when small farmers own their lands) (Articles 14–27). It creates a reward system according to an initial socialist stage (in anticipation of an ultimate communist society); i.e., 'from each according to his ability, to each according to his work' (Article 19). And it proclaims proletarian internationalism as the bedrock of the nation's foreign policy: supporting other socialist states, liberation movements, and progressive regimes opposing imperialism (Article 12) (Simons, 1980, pp. 99–134).

The Council of Ministers

The Council of Ministers constitutes the 'government of the Republic,' and is 'the highest-ranking executive and administrative organ' of the regime. It is one of the three institutional power pyramids in the system (the other two are the Communist Party (PCC) and the Organs of People's Power (OPPs)) comprising the bureaucratic structure of the central government. The Council of Ministers is headed by its Executive Committee, which is one of the four centers of power in the political system (the other three are the PCC's Secretariat and Politburo, and the OPPs' Council of State).

The Constitution covers in Articles 93–9 the organization, power, and accountability of the Council of Ministers (it is accountable to the OPPs' National Assembly's Council of State for its administrative decisions and performance), as well as other matters related to the Council of Ministers. The composition of this executive body includes a President (who becomes head of the government and state); First Vice President; several Vice Presidents, at least seven; the President of the Central Planning Board; the ministers, the secretary, and other members determined by law. In Article 96, the Constitution specifies in twenty entries the powers invested in this executive and administrative state organ. Castro presides over it, and Raúl Castro is the First Vice President.

The Executive Committee of the Council of Ministers is formed by the latter's President, First Vice President, and remaining Vice Presidents. It is a powerful state agency controlling the administrative apparatus of government, and is constitutionally allowed to 'rule on matters normally under the jurisdiction of the Council of Ministers' (Article 95). The functions centered in this body make it the highest layer of administrative and executive decision-making. Based on the principle of democratic centralism, its decisions apply downwards, first to the Council of Ministers, and then to the rest of offices, ministries, and other agencies that altogether constitute the administrative structure of the regime.

The Council of Ministers and its Executive Committee and the National Assembly and its Council of State are interlocked at different levels of their respective structures. They stand next to one another in a dual system of horizontal collaboration and vertical subordination, which again functions according to the principle of democratic centralism. This brings together and coordinates bureaucratic administration and decision-making (under the care of the Council of Ministers) and administrative policy-making, supervision of services and agencies, and legislation (under the care of the OPPs' National Assembly and Council of State). At a lower interlocking layer, medium and lower administrative offices of the central government work under the same principle with the provincial and municipal assemblies of the Organs of People's Power coordinating their politico-administrative functions with the state administration.

The Organs of People's Power

The Organs of People's Power (OPPs) comprise one of three institutional power pyramids in Cuba (the other two are the Communist Party and the Council of Ministers). Its National Assembly met for the first time on 2 December 1976. This terminated sixteen long years in which the Cabinet had centralized political power exercising executive, legislative, and judicial functions. It also eliminated the position of Prime Minister held by Castro since 1959. Under the new arrangement, the President of the National Assembly's Council of State and of the Council of Ministers' Executive Committee—the same person holds both positions—becomes then the actual President of the country. Castro was elected to these positions in 1976. In December 1986, he was reelected for the third consecutive five-year term. As expected, on all three occasions Raúl Castro was the First Vice President.

The system of OPPs is organized following 169 politico-administrative Municipal Assemblies, fourteen Provincial Assemblies (one for each munici-pality and province in the country), and one National Assembly. The Municipal Assemblies are headed by a president, vice-president, and secretary, and the Provincial Assemblies by an executive committee of seven to twenty-one members. The delegates to the former are elected directly by secret, popular vote of their neighbors for $2\frac{1}{2}$-year terms on the basis of one municipal delegate for each electoral circumscription. For a term similar to their own, the municipal delegates elect then their provincial counterparts (switching to an indirect electoral system). The number of provincial delegates is determined according to the population of each of the fourteen provinces on the basis of one delegate for every 10,000 citizens, or fraction greater than 5,000. Also, the municipal delegates elect the deputies to the National Assembly (an indirect election too) for a five-year term, with one national deputy for every 20,000 citizens, or fraction greater than 10,000.

The OPPs' Political and Administrative Functions

The Organs of People's Power's functions are constitutionally determined according to municipal, provincial, and national jurisdictional levels. They include significant political and administrative functions, and, at the national level, the National Assembly has legislative authority as well.

The Municipal and Provincial Assemblies. Both the Municipal and Provincial Assemblies 'govern in all that concerns them ... [directing] economic production and service units which are directly subordinated to them ... [providing] economic, cultural, educational, and recreational services' (Article 102). The authority of the Municipal Assemblies includes 'the operations of schools, of hospitals and clinics, of stores, movie theatres and ... transportation.' Meanwhile, the Provincial Assemblies are the 'supreme authority for the services and production units which cross over municipal boundaries, but which operate within provincial boundaries' (Bengelsdorf, 1979, pp. 12–14).

Established by the 1976 Constitution, the municipal and provincial OPPs' functions are complex. They include: (1) enforcing laws and regulations coming from superior state organs; (2) electing their executive committees, and revoking their mandates if proper cause demands such an action; (3) overseeing all matters related to the administrative units under their jurisdiction responsible for the different socioeconomic tasks entrusted to them; (4) electing and recalling the judges of the people's courts in the areas under their jurisdiction (in agreement with the 1977 reorganization of the judicial system); (5) studying and evaluating the rendering of accounts (*rendición de cuentas*) reports submitted by their executive committees, judicial organs and assemblies, and national deputies and provincial and municipal delegates, and adopting pertinent decisions regarding these reports; and (6) strengthening socialist legality and the country's defenses, and upholding internal order (Article 105).

The National Assembly.   Standing at the top of the OPPs pyramid, the National Assembly represents the 'supreme organ of state power,' and expresses 'the sovereign will of all the working people' (Article 67). It is invested with legislative and constitutional reform authority, and it can revoke the decree laws issues by the Council of State, which functions while the National Assembly is not in session. Its powers include: (1) declaring a state of war in the face of military aggression; (2) approving the national budget; (3) exercising control over the organs of state and government; and (4) appointing the members of such organs as the Council of State, the president, vice president, and other judges of the People's Supreme Court, and the Attorney General of the Republic (Article 73).

The National Assembly is made up of 492 deputies, and is headed by Flavio Bravo. Substantive legislation was approved in the last ten-year period, including yearly economic and social development plans, annual state budgets, and administrative, civil, penal, public, military, and other laws. The National Assembly's sessions are short, usually lasting two days. They are held twice a year, in July and December. If the need arises, an extraordinary session can also be called. In preparation for the regular sessions, twenty standing commissions work throughout the year drafting legislation. This is done in coordination with the National Assembly's Commission on Juridical and Constitutional Affairs. The national deputies are assigned to the different standing commissions, which are staffed with advisory and clerical personnel. In the National Assembly's second legislative period for 1986, 83 percent of the deputies worked in sixteen standing commissions, and drafted 112 social and economic studies that included 800 recommendations (*Granma Weekly Review*, 11 January 1987, p. 2). The national deputies (and the provincial and municipal delegates) continue holding regular jobs in addition to their OPPs' responsibilities—they are freed, however, whenever they need to attend regular sessions or other related meetings. No national deputy, or provincial and municipal delegate, receives a salary for his or her work in the OPPs; remuneration comes from regular jobs.

In addition to the national deputies, laws can be proposed by the Council of State, the Council of Ministers, the different commissions of the National Assembly, the trade unions and mass organizations, the People's Supreme Court, the Attorney General, and through a petition signed by at least 10,000 citizens who are eligible to vote.

The Council of State.   Functioning as the National Assembly's executive committee, the Council of State is the most powerful office within the OPPs. It stands at the top of the latter's power pyramid, and is one of the four centers of power in the political system. The members of the Council of State are elected by the National Assembly deputies from their own ranks. There are thirty-one members, including a president, first vice president, five vice presidents, and a secretary.

The President of the Council of State is elected by the members of this body. He becomes the head of state and government, which makes him also the President of the country. In consultation with fellow Council of State members, the President appoints the members of the Council of Ministers (the actual government of the country), over which he also presides.

In addition to representing the National Assembly while the latter is not in session, the Council of State has significant additional powers: a total of twenty entries listed in Article 88 of the Constitution. Since 1979 the decree laws issued by the Council of State have had equal standing and judicial validity with the laws approved by the National Assembly. This has tilted the balance of power in favor of the Council of State at the expense of the National Assembly, which functions as such only during its two brief yearly sessions. The additional powers granted to the Council of State have been used in major overhauls of the central administration agencies on several occasions.

Cuba's state and governmental institutions have been found to match those of the Soviet Union's. The National Assembly has been paired with the USSR Supreme Soviet and the Council of State with the Presidium of the Supreme Soviet (de la Cuesta, 1976, pp. 20–1; González, 1976, p. 8). Institutions like the Permanent Commission of Mexico and Venezuela could also be compared to the Council of State. In all these cases, however, each institution has its own peculiar features which correspond to the idiosyncratic nature of the political system. While Cuba shares a political tradition with other Latin American countries, its present Marxist-Leninist system brings it probably closer to those of the Soviet Union and other socialist countries.

Evaluating the National Assembly

The National Assembly has performed its formal functions properly since it was inaugurated. As reported in the official media, the national deputies appear to take their legislative roles seriously, bringing their constituencies' concerns, as well as their own, to the attention of the National Assembly. Seemingly, there has been thorough and open discussion of issues and proposed legislation. If anything, the trend appears to be toward more rather than less debate of proposed legislation, producing changes in the initially discussed laws and policies. And yet currently it does not seem possible for national deputies to exhibit an outright opposition to an official policy or legislation, particularly if it is supported by Castro or other major revolutionary leaders. The organically integrated nature of the Cuban polity is not geared to bring this kind of confrontational politics into fruition. The system is not aimed at pitting the National Assembly against the Council of Ministers, or at having national deputies posed against one another. This does not preclude debating policy; however, having a political organ like the OPPs blocking policy or legislation in an intra-institutional feud, as a way of opposing or weakening another powerful state agency, is not meant either.

The Effectiveness of the State Political Organs

The decentralization of decision-making sought in the 1970s through the newly created political institutions has been effectively established at the local level. By having placed substantive areas of responsibility and decision-making in the people's hands in matters directly related to their most immediate concerns, the system of OPPs has become an invaluable tool for the effective exercise of socialist democracy. The *rendición de cuentas* system has proved that it can assure accountability for the delegates and national deputies' actions. In particular, it addresses the question of whether the electorate's interests are truly safeguarded by their OPP representatives.

None the less, regardless of the obvious political significance of the local OPPs, national matters are not decided at this level. National and international policy fall under the Council of State and the National Assembly (in that priority order) within the OPPs structure. Thus, while decentralization and effective people's input have functioned effectively at the local level, it does not seem so (at least not as clearly) at the national level. This is, after all, where major policies addressing the issues facing the country as a whole are decided (Domínguez, 1982a, pp. 19–70; Ritter, 1985, pp. 270–90).

Relations Between the PCC and the OPPs

The nature of the PCC–OPPs relationship seems largely based not only on constitutionally differentiated areas of political authority but on what are the OPPs' members' priorities: is their primary allegiance to the OPPs or to the party? Do they follow the party's will (only a minority of the population belong to the party) while carrying out their OPPs functions? That is, to what extent are the OPPs' delegates and national deputies exercising independent political judgment upon representing the electorate? (However, these questions might be entirely inappropriate in such a political system as Cuba's, in which confrontational politics is not practiced for petty partisan gains.)

The examination of this problem leads to the PCC and OPPs' membership question. Although over half of the national deputies (55.5 percent) come from the ranks of the municipal delegates, and it is not necessary to be a party member to be elected to the OPPs, the reality of dual membership in both the party and the OPPs is central to this phenomenon. Of the national deputies 91.7 percent and of the Council of State members 100 percent belong to the PCC. In the provincial assemblies 90.6 percent belong to the party, and in the executive committees 99.2 percent. At the municipal level the party member–OPPs member ratio is the lowest of the three: 64.7 percent in the assemblies and 90.4 percent in the executive committees. However, if the Young Communist League's members are taken into account, the number of nonaffiliated OPPs members decreases: 24.2 percent in the municipal assemblies and 4.4 percent in the executive committees, and 6.1 percent in the provincial assemblies and 0.4 percent in the executive committees. At the National Assembly level, the nonaffiliated national deputies would then only be 3.3 percent (none are in the Council of State) (Azicri, 1980b, pp. 330–2; Ritter, 1985, p. 279).

Relations between the PCC and the OPPs are potentially problematic. As representatives of a politically sovereign institution, OPPs' members do not have to agree with, nor approve in their deliberations, PCC policies—they are not legally bound to do so by the 1976 Constitution. The presence of PCC members among OPPs deputies and delegates is seemingly the way used to secure the approval of party policies by the Organs of People's Power. Even if after debating—and many times modifying—them, the OPPs nevertheless consistently approve the party's policies.

The enforcement of the principle of democratic centralism in the party's decision-making process provides a channel for political participation and internal discipline for party members. This is not the case, however, for non-party members who do not participate in the PCC's decision-making. Given the significance the party's performance has for the political system's welfare, it seems imperative that party policies be properly examined and their merits convincingly demonstrated in OPPs' deliberations. As a regular political practice, this would have the beneficial effect of reducing and/or eliminating potential or actual intra-systematic conflict between the PCC and the OPPs.

The PCC's political leadership must be based on proven sound policies to be effective. This helps to explain the built-in pressure that exists in Marxist-Leninist regimes for the Communist Party to demonstrate effective political leadership by agreeing on sound policies and national objectives. The people's support for the system (i.e., the regime's legitimacy) must signify continuous agreement with the party's policies and performance. This would enlarge the system's democratic base while reminding the populace positively of a political reality among Marxist-Leninist regimes: that the entire nation lives formally under the Communist Party leadership and guidance.

In Cuba, however, besides the institutional changes made in the 1970s, the PCC, the political system, and the country still live under Castro's popular leadership. As a consequence of the strength of Castro's charisma and the wide support he enjoys, his policy choices are sometimes accepted without having their actual merits carefully evaluated—as happened in the past, particularly in the 1960s. Castro's leadership has been, and definitely is, an invaluable asset for the revolution, and he undoubtedly has many years of productive life ahead of him. But even though most political analysts would affirm that Castro and the Revolution are one, and that in order to understand the latter it is necessary to know the former well, reliance on a charismatic leader as the major support is not the kind of political foundation that a political system can be based upon indefinitely.[1] The 1980s is a period in which the state institutions established in the 1970s must gain permanence by enjoying a successful process of routinization.

Still, again and again, Castro's charisma seems to be the bedrock upon which the revolution relies to overcome new obstacles and to move ahead. The difficult problems discussed at the Third Party Congress seem to demand more, rather than less of Castro's leadership. Paradoxically, while Castro puts his customary imprint on the approach followed to face these difficult times, and he even defines the nature of the problems themselves, the system roots itself deeper in the invaluable source of his charisma in order to find strength and direction, as it has done all along.

Elections under the Revolution

In October 1976 national elections under the revolution were held for the first time. In the 1976–86 period, following an arranged cycle, a total of five elections were held: three electing OPPs' municipal and provincial delegates, for $2\frac{1}{2}$-year terms, and national deputies, for 5-year terms (1976, 1981, and 1986); and two electing municipal and provincial delegates (1979 and 1984). The electoral system is regulated in Articles 134–40 of the Constitution, and by the Electoral Law (Law 37 of 15 August 1982). Elections will follow in 1989, 1991, 1994, and so on, according to the law.

Allowing only for direct elections at the local level, the electoral procedure lacks the kind of political impact that national elections could have on a political system as a whole. This is reinforced by the type of campaigning allowed: a picture and a biography of a candidate is posted on a bulletin board at the electoral circumscription for everyone to see. The elections' political impact is narrowed further by the fact that provincial delegates and national deputies do not campaign seeking popular support. They are (indirectly) elected by the municipal delegates, who have been (directly) elected by the entire voting population. On behalf of the system, it could be said that it allows democratic elections by popular, secret, direct (at least partly) vote, even if in a peculiar fashion; and that it avoids having electoral campaigns become a disruptive influence in the nation's political life, as in other countries. The political system's reponsiveness to the electorate is increased by the fact that the national deputies are accountable to the municipal assemblies that elect them—to whom they have to render periodic accounts of their work at the National Assembly. Also, the provincial and municipal delegates render periodic accounts to their respective assemblies.

Since the 1976 elections the electoral process has produced some distorted political results. With a turnout of 95.2 percent of the total number of electors, in the first elections only 520 women were elected (6 percent of the total number of those elected). Rather than representing the impressive gains achieved under the revolution, this indicated a polity in which women would live a rather marginal political life. The election analysis indicated that female candidates had more political support in urban than in rural areas. Traditional values seemingly lingered among some sectors of the population. This was demonstrated by their favoring the allocation of political roles along ascriptive, rather than achievement lines (tradition rather than modernity).

In 1976 women represented 13.5 percent of all candidates, and 8 percent of those elected. Rather than improving, the situation got worse in 1979: only 9.9 percent of the candidates were women and 7.2 percent were elected. In 1981 the situation improved, but still was below 1976: 11.4 percent of the candidates were women and 7.8 percent were elected. A significant improvement took place in 1984: they constituted 16.3 percent of the candidates and 11.5 percent of the elected municipal delegates. Women's representation in the provincial assemblies increased also: from 16 percent in 1979 to 20.3 percent in 1984. In the National Assembly the situation was somewhat better: 21.8 percent of the national deputies in 1979 were women and 22.8 percent in 1984 (Espín, 1986, p. 52).

The Cuban voter has exercised a discriminating vote: 50 percent of the 10,752 municipal delegates elected in 1976 were not returned to office in

1979. Before the elections 108 delegates had been recalled (more male than female delegates), while others had been replaced for involuntary reasons— i.e., sickness, moving to another circumscription, and others. Recalling has been practiced more at the local level than at the national level—however, an agricultural worker caught cheating in a school examination was expelled from the National Assembly on charges of demeanor inappropriate to his responsibilities (Arañaburo, 1979). On the negative side of recalling OPPs municipal and provincial delegates and national deputies, Ritter speculates that 'it is possible that this mechanism could be used to induce conformity and, in the extreme, to weed out troublemakers and upstarts' (1985, p. 280).

The Judiciary

Similarly to the rest of society, Cuba's legal and judicial system was transformed under the revolution. The nation's legal basis is formulated in Article 9 of the socialist charter: 'The Constitution and the laws of the socialist state are the juridical expression of the socialist production relationships and of the interests and will of the working people.' Also, all citizens are expected to be law abiding members of society. Respect for the law places everyone 'under the obligation to strictly observe socialist legality and to look after the same within the whole context of society.' The new judicial institutions are meant to provide the structure guaranteeing the functioning of the socialist legal system (Articles 121–33).

The administration of justice in socialist Cuba has received mixed reviews from political and legal analysts. According to Domínguez, 'in the post-revolutionary period [the courts] retain some small degree of autonomy; state prosecutors do not always win their cases . . . The courts perform a limited role as defenders of individual rights . . ., though only for those accused of crimes not regarded as political' (1978, p. 6). On the state's social control of juvenile delinquency, Salas concludes that, 'Cuba has placed a strong emphasis on the correct upbringing of its youth . . . [Its] delinquency develops in many of the same ways found in other societies. It seems to be concentrated among lower class, male youth with low educational achievement who come from broken or maladjusted homes' (1979, p. 368). Regarding penal institutions, Elder states that, 'the Cuban prisons I witnessed compared favorably with US prisons I had visited in philosophical orientation, general atmosphere, and in the low rate of recidivism. Prisons in Cuba are not a business justifying a bloated crime-prevention superstructure. The goal is to return to society the prisoners as productive human beings' (1985, p. 87).

The courts are functionally independent from other state organs, but are subordinated to the National Assembly and the Council of State. The functions of the courts include: (1) protecting the socioeconomic and political system established in the Constitution; (2) protecting socialist (public) and personal (private) property of citizens and others (as recognized by the Constitution); (3) protecting the life, freedom, dignity, honor, family relations, and other rights and interests of citizens; (4) preventing violations of the law and antisocial conduct, and restraining and reeducating those who are guilty of such violations or conduct; and (5) increasing awareness (public education campaigns) as to the need for strictly observing the law, and the norms of socialist living (Article 123).

At the top of the judicial structure is the People's Supreme Court, which is ruled by its own Governing Council. It has the power to issue regulations, make decisions, and enact norms which are obligatory for all lower courts. The courts function in a collegial form, including professional and lay judges (the social significance of the latter's functions is emphasized as a court's priority). According to the Constitution, the judges are independent while administering justice and 'only owe obedience to the law' (Article 125). However, they have to render once a year an account of their work to the (OPPs') Assembly that elected them, which also has the authority to recall, and replace them.

Preceding and following the 1976 Constitution, the judicial system was reorganized twice in a period of four years, in 1973 and 1977. The reorganization of the judiciary was not an example of good planning. The judicial system had to be organized again and again in order to fit into the overall institutionalization process.

Under Law 1250 of 23 June 1973, the ordinary, revolutionary, people's, and military courts, which previously were handled separately, became unified. Later, Law Number 4 of 12 August 1977, sought to rectify some of the contradictions caused by Law 1250 and the modifications introduced by the Constitution, and, moreover, by the 1976 Law Organizing the Central Administration of the State.

The 1977 reorganization of the judiciary established three layers for the court system: (1) the People's Supreme Court; (2) the People's Provincial Courts; and (3) the People's Municipal Courts (the previous regional divisions were eliminated). There was also a Military Chamber of the People's Supreme Court, which had first instance and appellate jurisdiction to sentences given by Military Territorial Courts (Article 29 of Law Number 4). The administrative (governmental) functions of the judiciary fall under the jurisdiction of the Ministry of Justice. This is separated from actual judicial decision-making (sentencing), which remains the sole domain of the courts.

The power and functions of the Attorney General are regulated in Articles 130-3 of the Constitution. The National Assembly has the power to elect and recall him—he is subordinate to the National Assembly and the Council of State. The offices of the Attorney General are organized 'in a vertical manner all over the country' under his authority (independently of all local organs). At least once a year the Attorney General has to render an account of his work to the National Assembly. He is charged by the Constitution to 'control socialist legality by seeing that the law and other legal regulations are obeyed by state agencies, economic and social institutions, and citizens' (Article 130).

The Mass Organizations

The 1976 Constitution lists the main mass organizations and acknowledges their central social position while promising the state's recognition, protection, and stimulation. The mass organizations are the Confederation of Trade Unions (CTC), the Committees for the Defense of the Revolution (CDRs), the Federation of Cuban Women (FMC), the Federation of Secondary Education Students, and the Union of Pioneers of Cuba. Noticeably, the National Association of Small Farmers (ANAP) is not listed, although it is an important mass organization. The Constitution states, 'the state relies on the social and mass organizations which, in addition, directly fulfill the state functions that are intended to be assumed by the same, in accordance with the Constitution and the law' (Article 7).

The mass organizations' social and political role in socialist Cuba includes a close interconnection between them and the nation's political structure. The mass organizations cannot be wholly independent in this context—their close relationship with the political system is even acknowledged by the Constitution, which gives them the right to propose legislation (Article 86). However, while performing their functions, they seemingly operate with some autonomy in their own ascribed domains. This is evidenced by the different characteristics of each mass organization which go beyond their assigned functions and by the emulation campaigns launched nationwide. The campaigns appeal to different chapters within each mass organization and among mass organizations, to excel while competing with one another in the implementation of a given program, particularly a national one. (The winners become then models for ulterior emulation campaigns.) This seems to recognize implicitly that the different mass organizations and their membership respond to subjective, ideological, and cultural motivations that cannot be assumed to be a constant feature. Rather, they have been nurtured by the regime in order to guarantee a supportive response by the populace (Aguirre, 1984, pp. 541–66). That the government responded positively to this concern is evidenced by the fact that the mass organizations contributed to what political scientist Richard R. Fagen calls a 'subculture of local democracy.' Also, Black, *et al*., note that, 'the closer one comes to the issues and decisions critical to a particular neighborhood or place of work the more one finds vigorous debate and a democratic approach to policymaking' (1976, p. 289).

The Confederation of Cuban Workers

Organized labor had not been a leading force in the struggle against the Batista regime. The April 1958 general strike failed, so it could not seriously harm Batista as had been expected. Some labor leaders, who had been involved in the underground struggle upon joining Castro's organization, gained control of the Confederation of Cuban workers (CTC) after the revolution came to power. Initially, a power struggle had ensued between the 26 July Movement and supporters of the old communist party, the Popular Socialist Party, for the control of the labor organization. However, David Salvador, a labor leader initially favored by Castro, fell out with the regime and was later sentenced to prison for conspiratorial activities. Moreover, the revolutionary government had a labor policy based on mistaken assumptions regarding the role of labor organizations under a socialist regime. Jorge Risquet Valdés, then labor minister, admitted in the early 1970s 'the government had allowed the union structure to atrophy during the 1960s because it had mistakenly assumed that in a revolutionary system the workers rights would be automatically protected and promoted by the government' (Black, *et al*., 1976, p. 306).

During the institutionalization of the 1970s the role of labor under socialism was examined. Nevertheless, the question of whether labor should be the leading force under the 'dictatorship of the proletariat' still remained. According to Raúl Castro, 'It is necessary to keep in mind that the working class considered as a whole . . . cannot exercise its own dictatorship since . . . originating from bourgeois society, it is marked by flaws and vices from the past.' He elaborated further, 'One of the principal functions of trade unions under socialism is to serve as vehicles for orientation, directives and goals which the revolutionary power must convey to the working masses . . . *The Party is the vanguard. Trade unions are the most powerful link between the party and the working masses.*' (*Granma Weekly Review*, 26 September 1974; emphasis added.)

Pérez-Stable notes that, 'this official position coincided with Lenin's position in the 1921 Bolshevik party debate on trade unions between Worker's Opposition and Trotsky' (1985, p. 304). Thus labor would perform a mass organization function through its own CTC, providing a supportive, but still central service. Its major social role would be disseminating orientation and directives to workers (as a downward transmission belt), while the revolutionary vanguard would continue leading the transition towards socialism in Cuba.

By the mid-1970s, however, the labor movement was revitalized. New CTC chapters sprang up; collective agreements regulated worker-management relations; and workers' involvement in planning and management characterized their discussion of the enterprises' production plans. Also, work councils were instituted. Later, they lost their authority to solve disciplinary problems, when this power was given to management by the Council of Ministers. By the early 1980s, however, with more than 3 million workers affiliated, the labor movement had improved organizationally. Workers' revolutionary consciousness and activism increased, while the labor movement became an integral part of today's Cuba. This was not limited to labor's vanguard movement, as had happened in the 1960s. The workers' standard of living improved also. Representing eighteen trade unions, the CTC Congresses became relevant for the labor movement and the polity: both labor and national problems were discussed on such occasions by President Castro and the general secretary of the CTC, Roberto Veiga.

The Committees for the Defense of the Revolution

Probably no mass organization is as central to the revolution as the Committees for the Defense of the Revolution (CDRs) are. Organized in 1960 to maintain vigilance against the 'enemies of the revolution,' the CDRs are open to membership by practically everyone in society: are organized nationally on a neighborhood by neighborhood basis. In addition to being the most inclusive of all mass organizations, the CDRs are also the most multifunctional. Having replaced initial vigilance against the counterrevolution as the CDRs main objective, today they are engaged in all kinds of tasks, particularly educational (ideological) and mobilizational (aiming at community and national activities). The CDRs are the regime's ideal conduit to reach the population at large, and to engage it in a myriad of campaigns. By the mid-1970s, over 70 percent of the adult population belonged to the CDRs, representing more than 50 percent of the entire population (almost 80 percent of the adult population belonged to the CDRs by the 1980s).

Since the mid-1970s, however, the political centrality of the CDRs has decreased. While the mass organizations in general have increased their party membership and representation in such organs as the Politburo and Central Committee, the CDRs have lost, nevertheless, some of their broader political role. (In addition to having the heads of the mass organizations appointed to the Politburo, their membership increased from 6 percent of Central Committee members in 1975 to 19 percent in 1980.) The establishment of the Organs of People's Power in 1976 as the state political structure has been mostly responsible for the CDRs' relative loss of significance. The OPPs at the municipal level provide now the immediate open local forum that only the CDRs could provide before. Thus the CDRs' functions have been specialized further, focusing on those community projects that they are better suited to carry out. All in all, this has had the positive effective of broadening political participation opportunities at the local level. It provides more possibilities for people's input into the political process—albeit, within the limitations established by the political system already discussed (Rabkin, 1985, pp. 261-6).

The Association of Small Farmers

The National Association of Small Farmers (ANAP) is made up of independent farmers, who function outside of the collectivized state farm system. Their economic and political significance is underscored by the fact that they represent about a fifth of all cultivated land in the country—although they concentrate on such specialized crops as tobacco, coffee, and tubers. As other mass organizations, ANAP provides a channel of communication between the regime, particularly the PCC, and its members. Equally important, however, ANAP provides a direct opportunity to independent farmers for political participation and integration into the revolutionary process. This keeps them within the orbit of the revolution, preventing what otherwise could be scores of independent farmers (representing the largest private sector left in the country) drifting away, politically and otherwise.

The special conditions under which ANAP members function were institutionalized by the 1976 Constitution (Articles 20-2, 24). Only family members who are directly engaged in the cultivation of the farmland can inherit it (Article 24), but the right to own the land privately is not questioned (Article 20). The government, however, has a preferential option to purchase the land if it is for sale, and it has to approve whatever transaction might be agreed upon (Article 21). From the government, private farmers receive credits, fertilizer, seed, and tools. In return, they are required to sell a percentage of their crops to the state at official prices, which are below market prices (the *acopio* system).

In the long run, however, the private farmer may be an 'endangered species.' With the educational opportunities open to their children leading to careers other than farming, farms might move increasingly from the private to the public sector. The short-lived private farmers' market in the late 1970s and early 1980s provided an economic bonanza to the independent farmer (selling his products at inflated market prices). That kind of incentive is gone now, and is unlikely to return in the near future. The regime has favored all along the absorption of independent farmers into state-owned projects. A combination of subsidies and official regulations is used as incentive to motivate farmers to accept this policy. Hence, the current trend most likely will not lead to numerous generations of independent farmers in years to come.

The Federation of Cuban Women

The Federation of Cuban Women (FMC) is highly responsible for the progress achieved by Cuban women under the revolution. The modernization of Cuban women is one of the regime's most successful developmental experiences, which stands as a leading women's liberation movement today in Latin America. While the PCC's low female membership ratio and the low number of women elected for the OPPs (discussed earlier), and other shortcomings, detract from its record of achievements, it is still a movement credited with tangible and impressive results.

When the FMC was inaugurated on 23 August 1960, the different women's associations in existence were grouped under its organizational structure. The *federadas* (FMC's members) include women 14 years old and older. They grew rapidly in number, turning their movement into a leading mass organization. Starting with 17,000 in 1960, one year later they already were at 90,000. In 1970 they numbered 1,324,751, and 2,167,171 in 1976. For eighteen years they had a rate of growth of 132,475 new members per year (5.8 percent), declining later to 5.1 percent (Azicri, 1979, p. 32). Nevertheless, by the 1980s the *federadas* included over 80 percent of the total female population.

Different social rehabilitation programs were established in the early 1960s sponsored by the FMC. Schools were created for women working in domestic service who wanted to prepare themselves in new areas of employment. In Havana province alone 20,000 women used this program. However, some of them found employment in the day-care centers that were built in increasing numbers. Self-improvement schools for prostitutes from the pre-1959 period were also created. In spite of their pre-1959 conditions, characterized by tradition and political and economic marginality, women's active participation in such programs as the 1961 literacy campaign demonstrated early their revolutionary commitment. The FMC encouraged women to learn technical skills including agriculture, tractor driving, specialized farming techniques, cattle raising, and political instruction.

Since its foundation, the FMC has been headed by Vilma Espín. She is the wife of Raúl Castro and a revolutionary leader in her own right. Her impressive credentials date back to the underground struggle against the Batista regime. Espín was Castro's 26 July Movement coordinator in Oriente province until she was forced to leave its capital, Santiago de Cuba. By then she was placed high on the police wanted list. She met Raúl Castro when she joined his Second Front 'Frank Pais,' in the northern part of what was then Oriente province. At his request, she stayed there for the remainder of the insurrectionary struggle. They were married soon after the revolution came to power in 1959, and have several children.

The FMC's values and objectives are representative of women's conditions in the Third World. Its rationale is 'feminine' but not 'feminist.' Women are seen as men's equals, but not as their opponents. Rather than pitting women against men, as is done often by Western feminist movements, the FMC seeks to integrate the *federadas* into the revolutionary process. While structural social change is taking place remedying women's plight, it is understood by the FMC that its immediate and major task is to support the revolution effectively. According to Espín, '[The FMC's] work is to make everybody advanced. Then when everybody has a high level of consciousness, nobody will have to think of equality.' She states her dislike of the United States brand of feminism in rather strong terms:

In reality . . . we have never had a feminist movement. We hate that. We hate the feminist movement in the United States. We consider what we are doing part of the struggle. And for that reason we consider we are more developed. We see these movements in the United States which have conceived struggles for equality of women against men! . . . That is absurd! It doesn't make any sense! For these feminists to say they are revolutionaries is ridiculous! . . . That's what is more tragic. They are just being manipulated, being used. The feminist movement! Ha! [Quinn, 1977, p. B3]

As a mass organization working within a Marxist–Leninist system (where social equality is recognized as a value included in official policy), the FMC pursues women's development through an organically integrated social context (without pluralist interest groups pitted against each other). The FMC's philosophy of women's liberation is a product of this reality. Also, it recognizes the fact that in order to be part of the revolution, women had to contribute to it. But they needed to capacitate themselves first in order to do it. In Espín's words, 'We also knew that women in Cuba were not ready for the tasks that awaited them in a new society.'

Women's remarkable educational gains, their social and political work, and their incorporation into the labor force in all kinds of productive work since 1959 are major achievements. By 1986 1,144,045 women were working, representing 37.4 percent of the total labor force (they totalled 13 percent of the working population in 1953). In the City of Havana province women constitute 44 percent of the labor force, and there are eighteen municipalities in which they represent over 45 percent of the working population. Before 1959, women worked mostly in domestic service (27 percent of all working women), or as teachers (14 percent)—they constituted 82 percent of the teachers and performed 89 percent of the domestic service. Today, practically all kinds of work are open to women, including the professions and the armed forces. Nevertheless, the Labor Ministry approved Resolutions 47 and 48 in the late 1960s that allegedly protected women (the first one saved women from hard and risky work, and the second kept certain jobs from women arguing that they were hazardous to their health), but which were found to be discriminatory against women (Espín, 1986, p. 38). The Labor Ministry resolutions were also reinforcing notions of 'biological fatalism' allegedly affecting women.

In that case, and others, as when the Family Code was initially drafted, the FMC worked effectively as a catalyst bringing women's concerns to the revolutionary leadership's attention. As noted, it has not always been successful. The regime's overall needs, particularly the country's development, take precedence over women's sectorial interests. Thus it is fair to say that when their interests overlap (the regime's and women's), women's issues are then properly handled. But the regime's commitment to social equality and development makes women's progress a built-in objective of the revolution's social policy goals. To some extent, this gives credence to the assertion that under socialism women could find themselves truly liberated. In the Cuban case, the record indicates that while women have become a formidable social and economic force, total political success is still awaiting them down the road. Women will become equal partners in every political situation when all sectors of society have developed to a higher level of consciousness, according to Espín's characterization of the FMC's objectives. This new equality should include a higher ratio of the PCC's membership and leadership posts, and of the OPPs' elected positions.

Political Dissent

The clearest definition to date of Cuba's openness and/or restrictions on freedom of expression is Castro's 'Words to Intellectuals' speech. Addressing a gathering of writers, artists, and intellectuals at Havana's National Library on 30 June 1961, Castro explained to those present what was expected from the substance and direction followed in their work—and by extension from any other cultural activity as well. He stated that: 'Within the revolution—everything, against the revolution—nothing' (Karol, 1970, pp. 241–3; Szulc, 1986, pp. 564–7). While Castro made clear then that no artistic or literary school was being established or endorsed (i.e., socialist realism), and that a wide scope of creativity was permissible, he also made clear that no anti-revolutionary work would be allowed. By extension, his definition of what was culturally proper applied to the mass media. Any organized form of political opposition remained off limits, however.

Different forms of self-examination and criticism are widely practiced—albeit, always 'within the revolution.' While public expressions or actions 'against the revolution' are not acceptable (even sanctioned if considered subversive), freedom of expression for revolutionary thought and ideas is officially supported. How much of the latter is always practiced is debatable. For example, direct and open criticism of Castro is not exercised, and probably never will be. But nation-wide debates affecting public policy are regularly held. Public discussion of major legislation (including the Constitution, and major new Codes and laws) is an institutionalized practice. Notwithstanding the political and social benefits of such a participatory process, it is hard to determine how many recommendations made in those hearings are normally heeded, and added to the final legislative draft.

No political opposition to Communist Party rule is allowed. As a Marxist-Leninist political system, the regime functions on 'the assumption of a nonpluralistic, single truth in politics.' As articulated by the political left elsewhere, in socialist Cuba 'the nonliberal democratic connotations [present] in Rousseau's philosophy and political theory find proper expression' (Azicri, 1986, p. 71; Talmon, 1961, pp. 1–13, 17–65). Cuba's socialist democracy is meant to be an expression of the dictatorship of the proletariat.

For liberal democracy, this is more than just a limitation; it represents a practice based on nondemocratic values. While liberal democracy embraces the values of 'liberty' and 'individual freedom,' socialist democracy stresses 'collective' and 'group goals' as proper democratic values. Thus political dissent, as practiced in a pluralistic, liberal democratic system, is nonexistent in Cuba. Whether this makes Cuba less or more democratic becomes then both a philosophical and practical question. As Talmon puts it in his analysis of modern political thought, liberal democracy and the democratic values of the left ('totalitarian democracy of the left') are two political traditions that after having evolved from similar social enginering roots, moved into separate, even opposite directions (Talmon, 1961).

It is within such institutions as the PCC (the leading political agency), the OPPs (representative political institutions), and the mass organizations (the vehicle for direct, public political participation) that political life takes place. Opposition to any policy or program must take place within this institutional framework, and whatever decisions are arrived at must conform to the principle of democratic centralism. In Castro's own words: '[Cubans] don't understand the concept of liberty in the same way as . . . [liberal democrats do] and, as a matter of fact, the opportunities to carry out opposition against the revolution are minimal. They do not exist legally.' Moreover, while opposition as a social-class phenomenon is, in his opinion, nonexistent in Cuba, he still defines the context in which opposition 'within the revolution' is legitimately exercised: 'Yes, opposition exists. One carries it out within the Party, within the [mass] organizations, the factories . . . It has to be within the Party because the essence of the Party is precisely its democratic spirit, . . . the right to criticize and the duty to carry on self-criticism . . . There exists the right to disagree' (Mankiewicz & Jones, 1975, pp. 84–5).

The lack of opposition is also justified by Castro as a political necessity rather than as a principled policy:

The only really important enemy we have had has been the North American imperialism, a powerful enemy who would have liked to have opposition parties here against the Revolution—newspapers, radio stations speaking out against the Revolution—to use them against the Revolution. Look at the Chilean example, Allende respected all these rights. The opposition press conspired. There were newspapers clamoring for a *coup d'état* every day, and they finally gave a coup . . . [Mankiewicz & Jones, 1975, pp. 84–5].

The existence of such opposition parties and mass media is contrary to present political institutions, and the political values upon which the system is predicated. The political hegemony exercised by the PCC is not a temporary, or conjectural policy; it is central to the system itself. Neverthe-less, at lower levels, there is room for openness. The popular monthly *Opina* provides a forum for consumers' complaints exposing publicly managerial shortcomings of state enterprises. *Opina*'s section of classified advertisements popularized the practice of trading houses (*permutas*) among homeowners, but it was discontinued in mid-1986 after direct sales of houses and apartments from one private party to another were terminated.

Criticizing the main political and ideological features of the political system and the lack of political opposition in a human rights report, the Organization of American States (OAS) nevertheless recognizes 'the existence of political organs of a collective nature . . . as a positive feature, since they employ negotiating procedures designed to obtain a consensus for political action.' Moreover, '[these] collective organs constitute a sound basis to facilitate broad citizen participation in the formulation of national policy.' However, states the OAS report, 'The principal organs of the State and the Communist Party have been dominated by a small group [the revolutionary leadership] since the very beginning of the current political process' (Organization of American States, 1983, p. 177).

The human rights question is a sensitive issue in the West. Works by Cuban exiles like Armando Valladares and others, enabled the Reagan Administration to launch, mainly for propagandistic reasons, an inter-national campaign denouncing Cuba as a violator of human rights. In March 1987 Washington sought a declaration by the United Nations Commission on Human Rights condemning Cuba for alleged human rights abuses. Although it was rejected by the United Nations, the Reagan Administration's international campaign served to deteriorate further what has already been a rather poor state of relations between Cuba and the United States in the 1980s (*New York Times*, 2 May 1987, pp. 1, 7).

Valladares' *Against All Hope* has been described as a 'searing account of his personal experience as a political prisoner in Cuba for 22 years' (Mellanby, 1987, p. 230). Also, according to another reviewer, 'until the publication of this book . . . we had not had a full picture of the brutality meted out to real and imaginary opponents by the Castro dictatorship' (Radosh, *New York Times Book Review*, 1986). Seemingly, in addition to the Reagan Administra-tion, and conservative and liberal writers and academics, the 'Valladares campaign' has been fueled by additional publications from such anti-Castro organizations as the Cuban American National Foundation (Cuadra, 1986).

Valladares' account of a 'Cuban *gulag*' has been refuted by writers and academics with their own account of Valladares' association with the Batista police, his counterrevolutionary activities, and the numerous inaccuracies plaguing his work. According to an American law professor, 'Valladares was arrested in December 1960 and convicted of conspiring with others to engage in acts of sabotage . . . Much of [his] . . . book is made of one-page anecdotes about events to which Valladares was not a witness, yet he describes these incidents in minute detail including precise dialogue, even the color of a car' (Evenson, 1986, pp. 1–3). Another reviewer of his book comments that, 'Once Valladares entered prison, he chose to become an intimate of the most extreme counterrevolutionaries. These friends brag of their attempts to assassinate leaders such as Che Guevara and Fidel Castro.' Also,

the author of 'Against All Hope' appears to have forgotten that he worked for the [Batista] police, forgotten that rather than being executed by the new government he was offered the same job, and forgotten that he had admitted as much years before writing a book in which he denies any connection with the police and states he was a fervent opponent of Batista . . . [Georgakas, 1986, pp. 10–11]

The 'Valladares campaign' is the latest example of the kind of ideological barrier that stands against outside objective and validated assessments of the real state of human rights in Cuba, particularly as seen from the United States. Seemingly, lack of empirical evidence is not an obstacle to accepting anti-Castro Cuban exiles' testimonies at face value. A political analyst wonders reflectively,

What happened to the old journalistic axiom about checking your sources? . . . I was in Havana recently and took the trouble to check out Valladares' background. It is there for anyone to see, in the files of Batista's secret police, which the Cuban government has kept intact. Valladares was no 'poet' but was rather a . . . protégé of Armando Carratala, the most bloodthirsty of Batista's professional torturers. [Hinckle, 1986]

As discussed above, socialist democracy and liberal democracy stand for substantively different, even opposite modalities of human rights—while the former concerns itself with social rights, the latter concentrates on individual political rights. However, it seems that the Valladares controversy examined here is more an expression of the current confrontational state in East-West relations (in which United States-Cuban relations are currently hopelessly immersed), than a factual examination of human rights in Cuba. Because of this and other reasons, Cuba watchers' efforts in evaluating the Cuban human rights record appear to have produced mixed results at best.

6 The Economic System

Almost Three Decades of Economic Policy

When the revolutionary government was inaugurated in 1959 the economic conditions facing Cuba were difficult and complex. For the regime, however, the worst problem at the time was the lack of effective economic perspectives. Cuba's small volume of external trade did not justify the investment required to improve the country's economic and industrial development infrastructure, even if further investment was needed to improve both the level of exports and the internal living conditions. In 1957 and 1958 only 17 percent of imports had been for badly needed machinery and supplies for the sugar and non-sugar industrial sector, while 73.3 percent were for durable and non-durable consumer goods. Approximately 94 percent of exports were sugar, sugar-derivative products, tobacco, construction materials, and minerals. In the absence of a long-range developmental policy, the Batista regime did not use available short- and long-term external credits. Instead, reserves and credits with foreign financial firms were used as collateral for short-term obligations. From a rather weak financial position, the revolutionary government had to negotiate with private banks and foreign governments the debt it had inherited from the previous government (Banco Nacional de Cuba, 1982, p. 4).

The economic policies instituted since by the revolutionary government led to significant achievements in the redistribution of national income, and of people's basic needs satisfaction. Notwithstanding serious flaws attributed to the Cuban economy (i.e., systemic economic inefficiency due to its 'reliance on a centrally planned economy,' etc.), a Joint Economic Committee of the US Congress recognized in a 1982 study that Cuba has achieved, 'A highly egalitarian redistribution of income that has eliminated almost all malnutrition, particularly among children; ... [and] a national health program that is superior in the Third World and rivals that of numerous developed countries.' It also admitted the 'near total elimination of illiteracy and a highly developed multi-level educational system' (Theriot, 1982, p. 5). Cuba's basic-needs satisfaction economic policy was oriented towards a growth strategy as well. Moreover, while the basic needs of the population were properly met, 'since the early 1970s [Cuba's economic policy has] been accompanied by a relatively high rate of sustained growth.' However, 'this road towards equity with sustained growth has been both bumpy and difficult' (Brundenius, 1985, pp. 193–4).

None the less, after almost three decades of steady economic growth, Cuba is today under the combined impact of such negative external forces as the after-effect of the 1982–3 world recession. Still, Cuba has fared better than other neighboring countries. A 1984 Latin American economic survey found that the region suffered from 5.6 percent decline in GDP per capita, and an average annual inflation of 68 percent (Banks, 1986, p. 740). Also, Cuba faces increasing economic pressure from the Reagan Administration, which has tightened further the US economic embargo imposed by the Kennedy Administration. And, internally, it suffers from agricultural setbacks, inadequate planning, and waste of human and natural resources.

Reflecting on Cuba's economic troubles in the mid-1980s (which included failing to meet export commitments to socialist nations, and a continuous decrease in the share of trade with the West, which has slipped from 40 to 13 percent of its total trade in the last decade), President Castro was reported as saying to three American journalists: 'I want to know two things. Who is the genius who did away with the jack-of-all-trades in Cuba? And who is the genius who invented the coffee break?' Moreover, he said, 'What happened to the person who could do many jobs instead of just one? . . . Trade unions always try to create jobs, of course. But now, you find one person in charge of opening and closing the closet, another one cleans it, and a third one organizes what is in it' (*Washington Post National Weekly Edition*, 18 February 1985, pp. 9–10).

Ideology and Economic Decision-Making

While the economy faced rather serious problems, seeking ways to increase exports and to utilize domestic resources better, the Cuban leader discussed with American newsmen some issues stemming from the high level of social (job) security and division of labor provided by the regime. The economic problems seemed compounded by the dilemma of how to motivate the work-force properly so as to increase production in both quantity and quality. As official policy, the regime has shifted from moral to material incentives, and, more recently, back again to incentives based on moral motivations.

This time the stakes seem to be higher. Some of the economic mechanisms created in the late 1970s were rejected in 1986, the year of the Third Party Congress. According to Castro, they led to new social inequalities, which are unacceptable in a socialist society. The free farmers' market and its demise in 1986 is a case in point. The private intermediaries who distributed for profit the peasants' produce surplus destined for the privately-run markets took undue advantage of the situation, thus becoming a privileged population sector. They profited more than the peasants did. The national rectification campaign launched in 1986–8 is highly ideological in nature. It has turned to political consciousness and activity as necessary steps to deepen communist understanding among the population. In the eyes of the Cuban leaders the proper development of a socialist society that would eventually lead to communism might depend on it. Nevertheless, how this new turn in the history of Cuban socialism will affect present and future economic growth, and allow for effective management of the economy at the same time, is currently being debated inside and outside the island. Only time will tell, however, what the final outcome will be.

Understandably, ideological consciousness and economic performance at both individual and national levels are closely intertwined in a society such as Cuba. They have always been, but seem to be much more so today, Castro's televised report to the nation discussing the cases of Luis Orlando Domínguez and Rafael del Pino indicates clearly how corruption in the midst of scarcity could border on, or actually lead to, treason. (Domínguez was the former leader of the Communist Youth Union (UJC) charged with embezzlement of public monies, and del Pino is a pilot who fought valiantly against the 1961 Bay of Pigs invaders but defected in May 1987 to the United States with his family in a Cuban airplane.) According to Castro's report, unchecked personal greed for material possessions (which could not be properly satisfied under the limited availability of consumer goods in Cuba, particularly now, and which also ran contrary to the revolutionary values of egalitarianism and collectivism) led to improper conduct in both cases, and in del Pino's case to the betrayal of the revolution (*Granma Weekly Review*, 5 July 1987, p. 4).

However, the present policy paradox confronting Cuba is that while strengthening the ideological consciousness of the populace is necessary (in order to deepen people's commitment to sustain the revolutionary effort, among other reasons), it is also possible that reverting to moral incentives and ideological reasoning as a policy-making rationale, might lead to less pragmatic decision-making practices in economic production and otherwise, with possible counterproductive effects. Thus, rather than solving this dilemma, there is the potential that the current ideological phase might aggravate economic and other problems in the long run, even if unintentionally. When a similar rationale was used in the 1960s, it was regarded by outside critics as a mistaken approach that was wisely corrected: 'The romantic attempt in the second half of the 1960s to achieve development by rapidly raising consciousness and changing values through moral incentives, labor mobilization, and similar techniques has been reversed in the 1970s and is now criticized as an idealistic error' (Mesa–Lago, 1981, p. 3). Also, 'the most convincing indication of the significance and pervasiveness of the negative effect of the subjective factors upon the 1970 [sugar] harvest is the fact that the Moral Economy began to be dismantled in the aftermath of the costly experiment' (Roca, 1976, p. 65).

The Havana Enterprises Meetings

The second annual meeeting of Havana enterprises held in June 1987 indicated that proper corrective measures were being applied to solve different economic problems—at a time when the country's convertible, hard currency reserves were at their lowest for some years. Even if modest, production rates did improve: the Ariguanabo textile mill increased first quality production by 8 percent, and the Hilanderia de Balance textile mill increased production in April–May 1987 by 23 percent over the same period in 1986. However, the latter is still facing both quality production and labor discipline problems.

The first meeting of Havana enterprises had been held in 1986 in the wake of the serious problems denounced at the Third Party Congress, when urgent corrective economic measures, and a quantitative and qualitative increase in production, were demanded. At the 1987 meeting, in a non–ideological mood, Castro made clear that economic problems cannot be solved by subjective means alone, that proper objective conditions must also exist. Moreover, he stated that '[The] capitalists organize production better, have better methods, and [therefore] there are things that should be learned from them. *Not their ideology, but their technology*' (emphasis added). However, hinting also that some of the tendencies that characterized the highly centralized decision–making of the 1960s and early 1970s might still persist, Castro defended state centralized decisions on how to use hard currency reserves. Otherwise, he wondered, 'What is planification [good] for?' (*Granma Weekly Review*, 5 July 1987, p. 5).

Castro also said that it would be wrong to assume that the state could give away such prerogatives as deciding what kinds of investments should be made. Adding that, '[While] we want well trained economists, intelligent, that could help us . . . we do not want people pretending to tell us what to do.

I state it categorically: science and economics are political instruments; they are instruments of the revolution.'

The Rectification Process and Consciousness.   Castro's defense of the decision-making authority of the regime and its leadership during the present rectification process is a plausible stance. However, given past economic mistakes, particularly during the years prior to the institutionalization of the revolution, resistance to delegating authority to technical and lower decision-making bodies hardly leads to decentralization, making more difficult an increase in production and an overall improvement in economic performance. It rather raises doubts among some Cuba watchers, who fear that the strongly ideological mind-set of the past might be reigning again, even if temporarily.

And yet, there is a logic in President Castro's position. His approach seems more ideological on the surface than it may really be. For a small developing country, such as Cuba, consumerism as the West practices it is an untenable goal in the short run, and most likely in the long run as well. Cuba has become a consumer society under the revolution, but differently from what it was before 1959; i.e., without the polarization of haves and have-nots characteristic of developing nations.

The collective and egalitarian approach toward consumption followed after the initial consumerist stage of the early 1960s, is realistic and in keeping with the limited resources of a country that is planning its development towards the future and not simply satisfying today's needs. The question is what could the regime offer as effective incentives within this limited context? Determining the proper type of incentive, so that a socialist society would be solidly built in the process, is central. Castro's view of socialist consciousness as the bedrock sustaining revolutionary Cuba makes sense here, both ideologically and pragmatically. From the regime's perspective, consciousness rooted in revolutionary Marxist-Leninist values must provide the parameters for acceptable and desirable social actions. This also means a recognition that a country such as Cuba, while capable of satisfying the basic needs of its population in a way that is rarely, if ever, seen in the Third World, lacks the resources to motivate its workers on the basis of material incentives alone. Particularly, as workers are motivated by developed market economies, or increasingly so by more advanced socialist European nations.

The 1986-8 rectification process launched at the Third Party Congress renewed the debate on development strategies, and how to relate them to centralized planning. It centered on deciding again what kinds of incentives, moral and/or material, were a better, more effective choice to motivate the labor force to higher productivity. This critical question has been examined by Zimbalist:

The reconsideration of incentives [taking place in the mid-1980s] surely has an ideological component. It is less often recognized, however, that material incentives are severely limited in their usefulness in a non-market, shortage ridden economy. Given their limitations, it is imperative for the effective functioning of centrally planned economies to develop, as well, moral and internal incentives (i.e., workers' internalization of goals through greater participation in goal formulation). The limitations of material incentives become more pressing during periods of severe foreign exchange difficulties, such as Cuba is . . . experiencing [in the mid-1980s.] [Zimbalist, 1987, pp. 2–3]

However, the orderly decision-making channels established in the 1970s, providing the structure for more pragmatic and well-conceived policies, are as necessary today, if not more, than they were then. So they should not be undermined in any way. In a permanent sense they have not been yet, even if some recent decisions could give such an impression.

Structural Changes and Economic Models

Cuban revolutionary leaders found five major flaws in the economy in 1959 that needed urgent remedy. Seeking to eliminate them, the regime's major objectives included: (1) improving the slow rate of economic growth; (2) breaking away from sugar monoculture which dominated the country's external trade and generation of GNP; (3) eliminating the state of economic dependence on the United States which dominated Cuba's capital investment and external trade; (4) terminating the historical high rate of unemployment and underemployment; and (5) reducing, if not eliminating altogether, the significant differences in standard of living between different population groups, particularly between residents of urban and rural areas. (See: 'Transforming the Economy', in Chapter 2.)

Five Stages of Economy Policy

The first two decades of revolutionary economic policy can be divided into five consecutive stages. Each of these stages represents a different economic model adopted by the regime in pursuit of its developmental, and consumptionist policies. As the regime moved from one stage to another, the developmental objective prevailed over the consumptionist one—the latter became increasingly satisfied by collective and egalitarian means, guaranteeing an equal access to consumer products by the entire population.

The First Economic Stage, 1959–60. The first two years included the liquidation of the capitalist system and the erosion of the role of the market in the economy, among other changes. Rather than following a Marxist blueprint, this phase is seen as influenced by such economic notions as ECLAC's (United Nations Economic Commission for Latin America and the Caribbean) import substitution, industrialization, agrarian reform, tax reform, and others. Ernesto Ché Guevara was highly influential on economic policy-making in the early 1960s from the several posts held by him: as head of the Industrialization Department of the Institute of Agrarian Reform (INRA), president of the National Bank, and Minister of Industry. Economic policy for the period was imbued with attitudes like 'willingness, consciousness, morale, austerity, and loyalty,' which prevailed over 'material and human resources, technology, and knowledge and expertise' (Mesa–Lago, 1981, pp. 7–12).

The 1959 agrarian reform law (which expropriated land from farms exceeding the 400 hectares limit), and the establishment of INRA to direct the agrarian reform and direct agricultural production, allowed the regime to enforce its agrarian policy: '[It] eliminated the *latifundia* sector, with immediate [positive] results over land-and-cattle production ... The peasants ... were able to free themselves from the large warehouse owners' and intermediaries' long-held policy of imposing unfavorable prices for the peasants' products, while forcing them to buy overpriced industrial goods' (CEPAL, 1980, p. 24). The second agrarian reform law of 1963 ended the economic and social influence exercised by the rural bourgeoisie. But the rapid rate of transformation of the rural sector made impossible the development of a coherent agrarian policy during this period. It also meant increasing the state control over the economy, and the collectivization of the means of production. This was accelerated between June and October 1960, when major factories and other private businesses were also nationalized.

The Central Planning Board (JUCEPLAN) was also created. It became the agency in charge of state central economic planning. The Ministry of Finance became closely involved in financing the economy through the state budget (limiting private financing operations to agriculture), while the National Bank further extended its control over credit and foreign exchange.

The social benefits derived from the basic-needs-oriented strategy used were noticeable. Between 1958 and 1962, after three years of revolutionary policy, the total labor force increased by almost 12 percent (a total of 263,000 workers), and open unemployment was reduced from 11.8 to 9 percent (benefiting a total of 47,000 workers). The per capita availability of basic goods and services increased fairly well in food and beverages—the food situation remained critical during the 1960s, mostly due to inefficient planning and distribution. Social services like public health increased sharply, and education even more so. However, clothing was in short supply. The textile industry suffered from the economic embargo imposed by the United States, which forced a structural transformation including using low quality locally produced raw material to replace what had been imported. After having an average of 17,000 new dwelling units built annually during the early 1960s, between 1963 and 1970 construction dwindled drastically creating a housing shortage. Among other reasons, this was due to the priority given to building roads, schools, industrial plants, and other constructions at the expense of housing (Brundenius, 1985, pp. 195–7).

Three More Economic Stages, 1961–70

The three remaining economic stages of the 1960s witnessed major shifts in the regime's economic models: (1) introducing an economic model based on the Soviet experience (1961–3); (2) testing other alternative socialist economic models (1964–6), and (3) adopting a subjective model (emphasizing consciousness over objective conditions), based on economic ideas supported by Guevara (1966–70) (Mesa-Lago, 1981, pp. 14–27).

The collectivization of the economy continued throughout the entire period, while new organizational structure was put in place. It included a network of government agencies and ministries, with JUCEPLAN formulating new macro development plans. Government trusts (*consolidados*), created for those state controlled enterprises producing the same kind of goods, were placed under the direction of a central ministry. Government agencies' budgets included financing the *consolidados*' annual operational expenses. A rationing system was instituted in 1962, guaranteeing that needed consumer goods would be equally accessible to the entire population at subsidized prices, but in limited amounts.

The rate of collectivization of the means of production established in 1961 was increased in most areas: education, banking, wholesale and foreign trade were already 100 percent collectivized in 1961, but retail trade increased from 52 percent in 1961, to 75 percent in 1963, and to 100 percent in 1968. Transportation was 92 percent in 1961, 95 percent in 1963, and 98 percent in 1968. Construction increased from 80 percent in 1961, to 98 percent in 1963, and 100 percent in 1968. Industry was 85 percent collectivized in 1961,

95 percent in 1963, and 100 percent in 1968. And agriculture was 37 percent in 1961, 70 percent in 1963, and 79 percent in 1977. The 21 percent of agriculture belonging to the private sector was credited with owning 32 percent of the cattle, and a production share of the national output totalling 80 percent of tobacco, 50 percent of coffee, 50 percent of vegetables and fruits, and 16 percent of sugar (Mesa-Lago, 1981, pp. 33–5).

The Second Economic Stage, 1961–3.   During 1961–3 the regime attempted to apply an economic organization model that had been used in the Soviet Union. It included a heavy industrialization policy favored by Soviet planners in the 1930s. Some well-known Western economists like Leo Huberman and Paul Sweezy, and Soviet and Czech advisors, provided some of the ideas used during this economic stage. A new administrative structure was implemented, relying on centralized planning to command the economy through the newly created JUCEPLAN. However, the introduction of central planning and the erosion of market mechanisms met serious obstacles that led to a decline in productivity. Agricultural products from the *acopio* system (the private farmers' production quota sold to the state) were significant but were not always properly managed, which caused problems at a time when *latifundia* was being collectivized. A dislocation in the distribution of agricultural products in the cities ensued, exacerbating the shortage of food available to consumers in major urban centers.

None the less, the basic-needs-oriented dimension of the revolution's economic policy continued to improve the populace's living conditions. Notwithstanding the fact that approximately half of all medical doctors left the country in the first three years of revolutionary government, perhaps no social policy, with the exception of education, proved to be more effective than public health. And yet, there were problems in this area as well in the 1960s. The number of hospital beds per 1,000 inhabitants increased from 4.22 in 1958 (a total of 28,536 hospital beds) to 5.03 in 1962 (an increment of 7,951). But the rate of hospital beds per 1,000 inhabitants decreased to 4.95 by 1968. The total number of beds had actually increased by 4,540, but was not enough to move to a higher, or even keep an equal, ratio with the rapidly growing population at the time.

Also, unemployment had been practically cut in half from pre-1959 rates by 1963. Although the absorption of most of the formerly unemployed into the tertiary (service) sector of the economy did not add to any production increase, it served to guarantee a permanent income to many who had suffered unemployment, or seasonal employment at best in the past. The burden this measure represented for the national economy (as long as the productive sector was subsidizing the policy to some extent) was a calculated decision on the part of the revolution's leadership, in keeping with its objective of pursuing economic growth with social equity.

The Third Economic Stage, 1964–6.   New economic models were examined and tested during this stage. More significantly, a decision was made to return to agriculture (especially sugar) as the main goal for the economy, abandoning the heavy industrialization plans of earlier years. The rationale behind this turn in policy was a recognition that sugar still was, as it had been historically, the country's main resource. Profitable sugar harvests coupled with good prices in the international market could provide the necessary resources for future growth and development. Moreover, the regime seemed to reason that under the kind of trade relations it had entered with socialist nations, particularly the Soviet Union, the country could concentrate on a product such as sugar that could in return provide needed industrialized goods, which were not properly manufactured in Cuba. This could be done without risking the kind of exploitation by price manipulation that usually happens in trading with market economy countries, as most developing nations experience under existent unfair trading practices.

Two different, in some respects opposite, approaches were debated and tested during this period. Their roots go back to arguments among Marxist policy-makers as to the best strategy to build socialism, particularly in a developing country. The transition from capitalism to socialism, and then to communism, is complex and difficult. In the case of Cuba, this is magnified by the kind of dependent capitalism it experienced under the influence and control of the United States. Guevara favored the first approach, under which it was argued that the initial phase of building the foundation of socialism could be done by skipping capitalism properly speaking, and then moving directly to build socialism. Adjustments would be necessary, however, at both the ideological and material social levels, in order to enforce it properly.

Rather than relying on market mechanisms (even if limited to the restrictions of a socialist economy) and material incentives, under this approach it was suggested that moral incentives would be used in order to motivate the workers into higher production levels. A socialist consciousness and not pseudo-capitalist motives should be the rationale in a socialist society; thus a new person—Guevara's 'new man'—should emerge from the socialist revolution. State enterprises would operate as branches of a centralized economy, and would be financed through the state budget. Their profits would be added as state revenues, and their deficits would be covered by the central budget. So state enterprises would not have an independent financial status for either losses or profits. While money would still be used for accounting purposes, it would lose its significance as a measure of profitability in state enterprises, and in a general social sense as well. This approach was applied to the industrial sector, but not to agriculture.

The second approach examined and tested at the time supported a more pragmatic, less idealistic version of how to build the foundation of a socialist system. It was not at odds with the notion of developing a socialist conscious-ness among the masses, but it advocated the transformation of the economic infrastructure first. It also intended to use the resources of 'market socialism' (a selected utilization of market incentives and mechanisms adapted to a socialist context) in order to accomplish it. Although it seems to borrow from non-socialist, even capitalist, modalities, this second approach is closer to the logic of Marxist theory than the first one, which wanted to modify the ideological superstructure of society at a time when the economic base was not transformed yet. As Guevara so eloquently recommended, it also advocated egalitarian frugality if necessary, based on revolutionary and socialist *conciencia*, rather than material incentives. The second approach, the Cuban version of 'market socialism,' was championed by the economist Carlos Rafael Rodríguez, who was at the time director of INRA. Rodríguez' approach was used in the agricultural sector, but not in industry (Mesa-Lago, 1981, pp. 18–23).

Guevara's approach was implemented in two-thirds of the industrial sector; Rodríguez' plan was applied to one-third of the nation's enterprises. The centralized modalities used in Guevara's plan were more applicable to the industrial sector, but the more decentralized approach used in Rodríguez' plan was used in agricultural enterprises, which demanded broader autonomy.

The decision to return to agriculture as the central economic activity had additional significance given the revolution's objective of elevating the standard of living of the rural population, which had been traditionally neglected. Also, it made clear the regime's perception of major cities, particularly Havana, as bureaucratic centers practicing conspicuous con-sumerism at the expense of the nation and the population as a whole (CEPAL, 1980, p. 25). Consequently, the demand for additional labor force in the countryside increased, while job opportunities in the cities diminished.

The Fourth Economic Stage, 1966-70. The last years of the first revolutionary decade brought further collectivization of the economy and, more import-antly, Castro's decision to accentuate the support for Guevara's plan at the expense of Rodríguez' plan. With obvious reluctance to decentralize and delegate authority, the regime had problems using central planning in the decision-making process. The revolutionary leaders made economic decisions without relying fully on the technical planning advice of JUCEPLAN, which functioned in a lower capacity than its initially assigned central planning role.

On the expectation that somehow socialism would readily replace the anarchic capitalist market with the order of central planning, and with first-hand knowledge of the Cuban economy, Boorstein noted that 'even in an office or factory the manager does not decide everything himself. Think of the millions of decisions required to run a whole economy in just a single day. *Along with centralization, there must be decentralization. The problem is how to combine the two; what and how to centralize, what and how to decentralize*' (Boorstein, 1968, p. 253; emphasis added).

In keeping with Guevara's plan, important institutional and administrative changes were made, affecting the economy as a whole. The Ministry of Finance was abolished in 1966. Its functions were consolidated into the National Bank, which expanded its role to include overseeing the financing of the nation's economy. The budgetary financing system was expanded to cover the entire economy. In pursuance of developmental plans, investment ratios were increased. While the sugar industry involved approximately 100 mills and related operations (about 160 sugar mills existed at the time of the revolution, most of which had been built in the nineteenth century), the total number of state enterprises was limited to 300. Some of the enterprises' scope was rather inclusive, encompassing most productive units in a particular industrial sector. In the spring of 1968 the so-called 'Revolutionary Offensive' absorbed into the public sector the non-agricultural economy that was still operated by private individuals: a total of 56,000 small businesses, from street food outlets to restaurants and bars (Mesa-Lago, 1981, pp. 23–7).

Throughout the 1960s the revolutionary regime experienced significant policy changes, modifying substantively its economic models while pursuing major socioeconomic objectives. The initial goals of achieving social equality, full employment, elimination of illiteracy, lower prices of basic staples and services and other items, and a more equitable distribution of income and resources were pursued vigorously. The population as a whole was clearly the intended recipient of these benefits.

The most constant factors in this transitional decade have been identified as follows:

(1) *egalitarianism*: including effective opportunities to all citizens to become involved in all aspects of the nation's life;

(2) *rural development as a priority*: including both the transformation of the rural economy and rural life;

(3) *political participation*: as a means of integrating the populace into the revolutionary process, the population's political mobilization was based on a close, direct contact between revolutionary leaders, particularly Castro, and the masses;

(4) *union with the socialist camp*: after severing its long-held relations and dependency on the United States, Cuba sought in the socialist camp a substitute market for its products, and a source of industrialized goods, credits, and financing;

(5) *the migration of those disaffected with the revolution*: approximately 600,000 disaffected Cubans, 10 percent of the country's 1959 population, left the island between 1959 and 1973, which served to develop a solidly anti-revolutionary community in southern Florida, and provided a needed outlet for those who could not adjust to the demands and rigors of revolutionary life;

(6) *changes in the population and use of human resources*: partly due to heavy migration, the initial increment in population growth declined since the mid-1960s, reducing the number of the working age population from 60 percent in 1960 to 56.6 percent in 1970; this compounded, for those over seventeen years of age, the legal working age, the impact that the expansion of educational opportunities had already had on the labor market;

(7) *continuing the economic dependency on sugar*: the initial industrialization and agricultural diversification drive was reversed as infeasible for reasons beyond the regime's control, thus returning to agriculture and sugar as major economic resources. Developmental plans were cautiously continued, expanding the country's industrial base and diversifying its agriculture (CEPAL, 1980, pp. 21–35).

From 1963 to 1969 the global social product grew 20.3 percent (a yearly average of 2.9 percent). However, there were losses in three different years: 1964 (9.29 percent), 1966 (0.9 percent), and 1969 (1.29 percent). The 1964 and 1966 losses were recovered the following year with a 24.1 percent increase in 1965, and a 7.4 percent in 1967. In the seven-year period, cattle and agriculture increased 42.5 percent; industry 17.6 percent; construction 28.6 percent; transportation 103 percent; and communications 100 percent. While agricultural gains were substantive, industrial growth was not negligible. Transportation and communication experienced remarkable growth. But commerce decreased 3.2 percent. Even if rather small, the decrease indicates the scarcity of consumer products that afflicted the 1960s (see Table 6.1).

The Fifth Economic Stage, the 1970s

Although the per capita global social product rose from 835 pesos in 1966 to 868 in 1968 (7.5 percent increase), the 1960s proved to be creative but difficult years for the twin goals of economic growth and social equity. They led to the most controversial and history-making policy of the revolution ever: the 1970 Ten Million Tons campaign. This policy objective marked a definite turning point for the revolution. In its aftermath, subjectivism and consciousness were replaced with objective channels of policy deliberation and a broader input from different government agencies in the decision-making process. The Ten Million Tons sugar campaign also led to the 1970s institutionalization of the revolution movement.

Short approximately 15 percent of its 'ten million' target, the 1970 sugar harvest was an output record that will be hard to repeat. However, the price paid for it economically, politically, and even psychologically, was more than anyone had anticipated. Based on the expectation that a record sugar harvest would provide the needed resources to pay for industrialization projects, clear the debt with the Soviet Union, and increase the national standard of living, many sectors of the economy were neglected while a national mobilization effort concentrated on the 'ten million' harvest.

Later, more than with the harvest's aftermath, the regime had to reckon with the reorganization of the state, including the economy as well as the political system. By 1970, practically full employment had been achieved, while the egalitarian principles of Guevara's plan had moved the country into a socialist system where money had become relatively irrelevant—given the availability of free social services (from burials to sport and cultural events). But labor absenteeism and the black market had also increased in 1969–70. A sense of realism was needed in the economy, and free social services had to be restricted in order to restore financial accountability. Hence, a new economic model was implemented. With the same enthusiasm that guided its actions in the 1960s, the revolution sought new directions in the 1970s.

The Economic Policy Assumptions of the 1970s.   With the rising price of sugar lasting half of the decade, the 1970s started rather favorably. The sugar share of exports had risen from 80 to 90 percent in 1974 with beneficial effects to the economy as a whole. Better sugar prices allowed more imports for other economic activities which led to an 8 percent increase in industrial output in 1971–5, and a 6 percent growth in labor productivity.

Table 6.1 Global Social Product (GSP) Balance, 1963–1969 (m. pesos)

Item	1963*	1964*	1965*	1966*	1967†	1968†	1969†
Total Global Social Product	6,013.2	5,454.5	6,770.9	6,709.3	7,211.6	7,330.9	7,236.1
By Economic Sector							
Cattle and agriculture	904.2	958.5	1,074.0	1,041.9	1,119.9	1,352.4	1,289.2
Industry	2,700.7	2,813.5	2,913.0	2,858.5	3,185.1	3,129.9	3,178.0
Construction	348.3	421.7	521.8	517.5	597.5	525.8	448.0
Transportation	297.7	339.5	348.1	372.5	384.5	610.9	604.6
Communications	48.2	48.8	51.5	55.7	56.6	60.3	60.6
Commerce	1,714.1	1,782.9	1,862.5	1,863.2	1,876.0	1,651.6	1,657.7

* In millions of pesos at constant 1965 prices.
† In millions of pesos at current (1972) prices.
Source: Anuario Estadístico de Cuba, 1972 (Havana, Cuba, Junta Central de Planificación, Dirección Central de Estadística, 1974), p. 30.

Economic planning for the decade was based on the following policy assumptions: (1) The economic infrastructure built in the 1960s should permit further industrialization, while the amount of land dedicated to sugar should remain stable (mechanization and modernization of production techniques should receive priority attention). (2) Increased decentralization should bring financial accountability to enterprises beyond their earlier responsibility of responding only for the fulfillment of production quotas, but without changing basic procedures and developmental objectives—in reality, this kind of change took longer than initially expected for its implementation. And (3) the 1967–70 practice of disregarding JUCEPLAN's planning input in economic policy should be reversed, and short-term (1971–5) and long-term (1971–80) planning encouraged—JUCEPLAN presented its 1976–80 plan in 1975 (CEPAL, 1980, pp. 41–2).

The System of Economic Management and Planning (SDPE)

Although Cuba lagged behind most socialist nations in adapting economic procedures to the demands of central planning, the 1970s brought an increased acceptance of planning as a central economic tool. Sectorial and mini-plans were subordinated to the yearly macro plans initiated in 1973, which were complemented by the first Five Year Plan (1976–80), followed by a second (1981–5), and a long-range economic development and forecast plan (1980–2000). The recognition that planning had a place in a socialist economy was reinforced by the acceptance of such economic instruments as cost anlaysis, enterprises' profitability, depreciation, and others (reversing the economic modalities of Guevara's plan). National and provincial economic management and accounting schools were established in 1976.

The new System of Economic Management and Planning (SDPE) was introduced in the second half of the decade. It was expected to be completed in 1980, and in full operation by the mid-1980s. While recognizing that supply and demand have a place in socialist commerce (and production), it recommends (within the limits of a socialist system) monetary controls, budgets, prices, credit, interest, and even taxes. The SDPE was rated as a 'Soviet style' system that was applied to Cuba after being 'the model of economic reform . . . in force in the USSR' (Mesa-Lago, 1981, pp. 28–30). This kind of characterization was labelled as being 'at best . . . an accurate description of the *form* of Cuban planning. [However], the *content* or practice of Cuban planning is quite different from the *content* of Soviet planning.'

Moreover, it is important to remember that, 'Planned economies function on the basis of administrative decision-making. Market forces are broadly constrained and circumscribed by the plan. They are not permitted to play the role of providing ubiquitous (price) signals on a decentralized basis to all economic actors' (Zimbalist, 1985, pp. 213–15).

Nevertheless, Zimbalist also states, 'The SDPE in many respects is modeled after the 1965 Soviet reforms. It attempts to (1) put enterprises on a self-financing basis, (2) introduce a profitability criterion with its attendant incentives, and (3) generally promote decentralization, organizational coherence, and efficiency' (1985, p. 223).

In the early 1970s steps were taken by the regime to include workers in factory management. The 13th CTC Congress supported the remuneration principle of 'to each according to his/her work' that corresponds to a socialist stage of development—preceding the communist remuneration stage of 'to each according to his/her needs.' Also, the trade unions' congress approved strengthening and extending workers' participation in collective management. Studies made in the mid-1970s by Cuba watchers indicated a growing willingness to be involved in decision-making on the part of the workers, who wanted to have a say in managing the factory.

Wages were also tied to work norms, increasing or decreasing according to productivity. But the process of strict production accountability was done rather slowly. By the end of the decade only 46.6 percent of workers in the productive sector were included in this plan. But by 1985 there were 1,167 enterprises involved, including fourteen enterprise unions, with over a million workers competing for awards, a total of over 53 percent of the enterprises' labor force (Martínez Fagundo, 1986, p. 167). Material incentives were also awarded along collective lines. Consumer durables made available to work centers—such as television sets—were awarded individually according to merit criteria approved by the workers. The system was extended to include new houses built by workers' 'microbrigades.' The microbrigades are formed by 15–40 workers per work center who leave their jobs to work in a construction project while their regular work is done by fellow workers. The new houses are also allocated according to a merit criterion collectively established by the workers, including high productivity, low or no absenteeism, family needs, and other factors.

The establishment of the Organs of People's Power (OPPs) at the national, provincial, and municipal levels in 1976 also contributed to the overall decentralization of the political and economic system—reinforcing the economic principles and assumptions of the SDPE. Approximately 34 percent of local enterprises in service, commerce, and industrial activities became subordinated not to a central ministry but to the Municipal OPPs, which also served as a link between the enterprises and JUCEPLAN.

Centralized planning combined with material gains as an incentive for higher and better economic production could have had contradictory results as well. This was particularly true in an economy such as Cuba's: from the early 1960s the regime sustained a policy of economic growth coupled with the satisfaction of the population's basic needs, or social equity. The problem was then that 'Since almost all prices in planned economies are centrally administered . . . the use of material incentives inevitably engenders behavior inconsistent with welfare maximization as defined by the plan' (Zimbalist, 1985, p. 214). Reportedly, the Soviets experienced this kind of unintended result as early as 1965 when they attempted to measure some enterprises' performance not by physical quantity of output but by profitability standards.

Different problems could occur when simulated market signals are used to run the economy under centralized planning. Some of them became real in Cuba due to the shortages that still exist today. As an economist observed, 'it is difficult to motivate greater work with higher pay, if the desired goods are not available to be purchased.'

At the end of the 1970s Cubans seemed rather satisfied with the results from SDPE. Humberto Pérez, then head of JUCEPLAN, commenting on a 1980 government study stated: 'There are still several difficulties, but in view of the goals set at the First Party Congress (1975) the final balance of this study is completely positive.' Later, in a 1983 interview, Pérez stated, 'The system has produced advantageous results . . ., it has helped to raise the economic consciousness of all our cadres in administration and management, the consciousness that they must save every possible resource, every peso, every *centavo*' (Zimbalist, 1985, pp. 223–4).

None the less, the pressure to increase productivity remains. The question is how to overcome both internal (increasing quantity output and availability of goods) and external (modifying unfair trading and pricing and credit conditions) complex problems so that material gains motivating workers to production increases could be made readily available to them. Under present conditions, more than any material gains awarded to workers and management, significant monetary gains have accrued mostly to those sectors of the population engaged in certain economic activities—as it happened, to peasants associated with the free farmers' market; and to a higher degree to profiteers, like the private intermediaries who transported the farmers' produce to the free markets.

During the farmers' markets' brief existence, differences in monetary and material resources among the population increased, bringing potential social dislocation. That is not to say that the markets did not provide a service for the consumer, that the need for the products offered was not real, or that the consumers' plight has not worsened since the farmers' markets' demise in 1986. Precisely because the need is so real, it was possible to profit beyond acceptable limits for an egalitarian society. Even before 1986 some limits restricting how far high achievers can go, without disrupting the precious egalitarian social balance, had been established:

The size of the economic incentive fund, introduced in 1979 in 7 percent of the enterprises, is determined by enterprise profitability. It is partly used to provide economic rewards for its workers—both collectively ... and to individuals ... In order for these new incentives to be effective, 'socialist inflation,' which is monetary surplus, has been reduced by curtailing demand through higher prices and increasing supply of consumer goods ... [Mesa-Lago, 1981, p. 30]

However, from a material incentive standpoint, such limits could also work as disincentive mechanisms, giving the wrong signal to current efforts to increase production. It becomes a difficult task for centralized planning to work effectively under these conditions. And yet, as Castro stated at the Third Party Congress, the blend of moral and material incentives at that time available—some of which were awarded to work centers through collectively defined criteria—must spur all workers to higher quantitative and qualitative efficiency and productivity.

Evaluating the 1970s

The first half of the decade was marked by impressive economic growth, but it declined in 1976–80. Both events were related to ups and downs of sugar prices in the international market. Although the 1971–5 sugar harvests were lower than in 1976–9, the high price of sugar of the early years compensated in value for it. The 1971 half a billion pesos in trade deficit was turned into a small surplus in 1974. While sugar continued its central role in the economy (with a record high in 1975), the industrial approach followed was quite different from the 1970 sugar harvest. Mechanization rather than labor mobilization, and limiting the use of labor and other resources to what had been allocated without affecting other economic sectors, defined the sugar policy and new economic practices of the 1970s. Trade relations achieved a higher level of integration with socialist nations when Cuba entered COMECON in 1972 and signed trade agreements with the Soviet Union, first for 1973–5, and later for 1976–80.

As measured by the global social product (GSP) and gross material product (GMP), production grew steadily during the decade. From 1970 to 1975 the GSP increased by 89 percent, a yearly average of 14.8 percent. During the same period the GMP increased 111 percent, an annual increment of 18.5 percent. The second half of the decade showed lower growth rates. From 1976 to 1979 the GSP increased 18.7 percent, a yearly growth of 4.67 percent (10.2 percent less in the last four years than in the preceding six). During the last four years of the period, the GMP grew 18.7 percent, or 4.68 percent yearly (a loss annually of 13.8 percent as compared with the first six years). The higher annual loss in GMP than GSP suggests that material services connected with the production of material goods (which are excluded from GMP) were not affected as much during the ten-year period. Also, material goods included in both GSP and GMP seemed equally affected (see Table 6.2).

Contrary to what might be expected, the GSP rates included in Table 6.2 (a computation by Mesa-Lago from Cuban sources and his own estimates) are somewhat higher than rates provided by Cuban official sources (see Table 6.3). This may be explained by 'shifts in [Cuban statistical] methodologies and because inflation affected data, particularly since 1967' (Mesa-Lago, 1981, p. 34), and also because the *Anuario Estadístico de Cuba, 1980* was not included in Mesa-Lago's computations, which is the source for Table 6.3. The differences between Tables 6.2 and 6.3 during the last five years of the decade are lower estimates in the latter than the former (the difference in the first three years was almost the same, but it was somewhat smaller in the last two): 1975, 11.9 percent; 1976, 11.1 percent; 1977, 11.3 percent; 1978, 9.8 percent; and 1979, 10.2 percent.

The GMP rate of growth between 1970 and 1978 was 9.8 percent. This was largely based in the high price of sugar in the international and socialist markets: 1973, 12.02 and 9.45 cents per pound, respectively; 1974, 19.64 and 29.66, respectively; 1975, 30.40 and 20.37, respectively; 1976, 30.95 and 11.51, respectively; and 1977, 35.73 and 8.14, respectively (CEPAL, 1980, p. 75).

The GSP rate of growth between 1975 and 1979 recorded in Table 6.3 is 21.4 percent, 4.2 percent yearly. The best year in the period was 1978, with a growth rate of 11.2 percent over 1977. The period showed a steady increment in all economic sectors: cattle and agriculture, 21.6 percent (4.3 percent yearly); industry, 17.7 percent (3.5 percent yearly); construction, 25.4 percent (5 percent yearly); transportation 21.7 percent (4.3 percent yearly); communications, 72.2 percent (14.4 percent yearly); and commerce, 25.5 percent (5.1 percent yearly). As in previous periods, cattle and agriculture had higher rates of growth than industry, but the latter had healthy gains too. Construc-

Table 6.2 Economic growth, 1970–79 (m. pesos)

Year	Global Social Product (GSP)*	Gross Material Product (GMP)*†
1970	8,355.6	4,203.9
1971	8,936.4	4,818.2
1972	10,349.2	6,026.9
1973	11,910.3	6,710.4
1974	13,423.5	7,414.1
1975	15,799.3	8,886.3
1976	15,860.5	8,881.8§
1977	16,510.8‡	9,246.0§
1978	18,062.8‡	10,115.2§
1979	18,830.5‡	10,545.1§

* The GSP and GMP include the production of goods in such economic activities as industry, mining, construction, fishing, and agriculture. While GSP includes the value of services involved in the production of goods, like trade, communication, and transportation, GMP excludes them. Also, GSP and GMP exclude the value of such services as health care, education, and others, which are not of a 'material' nature.

† GMP in 1970–9 current prices.

‡ Official estimate.

§ Estimate based on the average ratio of GMP/GSP in the previous ten years.

Source: Carmelo Mesa-Lago, *The Economy of Socialist Cuba—A Two Decade Appraisal* (Albuquerque, New Mexico, University of New Mexico Press, 1981), pp. 33–4.

tion and transportation had similar proper growth rates, while communication's was outstanding, the highest for all economic sectors. Contrary to the experience in the 1960s, when it had negative marks, commerce grew satisfactorily from 1975 to 1979. Only in 1976 did it fail to grow (a loss of 8.7 percent that was recovered in 1977 with a 5.2 percent gain over 1976, and 0.4 percent over 1975). The growth in commercial rates indicate the increased attention given to consumer goods during the last years of the decade (see Table 6.3).

The combination of economic growth and social equity pursued by the regime brought substantive social gains to the population and an overall increment in its standard of living. This occurred throughout the 1970s and

Table 6.3 Global Social Product (GSP) balance, 1975–79 (m. pesos)

Item	1975	1976	1977	1978	1979
Total Global Social Product	13,913.1	14,086.1	14,635.2	16,281.5	16,897.6
By economic sector					
Cattle and agriculture	1,537.7	1,595.3	1,664.9	1,765.5	1,870.8
Industry	6,724.2	7.015.6	6,995.8	7,562.5	7,916.8
Construction	1,250.3	1,320.1	1,450.2	1,557.1	1,569.1
Transportation	1,006.3	1,035.9	1,095.7	1,169.4	1,225.3
Communications	78.1	82.1	90.1	107.8	134.5
Commerce	3,218.8	2,935.9	3,234.2	3,988.8	4,039.9

Source: Anuario Estadístico de Cuba, 1980 (Havana, Cuba, Junta Central de Planificación, Dirección Central de Estadísticas, 1981), p. 50.

continued into the 1980s. The total education enrollment from 1970 to 1982 increased by 38.7 percent, from 2,323,600 to 3,223,400. It was 811,100 in 1958. This reflected increases in the secondary, pre-university, university, and other educational levels; and a minor (0.01 percent) decline at the elementary level. The improvements in public health included both the availability and quality of medical services. Life expectancy was extended from 69.3 (1970) to 70.2 years (1980) for men, and from 72.6 (1970) to 73.5 years (1980) for women. The mortality rate per 10,000 babies born alive decreased from 38.7 (1970) to 19.6 (1980); and the mothers' mortality for every 10,000 babies delivered alive decreased from 7 (1970) to 5.3 (1980).

Living conditions had also improved as measured by the population's daily per capita nutrient consumption: calories, from 2,565 (1970) to 2,867 (1980) (needed: 2,980); proteins, from 69 (1970) to 75 grams (1980) (needed: 89 grams); fats, from 60 (1970) to 72 grams (1980) (needed: 84 grams); and carbohydrates, from 441 (1970) to 479 grams (1980) (needed: 470 grams). Actual salaries increased throughout the 1970s for an average of 75.5 percent above their rate at the end of the 1960s, and women's share of the labor force had reached 38 percent by the 1980s. The rate of appliance ownership per hundred inhabitants in 1974 was seventy-five radios, twenty-four television sets, twenty-eight refrigerators, and two washing machines (Banco Nacional de Cuba, 1982, p. 28; Pérez González, 1982, p. 31; *Granma*, 6 July 1984).

For Mesa-Lago, the fulfillment of the economic goals of the 1970s was characterized by 'The reintroduction of material incentives, the increasing use of prices, the halt or curtailment of some free social services, and the restoration of the value of money as a buying tool [which] resulted in a retrenchment in egalitarianism and some stratification.' Also, 'The new model of economic organization stresse[d] efficiency and [gave] more power to enterprise managers for dismissals . . . [while] voluntary labor [was] . . . only used when its net productivity [could] be proved beforehand' (Mesa-Lago, 1981, p. 31).

The economic policies Cuba pursued in the 1960s and 1970s have an additional positive correlation. It is the relationship that seemingly exists between a high rate of basic-needs-oriented economic strategy and economic growth, including their present and/or future performance record: 'Countries making substantial progress in meeting basic needs do *not* have substantially lower GNP growth rates; and . . . the attainment of higher levels of basic-needs satisfaction appears to lead to higher growth rates in the future' (Hicks, 1979, p. 992). For Brundenius, Cuba illustrates Hicks' theory much better than probably any other Third World country:

There was a vigorous growth of virtually all industrial activities in the 1970s, with the manufacturing industry as a whole growing at a rate of 7 percent per year and the capital goods industry growing at 15 percent per year. Most spectacular was the growth of the construction industry, which increased at a rate of 14.2 percent per year during the period . . . [Brundenius, 1985, pp. 206–7]

After changing economic models in the 1960s and 1970s, the regime was ready to enter its third decade, the 1980s, with a higher level of systemic institutionalization than ever before. Many of the mistakes of the 1960s had been corrected, and important lessons seemed to have been drawn from them. In spite of all the changes, however, that developmental policies were aimed at attaining economic growth with social equity appears to be a constant in revolutionary economic and social objectives.

7   The Cuban Economy in the 1980s

The Decline of Western Credit and Trade

Cuba's Western credit has suffered since 1979 in spite of its improved economic performance in the 1970s. The fact that the country had organized itself with new political and economic institutions did not seem to matter much to Western lending banks. Neither did it matter that its trade balance in convertible currency had improved in 1979 and 1980, and continued growing favorably in 1981 and 1982 (see Table 7.1). After another positive performance in 1983 ($450.7 million exports over imports, including re-exports), the trade balance turned negative in 1984 with a $66.5 million deficit. Exports had plummeted 14.7 percent below the 1983 level, while imports had increased 40 percent over the same one year period. However, the 1986 deficit was turned into a surplus in 1987, following the rectification process launched at the Third Party Congress.

Table 7.1 Trade transactions in convertible currency, 1979–82 (m. pesos)

	1979	1980	1981	1982*	Total*
Exports	680.3	1,247.7	1,405.8	1,337.6	4,671.4
Imports	581.4	881.2	1,121.5	733.6	3,317.7
Trade balance	+98.9	+366.5	+384.3	+604.0	+1,353.7

* Partial estimate.

Source: *Informe Económico*, Havana, Cuba, Banco Nacional de Cuba, August 1982, p. 33.

The looming external debt crisis in which one developing country after another could not service its debt was seemingly uppermost in the creditors' minds. The situation worsened after President Reagan's inauguration in early 1981. His Administration embraced a policy against improving relations between Washington and Havana, and launched a campaign aimed at undermining Cuba's chances to negotiate improved credit conditions with Western banks.

Cuba had a favorable trade balance with market economies from 1979 to 1983 (it grew from $98.9 million in 1979, to $604 million in 1982). But the volume of trade had declined from the 1960s level; in 1982 there was 47.3 percent to 55.4 percent less trade than in 1975. In 1980 the trade balance gained $267.6 million over 1979, but lost $16.7 million in 1981. This was followed by substantial growth in 1982, when it more than doubled by gaining $319.7 million over 1981. In 1983–5 there was a combined trade surplus of $810.8 million (93 percent of imports were intermediate and capital goods, while consumer goods were limited to 7 percent in 1983 and 1984).

From 1959 to 1985, the rate of external commerce grew an average of 8.9 percent annually, including 9.4 percent imports and 8.4 percent exports. The predominance of the former over the latter, caused a negative balance of $12.294 billion. Trade with socialist countries amounted to 70 percent of the trade deficit accumulated in twenty-six years. The socialist bloc provided additional preferential credits and payment facilities. The trade structure was modified according to developmental plans after 1959: consumer imports decreased from 39.1 percent in 1958 to 10.8 percent in 1985, and intermediate goods increased from 34.1 percent to 67.9 percent. While sugar and sugar-based exports decreased from 80.6 percent to 74.4 percent in the same period, non-traditional exports increased from 8.8 percent to 18.9 percent (Rodríguez, 1987a, pp. 5–27).

However, in addition to adopting protectionist trade barriers, some of the countries involved had increased their sugar production to become exporters. From 461,000 metric tons of sugar imported in 1959–63, the European Economic Community bought only 13,000 in 1980. Japan reduced its Cuban sugar imports from 324,000 metric tons in 1959–63 to 299,000 in 1980. As before, the price of sugar in the free market (the price of a pound of sugar fell from 29.01 cents in 1980 to 4.04 cents in 1985) and the volume of exports still determined Cuba's good and bad economic periods.

Worsening conditions in existent trade relations cost Cuba in lost revenues approximately $3.741 billion in 1976–80, and $2.084 billion in 1981–5. This amounted to $5.825 billion in a ten-year period, equal to the total exports of a year like 1985.

An effort was made to reduce the negative trade balance in convertible currency. The 1986 deficit of $199.4 million ($390.1 million exports, including re-exports, against $589.5 million imports) became a $22.5 million surplus in 1987 ($460.1 million exports, including re-exports, against $437.6 million imports). In one year exports increased by 17.9 percent, while imports decreased by 25.8 percent (Banco Nacional de Cuba, June 1987, p. 6). The 1987 trade volume with market economies was 15.5 percent below the 1986 level. Exports had increased by $19.5 million (8.05 percent), but imports decreased by $146 million (25.4 percent). Thus the trade deficit was reduced by $165.5 million from 1986 (see Table 7.2). The growth in commercial exchange that still took place, $276.4 million (3.7 percent), was mostly due to the higher trade volume with socialist countries.

Table 7.2 Total trade transactions, and trade with market economies, January–June 1986–87 (m. pesos)

	1986	1987
Trade with market economies		
Exports	242.2	261.7 (+8.05%)
Imports	575.0	429.0 (−25.3%)
Total trade transactions		
Exports	3,942.1	4,162.5 (+5.6%)
Imports	3,571.6	3,627.6 (+1.6%)

Source: *Cuba–Informe Económico Trimestral*, Havana, Cuba, Banco Nacional de Cuba, Comité Estatal de Estadísticas (June 1987), p. 5.

Economic Grains but Less Credit. Cuba achieved respectable economic growth in 1981–2: 101.2 percent fulfillment of the national economic plan, a sugar harvest of 8,207,178 tons, and 5.5 percent economic growth. The food, basic, and light industries fulfilled 99.5, 101.4, and 98.4 percent of their economic plan, respectively, while construction completed 111.8 percent. Some industrial gains in the first six months of 1982 over the same 1981 period included food, 11 percent; spare parts, 27.9 percent; construction maintenance, 17.4 percent; fishing, 7.6 percent; and cattle and agriculture, 3 percent (sugar, 6.8 percent; and non-sugar agriculture, 11.8 percent) (Banco Nacional de Cuba, 1982, pp. 33–4, 39–40). Moreover, according to official reports, the economy achieved in 1984 a 7.4 percent growth in the Global Social Product (GSP) on 1983 prices, and had maintained for five years (1980–4) an annual GSP average growth of 7.2 percent (Pérez, 1985, p. 13).

But the GSP growth achieved in 1986 was a modest 1.4 percent over 1985, $27.457 billion on 1981 prices. Serious internal and external factors had created rather adverse economic conditions. Internally, they included the hurricane Kate, which affected badly the 1985–6 sugar harvest; the 1986 rainfall that reached only 937 millimeters, the lowest in over a decade (the combined effect of hurricane Kate and the drought reduced sugar production by 1,240,000 tons, representing at 1986 prices a loss of $160 million in convertible currency); the mistakes made by economic planners and enterprise managers; and the low level of labor productivity and efficiency.

Externally, economic problems included the value of 1986 re-exports, which decreased by 55 percent in comparison to 1985 due to a 40 percent fall in the price of oil (a $320 million loss); the drastic fall in the price of the US dollar, which reduced export earnings in convertible currency by approximately $120 million; and the protectionist barriers created by some market economies to safeguard their domestic markets. Total convertible currency earnings for 1986 was 50 percent below 1985, a $600 million loss in twelve months (Banco Nacional de Cuba, May 1987, pp. 1–4).

In spite of the respectable economic gains of the early 1980s, Cuba's credit with Western banks had been deteriorating. A negative balance accrued in the loan-deposit funds maintained by market economy banks with Cuba's National Bank. In only two years, from October 1981 to August 1982, withdrawals from such funds totalled $470 million. By the end of 1982 the negative balance had reached $520.1 million.

Unstable Sugar Prices, and Oil Re-exports

From the 1960s to the 1980s at least six sugar price-cycles affected the nation's convertible currency income, with low price periods lasting longer than higher ones. Before the First Five Year Plan (1976–80) the London stock market price fluctuated between 20 and 30 cents (US dollar) per pound—in November 1974 the daily price had averaged 57 cents per pound. After having anticipated in 1974 at least two years of revenues based on 15 cents per pound of sugar in the international market (which was considered at the time a conservative estimate), a sudden fall toward the end of 1975 forced a revision of economic plans. The price averaged four cents below the expected price—in 1976–9, the price of sugar fell from 11.51 cents per pound to 9.65. This happened again during the Second Five Year Plan (1981–5), when the price fell sharply from 29.01 cents per pound in 1980 to 4.04 in 1985. The value of sugar exports decreased from $866.3 million in 1981 to $171.2 million in 1985. The downward trend in the price of sugar reduced drastically Cuba's convertible currency reserves, which exacerbated economic problems in the mid-1980s. Difficult trade and financial conditions caused the loss of 60 percent of hard currency reserves in a six-month period, falling to $120 million in August 1982.

Cuba has re-exported Soviet oil since the early 1980s with Moscow's approval. Since the Second Five Year Plan Havana has sold in the international market whatever Moscow-supplied oil it could conserve. Because oil had higher prices than sugar in Western markets, after buying more Soviet oil in transferable rubles than it needed, Cuba resold the difference for hard currency, becoming in practice an oil exporter. During 1981–5 oil revenues amounted to $1.922 billion, 30.2 percent of total convertible currency earnings. In 1983, 40.3 percent of convertible currency income came from oil re-exports; in 1984, 42.65 percent; and in 1985, 42.34 percent. But in 1986 it fell to 27.38 percent, reducing hard currency earnings by 27.08 percent (approximately $300 million), which caused the cancellation of 25 percent of needed hard currency imports (Banco Nacional de Cuba, May 1987, p. 21; Rodríguez, 1987a, pp. 11–12).

Given its new dependence on revenues from Soviet-supplied oil sales, the falling oil price in the international market affected Cuba's economy badly. This was compounded by the low sugar price, and the falling US dollar since 1986 in relation to other convertible currencies. It was estimated that by 1985, 'Cuba's hard currency earnings from petroleum reexports were three times greater than its hard currency earnings from sugar exports' (Domínguez, 1986, p. 132). Lower oil prices in 1986 brought losses to over one-fourth of the expected hard-currency earnings.

The External Debt

A decrease in Cuba's international credit represented a serious financial liability. The country's capacity to service its convertible currency debt, as well as the chances to have it rescheduled in more favorable terms were reduced. The foreign debt in 1969 amounted only to $291 million, but by June 1982, thirteen years later, it was $2.913 billion (a tenfold increase). To some extent, the large debt growth came as a result of the emphasis put on developmental programs in the 1970s. Cuba took advantage of improved relations with market economy countries and financial institutions, using its credit to borrow substantively. Contrary to some Latin American nations' programs, Cuba's were seemingly sound and properly supported by its own domestic economy. But similarly to neighboring countries' experience, the crisis that developed in the world capitalist economy in the 1980s nearly caught the Cuban leadership by surprise, wrecking their immediate economic plans and growth objectives.

By 1984 the foreign debt was $3.32 billion; $242.8 million higher than in 1983, but 6 percent lower than in 1981. By the end of 1986 it was estimated at

$3.87 billion, $249.4 million over 1985 (a growth rate of 6.9 percent). The official bilateral debt was reduced by 10.6 percent (after a reclassification that had been agreed upon earlier in May), and the official multilateral debt by 16.3 percent. In 1986 the debt grew mostly in the areas of credits from suppliers for current imports (98.9 percent), and financial institutions (1.3 percent). Lacking credit from banks, imports were financed with credits from exporters. The debt estimate reached $5 billion in 1987, when the Cuban peso was computed on a par with the US dollar.

The official (government) debt amounted in 1986 to $1.645 billion (43 percent), all in medium-term credits. The private (banks and commerce) debt was $2.224 billion (57 percent)—$1.349 billion in short-term credits, and $875 million in medium-term credits. In 1986, the total debt was 35 percent in short-term credits, and 65 percent in long-term credits (Banco Nacional de Cuba, May 1987, pp. 26–8).

Cuba issued a critical report in 1985 to the Chairman of the Group of Creditor Countries and the Steering Committee of the Creditor Banks, which were signatories of the 1984 rescheduling agreement approved by Cuba and market economy creditors. It compared its increasingly adverse financial status with those of other Third World countries: all were facing growing trade problems and were unable to service their foreign debt. Havana stated that,

The unfavorable behavior of Cuba's financial relations with the developed market-economy countries has been accompanied by trade relations that do not correspond to the needs and aspirations of the developing countries. In the 1983–1984 period, the terms of trade registered an unprecedented deterioration. The evolution of the price of sugar on the free world market, whose levels do not even cover the costs of the most efficient producers, implies the forced transfer of large sums of resources to the market-economy countries. An estimate for the 1983–1985 period, conservatively based on the minimum price set in the 1977 International Sugar Agreement, shows a loss in income to Cuba of more than $640 million . . . [Banco Nacional de Cuba, 1985, p. 2]

Trade relations with market economy countries worsened in 1985–6, reducing severely Cuba's hard currency earnings. Several factors accounted for this turn of events: (1) earnings from Soviet crude oil re-exports were more affected than initially expected (after 1983–5 the price of oil fell from $30 to $12–$15 per barrel); (2) the low price of sugar in the world market continued; and (3) the rapid devaluation of the US dollar in 1986–7 cost Cuba approximately 150 million pesos in international purchasing power (Zimbalist, 1987, p. 4).

However, according to Turits, by using its resources wisely, Cuba was able to manage its hard currency obligations with 'unexpected ease,' to meet 'its interest payments on time,' and to avoid making 'precarious cuts in welfare spending, or subtantially-reduc[e] growth rates.' Also, it 'witnessed a build-down of its debt probably unique in Latin America. Commercial debt reported to the Bank for International Settlements (BIS) decreased from $2.1 billion in 1979 to $0.9 billion in 1982.' Although it had increased since 1982, its total debt in 1984 was 5 percent below its 1981 level. Meanwhile, Latin America's debt had risen 30 percent (Turits, 1987, p. 165).

Servicing the debt became more costly after 1978 when interest rates were raised. From 1978 to 1985, Havana's payments increased $888 million above initial interest rates. A negative balance of $12.2 million accrued in 1986 while servicing the debt, following credits for $249.4 million and interest payments of $261.6 million (Banco Nacional de Cuba, May 1987, pp. 27–8). But since 1979 Cuba has not received what could technically be called 'fresh [capital] money' (interview, J. L. Rodríguez, CIEM, December 1987).

Even though Cuba's international debt is relatively small in comparison with other Latin American countries' debt, this applies only to its convertible currency debt, which includes 14 percent of its total commerce. Its additional debt to the Soviet Union totals approximately $6 billion and is handled separately. After a mutually agreed moratorium between Havana and Moscow, payments are not due until 1990. Nevertheless, problems exist in this area, too. Cuba had to spend hard currency buying sugar in the international market to fulfill its trade obligations with the Soviet Union. For this and other reasons, in 1984 it spent $101 million importing sugar; $106.4 million in 1985; and $89.6 million in 1986. These purchases reduced the convertible currency income from sugar sales in the free market to $416 million in 1984, and $912 million in 1985.

Renegotiating the External Debt

During several rescheduling negotiations held in the 1980s, Cuba argued that it deserved a better hearing than Western creditors were giving. It charged the Reagan Administration with having pressured lending banks to ask for harsher terms than they would normally request (Banco Nacional de Cuba, 1982, pp. 42–5). Cuba sought to reschedule these obligations under conditions no less favorable than lending banks had granted to other Latin American countries. Part of the debt was rescheduled through the Club of Paris, an agency representing Western banks making loans outside the jurisdiction of the International Monetary Fund (IMF).

There have been four different phases so far in renegotiating the debt: in 1982, 1984, 1985, and 1986. In September 1982, Cuba's National Bank requested to renegotiate 36 percent of the medium-term debt. It included 95 percent of payments due in March 1983, asking for ten years to pay and a three-year grace period. The payment schedule agreed upon provided for eight years and four months to complete payments, and a three-year and ten-month grace period. Postponed payments totalled $578 million, while servicing the debt included 2.25 percent interest payments and 1.25 percent in commissions. The 'adjustment program' agreed to in Paris in March 1983 was satisfactorily followed by Cuba, which was helpful in the next renegotiating session (Rodríguez, 1987a, pp. 14–18).

The second discussions were held in the spring of 1984. Cuba sought a longer grace period this time. The final agreement included nine years and six months for payments, and a five-year and six-month grace period, with 1.88 percent interest and 0.88 percent commissions.

The third renegotiation took place in 1985. Cuba wanted to delay payments for $229 million of the official debt and the banks' debt combined—$145 and $84 million, respectively. Also, $468 million in short-term deposits that commercial banks had been rolling over on a year to year basis had to be negotiated. Cuba asked for payment conditions similar to those granted to other Latin American countries, and more trade with creditor nations during the 1986–90 period. It obtained a six-year and six-month payment schedule, and six-year and six-month grace period. It had to pay 1.5 percent in interests and 0.38 percent in commissions.

The fourth session was held in May 1986, under extremely adverse financial conditions for Cuba. These included the low price of sugar, the falling oil price, the adverse natural conditions causing poor harvests, and the re-evaluation of the convertible currencies covering Cuba's debt after the fall of the US dollar.

Cuba requested a renegotiating package including:

(1) postponing payment of principal (capital) due in 1986 and 1987 (including the renegotiated 1982 and 1983 debt, and new debts contracted afterwards);

(2) postponing interest payments due in 1986 and 1987, from the 1982 and 1983 debt, and from the debt renegotiated in 1984 and 1985;

(3) postponing short-term deposits deadline overdue in September 1986;

(4) receiving a new 'fresh (capital) money' loan that would bring an orderly process to the balance of payments.

A twelve-year payment schedule, and a six-year grace period was requested as part of the new terms. A meeting held in Paris in July 1986 agreed to postpone the payments due that same year, but failed to agree on new terms for 1987 payments. Nor was any agreement made with representatives from private banks (Rodríguez, 1987a, pp. 14–18). A Paris Club meeting scheduled in Havana for 26–9 May 1987, to consider renegotiating $1.9 billion of foreign debt, was postponed at Cuba's request.

Servicing the debt amounted to $1.029 billion in 1982 (63.4 percent coefficient of $2.668 billion total debt); $719 million in 1985 (57.8 percent coefficient of $3.558 billion total debt); and $1.775 billion in 1986 (172 percent coefficient of $3.870 billion total debt) in convertible currency payments. During the 1981–5 period, servicing the debt totalled $3.745 billion, the equivalent of 58.7 percent of all exports in convertible currency in those five years (Rodríguez, 1987a, p. 18).

Preserving the Social Welfare Program

Cuba's social welfare program continued growing during this difficult period. By using other financial outlets for its convertible currency debt and managing to safeguard the social priorities of its socialist system, the island spared itself the negative social effects of the draconian measures imposed by the IMF on Third World debtor countries. Cuba's relationship with the IMF had been terminated in the early 1960s.

From 1980 to 1986 investment on social assistance and security increased by 36 percent (from $709.3 to $965.2 million), education and public health by 45.9 percent (from $1.800 to $2.626 billion), and sociocultural and scientific activities by 49.3 percent (from $1.315 to $1.964 billion).

Day care centers increased by 2.76 percent, and the number of mothers using this service by 22.2 percent. The number of primary schools increased by 77 percent; enrolled students by 42 percent, and those who graduated by 38.9 percent. At the superior educational level, the number of schools increased by 20.6 percent, enrolled students by 45 percent, and those who graduated by 28.7 percent. The infant mortality rate decreased from 19.6 to 13.6 for every thousand children less than one year old. The mothers' mortality rate decreased from 53.3 to 36.7 for every 100,000 babies born alive. Medical doctors increased from 15,247 to 25,418, while the ratio of one medical doctor per 637 inhabitants decreased to 399. The rate of calory intake increased from 2,867 to 2,967, and of protein from 75 grams to 79.9. And the minimum monthly wage at 1981 prices increased from 147.8 to 187.7 pesos (Rodríguez, 1987a, pp. 22–4).

In spite of the critical financial and international credit problems and economic difficulties, Castro could speak with pride of Cuba's social welfare program, stating that, 'we do not take such measures as leaving senior citizens without help, reducing pensions for retired people, giving less medical care to the sick, or less resources to hospitals and schools; we do not sacrifice our social programs' (*Granma*, 10 July 1985, p. 4).

Soviet Aid and Socialist Trade

Soviet economic and military assistance have been vital for the survival of the Cuban revolution. Economic aid is not as large as claimed by Western observers and official US sources, however. While sugar subsidies are overestimated, the price paid for Soviet aid is underestimated. Missing in such calculations is 'the high cost and poor quality of Soviet imports that must be purchased with the rubles received for Cuban exports' (Zimbalist & Eckstein, 1987, p. 19).

Although it applied to most of the economy (including price subsidies for sugar and nickel, and technological transfers and development and payments aid), during the first thirteen years, 1960–73, Soviet aid concentrated heavily on the industrial sector: industry, 76.1 percent; agriculture (irrigation and drainage), 5.2 percent; geological surveys, 8.3 percent; transportation and communication, 8.2 percent; education and health, 1.9 percent; and other sectors, 0.3 percent. By 1972 Soviet aid had already totalled 616.2 million rubles. However, out of the socialist countries' 62.23 percent share of Soviet aid granted in 1972, Cuba received only 4.58 percent (the fifth recipient after Bulgaria, the German Democratic Republic, Mongolia, and Poland) (Blasier, 1979, pp. 230–2).

Cuba had received approximately $10 billion in assistance from Moscow by 1977 (almost $600 milion annually), of which only half ($4.9 billion) had to be repaid. Also, it received $459 million from 1960 to 1964, and $402 million from 1973 to 1976, in development loans. Credits to finance trade deficits totalled $4.05 billion from 1962 to 1976. The combined total of credits received from socialist countries, including the Soviet Union, amounted to $5.178 billion by 1976. However, credits from the People's Republic of China, Hungary, Poland, and Bulgaria granted after the early 1960s, from Romania after 1969, and the Soviet Union after 1976, were not included in this total (Mesa-Lago, 1981, pp. 103–4). Total Soviet aid for the 1972–82 period was estimated by an official US source at $13 billion—a yearly average of $1.3 billion (Theriot, 1982, p. 6).

Castro has acknowledged the extent and significance of socialist assistance, and particularly of Soviet aid, on several occasions. At the First PCC Congress, in December 1975, he stated:

Without the decisive, steady, and generous aid of the Soviet people, our country could not have survived the confrontation with imperialism. They bought our sugar when our market was brutally suppressed by the United States, they supplied us with raw materials and fuel which we could not have acquired in any other part of the world; they caused to arrive free arms with which we opposed the mercenaries at the Bay of Pigs and equipped our Revolutionary armed forces in order to impose the highest price on any direct aggression by the United States; they supported our economy in exemplary fashion in the critical years of the blockade . . . [Blasier, 1979, p. 229]

The trade volume with socialist countries increased in the 1980s. They paid higher prices for Cuban goods under more favorable trade relations. Meanwhile, the share of Cuba's trade with market-economy countries had declined from 22 percent in 1977–80 to almost 13 percent in 1982–4. Sugar exports to these countries had been purposely reduced as part of a strategy to diminish the adverse effects of existing trade relations.

Cuba's total trade turnover increased from $11.74 billion in 1983 to $12.66 in 1984 (7.9 percent). The lion's share of the trade turnover was taken by the socialist countries. The total trade volume with the latter increased by $794.1 million from 1983 to 1984 (7.8 percent). But the trade deficit was aggravated when exports increased by only 2.9 percent, while imports grew by 12.1 percent. The negative balance of trade in 1984 was $516.3 million over 1983 (79.5 percent). Trade with socialist countries by 1984 accounted for 86 percent of the total trade, and 67 percent of the trade deficit. However, in 1986 the total volume of trade with socialist countries amounted to $6,696.5 million, although it increased to $7,099.4 in 1987 (for a total of $403 million, 6 percent). In 1986 and 1987 there was a positive balance in Cuba's trade with socialist countries ($703.3 million and $702.2 million, respectively), even though the trade increment was due more to imports than exports (see Table 7.3).

While increasing the level of trade with socialist countries provided higher revenues for Cuba (an economic outlet not always available to other developing nations), this measure did not adequately address the problem of earning convertible currency. It limited the country's financial capacity to import needed commodities from Western countries, and to service its external debt. The government acknowledged that limiting trade with Western markets was not the most desirable alternative. Only because it faced such adverse terms had Cuba decided to reduce (sugar) sales to those

Table 7.3 Trade turnover with socialist countries, 1983–84, and 1986–87 (m. pesos)

Socialist countries	1983	1984	1986*	1987*
Exports	4,753.9	4,892.8	3,699.9	3,900.8
Imports	5,403.1	6,058.3	2,996.6	3,198.6
Total	10,157.0	10,951.1	6,696.5	7,099.4
Balance	−649.2	−1,165.5	+703.3	+702.2

* At current prices.

Source: *Economic Report*, Havana, Cuba, Banco Nacional de Cuba, February 1985, pp. 12–13; *Cuba—Informe Económico Trimestral*, Havana, Cuba, Banco Nacional de Cuba, June 1987, p. 5.

countries: 'The Cuban economy needs to complement ... [its trade with socialist countries] with trade with the market-economy countries.' Cuba wishes 'to maintain an open approach to relations and trade with the whole world and to honor the confidence bestowed on her by her creditors, thereby honoring her commitments' (Banco Nacional de Cuba, 1985, pp. 2–3).

Looking for More Western Trade

More exports to market economies were needed to increase hard currency reserves. But to regain the lost trade volume with Western markets, it was necessary to achieve a sizable $130 million export increase over 1984 figures—a $57 million increment over the highest trade level accomplished earlier. It was an ambitious goal. It meant that by the end of the 1986–90 five-year period, non-sugar exports to Western countries should be $1 billion above the 1984 mark. The income increase in goods and services for 1990, above the 1984 level at that year's prices, was planned for $1.12 billion. In spite of mounting economic problems, the government argued that this was a feasible plan if only Western nations would take advantage of the 'favorable domestic conditions that have been created in terms of infrastructure, skilled personnel and productive potential,' and increase their trade with Cuba.

In addition to a highly qualified work-force already in place, during 1986–90 7,516 university-trained workers and 1,169 doctoral candidates and doctors will complete their training. They will cover fields as varied as energy and fuel, sugar, electronics, machine construction, chemistry, food, agriculture, cattle, and fishing. By pointing out its human resource capabilities to international leaders, Havana was making the most of its high quality educational system. The built-in expectation was that this would enhance the chances for better credit terms. Also, it was a reminder to Western banks that the revolution had improved Cuban society in ways not commonly found in developing nations—the present credit and foreign debt problems notwithstanding.

Castro's criticism of the economy at the 1986 Third Party Congress, when the rectification process was launched, gained an additional urgency in this context. Cuba's Third Five Year Plan, for 1986–90 (which includes a projected 5 percent annual growth), was born under rather difficult auspices. Achieving such a goal depended on correcting past mistakes and improving economic performance. It included increasing efficiency in the use of resources; reducing material consumption (including fuels and their by-products); servicing the foreign debt with Western (and socialist) creditors; meeting export commitments to socialist countries; curbing consumption without reducing the population's standard of living; and adjusting investment in development programs to assure the external trade sector of the economy (Banco Nacional de Cuba, 1985, pp. 3–5, 44–7).

Also, the government committed itself to 'cut back hard-currency imports, aggressively pursue hard-currency exports, restrict investment more tightly to productive ... purposes, encourage joint ventures and other economic relations with market economies, earn hard currency through the export of services (e.g., construction workers), and cooperate in international efforts to stabilize sugar prices' (Pérez-López, 1986, p. 23).

The domestic austerity program approved in December 1986, at the conclusion of the Third Party Congress, includes:

Increases in public transportation fares, consumer utility costs and select parallel market prices [the dual subsidized and non-subsidized price system in stores and food markets], as well as cutbacks in the number of state-assigned automobiles, per diem payments to government officials, and foreign travel budgets. Together with the retrenchment of the private sector, these measures may save the state up to 500 million pesos a year ... [Pérez-Stable, 1987, p. 300]

Cuba's serious but not unique economic problems of the mid-1980s— most developing nations, and many industrialized countries, were also adversely affected—were noted and widely publicized. A US publication characterized the situation as a major crisis:

Money is more than ever in desperately short supply. 'Cuba is suffering an economic crisis of massive proportions,' says a foreign diplomat. 'Here is a country with ... a controlled economy and $4.6 billion from the Soviets each year—and they're still, in hard-currency terms, almost bankrupt' ... [*Time*, 21 September 1987, pp. 46–7]

Without resorting to such hyperbole, a scholarly study also noted recent changes and current problems by stating that,

[Vice President Rodríguez'] ... economic responsibilities were assigned to fellow Politburo member Osmany Cienfuegos Gorriaran ... Additional powers were assigned to a Cienfuegos 'central group', with speculation that the latter might evolve into an 'umbrella ministry' to provide coordination across a variety of economic sectors ...

Moreover,

Faced with a manifestly worsening economic situation, President Castro launched a major campaign against bureaucratic corruption and inefficiency ... [He] later announced a major austerity program to compensate for a severe decline in foreign exchange earnings and Soviet subsidies, which had earlier been estimated at $6 billion a year ... [Banks, 1987, pp. 139–40]

The negative effect that reductions of Soviet supplied oil and sugar price subsidies had on an already troubled economy was also noted by another scholar:

Cuba's open economy remained as vulnerable as ever. Its annual export earnings had in the recent past provided sufficient hard currency for imports between $1.2 billion and $1.5 billion, but in 1986 those had been reduced to some $600 million. Today, real sugar prices on the world market have fallen to 1930s levels, and the value of petroleum exports (domestic savings from the crude oil that the Soviet Union supplies to Cuba) has declined by half. While the Cuban–Soviet relationship is stable, Soviet sugar price subsidies and oil supplies beyond the island's domestic needs are reportedly being reduced ... [Pérez-Stable, 1987, p. 298]

Cuba's financial problems and their possible cause were being examined closely—notwithstanding the discrepancy between *Time* and Banks on the exact amount of Soviet yearly subsidies. Castro had puzzled many observers before by devising bold initiatives under adverse conditions. He confronted this time the pressing problems affecting the economy with austerity measures and an urgent plea for higher productivity. A rectification process campaign stressing ideological consciousness was also launched seeking to amend the nation's past economic mistakes. Neither the problems nor the solutions were entirely new, however. Neither was Castro and his country-men's longstanding determination to keep moving forward. They have persevered for almost three decades in their objective of develping Cuban socialism fully, despite the numerous obstacles frustrating their efforts.

Economic Performance in the Mid-1980s

By the fall of 1987, the second year of the rectification process, President Castro claimed significant economic gains: exports had increased by 8.8 percent and imports decreased by 6.6 percent, as compared with the same period in 1986. The policy of restricting imports from market economies was being firmly implemented. In the first nine months of 1987 only half of the country's import requirements had been satisfied: 550 million pesos, with the expectation of not exceeding 700 million by the end of the year, which was well within the established goal. (But imports from the socialist area had increased by 1.2 percent.) Also, accumulated commodity production had reached 71.8 percent of the annual plan, while salary savings amounted to 158 million pesos. Reversing the trend of several years, inventories had been reduced by nearly 332 million pesos. Recovery of raw materials had increased by 4.1 percent. Approximately 37,000 new housing units were expected by the end of 1987, while 42,340 more are under construction (23,443 by the Ministry of Construction, and 7,445 by Havana minibrigades) (*Granma Weekly Review*, 8 November 1987, p. 9).

Moreover, hard currency reserves had experienced a 4 percent growth (excluding fuel re-exports). Regarding trade with socialist countries, the growth in reserves was even better: a total of 8 percent in the 1986–7 period.

On the negative side, Castro underscored the need to increase exports of light industry products, and to end production delays in the soft drink and beer industry, which affected products earmarked for export. In order to overcome these and other deficiencies, old practices had to change, including improving the organization and quality of industrial production, ending defaults in the iron and steel and machine industry, and guaranteeing the availability of manufacturing spare parts. The export of citrus had suffered because of a shortage of cardboard boxes used to package it. Delays in the arrival of imported raw material needed to make cardboard boxes had created the problem.

In agriculture, the low yield in the coffee, cacao, citrus, and other fruits and corn crops, caused by a severe drought in the first quarter of 1987, was later recuperated, including milk production. However, many state agencies developed production problems too, affecting projects like the manufacturing of concrete pipes to carry water under high pressure. Unavailable spare parts delayed completing the El Gato waterworks project, which is now carrying water to some areas of the capital (*Granma Weekly Review*, 8 November 1987, p. 9).

While policies implemented under the rectification process were rendering tangible, positive results, they also had countereffects, even if unintended. Saving hard curency reserves by restricting imports is a necessary objective, but it could also have undesirable effects. Shortages in imported raw material affect the production of export commodities. It also creates shortages affecting the consumer at home. Although austerity measures are necesary to cure a troubled economy, they can also restrict the number of choices for both production and consumption plans. It seems that their immediate effect is to reduce the volume of economic activity. In the long run, however, it is expected that the economy will grow on a sound basis, because of such measures. This assertion, accepted by most market economies, appears equally valid for a socialist economy, such as Cuba's.

During the first six months of 1987 the economy decreased by approximately 297 million pesos (3.6 percent) the level of mercantile production from the similar period a year earlier. However, during the second quarter there was a 3.7 percent increase in production above the level of the first quarter. The agrarian and cattle sectors achieved 0.6 percent growth in production, and communication had a major increase, 5.7 percent. While most sectors lowered their production levels, only construction and other (nonspecified) areas decreased by more than 5 percent during the second quarter of 1987. The sugar sector had a 4.2 percent decrease from the first six months of 1986, while the non-sugar economy decreased by 3.5 percent. However, the downtrend of the first quarter in production was reduced in most areas by 50 percent during the second quarter (see Table 7.4).

Table 7.4 Mercantile production, January–June 1986–87 (m. pesos)

	1986	1987
Sugar economy	1,502.1	1,438.8 (−4.2%)
Non-sugar economy	6,683.6	6,449.0 (−3.5%)
Total	8,185.7	7,887.8 (−3.6%)

Source: *Cuba–Informe Económico Trimestral*, Havana, Cuba, Banco Nacional de Cuba, Comité Estatal de Estadísticas (June 1987), p. 1.

Castro's current policies promote cost-efficiency planning and a more productive economy. Its philosophical objectives, however, are aimed at reinforcing the populace's commitment to Marxist-Leninist ideological beliefs. On this central point, Cuba's rectification process parts company with market economy countries. Whenever the latter apply austerity measures to their economic problems, their objectives are quite different.

Cuba, 'Perestroika', and 'Glasnost'

Cuba's rectification process also parts company with other socialist countries' current policies; i.e., Mikhail Gorbachëv's innovative and controversial twofold system–change policy: restructuring, *perestroika*, and openness, *glasnost*. For Cuba, however, this seems to validate rather than contradict the notion that the construction of socialism is a unique national experience. A socialist system must come out of the country's historical background. It should also respond to its socioeconomic conditions, even if most socialist countries seem to be guided by common operational guidelines. The latter constitute a set of principles derived from their common experience while pursuing similar political and socioeconomic objectives, and not ironclad laws for all to follow in every instance.

Hence, Cuba's so-called rectification process constitutes a self-styled approach to economic problem-solving, well within the boundaries of socialist policy-making (particularly under a revolutionary government). It is intended for domestic consumption, and not as a rejection of other socialist countries' policies.

It was reported that Castro criticized publicly current Soviet system–change policies, even if rather obliquely and without giving names, and apparently mostly directed at *glasnost* (*Miami Herald*, 10 October 1987). Nevertheless, if not in agreement with specific policy objectives and particulars of the rationale behind such policies, the general nature and aims of Gorbachëv's *perestroika* (the bedrock of his transformation program) is not alien to Castro's rectification process. In reality, Gorbachëv's reasoning for the urgent need to overhaul the Soviet system could have come from Castro's mouth. Both Gorbachëv's rhetoric and substance (but not the methods used to implement them) are seemingly akin to the policies launched at the Third Party Congress in Havana. One could even speculate that by launching its rectification process today, Cuba is saving itself from a *perestroika* tomorrow. Whether it will implement sooner or later its own *glasnost* is another matter. However, in the Soviet way of thinking, both *perestroika* and *glasnost* are part of a single policy-complex that need and reinforce one another. According to the Soviet leader,

Perestroika is no whim on the part of some ambitious individuals or a group of leaders ... [It] is an urgent necessity arising from the profound processes of development in our socialist society ... Any delay in beginning perestroika could have led to an exacerbated internal situation in the near future, which, to put it bluntly, would have been fraught with serious social, economic and political crises.

Moreover,

At some stage . . . the country began to lose momentum. Economic failures became more frequent. Difficulties began to accumulate and deteriorate, and unresolved problems to multiply. Elements of what we call stagnation and other phenomena alien to socialism began to appear in the life of society . . . [Gorbachëv, 1987, pp. 17, 19]

None the less, reportedly there have been complaints that Gorbachëv's innovative policies have not been properly heeded. In a meeting held at Havana University in October 1987, journalism students confronted Castro with requests for some kind of domestic *glasnost* in news reporting. Soviet publications reporting openly under new policies receive now unusual attention, to the point of being sold out in a few days. As soon as 'the Spanish language edition of *Moscow News* is . . . on the stands . . . it is snatched up, borne off and passed from hand to hand' (Hitchens, 1988, p. 79). New Soviet films critically discussing social problems have gained a more attentive audience.

According to the Soviet Embassy Press Attaché in Havana, Anatoly Shevchenko, '*Glasnost* and *perestroika* have aroused a great interest among Cubans, not to copy but to study them. People want to know about the radical changes that are taking place within socialism.'

In less diplomatic language, the Soviet magazine *New Times* published several articles critical of the Cuban economy and the direction it is taking. In an article published on 17 August 1987, authored by Soviet journalist Vladislav Chirkov, the economy was criticized for such problems as shortages of housing and electricity, food rationing, low labor productivity, and the foreign debt. Cuban Vice President Carlos Rafael Rodríguez, responding on 9 October in the same magazine, listed economic statistics contrary to Chirkov's allegations. Rodríguez characterized Chirkov's article as 'shallow and one-sided' (*Miami Herald*, 18 October 1987).

However, in an exercise in tropical *glasnost*, the Cuban magazine *Somos Jóvenes* recently published a controversial article denouncing the existence of about a thousand prostitutes working in Havana, some of them making 6,000 pesos per month (*El Nuevo Herald*, 8 December 1987, pp. 1A, 4A). Indeed, if factually correct, it is an astronomical and unmatched income in the country. More importantly, a social objective of the revolution was to eradicate prostitution. In the early 1960s most of the active prostitutes were rehabilitated and re-educated for a useful social life. The alleged existence of major prostitution in the 1980s stands as a stark reminder of still unresolved social problems that were thought gone long ago.

Cubans Working Overseas

When it became known in the early 1980s that Cuban construction workers were being sent overseas to work in different projects, some analysts concluded that this was an indication of renewed unemployment and the need to generate revenue for the country's sagging economy. The program helped to reduce unemployment in the eastern provinces, but it appears that the decision to send workers abroad responded mostly to national developmental objectives, which were now feasible through new international opportunities (interview with J. L. Rodríguez, CIEM, December 1987).

The overseas workers program gained full strength by 1983. The main objective was to have workers receiving qualified training in a socialist country with an economy and technology similar to Cuba's. Upon returning to their homeland they could then use their newly learned skills as qualified workers. The program saves Havana from building the infrastructure for the worker's training (which is already available in more industrialized socialist countries), while, in return, it provides the host country with the necessary manpower. By 1986-7, Bulgaria, Czechoslovakia, German Democratic Republic, and Hungary had the highest number of Cuban workers, altogether close to 20,000.

Workers serve from three to five-year periods in cold winter weather, which is to some extent compensated by comfortable living quarters. But they live in their own communities, separated from major urban centers, or even villages (which gives them protective insulation, but also keeps them isolated from the social milieu of the host country). The workers can renew their contracts for a new term, and those who do are known as *cooperantes* ('those who cooperate'). Mostly single males are chosen to avoid the assimilation problems of entire families (workers undergo an initial test to check for possible assimilation problems). In addition to learning qualified skills, the workers also learn a foreign language that might allow them to work as interpreters at home later.

The program is planned to continue into the 1990s, but without increasing the number of workers. The new direction, instead, seems to be mixed enterprises similarly to Jabaros, a lumber enterprise in the Soviet Union. Jabaros is a Havana–Moscow joint venture located nearby Vladivostok. Cuba provides and pays the workers, and the transportation to carry back its share of lumber (less than half of total production), and the Soviet Union provides the forests for Jabaros' lumber. It seems a mutually satisfying agreement for both parties. The Cubans get a steady supply of lumber (at negotiated price rates), which they lack and which Moscow could not provide otherwise. And the Soviets get to exploit and benefit from a natural resource that would remain largely untouched without this agreement, because of their labor shortages for such work (interview with J. L. Rodríguez, December 1987).

Three Major Economic Areas

Historically, to talk of the Cuban economy was to talk of agriculture. And, it was to talk of the fact that in a mainly one-crop open economy sugar has reigned supreme for at least a century—notwithstanding the importance of coffee, tobacco, and cattle as national resources. Still today, sugar stands at the center of the island's economy, even though the country's economic system and trade patterns have been entirely transformed. But after its price fell in the 1980s to the low levels at which it had been during the world economic depression half a century ago, sugar seems unable to provide the amount of income needed for the nation's treasury. Thus, preserving the country's standard of living at the level it enjoyed in the late 1970s demands drastic solutions today and certainly in the future. Some of these are already in place under the so-called rectification process, while new ones are most certainly in the making.

Agrarian Policy

The revolutionary government's objective was to transform as well as to foster the nation's agricultural economy. The social and economic impact of agrarian policy was felt almost immediately. From 1958-9 to 1960-1 the percentage of the economically active population working in agriculture increased slightly, from 37 to 38 percent. Sugar and related products, tobacco, and coffee's share of exports grew from 1958 to 1960 from 87 to 92 percent, even though total exports had decreased from $699 to $650 million in the same period (Aranda, 1980, p. 11).

The rural reality the revolution encountered included 1,342,000 hectares of land that were never used, or were mostly unattended and used only marginally for cattle grazing. The land tenure system was characterized by the extremes of *latifundia* (large landholdings) for some crops, and *minifundia* (small landholdings) for others. This resulted in three-fourths (73.3 percent) of the land belonging to a tenth (9.4 percent) of the owners, while less than a tenth of the land (7.4 percent) belonged to two-thirds (66.1 percent) of the owners.

The negative impact that this had on the country's development created rather poor rural working opportunities with 361,000 unemployed and 370,000 partially employed workers. A continuous cycle of low level of employment during the sugar harvest and higher unemployment during the off-season (*tiempo muerto*) period paralleled one another. While approximately 200,000 workers remained unemployed during the former, the number increased to 457,000 in the latter. From 423,690 agricultural workers, approximately 201,771 (47.6 percent) worked only three months or less in the year, and 358,509 (84.6 percent) labored six months or less. At the same time, $200 million in food was imported that could have been produced domestically like rice, vegetables, poultry, eggs, and pork. The first agrarian reform, signed on 17 May 1959 in Sierra Maestra, put an end to this situation. Even so, it was followed by a second agrarian reform on 3 October 1963.

[The 1959 agrarian reform] began with the abolition of latifundios and had as social objectives reserving for the state economy all those lands which were not under cultivation and guaranteeing property rights for the small and medium size farmers who worked the land without owning it. From the economic point of view, the idea was to create an internal market needed for industry, by raising the standard of living in the countryside . . . [Rodríguez, 1987b, p. 27]

Some of its features included: (1) limiting the maximum extension of land to 402.6 hectares (extended in some cases to 1,342 hectares); (2) limiting land ownership to Cuban citizens or entities only; (3) creating a vital minimum of 26.8 hectares for those working the land; and (4) allowing beneficiaries to own up to 67.1 hectares.

The newly expropriated land was used almost immediately, and the results were seen rapidly. In only eight months, by the summer of 1961, 308,000 hectares of nationalized land were already cultivated. Agricultural products, particularly sugar, had record harvests (6.8 million metric tons of sugar that year). Rural unemployment ended. Also, after joining new education programs, rural youth was not available to work in the fields as it had been before. The ensuing shortage of labor affected agriculture badly. The fields were not carefully attended, and many crops were not properly harvested. The agricultural phase of sugar production was completed with the help of urban workers. The ongoing program of public works in cities across the country competed for workers, draining further needed rural labor.

The National Institute of Agrarian Reform (INRA) was created in 1959, as well as the National Association of Small Farmers (ANAP), which represented private farmers not affected by the nationalization of large estates. INRA became the economic and developmental center of the nation in charge of agriculture, cattle production, and sugar and other industrial enterprises. By keeping a balance between workers' and peasants' interests, INRA sought to safeguard an alliance that had major implications for the ultimate direction of the revolution.

Che Guevara served as director of INRA's department of industrialization, which initiated central economic planning through its Section of Planning and Studies. Agrarian production was carefully planned, including supportive and technical infrastructure. This included transportation, communication, and electricity, as well as warehouses and workshops, and storage centers for farmers' *acopio* (INRA's farmers' assigned production quotas).

In spite of many dislocations in production the early 1960s were still good years for sugar, tobacco, coffee, and other leading products. However, a food scarcity ensued, which worsened throughout the 1960s. The staples of the Cuban diet were difficult to find in city markets. Agricultural diversification and a lower rate of sugar production were replaced with an emphasis on sugar at the expense of other crops. The main economic objective at the time was industrial rather than agricultural. This changed in the mid-1960s when the initial industrial goals were realistically re-evaluated and new agricultural objectives were set up (Aranda, 1980, pp. 5–18).

From 1961 to 1963 agricultural planning moved into low cost intensive crops, and away from extensive agriculture. This was changed in 1964 when developmental plans were based on economic accumulation. Using the sugar cane monoproducing and monoexporting structure, the new strategy was applied from 1964 to the mid-1970s. The idea was to build a technical/ material base that would sustain the country's industrialization program, while agriculture was being technically re-equipped.

From 1960 to 1985 $11.179 billion were invested in agriculture (26.1 percent of total investments made in the country during this period), which brought an increase of 16.5 percent of cultivated land. It also brought an eight-fold increase of tractors; a ten-fold and four-fold increase in the application of fertilizers and pesticides, respectively; the construction of 3,000 new agricultural and industrial facilities; and a 125-fold increase in the capacity of dammed water, including one million hectares of irrigated land. More important, however, was the radical improvement in the living conditions of the rural population. Education, employment, salaries, income, social security and assistance, and health benefits were made available to the extent that the quality of life was transformed entirely in rural Cuba (Rodríguez, 1987b, pp. 28–33).

Sugar Policy

Cuba was in the pre-revolutionary period the world's leading sugar exporter, but this prominent position was not properly supported at home. The revolution inherited in 1959 a sugar industry afflicted by serious structural problems. Neither the agriculture, nor the sugar industry was advanced enough to support such a leading role—at best, the latter was three decades behind. Paradoxically, Cuba's sugar industry had been regarded in 1915 as probably the most advanced in the world.

But since 1920–30, systematic industrial neglect had become an accepted practice. National and foreign investors alike sought to maximize their assets by doing routine maintenance work in their sugar mills, but without bothering to reinvest their profits in industrial improvement or expansion. Cubans owned 62.13 percent of sugar mills in 1958, while investors from the United States, Spain, and France owned 36.65 percent, 0.95 percent, and 0.27 percent, respectively. The sugar industry ocupied a large part of the labor force during the harvest season, but thousands of workers would be adrift later, crisscrossing the country unemployed and poor during the dead-season looking for any menial job. Meanwhile, the industry's technical personnel were aging: most sugar technicians were age 45 or older, with some in their early and mid-sixties (Charadán López, 1982, pp. 115–18).

The socialist transformation of the sugar industry started on 4 February 1960. That day fourteen sugar mills owned by members of Batista's regime, most of whom had fled the country in early 1959, were nationalized by a decree from the Ministry (in charge of) Recuperating Missappropriated Property. This was followed four months later, on 27 June by a Washington decision to reduce Cuba's sugar quota in the US market. A week later, on 2 July, the Eisenhower Administration cancelled any further purchases of Cuban sugar, which terminated the island's quota. Castro responded defiantly to these punitive measures. Threatening to nationalize US property valued at $800 million, he said: 'So we could lose part of our sugar quota? They could lose then part of their investment here. So we could lose our entire sugar quota? They could lose then their entire investment in Cuba. We will trade [sugar] quota for [US] investment [here].' The US-owned sugar mills became the property of the Cuban government, thirty-six in total. Approximately 50 percent of all sugar production was already under state control. The remaining sugar mills would follow (Charadán López, 1982, pp. 120–4). Indeed, a new era had began in Cuban history.

The early developmental policy based on diversification and non-sugar agriculture was replaced in the 1960s by one based on sugar and primary activities. The focus of state investment moved from industry to agriculture, and finally to sugar. The production record was erratic, however: after two good sugar harvests, 1959 and 1960, a 6.7 million tons peak in 1961, it decreased in 1962–4, climbed again in 1965, but then declined in 1966. Total agricultural productivity had increased by 14 percent between 1958 and 1961, but decreased by 27 percent in 1961–3. Moreover, according to French agronomist René Dumont, state farms' productivity ratio in 1961 ranked 50 percent below the private farmers' ratio (Mesa-Lago, 1971, p. 286).

Sugar exports were reorganized in 1964–5 according to the demands of the international market, and the newly established trade with socialist countries. The first sugar production plan, the Prospective Sugar Plan, was set for 1965–70. According to Mesa-Lago, the plan was never successful: only in 1965 was the plan output target met. Moreover, the total accumulated output for the period was 25 percent below its target (Mesa-Lago, 1981, p. 59).

The 1965–70 plan had a comprehensive outlook, including a technical support system; the supply of quality spare parts (which were highly scarce after the US-imposed trade embargo); an economic investment plan; longer sugar harvest (beyond the traditional hundred-day harvests); the improvement of the personnel technical qualification; an *acopio* distribution system (the system of private farmers' procurement quotas sold to the government at officially fixed prices); and a maintenance and repair system. But its ultimate objective was the 1970 Ten Million Tons sugar harvest. This was meant to be the largest ever in the country's history. However, under the 1971–80 plan production output was originally targeted for 11–12 million tons of sugar. The 1970 target was never accomplished in its entirety. It felt short by 1.465 million tons. Sugar amounted, however, to 47.3 percent of total agricultural production that year, and the harvest grinding period was one of the largest, totalling 143 days (surpassed in 1978 with 153 days). The 1970 harvest was a fateful event in the development of the revolution. Its failure unleashed the institutionalization movement of the 1970s which accomplished the transformation of the revolutionary polity to its present form.

In August 1971 Castro discussed the new Five Year Plan, 1971–5, in a plenary meeting. He urged the re-establishment of tighter controls and discipline in the management of the sugar mills, but not by self-imposed production limits. 'We should not follow a conservative line,' he said. 'If a sugar mill could produce 1.2 million tons, let's not start aiming only at 900,000, or even 1 million.' Regarding workers' qualifications and promotions, he suggested linking stability with promotions. Castro thought it plausible to have 100,000 highly qualified workers producing some day 10,000 million tons of sugar. 'It is perfectly possible. This would mean

100 tons for every man working in the sugar industry,' Castro said. But the period witnessed instead the repairing of the sugar mill network, which needed special attention after the excesses of 1965–70 and the Ten Million Tons campaign. The use ratio of the country's industrial capacity improved, however. The percentage of sugar cane cut by machine grew from 2.4 in 1971, to 5.8 in 1972, 9 in 1973, 16.1 in 1974, and 25 in 1975. Other production indicators improved similarly.

Cuba's leading position as sugar producer and exporter continued in the 1980s. It still is the world's number one raw sugar exporter, the second largest producer of raw sugar, and the third leading producer of sugar cane. Post-1959 achievements in the sugar industry include: (1) the mechanization of the sugar harvest (two-thirds of the sugar cane is now cut by machine, which freed thousands of *macheteros*, cane cutters, from such a painful job); (2) the marked improvement in the standard of living of sugar workers (including steady work and all kinds of social security benefits); (3) the increasing modernization of the country's industrial infrastructure (new agro-industrial complexes are replacing the old sugar mills); (4) the major role played by cooperatives and state farms in growing sugar cane (four-fifths of the total is grown on state farms); and (5) the transformation of old sugar trade patterns in commercial exchange (particularly in sugar sales to the Soviet Union, and other socialist countries) (Feuer, 1987, pp. 69–75).

Problems troubling the sugar industry today include: (1) the deplorable conditions of the world sugar market; (2) the low profitability of sugar sales in the mid-1980s (sometimes producing at a loss regardless of how cost efficient the producer might be); (3) the inadequate levels of sugar cane productivity; and (4) the uncertainty caused by disease and other natural disasters (Feuer, 1987, p. 69).

The tons per hectare yield achieved by private farmers is still consistently higher than the state farms' yield: 61.3 tons per hectare in 1981, 61 in 1982, 63.6 in 1983 by private farmers, and 53.8 in 1981, 53.9 in 1982, and 56.7 in 1983 by state farms. However, the yield achieved by private farmers has declined from the late 1970s to the mid-1980s: from 64.6 in 1979 to 54.3 in 1985.

The country's sugar performance followed an incremental production output. The 1962–70 average was 5.3 million tons; in 1971–5, 5.5; in 1976–80, 6.9, and in 1981–5, 7.7 (Feuer, 1987, p. 73). But sugar production was declining in the mid-1980s. The sugar harvest totalled 7.8 million metric tons in 1985, 7.4 in 1986 (5.12 percent less), and 6.7 in mid-1987 (9.4 percent less), a 1.1 million metric tons production loss in three years (14.1 percent) (Banco Nacional, May 1987, p. 7; June 1987, p. 10).

The centrality of sugar in Cuban life today is underscored by the fact that almost 360,000 men and women work in the sugar industry, representing about 12 percent of the labor force. Sugar workers and their families amount to approximately one-sixth of the entire population. Also, almost one-third of all industrial resources are invested in sugar production, and 1.7 million hectares are used for sugar cane. In 1983 sugar and related products represented four-fifths of the total value of exports, and the industry's output as a whole amounted to a tenth of the country's Global Social Product (GSP). The new agro-industrial complexes, the diversification of sugar related industrial products, the improvement of the industry's infrastructure, and other changes made in the last years have not been able to increase revenues in the 1980s. However, whenever the producing countries' trading conditions improve in the international sugar market, and the price of sugar regains its fair value, Cuba will be ready to profit from it.

Industrial Policy

Industrial policy has been a central component of the reorganization and development of the economy since 1959. Contrary to initial expectations, however, the limited economic resources available did not support achieving industrialization in a relatively short period of time. Also, the absence of a proper socioeconomic infrastructure forced the regime to accept a slower industrial growth pace. Accelerated growth needs the proper kind of social and economic relations of production capable of sustaining it (Rodríguez, 1980, pp. 170-6). This was characteristically absent in an underdeveloped island that had complicated matters further by choosing a socialist economic modality. Regardless of how sound the political reasoning behind choosing such a modality was, the transition from underdevelopment and dependent capitalism to development and socialism promised to be unreasonably difficult.

The revolutionary leadership accepted the reality of things later in the process. The PCC saw it in these terms in the 1970s:

Cuba inherited from capitalism a deformed economic structure with a backward agricultural basis and little industrial development, mainly concentrated in the sugar industry . . . [After 1959 the] focus of activities and the orientation of investment policy were mainly directed toward the agricultural sector, and while working to create the necessary infrastructure . . . to set up the basis and conditions for the process of industrialization, the central task of the plan for the development and promotion of the national economy beginning with the coming 1976–1980 Five-Year Plan will be the industrialization of the country.

Moreover,

In this sense, it will be necessary to maintian the efforts to give the national economy an infrastructure responsive to the requirements of future development. The main task of industrialization is that of creating the necessary internal basis for the systematic development of the productive forces, supplying industry, land cultivation and cattle-raising with equipment and materials; of increasing the exportable resources, of substituting for imports; and of producing a wide range of commodities for the population . . .[Programatic Platform of the Communist Party of Cuba, 1976, pp. 72–3]

There were some basic facts involving Cuba's economic potential and limitations impinging upon industrial policy. One was the open nature of Cuba's economy. This demanded eliminating the nation's dependence on external trade—so far an elusive goal—and realigning its trade from market economies to the socialist market, which has been accomplished to a large extent. However, trading with the former is necessary to earn valuable convertible currency. Secondly, the punitive trade embargo imposed by the United States created serious and additional problems for the economy, particularly in the first ten years of revolutionary rule. Well-qualified labor was in short supply. This became even more urgent in the early 1960s after the exodus of such qualified personnel as professionals and technicians to the United States and other countries. At that time the country lost half its medical doctors.

The industrialization program inaugurated in the 1960s sought several objectives:

(1) to accumulate a large percentage of the national earnings;
(2) to use the agrarian and cattle sectors as the main vehicle for a broader distribution of the national income, and to modernize the agriculture for further industrial development;
(3) to use the industrial sector as a major investment recipient after agriculture, especially the mechanical, construction materials, chemical, and energy industries (this should bring a better balance between agriculture, industry, and the economic infrastructure, and an orderly development of the three areas);
(4) to seek the best possible terms in the socialist market for Cuban products based on the international division of labor established among socialist countries (this included modernizing and expanding the sugar industry, and other marketable commodities);
(5) to give priority to educational programs above any economic and social programs, with the exception of public health;

(6) to look for financial opportunities abroad in addition to maximizing domestic resources.

After the conclusion of the initial phase, a high rate of capital accumulation during an accelerated industrialization process was targeted for the second phase. The manufacturing of production equipment was to prevail then over the production of consumer goods, but an acceptable rate of industrial growth was always to be safeguarded.

The regime considered the first phase completed by 1975, so it moved under the new economic management and planning system (SDPE) into its First Five Year Plan, 1975–80. While the massive agricultural investment made earlier was visible after 1975, the rate of investment and growth that was taking place in the First Five Year Plan was not apparent yet. This would become evident during the following period, 1980–5. In this sense, 1975–80 was a transition period from years of economic reorganization into a new stage of accelerated industrialization (Rodríguez, 1980, pp. 174–5). In reality Cuba confronted major problems all along, but it was still able to achieve significant gains as well.

During the initial phase, the value of industrial output, in 1965 prices, grew from $2.7 billion in 1967 to $4 billion in 1970 (45.8 percent), and to $5.3 billion in 1974 (34.8 percent). The thirteen-year period had a 96.6 percent total growth. This included the mechanical, metalurgic, construction materials, chemical, oil and by-products, electricity, mining, food, textile, and sugar industries (Rodríguez, 1980, p. 214). In the first two decades the total industrial output had doubled to an annual average rate of 5 percent, from 86.2 in 1962 to 197.1 in 1977 (a much better record than in agriculture). In per capita terms, this meant approximately 70 percent or 3.5 yearly (Mesa-Lago, 1981, p. 39).

But after a 48.5 percent peak in 1978, the industrial output share of the Global Social Product decreased from 47.8 percent in 1975 to 43.5 in 1982 (*Anuario Estadístico de Cuba, 1982*, 1983, p. 99). In the first six months of 1987 there was a 2.4 percent decline in the mercantile production of some industries from the same period in 1986. This was due to the decline in mercantile output of such industries as sugar, non–electric machines, energy, beverages, and tobacco—which amount to 57 percent of the entire industrial sector. Total industrial mercantile production for the same period decreased by 3.9 percent from the year before, although mercantile production totalled $7.887 billion (Banco Nacional de Cuba, June 1987, p. 11).

The Industrial Sector and the Consumer.   The Cuban Institute of Research and Direction of Internal Demand (ICIODI), which functions under the supervision of the Council of Ministers, provides most communication between industrial enterprises and the consumer. The ICIODI was founded in 1972, and Eugenio R. Balari was its director until the mid-1980s. As a multidisciplinary agency with a staff of over a hundred researchers specialized in economics, sociology, psychology, mathematics, statistics, marketing, and even fashion design, architecture, publicity, and communications, it covers a wide array of research subjects. ICIODI's studies center mostly on food, clothing, footwear, housing, furniture, appliances (and other items related to needs for people's living quarters), national and international tourism, leisure time activities, and other subjects (Balari, 1985, pp. 92-7).

ICIODI also studies the way the population uses its time, particularly its free time. These studies have shown how women working outside the household are more prone to engage in other activities complementing their lives than housewives are—i.e., taking evening courses, participating in political, cultural, and other kinds of activities, etc. Cultural values and attitudes supporting women's modernization are reinforced by this kind of research.

The administration of the family budget, and how the population prefers to spend its money are studied. Making an inventory of the probable number of footwear, clothing, home appliances, and other items of personal and family use that people have provides essential information for the government to use in deciding how much the population needs and what the country's economy could then afford. The actual habits and preferences of the consumer led to a model defining what should be 'the rational norms of consumption by the socialist Cuban society.' While the revolution has fostered consumption on an egalitarian basis by providing free social services to all and elevating the national standards of living of the population, highly priced items for individual consumption (considered conspicuous and unaffordable by Cuban standards) are not available, so their possession is purposely discouraged as unnecessary consumerism.

Many educational campaigns dedicated to teach the public about consumption habits (i.e., the need to eat high protein food other than beef, like fish and others, to stop smoking, etc.) have been conducted by ICIODI as a result of its own studies. Its popular monthly magazine, *Opina*, has a wide circulation and serves as a forum for consumers' complaints and prospects. It also publishes a scholarly publication, *Demanda*, written by its professional staff and dedicated to theoretical and empirical questions of consumer research. Marketing is another important area of investigation. Market research is done for government agencies and industrial enterprises concerned with how saleable available products are, or what might be sold in the future. Short- and long-term market forecasts are conducted, as well as micro- and macroeconomic research. Market forecast research is sometimes related to government policy determining the future direction of the consumer's market. Hence ICIODI functions as both a government agency that studies the consumer and that, also, decides the future direction of the consumer's market to some extent. Altogether ICIODI conducts between 100 and 120 studies every year (Hernández del Campo, 1975; Balari, 1985).

ICIODI uses modern research methods, and its mathematical and statistical models are calculated using Cuban-made computers. The studies are conducted following simulation, multivariate, experimental, and non-parametric models, and other research techniques such as system analysis and public opinion surveys. A network made up of approximately 50,000 families serves as the population sample informing on consumer-related subjects. The families involved as well as the locations are rotated systematically in order to enhance the randomness and representative value of the sample. There is a second network of 1,000 observers directly supervising commercial enter-prises. Its purpose is to verify which items are liked and which are rejected by the consumer. Responding by mail to ICIODI's monthly questionnaires, the observers give valuable feedback regarding the quality and marketability of the products that are sold to the public.

ICIODI is also in charge of fashion designing and sponsoring fashion shows. It strives for fashions suitable to Cuba's tropical climate that would be attractive and sell well at home and internationally. It designs workers' uniforms, too. It designed a shirt for *macheteros* that would use fabric more resistant to the hard wear of such a demanding job, more tolerable for long working hours of hot weather, and that would allow freer movements for cutting sugar cane.

It also regularly sponsors seminars and conferences for its staff and other experts. The progress made in the first five years of studying the problems of the consumer and the internal demand scientifically was examined in a seminar held in 1977. Its social scientists and statisticians presented on that occasion thirty-four papers examining a broad range of consumer and internal demand questions. They also examine the direction taken by Cuba's internal demand since it had been scientifically studied (Balari, 1979, p. 3). The first international seminar sponsored by ICIODI was conducted in 1975 with representatives of leading consumer research institutes from socialist countries. The second international seminar was held in 1980 with experts from socialist and market economy countries. Particularly, the second international seminar provided an opportunity to examine the progress made by ICIODI as a consumer research institution, and for its staff to present scholarly papers on their consumer research.

Given its more limited personnel and material resources, Cuba has concentrated in one single agency a rather broad area of study and expertise usually subdivided into different agencies in other countries, including socialist nations. None the less, Cuba's record has not been evaluated negatively by European socialist countries. According to Balari, 'the knowledge we have of the country's general economic problematic, given ICIODI's hierarchical standing, has put us in an advantageous position. We can see both sides of the problem. We are aware of the general economic problems—and sometimes also of the particular ones—as well as of the needs, demands, and expectations of the population' (Balari, 1985, p. 94).

8 Domestic Policies

The policies Castro initially conceived and implemented did not have to be Marxist in order to be revolutionary. They were revolutionary because they sought a radical transformation of the Cuban policy. Later, in the early 1960s, when Cuba decided to embrace Marxism–Leninism as its official ideology, revolutionary policy-making became identified with Marxist-Leninist goals. But the regime's policies would have been revolutionary even if Cuba had not become Marxist-Leninist. The significance of this distinction is central for the Third World in general, and Latin America in particular. It would be a serious political mistake for Western analysts and policy-makers to identify developing polities' radical societal change as being necessarily Marxist-Leninist inspired. While the Cuban case can help to clarify such a distinction if it is objectively examined, it can obscure the analysis even further if it is examined through a narrow, ideological approach.

In the eyes of the revolutionary leadership, so much demanded change that the only possible solution to Cuba's ills was through a radical social transformation that would end the old regime and its supportive social, economic, and political institutions, and especially the international relations structure that made such a system possible: American political and economic dominance over Cuba. Having created the system, Washington sought to perpetuate it.

In 1959, with or without Marxism–Leninism, Cuba was headed for radical change under revolutionary rule. As an ideology and the basis for official policy, however, Marxism gave the regime a level of philosophical coherence that in all likelihood it would not have had without it—the contradictions and erratic course followed on so many occasions by revolutionary policies notwithstanding. The domestic and external context of revolutionary policy-making changed after Castro officially embraced Marxism–Leninism in 1961. After the regime became associated with the Soviet Union and other socialist countries, its solution to Cuba's long-held political and socio-economic ills became identified with the pursuit of a socialist society. By the end, Cuba should become a developed communist nation, not just another modern country.

Education and Revolution

It is not possible to think of the revolution and ignore the 1961 Literacy Campaign and the radical transformation of the educational system. That education policy has been central to the revolution and that educational opportunities are now available to all citizens cannot be ignored either. In Castro's words, 'education is the revolution.' The facts that the island's educational system had deteriorated notably in the decades prior to the victory of the revolution, and that very few people were well educated (a good eduation was not generally seen as a highly desirable objective), make the educational renaissance started in 1959 all the more important.

A well-known student of Cuba's educational system, Marvin Leiner, reflected positively on twenty-five years of changes in education,

After my first visit to Cuba in 1968–69, I reported that 'throughout Cuba, in the city streets and alongside rural roads, banners proclaim education as one of the most important themes of the Revolution.' I recognized that slogans like 'The path up from underdevelopment is education' or 'The School plan is your responsibility' were not simply propagandistic platitudes but rather reflected the high priority given to education there.

Moreover,

Now 25 years after its revolution, Cuba's highest flag is still the banner of education. More than one-third of the people—3.5 milion—including nearly all children between the ages of 6 and 12, are enrolled in school. The number of teachers committed to the educational enterprise is a source of national pride. During the 1982–83 school year Cuba had approximately 250,000 teachers and professors, more than 83,000 in the primary schools, almost 8,600 in special education, approximately 25,000 in adult education, and nearly 12,500 in university centers. The present teaching population is approximately 11 times higher than before the Revolution with 130,000 having been added to the teaching force since the early 1970s . . .[Leiner, 1985, p. 27]

For the regime, education is a central component of the social engineering process that has modified Cuban society. So education means more than just learning how to read and write, to master trade skills and technology, and to receive professional degrees. Along with elevating the national educational standards, the regime's goal has been to communicate the revolution's value system. The new political culture sustains the egalitarian society that will make possible the emergence of a new socialist man. The new man will be both educated and socialist, and will live in an educated socialist Cuba.

Different social and political objectives are built into the educational programs. The educational system has been charged with ending racism and sexism, and with eroding the traditional barriers between the urban and rural population so a well integrated population can be formed. *La escuela al campo* (the schools in the countryside) program is geared toward overcoming the traditional gap between the city and the countryside. Students perform agricultural voluntary labor in addition to their school work. Many other combinations of study–work programs range from elementary school to the university level. Such revolutionary values as cooperation (helping one another while performing collective tasks) and participation (becoming actively involved in social and political affairs) are taught in the schools first, so people will act them out later in their daily lives.

The school population quadrupled in the first two decades of revolutionary rule. Practically all school-age children were enrolled in school, and continue to be. In the 1950s, before the revolution, only about one-half of the country's primary-school age children attended school. Rural educational neglect ended. The rural population began to enjoy as much access to education as its urban counterpart. National campaigns upgrading the nation's educational level were launched: unschooled adults completed elementary school, and then moved on to higher school levels. The 1961 Literacy Campaign had achieved a first grade level for 96.1 percent of the population (the estimated national illiteracy level in the pre-revolutionary period was 20 to 25 percent). It was followed by the 'Battle for the Sixth Grade.' From 1962–3 to 1973–4 more than half a million adults completed the primary school adult program.

The education system was transformed, new programs were added, and schools sprang up everywhere. Education became available to all, so workers received university degrees after attending evening classes in any of several universities. Better wages and job opportunites awaited those who bettered themselves through easily accessible educational opportunities. It is generally recognized that Cuba has built the most comprehensive educational system in all Latin America, but opponents of the system have found the quality and political objectives of the regime's education objectionable. A network of schools and programs now reaches the population in all areas of the country (Black, *et al*., 1976, pp. 135–6). A well–educated person is not an exception anymore, but a common reality in Cuba.

Change and Growth in Education

The present educational system functions under the vice–Prime Minister in charge of education, science, and culture, and the Minister of Education.

Below them are five vice-ministries and six general departments. Primary and secondary general education have their own vice-ministry, and technical and vocational schools at the secondary level have their own vice-ministry. Universities and higher specialized institutes work under the direction of the vice-minister for higher education, and a vice-ministry in charge of services and economic matters supervises support services. The vice-ministry of adult education is in charge of the numerous adult education programs.

The ministry of education has a vertical structure subdivided into provincial, regional, and municipal administrative authorities. Since 1976, however, the local Organs of People's Power have been directly involved in educational matters. They 'are vested with the highest authority for the exercise of their state functions . . . [including governing] in all that concerns them . . . the activities required . . . to meet the needs for welfare, economic, cultural, *educational*, and recreational services of the collective in the territory under the jurisdiction of each' (Article 102 of the Constitution, emphasis added). The OPPs coordinate their work with the ministry of education, voicing the local community's concern while directing the schools in their jurisdictions.

The school ladder starts at the *circulos infantiles* (day-care centers) level, which are open to children through the age of 5. Elementary school has six grades, serves children aged 6 to 12, and is mandatory. Secondary school is divided into basic and general secondary levels. Basic secondary schools (junior high schools) run from grades seven through ten, and are attended by students 13 to 16 years old. These schools are designated as basic boarding countryside schools (*escuelas basicas en el campo*) when they are located in rural areas. Preuniversity institutes (*institutos preuniversitarios*) offer secondary studies in grades eleven through thirteen.

Different secondary and higher level schools branch off above the primary level. Technical and vocational schools offer programs for skilled workers, and training schools for primary teachers include courses for elementary school graduates. A variety of schools and institutions are charged with training technicians and secondary-level teachers. The school year runs from September to June or July and ends with several weeks of student evaluation. Teachers' vacation periods last only a month to five weeks. They report to work in early September and stay after the school year for a training period (Black, *et al*., 1976, pp. 148-9).

Following the changes in lower levels, university studies were reorganized according to national needs and priorities. Traditional curricula was discouraged and more attention was given to technical fields. Law, humanities, and social science students decreased. Between 1959 and 1967 student enrollment increased in education (32 percent), natural sciences (51 percent), medical sciences (34 percent), engineering and architecture (82 percent), and agricultural sciences (128 percent). By 1967 these disciplines represented 90 percent of student enrollment. If preparatory courses for workers and peasants had been included, the percentages in these disciplines would have been even higher (Black, *et al.*, 1976, p. 169).

Growth in student enrollment throughout the entire system was remarkable. It included day-care centers, kindergartens, elementary, secondary, and special, adult, youth, and higher education, and other types of school. The school population grew from less than 1 million in 1959 to almost 3.1 million in the mid-1970s (210 percent). From 1958–9 to 1982–3, enrollment in kindergarten grew from 91,700 to 118,072 students (28.7 percent), with a total of 5,258 teachers. In elementary education the number of students grew from 625,717 to 1,363,078 (117.8 percent), schools from 7,567 to 11,215 (48.2 percent), and teachers from 17,355 to 83,358 (380.3 percent). Secondary student growth was even more striking: from 88,135 to 1,116,930 (1,167.2 percent). But schools and teachers increased at a similar level: from 7,567 to 11,215 (48.2 percent), and 17,355 to 83,358 (380.3 percent), respectively. The higher education student increment was also outstanding, from 25,999 to 200,000 (669.2 percent), while the number of facilities grew from six (only three were universities, all located in provincial capitals) to forty (566.6 percent) spread throughout the country, staffed with 12,433 teachers. The university curriculum includes 150 different specialities, with male and female, black and white students taking courses in all fields (Black, *et al.*, 1976, pp. 148–51; Leiner, 1985, p. 30).

The school budget amounted to $1.640 billion in 1986. The 1987 estimate was $1.613 billion (a 1.64 percent decrease), but the budget planned for 1988 was $1.664 billion (a 3.16 percent increase). Almost a quarter (23 percent) of the 1988 national budget was earmarked for education. At a particularly difficult economic time for Cuba, the monies for education guaranteed that all people of school age could continue studying.

Preschool, elementary, and intermediate education, the areas that have experienced the highest growth rate for years, received over four-fifths (83 percent) of the budget. However, the school enrollment in elementary and intermediate education in 1988 had only reached 96 and 99.4 percent of the 1987 level, respectively. A decrease in the population in the 6–17 age group accounted for it. In spite of this, the distribution of the school population in the different school levels still demanded additional monies for boarding schools at the elementary level and for intermediate education. Also, 138 day-care centers with room for 24,570 children had been opened, twenty-five special schools had been finished, and fifty-four were under construction. The day-care center, elementary day boarder, intermediate boarder, and special education categories increased their student numbers from 1987–8 to 1988–9, but the elementary school and intermediate categories declined in enrollment (see Table 8.1).

Table 8.1 Day–care center, elementary, intermediate and special education students at the start of school year 1987–8 and 1988–9 (in thousands)*

	1987–8	1988–9
Day care centers	109.4 (3.57%)	135.4 (4.39%)
Elementary school	937.1 (30.62%)	904.6 (29.37%)
Elementary day boarders	315.3 (10.30%)	326.1 (10.59%)
Intermediate	1,143.4 (37.36%)	1,139.0 (36.98%)
Intermediate boarders	506.4 (16.54%)	520.2 (16.89%)
Special education students	48.7 (1.59%)	54.0 (1.75%)
Totals	3,060.3 (99.98%)	3,079.3 (98.97%)

* Projected enrollment.
Source: *Granma Weekly Review*, 24 January 1988, p. 4.

Many educators have noted the significance of Cuban educational achievements since 1959. A scholar who has studied the island's innovations and changes in terms of the role that education plays in social development, stated: 'It is clear that education has played a central role in replacing the old elitist, hierarchical society with a new social order dedicated to egalitarianism and development.' He added, 'As Cuban education begins to shift from its revolutionary function back to one maintaining the new social order, other third-world countries, and especially those in Latin America, continue to watch Cuba with its promise of rapid and thoroughgoing sociocultural and economic reformation' (Paulston, 1971, pp. 394–5).

Cultural Policy

A Cuba watcher is tempted to say official support for Cuban culture started in 1959, even though that is not factually correct. The Cultural Division of the Ministry of Education dates as far back as 1934. But the cultural ambiance and the government support provided today are strikingly different from pre-revolutionary years. Currently all artistic expressions are productive and reach most sectors of the population. Yesterday, art and literature were usually the effort of a dedicated minority with little or no official support and minimal effect on the country's life. The poetry magazine *Orígines*, founded by the author of the novel *Paradiso*, José Lezama Lima, which included playwright Virgilio Piñera and poet Eliseo Diego, is an important example. Despite its proven quality it had limited circulation. Beyond literary and culturally active circles (where it was held in high esteem), it had little impact on the country's cultural life. It was also void of social and political content. The intellectual left was mostly grouped in the cultural association Nuestro Tiempo, which published a magazine of the same name (1951-9). Film-makers Alfredo Guevara, Julio García Espinosa, Tomás Gutierrez Alea, Santiago Álvarez, and José Massip, composers Harold Gramatges and Juan Blanco, and music critic Edgardo Martín belonged to Nuestro Tiempo.

Writers and poets under the revolution have been grouped into three different generations (Casal, 1971, pp. 447-69). While Alejo Carpentier, Nicolás Guillén, Enrique Serpa, José Z. Tallet, Cintio Vitier, Eliseo Diego, Fina García Marruz, and others had established themselves as influential writers and poets before 1959, the new generation expressed thematically the new challenges and opportunities present in Cuban life. Born around 1930, but flourishing under the revolution, Roberto Fernández Retamar, Pablo Armando Fernández, Lisandro Otero, Edmundo Desnoes, Severo Sarduy, José Álvarez Baragaño, Guillermo Cabrera Infante, and Heberto Padilla, were all members of the first generation.

The second generation branched out into two separate groups. The private publishing house El Puente (The Bridge), 1960-5, became the nucleus for one group. Their concern indicated aesthetic and moral questions. While some of them went into exile, others, like Nancy Morejón and Miguel Barnet, stayed and became highly regarded poets and writers. The other group, centered around the publication *El Caimán Barbudo*, still exists. This latter group wrote about events leading to 1959, and what happened since. Fully integrated into the revolution were writers like Jesús Díaz, Luis Rogelio Nogueras, and Victor Casasús. The third generation was formed independently from both El Puente and *El Caimán Barbudo* groups. Poets Lina de Feria (who later became editor of *El Caimán Barbudo*), and Excilia Saldaña belong to this younger generation.

In 1961 Castro addressed the problem of artistic freedom under the revolution in a talk to Cuban intellectuals at the National Library in Havana. He acknowledged that on different occasions the question of cultural freedom had been raised, as when he had talked to writers like Jean Paul Sartre and C. Wright Mills. The main problem for the regime was that it had not had enough time in 1961 to develop a policy on this matter. There had never been a proper dialogue between revolutionary leaders and artists and writers. 'This is a revolution,' Castro said, 'that was conceived and attained power in "record" time.' Acknowledging that what writers and artists wanted to know at the now famous meeting was whether they would be free to express themselves, Castro stated the revolutionary position on this major issue: 'Within the Revolution, complete freedom; against the Revolution, none.' There have been more statements by Castro and other leaders, particularly the Minister of Culture, Armando Hart, on cultural questions, but this initial broad and imprecise guideline remains as the main stated policy (Castro, 1977, pp. 3–48).

But the issue was not entirely settled in 1961. Major problems arose because of the uneasy relationship between some writers and poets and the revolution. The defection of writers like G. Cabrera Infante, an initial supporter of the revolution, was repeated by others before and after him. The one month imprisonment of the poet Heberto Padilla in 1971 turned into the now famous 'Padilla Affair,' which had damaging international political repercussions for the regime. It alienated, even if temporarily, well-known foreign intellectuals who had been supportive of Cuba. In the 1980 Mariel boatlift several writers, poets, and artists joined those leaving their homeland for other countries, mostly the United States.

Cuba's cultural policy is not neutral, nor is it dedicated to promote art as an end in itself. It has a pronounced political and social content, a direction that is clearly revolutionary, anti-imperialist, anti-colonial, pro-Third World, and socialist. It purposely strives to cleanse itself from other countries' cultural influence, particularly that of the United States. Furthermore, it promotes studying the nation's cultural past through its Afro–Cuban traditions so a legitimate national culture will flourish. It is a popular culture, a non-elitist, people's culture. It is also Latin American, and even Third World in its broadest sense. But it is mainly socialist, the cultural expression of a Marxist–Leninist society.

The revolutionary government has supported culture so decisively that it has turned Cuba into probably the most culturally active Latin American country today. Run jointly by the Ministry of Culture and the local Organs of People's Power, *casas de cultura* (cultural centers) exist in every municipality. They sponsor a wide range of activities including classes in photography, art, and ballet, art exhibits, and a community theater. Their facilities usually include an auditorium for recitals and other events, a library, conference rooms, music rooms, and studios (Weiss, 1985, p. 124).

Cuba's cultural events are internationally recognized. Actors, filmmakers, writers, poets, painters, ballet dancers, musicians, and others from Latin America and other parts of the world, all look at Cuban art, ballet, drama, film festivals, literary contests, and art exhibits as cultural events of great import.

Casa de las Américas is a prestigious cultural organization founded in 1959 that promotes cultural exchange between Cuban and Latin American writers and artists. Its well-known annual literary contest is highly praised internationally. It includes poetry, short stories, novels, plays, essays, and memoirs. An international jury made of famous writers and intellectuals decides who among the many entrants are the recipients of the sought-after awards. It also publishes the bimonthly review *Casa*, under the direction of the award winning poet Roberto Fernández Retamar.

The Cubanacán National School of Fine Arts was established in 1961 in a formerly private residential section of Havana. It teaches students from all parts of the country plastic arts, drama, music, modern dance, and ballet. Students receive scholarships covering all expenses, including spending money. This arts-training complex serves as the center of a national arts educational system that includes twenty-four schools in provinces and cities across the country. Plastic arts students join a national tradition of great painters and sculptors. Cuban artists like Wilfredo Lam, René Portocarrero, Amelia Pelaez, Mariano Rodríguez, Fidelio Ponce de León, Victor Manuel García, Luis Martínez Pedro, Jorge Arche, Eduardo Abela, and many others, are internationally known and recognized for their lasting contribution to twentieth-century art.

Books Published at Low Prices.   The books published before 1959 were limited mostly to school, trade, and professional textbooks. Books had such a limited market that publishing other subjects in large numbers was not seen as profitable enough for private business. Today books are published in large quantities by the government through different publishing enterprises at very low prices. The list includes a wide array of subjects and authors. Although there is a clear political orientation in publishing policy (as in every facet of Cuban cultural life), the visitor from abroad is positively surprised by the diversity of subjects and the very large number of local and foreign authors included.

Developing a Film Industry.   Another first under the revolution has been the development of a film industry. The Cuban Film Institute (ICAIC) is in charge of the production of films, documentaries, cartoons, and newsreels. It functioned under the able direction of its founder, Alfredo Guevara, until he was succeeded in the early 1980s by Julio García Espinosa, a notable filmmaker. ICAIC operates with an annual budget of $7 million which covers all production expenses and the salaries of its 1,100 employees. It produces annually forty documentaries, from five to ten animated cartoons, from four to six major feature films, and fifty-two weekly newsreels (Burton, 1985, p. 148).

Following a well-defined cinematographic documentary style, highly influenced by post-Second World War Italian Neorealism, Cuban films are known for their artistic quality. They have received awards in many film festivals, including those of Western countries. Filmmakers like Tomás Gutiérrez Alea (*Memories of Underdevelopment*), Pastor Vega (*Portrait of Teresa*), José Massip (*For the First Time*), Jesús Díaz (*Red Dust*), Humberto Solás (*Lucia*), and many others, are internationally known and have received praise from film critics for the high quality of their work.

ICAIC has sponsored since 1979 the annual International Festival of the New Latin American Cinema. The festival has become a major event for Latin American filmmakers, attracting directors and critics from all over the world. It provides a forum for quality art films dealing with social and political problems from a progressive political point of view. Some Hollywood luminaries like actor and performer Harry Belafonte, director Francis Ford Coppola, and others have attended Havana's film festival. Also, ICAIC publishes the magazine *Cuban Cinema*. Despite appearing rather irregularly, it is an invaluable source to the student of the Cuban outlook and direction in film making.

The Cuban National Ballet. Ballet in Cuba was always centered on Alicia Alonso, the internationally known Cuban ballerina. She is the founder and director of the Cuban National Ballet, which had functioned since 1948, until the triumph of the revolution, under the name of Alicia Alonso Ballet. Under her leadership a special Cuban school of ballet has been developed. '[It] has a mixture of Spanish and African blood ... [The Cuban school of ballet] glorifies in its pluralism ... Specialization is discouraged, so is stratification. A solid base of classical technique equips the dancers to cultivate versatility' (Littler, n.d.).

The Cuban National Ballet holds regular seasons at home and also travels all over the world. Its repertoire includes classical ballets like *Swan Lake*, *Giselle*, and *Coppellia*, and modern ballets like *Late in the Afternoon*, *Blood Wedding*, *Vital Song*, and *Carmen*. Alicia Alonso, Alberto Alonso, her husband, and Alberto Menéndez, José Parés, and others, choreograph some of the new ballets, and sometimes some of the classical ballets, too—such as

Alicia Alonso's remaking of *Swan Lake*, which was performed at Washington's Lincoln Center. Continuous official support made it possible for new dancers like Loipa Araujo, Aurora Bosch, Marta García, Jorge Esquivel, Orlando Salgado, and many others, to form a ballet company of fine quality that has gained well-deserved international recognition.

An annual international ballet festival is celebrated in Havana. This event has increased Cuba's reputation as an international ballet center. Dancers, choreographers, teachers, and directors from all over gather to see ballet companies from different countries on the stage performing new and older ballets.

Cuba's New Theater. Pre-revolutionary Cuba did not have a strong theatrical tradition. The Association for the Fomentation of the Theater, founded in 1910, was an early effort to create some theatrical interest. It was followed by the Association Pro-Cuban Theater in 1915. This group was dedicated to seeing that Cuban playwrights were included in the repertoire of foreign visiting companies. The foundation of the University of Havana Theater, directed by playwright Luis A. Baralt, contributed to increased interest in the theater, while providing the training grounds for new actors. By the late 1950s several small playhouses had been opened in Havana and were able to function with some degree of professional success. The very fact that they could continue working was in itself an important achievement. Plays like Jean Paul Sartre's *Respectful Prostitute*, and Jean Genet's *The Maids*, were major successes at the time, but Cuban playwrights' works attracted smaller audiences (Matas, 1971, pp. 428-32).

The National Theater of Cuba was opened in late 1959. The support given by the revolutionary government to the different theatrical groups raised great expectations among theater people. The enthusiasm generated among different artists with the opening of a new cultural era was extended to the theater as well. The Ministry of Education assigned cultural activities to a newly created agency, the National Council of Culture. New groups were founded, and most of the playhouses from the pre-1959 period were functioning in the early 1960s. After important early successes, the activity of the different playhouses declined later in the decade.

The Grupo Teatro Escambray (Escambray Drama Group) led to a theatrical revival in 1969 with the New Theater movement. The new plays touched upon such social and political issues as the struggle against counterrevolutionaries in the 1960-5 period in the Escambray region, the condition of women, the collectivization of dairy farming, and the problems encountered with the proselytizing activities of Jehovah's Witnesses in Cuba.

These themes had a powerful message that audiences could identify as relevant to the historical moment the country was living. This helps to explain the success that the New Theater movement had in reviving theatrical interest, and in generating a following among sectors of the public that had never been exposed to theater.

More than twenty drama groups now are part of the New Theater movement. Their artistic objective is to involve the audience in the drama played on the stage. Sometimes the performance is turned into an assembly, or ends involving the spectators with the actors in 'a dance party' (*guateque*) (Weiss, 1985, pp. 127–30).

The Union of Artists and Writers.   The National Union of Cuban Artists and Writers (UNEAC) was founded during the 1961 Congress of Writers and Artists. During most of its existence, Nicolás Guillén, the Cuban national poet, presided over it. But in 1986 an award winning writer, Lisandro Otero, became acting president. Guillén, already in his eighties and in poor health, had been unable to attend to his duties as head of UNEAC for months by then. The writer Abel Prieto was elected president in January 1988.

UNEAC's members represent all artistic specialities. Artistic quality, originality, and technical expertise in the artist's work are the criteria for admission. Its purpose is to promote artistic and literary work and to better the conditions under which artists and writers have to work. It establishes links between Cuban artists and writers and those from socialist and non-socialist countries. It publishes an art bulletin and two literary magazines, and its publishing department has the reputation of supporting a broader publication policy than the more restrictive approach followed by other publishing agencies. UNEAC sponsors art exhibits and literary and musical competitions for both professionals and amateurs.

Like other cultural and artistic organizations, UNEAC went through difficult times in the late 1960s and early 1970s. The regime's political and cultural objectives were not always in tune with artists' and writers' need for independent artistic freedom. Also, government bureaucrats, with a narrow view of the artists' needs and the revolution's best interests, compounded the problem further. A low point in this period was when homosexual artists and writers were sent to military labor camps, Military Units of Aid to Production (UMAP), to be rehabilitated. Some of them were members of El Puente, who felt they had been singled out and persecuted. UNEAC's sensible intervention on their behalf, as well as the additional pressure of an international protest, put an end to this practice (Black, *et al.*, 1976, p. 253). UMAP was terminated altogether later.

Guillén's replacement by Otero at the helm of UNEAC seems to have occurred at a critical moment, too. 'The first problem we had at UNEAC,' says Otero, 'was Nicolás Guillén's absence . . . This vacuum in leadership created a stagnating situation. UNEAC . . . wasn't functioning as it should.' In his opinion, under more difficult conditions, as when intellectuals and artists were being organized in 1961, UNEAC had functioned well. Once a Catholic intellectual asked Castro if he could 'write from a non–revolutionary, non–Marxist point of view or non–materialist point of view.' In his 'words to the intellectuals,' Castro answered by saying, 'Yes, you can, you can express whatever you want, your personal views, feelings, so long as you do not attempt to assassinate the politcial process that guarantees your freedoms.' According to Otero, '[At that] time UNEAC played a unifying role. But by the time I came to UNEAC, certain structures had broken down . . . there were too many sacred cows, too many father figures, a kind of paternalism, and there is nothing young people hate more than sacred cows . . . and the younger artists reacted against [it]' (Otero, 1987, p. 11).

UNEAC's policies and decision-making practices were changed. Otero states that

The policy we are working toward now is the democratizing of UNEAC. We want to avoid monolithic decisions. Instead of making unilateral decisions in certain areas, we have created commissions that will really work . . . There isn't an individual or a president that decides these things; rather, the group decides . . . We've tried to create a kind of legislative checks and balances system, so that the legislative checks the executive.

According to Otero, another major problem was that

Instead of acting as an ideological and cultural organization, UNEAC was turning into a business, a merchandising business, offering artistic services. It became a kind of interior decorating business . . . There were people who . . . were making a lot of money, . . . who earned 500,000 pesos in two or three years. A certain percent stayed in UNEAC, which served as the agent for these artists . . . [who altogether] were perhaps 25 individuals.

Otero explains the decisions made to improve UNEAC's record: 'We stopped the sale of these services and closed down the agency that took care of those requests, FELA (Artistic and Literary Economic Fund). It was dissolved, and these activities came to an end.' However, he said, 'The people who had made that money kept the money. This had been happening throughout '84 and '85, and we discovered it at the beginning of '86.'

Revolution and Religion

State–Church relations are different from the early 1960s, when they were characterized by mutual antagonism and confrontation. Anti-Batista activism among the members of Catholic Action student and labor groups brought many Catholics to the ranks of the revolutionaries, and Batista's police tortured and killed many of them. Castro acknowledged the Catholic contribution to the anti-Batista struggle when he stated that, 'The Catholics of Cuba have lent their most decided cooperation to the cause of liberty.' However, the Catholic Church acted contrary to these facts by either overlooking or approving militant priests and nuns promoting counter-revolution among the laity, rather than ministering to their religious needs.

The Church had supported Spain during Cuba's struggle for independence in the nineteenth century, and had continued such ties with the support many priests and nuns gave to Franco's regime. The Church hierarchy and some priests thought that revolutionary changes were too radical, but the Franco regime continued its diplomatic and commercial relations with Cuba. The Church had exercised a strong influence in Cuba for so long that its power had become ingrained in the national ethos and social order. This made accepting a role strictly limited to religious matters more difficult for the Church. After a brief initial period supporting the revolution, conservative priests and laity were united in their opposition to its radical course. Years of confrontation between the Church and the revolution ensued.

A student of Cuban State–Church relations has noted that the Church was in a state of disarray at the time of the revolutionary victory, and that there was 'growing dissatisfaction with Church leadership' by 1959. Also, 'facing stiff competition from the Protestant Churches and Santería [an Afro-Cuban folk religion], the Church was falling into an increasingly marginalized position.' It was the revolutionary victory that 'helped to reassert Catholic unity and developed an identity' (Kirk, 1985, p. 96).

In a survey conducted by the University Catholic Association in 1954, 96.5 percent answered that they believed in God's existence, but almost a fifth (19 percent) claimed to have no religion. While a quarter of the 72.5 percent who admitted being Catholic attended Sunday masses regularly, 42 percent attended irregularly, and 31 percent only every few years. Reasons for the religious detachment among the poor became clearer in a 1957 survey when only 3.4 percent of agricultural workers expected any assistance from the Catholic Church in improving their lot (Crahan, 1979, p. 171). The number of priests had decreased since the mid-1950s, which increased the priest–population ratio: one priest per 13,200 inhabitants in 1955, and one per 14,100 in 1960 (a 6.81 percent increase). But the priest–population ratio really grew under the revolution: one per 62,700 inhabitants in 1965 (a 344.6 percent increase, for a yearly average growth of 57.43 percent) (Jover Marimón, 1971, pp. 401–2).

The first decade of revolutionary rule witnessed several phases in State–Church relations: (1) mutual aceptance and cordiality (1959); (2) confrontation and antagonism (1960–1); (3) lessening of tensions (1962–4); (4) re-establishing coexistence (1965–8); and opening the Church again to dialogue (1969–). Once the hegemony of revolutionary power was well established after a bitter struggle between the Church and the regime in 1960–1, both parties gradually learned to coexist. The Church, however, could no longer enforce its own terms, so it had to accept the revolution's.

The revolution's socioeconomic policies ended the 1959 friendly phase in State–Church relations. Educational reforms affected Catholic education, while radical revolutionary change affected the interests of supporters of the Church's traditional status. A National Catholic Conference convened in Havana in November 1959 brought almost a million Catholic and non-Catholics together protesting the radicalization of the revolution. With a growing fear that exercising religious values and the practice of religion would soon be prohibited, the opposition used religion to launch a popular mobilization against the revolution in defense of the propertied class' economic interests.

No religious instruction was allowed in public schools, and parochial and non-religious private schools were nationalized after the Cuban exiles' Bay of Pigs invasion on 17 April 1961. The presence of three Spanish priests and a Methodist clergyman in the invading 2506 Brigade aggravated an already tense State–Church relationship. Several priests were arrested and the Cuban Cardinal, Monsignor Manuel Arteaga, had to seek refuge in the Argentinian embassy. Havana's Catholic University, Villanueva, was also closed. Nuns and priests, many born in Spain, and Protestant ministers began to leave the country. The closing of religious schools accelerated their departure. After a religious procession turned into an antirevolutionary demonstration in September 1961, 130 priests were expelled (approximately half of the priests left in the country). Of more than 2,500 nuns, less than one-tenth remained, approximately 200. In a few years the number of priests had gone from 723 to less than one-third that number.

Closely identified with American churches, the Cuban Protestant churches were also affected. These included 609 evangelical pastors ministering to between 150,000 to 250,000 people. In a ten-year period approximately half of Eastern Baptists, Methodist, Episcopal, and Presbyterian congregations left the island. Protestants became as involved in counterrevolutionary actions in the early 1960s as Catholics were. In an attempt to calm down a difficult situation, the regime redirected its attention after 1962 from organizations to individuals. Clergy and lay people were sent to the Military Units of Aid to Production (UMAP) to be rehabilitated politically, but they returned with divided loyalties: some became supporters of the revolution, while others deepened their sentiments against it (Black, *et al.*, 1976, pp. 129–33).

By 1965 a period of cautious coexistence between the Catholic and Protestant Churches and the revolution started, and both avoided criticizing each other openly. But relations between Havana and the Vatican had been strained. Rome showed its displeasure by downgrading its diplomatic representation in 1962. They were fully restored in 1974 when the Vatican elevated its representative, Bishop Cesare Zacchi, a skillful diplomat, to the rank of Papal Nuncio. Bishop Zacchi is credited with avoiding the worsening of a bad situation by tactfully establishing some rapport between the Church and the regime despite all the existing problems, and even developing a close relationship between himself and Castro, with whom he spent some time playing chess (Kirk, 1985, p. 101).

The Second Vatican Council (1962–5) called by Pope John XXIII also helped to change Rome's attitude towards Cuba. A dialogue between the Vatican and secular political forces committed to social welfare that began during his papacy contributed to improving Rome–Havana relations. Pope John XXIII and Castro had also opened channels of communication by writing letters to one another. Talking to a group of Cuban–American academicians in Havana in August 1980, Alfredo Guevara, then vice-Minister of Culture, said that Pope John XXIII wrote to Castro addressing his letters to 'my little son,' and that the Pope issued an invitation to Castro to visit the Vatican. Castro welcomed the Pope's invitation, but his visit to the Vatican never took place.

In the mid-1960s, after undergoing a soul-searching process, Catholic and Protestant clergy and laity recognized that socialist ethics did not conflict with their own beliefs, that the dignity of human beings was as much a core value for the revolution as it was to their own faith, and that socially conscious Christians could readily accept such revolutionary values as social equality, moral incentives, and cooperation rather than confrontation. This led to their increasing integration into the revolutionary process, paving the way for the era of greater cordiality in State–Church relations in the late 1970s, but especially in the 1980s.

The regime took important steps toward reconciliation with the Catholic and Protestant Churches. A religious procession was allowed in 1979 on the occasion of the installation of the new bishop in Pinar del Río province, the annual assembly of the Ecumenical Council was addressed by an official of the Cuban Communist Party in charge of religious affairs, and an increasing coverage of religious activities has appeared in the government controlled press (Kirk, 1985, p. 108). Christian Cuban exiles have attended numerous Catholic and Protestant conferences in Cuba strengthening their religious ties. Currently, 'there are 500 Catholic and approximately 700 Protestant churches, along with some 600 chapels, pastoral homes and missions' offering religious services (*Granma Weekly Review*, 14 February 1988, p. 12).

The Church hierarchy also undertook conciliatory steps. The Catholic pastoral letters of 1968 and 1969 marked a shift in attitudes: it ended its opposition to voluntary labor, denounced the US economic embargo of Cuba, and stated that it was necessary to respond to the economic and social problems of the population. The Catholic hierarchy produced an even more progressive document in 1976 calling for a renewal within the Church and broader social participation by the faithful. While the traditional sectors within the Church were losing ground, especially under the impact of Vatican II (1962–5), and the Latin American Conference of Bishops (CELAM) in Medellín (1968) and Puebla (1979), the progressives were gaining support. Monsignor Carlos Manuel de Céspedes, secretary of the Permanent Council of Cuban Bishops, was a decisive force behind the modernization of the Cuban Church.

Addressing a Washington audience in 1986, Monsignor Céspedes said that in his own opinion President Castro, already in his sixties, is looking to reconcile the 'different epochs of his life (which does not mean conversion).' Castro is putting together the religious education and formative years of his youth with his present Marxism–Leninism. An invaluable source for the understanding of the Cuban leader today, said Céspedes, is Friar Frei Betto's book *Fidel y la Religión* (*Fidel and Religion*), a bestseller in Cuba and Brazil. With 800,000 copies sold in Cuba of this book, stated Céspedes, it refutes the often repeated statement that the Cuban people are not interested in religion.

The Brazilian friar recorded in his book a long, candid conversation between Castro and him that took several days, and more than one trip by Betto to Cuba. Castro talks of his family life as a child, of his Catholic (Jesuit) education, of the different political influences he received during his formative years, and of his present vision that Christians and Marxists should work together for common, revolutionary goals in Latin America, and elsewhere. Also, Castro said that 'He believes that his [main] contribution to the Cuban Revolution has been to achieve a synthesis of Martí's ideas and

Marxism–Leninism, and to have applied them properly to [the Cuban revolutionary] struggle' (Betto, 1985, pp. 163–4).

The Protestant clergy also underwent important changes. The Cuban Council of Evangelical Churches (CIEC) was established with the purpose of helping member congregations adjust to the changes taking place under the revolution. Expressing a consensus among CIEC members, the head of the Council said in mid-1975, 'We feel that Marxism offers an effective methodology to carry out Christ's mandate to feed the hungry and clothe the naked' (Black, *et al*., 1976, p. 131). Although differences in the substance of Marxism and Christianity still separate them, CIEC's statement accepting similar social objectives recognized shared common grounds, which could lead to a non-adversarial, even cordial relationship between the two. The distance separating Marxism and Christianity has been closed even further with the annual celebration since 1971 of a conference seeking to bridge those differences. Pointedly, the conference is named after the martyr and revolutionary Colombian priest, Camilo Torres.

Reflecting the profound changes that have taken place in State–Church relations, the Cuban theologian Sergio Arce Martínez, who openly supports the revolution and teaches at the Protestant Seminary in Matanzas, has said:

The churches must prepare themselves for the changes in Cuba through new biblical and theological studies; a renewal of pastoral life; an analysis of their relationship to the political, economic, and social realities of both the past and the present; and a cultivation of flexibility, self-awareness, and imagination in response to the situation in contemporary Cuba . . . [Black, *et al*., 1976, pp. 132–3]

The Cuban Jewish Community.　By the time of the revolutionary victory in 1959, the Cuban Jewish community was 12,000–15,000 strong. Six synagogues and most Jewish religious, social, and commercial life were concentrated in Havana. Two waves of migration brought Jews to Cuba in the first half of the twentieth century, but the bulk of the community was formed in the 1920s. Just before and after World War I, Jews came initially from Turkey and the Eastern Mediterranean. They formed the Sephardic community (Spanish and/or *ladino* speaking, and known as *turcos*), constituting later approximately a quarter of the entire Jewish population in Cuba. Prior to and during the Second World War Jews migrated from Central and Eastern Europe, establishing the Ashkenazim community (Yiddish speaking, and known as *polacos*, a term used to refer to Jews in general). Jewish presence in Cuba can be traced, however, to the late nineteenth century, when some recently arrived Jews supported the cause of

Cuban independence. A Jewish American lawyer, Horatio Rubens, represented José Martí legally in the United States in connection with arms shipments to Cuba for the struggle against Spain (Greenberg, 1982, p. 13).

The Jewish community flourished in a relatively short period of time. There was no history of anti-Semitism in Cuba until the 1930s, when the Spanish upper class demonstrated its sympathies for Franco and Hitler, and showed its resentment for the commercial competition that some Jewish businessmen posed to its own business. But all in all, 'no one bothered the Jews as Jews.' The first arrivals concentrated on commerce and industry, but many from the second, Cuban-born generation moved into the liberal professions after graduating from Havana University.

Jewish religious life was mostly Orthodox, including both the Sephardic and Azhkenazim communities. A small group of North American Jews founded a reform temple in Havana, the United Hebrew Congregation. The Cuban B'nai B'rith Chapter was housed in this temple. The two major synagogues, built in the 1950s, are the Patronato de la Comunidad Hebrea (Ashkenazim), and the Centro Sefaradí (Sephardic). All three temples are located in the residential Vedado section of Havana. Older synagogues and social centers are located in the Habana Vieja (Old Havana) district, like the Centro Israelita, Adath Israel (Ashkenazim and Orthodox), and Chevet Ahim (Sephardic and Orthodox).

The location, character, and style of the synagogues and social centers reflected the socioeconomic development of the community. Initially, they were built in the lower income section of Old Havana, where most Jews lived at the time. Later, as many in the community became more affluent, Jews moved to the Vedado and Miramar residential sections. The temples were then built in the Vedado area, and one Jewish school, Albert Einstein, located in Miramar, was directed by a Cuban Jewish educator, David Pérez.

Relations between the Jewish community and the revolutionary government were initially very friendly. But most of the Jewish community left the country in the early 1960s. The decision to leave Cuba and migrate mostly to the United States, or to Israel or other countries, was made on economic and political, not on religious grounds. Cuba and Israel had diplomatic and consular relations, and several Israeli technical missions were sent to Cuba in the 1960s.

For the smaller part of the community that stayed behind (approximately 1,500), life became politically more difficult after Cuba announced in 1973, at the Algiers Nonaligned Summit Conference, that it had broken diplomatic relations with Israel. The issue of divided loyalties had emerged in Cuban Jewish life. An open pro-Israeli stance by Cuban Jews was not in harmony now with their true integration into the revolution, and the exercise of revolutionary *conciencia*. This sensitive problem did not alter religious life as such, however. The regime made very clear that breaking relations with Israel was a political and not a religious matter, and that while Cuba has an anti-Zionist political stand, it has never taken a position against Judaism as a religion. Hence synagogues and social centers continue open and hold religious services regularly. The problem for the community was keeping several synagogues operating with such a small number of Jews left. Reportedly, only one synagogue was offering religious services in 1988 (*Granma Weekly Review*, 14 February 1988, p. 12).

According to Dr José Miller, president of the Patronato, Cuban Jewish reaction to the regime's Israeli policy is separated from the practice of their own religion:

The foreign policy of Cuba is not a secret. That's not the question, not our business. In Cuba we have freedom of conscience. We can feel and we can speak as we want. That we do . . . Maybe some Jews share [the official] policy on Israel and some not. So this is not something we can approach as a whole. As a Cuban, I think the policy of the Cuban government is OK, but as a Jew, it's not my business.

Regarding being a Jew and having opportunities for advancement within the system, Miller states that Jews 'have taken part in socialism, they have prominent positions in the government or in political organizations; that is not new. But they aren't in touch with us . . . they never come here [to the Patronato] . . . There are no leftists in [the] community . . . because leftists don't come here.' But foreign leftists visit the Patronato when they are in Cuba, as a delegation from the Communist Party in Argentina did. [They wanted] to see how Jewish life is. But Cuban Communists don't [come],' says Miller, 'I don't know why. I would like that.'

Jewish religious life continues, but is more difficult than before to keep it alive, according to Miller.

Although . . . we pray and have services on Saturdays—for people who want to live according to Jewish customs, we really do not have a very Jewish life. That is the truth. It is difficult to have a *bris* (the traditional Jewish circumcision ceremony), or a *bar mitzvah*, or a wedding. There isn't a rabbi . . . It would be very expensive and more than we can afford . . . [There has not been one] for more than 20 years . . . [Greenberg, 1982, pp. 15–29]

However, the Patronato offers Hebrew classes to the children of the community (the teacher was born in Cuba but is not Jewish), and continues operating its library with a fine collection of Jewish literature. The library founder and director for many years was a Cuban Jewish journalist, the late Marcus Matterín.

A rabbi travelled to Cuba from the United States until the 1970s during the major Jewish holidays, Rosh Hashanah and Yom Kipur. Also, a cantor travelled to Havana on weekends and returned to Miami, where he lived for the rest of the week, in the early 1960s. But not anymore. The community has been assisted by the Canadian Jewish Congress for years, which sends matzah, meat, wine, and other kosher products at Pesach, and other Jewish holidays. Similarly to other churches and temples, the several synagogues and social centers are registered with the religious affairs section of the Central Committee of the Cuban Communist Party, which is responsible with overseeing that all religions operate freely, and for listening to and taking care of their requests and complaints.

Afro-Cuban Religions.   Among the different religions brought to Cuba from Africa, Santería (things of the saints) is probably the most widespread. It is the religion of the Lucumí, who are descendants of the Nigerian Yoruba. Another religious belief is that of the Ñáñigos, who were influenced by the Efik of eastern Nigeria, and are located in Havana and Matanzas provinces. Another religious practice is that of the Bantú and Congo, who live in the eastern provinces.

Santería offers the best example of religious syncretism, fusing both African and Roman Catholic religions into one entity. There is a duality in the practice of Santería, paralleling Catholic ritual, mythology, and saints with African practices, beliefs and spirits. This parallelism is based on the comparable existent array of Lucumí spirits and Catholic saints, and in the similar status they receive in the juxtaposition of both religions. Their names and symbols are interchanged in Santería altar rituals. In Spanish they are Catholic saints with a history of great deeds that justify their being called *santos* (saints), and in Yoruba *orishas* (spirits). As they have been elevated to the category of saints, the Lucumí spirits represent great men who have died, who were kings and founders of tribes in their lifetimes. According to the preference of the *santero* (leader or priest), the Santería ritual could follow closely the Roman Catholic ritual. It promotes, however, a hysterical atmosphere in which some of the persons present become possessed (*les dá el santo*). The possessed person takes on the personality and mannerisms, and speaks with the voice of the *orisha* (spirit) that has taken possession of his body. While remaining in a state of trance, he offers advice (acting only as a conduit, because it is the *orisha* who is 'speaking') to the persons present, who want and are expecting it (Black, *et al*., 1976, pp. 125–8).

Religious syncretism has moved in Cuba beyond its initial religious domain. African values and beliefs have had a profound impact in forming Cuban culture as well. The 'black' poetry of Nicolás Guillén and other poets brought the African roots of Cuban culture to the surface, transforming such roots into works of exemplary beauty and universal meaning. Other artists also used these religious and cultural themes in their music, literature, and paintings. Afro-Cuban religions contributed greatly to making Cuban culture richer and more expressive, expanding its appeal with its strength and magic.

It was not until the triumph of the revolution, however, that Afro-Cuban beliefs and rituals were properly treated as religions. Even though they were quite accepted by non-black population sectors (but not publicly admitted), Afro-Cuban religions were regarded as superstitious and objectionable religious practices in pre-revolutionary days. This has changed. The official policy for Afro-Cuban religions today is similar to that of other organized religions. They are treated with the same kind of respect that other religions receive from the government. As a worthy cultural expression, the Afro-Cuban heritage is also cultivated in the arts—to an extent not done before. New dance groups are centered around Afro-Cuban culture, using its music and symbols, and narrating its legends and mythology. In a memorable return to their cultural roots, Afro-Cuban dance ensembles have toured African countries with great success and general acclaim.

The vitality of Afro-Cuban cults was underscored by the current plans to hold the forthcoming Fourth International Congress of Orisha Tradition and Culture in Cuba. During a visit to Havana in 1987 of the King of the Yorubas, Alaiyeluwa Oba Okunanda Sijuwade Olubuse II, it was suggested creating a Yoruba cultural center in Cuba, that Cuban Yorubas should travel to Nigeria, and that the next congress should be held in Havana. This international event will bring together men and women, students and followers of the Yoruba culture in Cuba and elsewhere. Previous congresses have been held in Nigeria, United States, and Brazil (*Granma Weekly Review*, 28 February 1988, p. 1).

Critics of the revolution have noted that Afro-Cuban religious values have worked contrary to the successful political cultural transformation of the population sectors associated with such values. Accordingly, Marxism-Leninism as the official ideology has not been properly accepted by Afro-Cuban cults because it disagrees with their deeply seated religious values. In practice, then, dialectical materialism has not been able to conquer Afro-Cuban fantasy and beliefs (Matas, 1983, pp. 17–23). What they have not considered in their analysis, are the political and socioeconomic conditions in which blacks and other low income groups used to live before the revolution. Moreover, the revolution has provided more than just better living conditions. The Marxist–Leninist revolutionary political culture has brought into focus the realities of today's world, working as a political map to explain and describe it. Perhaps a new kind of syncretism has been in the making: Afro–Cuban religious values have been mixed with Marxist ideology, which are then acted out according to people's *conciencia*.

Military Affairs

Cuba's Revolutionary Armed Forces (FAR) were born out of the Rebel Army, Castro's fighting force in the Sierra Maestra. Despite the fact that it lacked formal training, proper material appearance, amounted to less than a tenth of Batista's 46,000–man army, and was made up of peasants and urban revolutionaries, it prevailed and won the war for the revolution. Some analysts argue, however, that the success of the revolution was not as much a military victory by Castro's forces against Batista, as it was evidence of the mounting resistance by underground revolutionary groups in the cities, and the debilitating crisis of the unpopular and corrupt Batista regime that demoralized the traditional army and turned it into a rather ineffective military outfit. But the civil war that engulfed the island by 1958 was the result of Castro's fighting in the mountains of eastern Cuba. Most likely the cumulative effect of all the different factors allowed Castro to win the war.

Rebel Army forces from the Sierra Maestra and Escambray mountains, and members of the 26 July Movement and Revolutionary Directorate urban guerrillas, were organized into the FAR in October 1959 and placed under the direction of Raúl Castro, who became Minister of the Revolutionary Armed Forces. But Fidel Castro was very much in charge as commander in chief and Prime Minister. The citizens were organized into the National Revolutionary Militia, which was responsible for mobilizing the population in defense of the country if it came under attack by internal or outside forces. The United States Central Intelligence Agency (CIA)-sponsored 1961 Bay of Pigs invasion by Cuban exiles furnished an opportunity for the civilian militia to engage in battle.

The effective organization of the FAR under Raúl Castro, including officer training in the Military Study Centers (CEM), and courses in conventional and guerrilla warfare and ideological and political education for officers and troops, provided the regime with a first–rate military structure. The FAR and popular militia combined became one of the best military establishments in Latin America, equal to those of large South American countries like Brazil and Argentina. Regime survival is normally central to all political regimes, but the defense of the revolution from actual internal and external enemies was a paramount and very real concern for the revolutionary leadership.

The revolutionary armed forces go beyond defense; they play an important political, economic, and social role. The military presence at the highest level of the PCC has decreased over the years, but it is always politically significant. This close association has allowed the military to be part of the social penetration exercised by the Communist Party in socialist Cuba. As any other governmental or political institution, the FAR should function under the party's guidance and control. President Castro's and Raúl Castro's dual roles as heads of the PCC and the armed forces have maintained the ultimate supremacy of the party (political) over the FAR (military), but at the expense of a clear distinction between the two. The regime's leadership has used either a civilian or military option in internal matters as the needs of the particular moment dictate.

The military role in economic matters was at its peak during the years leading to, and during the 1970 Ten Million Tons harvest. Political and economic analysts characterized the period as the militarization phase of the revolution. But Cuba did not become a militarized country in the true meaning of the term. It was a more case of fusing civilian and military roles into one and downplaying the importance of the distinction as irrelevant to Cuba's revolutionary needs and circumstances. The strong presence of military officers in the higher echelons of the PCC at the time and the political influence wielded by them were the outcome of this kind of practice.

The regime lacked the bureaucratic (civilian administrative) and political (Communist Party) capacity to run the Ten Million Tons campaign effectively. The only institution capable of undertaking such a complex task at the time was the military, so the regime turned to it for assistance. The administration of the economy was reorganized along military lines as a means of fostering efficiency and higher productivity. The military continues today its technical and administrative assistance in economic production, but is not involved as directly as before. It assists agriculture, construction, and an array of social tasks. It also functions, in conjunction with the Ministry of Interior, in internal surveillance, combatting hostile actions by enemies of the revolution.

PCC control over the military has been a matter of contention between political and military authorities. The FAR has protected itself from political and civilian encroachment. According to a student of Communist Party and armed forces relations,

Initially, no criticism [by the PCC] of commanding officers was allowed, though later this restriction was eased to allow criticisms of an officer's personal and political behavior. Criticism of his military performance (and especially his orders) was still proscribed . . . The party in the armed forces concentrated its energies on supportive activities (e.g. combat readiness, military maneuvers, troop morale, etc.) rather than on party control activities (political education, criticism and self-criticism, etc.). Even this limited role, however, continued to provoke criticism and resistance from some military officers . . . [LeoGrande, 1979, p. 3]

The revolution's military was modeled on the civic soldier (i.e., revolutionary military leaders ruling simultaneously over the military and civilian population). As long as the armed forces were conceived as an integral part of society, the civic soldier was fully integrated into it while providing a role model for others to emulate. President Castro's and Raúl Castro's political, administrative, and military functions created a pattern other revolutionary leaders imitated. This helped reinforce the civic soldier as a model for society, while civilian and military roles became indistinct at different levels of the regime structure. The entire phenomenon seemed a case of revolutionaries approaching the administration of government in a revolutionary fashion—the only way they knew how. Thus, differentiating between the civilian and the military issues did not seem relevant. But despite building a respectable military structure, the regime did not foster a military mindset in the traditional sense. The military was not allowed to threaten revolutionary authority, which was already both civilian and military, as represented by Castro and Raúl Castro at the top of the pyramidal structure.

Discussing the pervasiveness of the civic soldier in earlier periods of the revolution, a Cuba watcher noted,

Cuba is governed in large part (though not exclusively) by civic soldiers, that is, military men who actually rule over large sectors of military and civilian life, who are held up as symbols to be emulated by all military and civilians, who are the bearers of the revolutionary tradition and ideology, who have civilianized and politicized themselves by internalizing the norms and organization of the Communist Party and who have educated themselves to become professionals in military, political, managerial, engineering, economic and educational affairs. *Their civic and military lives are fused* . . . [Domínguez, 1974, p. 210, emphasis added.]

The institutionalization of the revolution in the 1970s meant a decrease of military involvement in non-military affairs—especially in the state administration. The outcome of such a state-building phase was the development of political and social institutions that had not been properly developed in the 1960s, or that simply did not exist then. Also, relations between the PCC and FAR changed. The FAR exercised less influence over the PCC and at the same was becoming a more professional military force.

More permanent than the civic soldier model in civilian–military relations has been the FAR's revolutionary symbolism. Imbued with revolutionary values and traditions stemming from the Sierra Maestra struggle against Batista, it has been articulated and disseminated by the regime's mass media, especially by FAR's monthly magazine, *Verde Olivo*. A main ingredient of this symbolism is the notion of the continuity of Cuban history from the nineteenth century wars to today's revolution. It includes over a century of nationalist struggle by several generations of Cubans in pursuit of their independence. Castro was linking his struggle to Martí's, and rooting it at the core of Cuba's nationalism and identity, when he proclaimed José Martí as the intellectual author of the events of 26 July 1953. The nineteenth anniversary of the attack on the Moncada barracks was celebrated with a commemorative 1972 poster portraying Martí as the 'intellectual author' of the Castro-led action that ignited the revolution. The revolution's and the military's symbolism was thus perpetuated and glorified (Judson, 1985, pp. 233–50).

Among other important values present in military symbolism is the belief that proletarian internationalism is a revolutionary duty. It is even recognized in Article 12 of the 1976 Constitution as an objective of the country's foreign policy. It legitimizes Cuba's support for Third World revolutionary regimes and wars of national liberation. The practice of proletarian internationalism represents a higher level of *conciencia* by an entire people. Cuba's wars in Angola and Ethiopia are two examples of how the country is living up to its commitment to proletarian internationalism. Its military presence in Grenada until President Reagan's 1983 invasion, and today in Nicaragua and elsewhere are additional examples. The April 1980 events in the Peruvian Embassy in Havana that led to the Mariel boatlift provoked massive demonstrations in support of the revolution: first, in front of the Peruvian Embassy, and weeks later, in May, in front of the US interest Section in Havana. A long line of unarmed veterans of international military missions was positioned in front of the US Interest Section to guard the building during the demonstration. As internationalists the veterans were the standard bearers of the nation's dignity at a difficult moment. Also, they were keeping alive, with their example to others, an important ingredient of the military's symbolism.

The FAR includes over 297,000 men and women distributed among three geographically located branches: the Western Army, Central Army, and Eastern Army. Under these three army umbrellas, each of the fourteen provinces has its own army corps. This structure frees each provincial army to operate on its own if the higher military echelon is disabled by the enemy. The Navy's personnel is close to 10,000 and the air force and antiaircraft forces exceed 20,000. The active reserve force is over 100,000. The combined strength of the newly organized territorial militias alone exceeds the 100,000 level—each territorial militia outfit is responsible for the defense of a given territory.

Also, the Youth Labor Army (EJT) is a 100,000 strong work-force made up of young recruits working under the direction of the armed forces Ministry. As a civilian-military force, EJT recruits perform such civic action tasks as building roads, clearing land, constructing buildings, cutting sugar cane, and others. The Youth Labor Army provides significant services to the national economy in addition to its character formation and educational function (Black, *et al*., 1976, p. 462; Sweet, 1980, p. 10).

The FAR's military equipment is supplied by the Soviet Union and other socialist countries. It is free of charge and modern. In 1959–75 socialist military aid was estimated at $2.5 to $3 billion ($166 million to $200 million per year). In a five year period, 1981–5, military aid was estimated at $4.010 billion ($802 million per year): $3.5 billion (87.2 percent) from the Soviet Union, $40 million (0.9 percent) from Poland, $160 million (4 percent) from Czechoslovakia, and $310 million (8 percent) from other socialist countries. Arms imports in 1985 were valued at $800 million—9.3 percent of $8.616 billion of total imports (it was 8.59 percent in 1984).

Socialist countries also provide technical advice on military matters, including administrative, organizational, and tactical questions, and new weapon systems training. The military share of the national budget is rather large by Latin American standards. Military expenditures for 1984 were estimated at $1.6 billion (5.94 percent of an estimated $26,920 billion Gross National Product), which amounts to $154 defense spending per person. The expenditure ratio amounts to $5,089 per soldier (ranking eighty-ninth out of 144 countries) and the military ratio per 1,000 people is 29.72 (ranking seventh out of 144 countries) (US Arms Control and Disarmament Agency, 1987, pp. 16–17, 71–145; see Table 8.2).

Cuba's military forces have been capable of guaranteeing the nation's security and of projecting the internationalist values and objectives of the revolution abroad. Their main objective is still to defend the country from the threat posed by the United States, which has been, and continues to be, the major enemy of the revolution. They also guard the country from attacks

Table 8.2 Cuba's ranking by military and other variables, 1984*

Military and other variables	Total and ratios†	Ranking
Military expenditures (ME)	$1.600 b.	45
Arms imports	$700 m.	13
Arms exports	$10 m.	41
Gross National Product (GNP)	$26.920 b.	52
Central government expenditures (CGE)	NA	42
Armed forces (AF)	297,000	22
Population	9,990,000	60
ME/GNP	5.94%	37
ME/CGE	NA	67
ME per capita	$154	40
ME per capita	$5,207	89
Armed forces per 1,000 people	29.72%	7
Arms imports/total imports	8.59%	31
Arms exports/total exports	0.16%	40
GNP per capita	$2,603	49
CGE per capita	NA	41
CGE/GNP	NA	24

* Cuba's ranking out of 144 countries.

† Dollars are in 1984 prices, except Central Government Expenditures (CGE), which are in 1983 dollars.

Source: US Arms Control and Disarmament Agency, *World Military Expenditures and Arms Transfers 1986*, Washington, Defense Program and Analysis Division, 1987, pp. 16–19.

by Cuban exiles, although the counterrevolution has not been a major problem since the 1960s. Cuba's military capability has provided the necessary wherewithal to advance foreign policy objectives, either by acting alone or together with the Soviet Union. Cuba's international standing has increased as a result of the prowess demonstrated by its military in Third World conflicts. Its military missions include countries extending from Latin America to Africa, the Middle East, and Asia. Cuba's internationalism has been served well by its revolutionary armed forces.

9 International Relations

Pre-1959 Foreign Policy

Cuba's strategic location in the Caribbean has always made it attractive to major powers; i.e., Spain, the United States, and the Soviet Union. It has also prompted Cubans to be in close contact with other countries and political leaders throughout their history so they could escape the isolation thrust upon them by their insularity. An internationalist outlook and practice have existed all along in Cuban history. Its independence was fought using hemispheric connections through which Latin America and the United States became closely involved. Cuban exile communities in Tampa, New York, and other cities were operating from American soil prior to US military involvement in the Spanish–Cuban–American war in 1898. For over half a century, 1902–58, the Cuban Republic was a faithful ally of the United States. Havana's stand on major international issues was usually in agreement with Washington's wishes.

Within a limited foreign-policy context, a tradition of internationalism existed before 1959, but without the ideological conviction and commitment associated with it under revolutionary rule. Cuba's internationalism is not a revolutionary aberration; what has changed is its meaning and direction. It is known now as proletarian internationalism with a clear social-class, anti-imperialist, pro-Third World, and socialist character. Its purpose is to support revolutionary and progressive regimes, and national liberation movements, and to bind Cuba to fellow socialist countries. However, some of these issues were present in Cuban internationalism before (with no ties to the socialist bloc, of course), but to a lesser degree and without the clear direction of today.

During the early years of the Cuban Republic, 'international relations expanded on two levels: first, formal policymaking was carried out by a corrupt and firmly implanted group of politicians (supported by the United States), and, second, informally, a network of opposition (including the student movement, the Anarchist–Syndicalist movement, and the Cuban Communist Party) was making international contacts' (Falk, 1986, p. 11).

The Sixth Pan-American Conference was held in Havana in 1928. Cuba joined a five-member peace-keeping international commission that mediated the Chaco War between Paraguay and Bolivia (1932–5). The

Machado regime had undertaken those international initiatives at a time of increasing domestic repression, while still enjoying US support. Fear of American renewed military intervention fueled opposition to the Platt Amendment, but the issue was not solved until May 1934, when it was finally abrogated. In the Spanish Civil War (1936–9) over a hundred Cubans, members of the Communist Party, fought in defense of the Republic. Right-wing political factions supported Franco's Nationalists but did not participate in the war.

Members of President C. Prío Socarrás' (1948–52) Auténtico party were associated with the antidictatorial Caribbean Legion, which included social democrats committed to end the several dictatorships in Central America and the Caribbean that existed in the 1940s and 1950s. José António Echeverria, assassinated by Batista's police on 10 March 1957, during the attack against the Presidential Palace by the Revolutionary Directorate, had led a group of Havana University students to Costa Rica in 1955 in support of José Figueres, and fought alongside his forces. President Figueres (1953–8, 1970–5) was putting down an invasion from Nicaragua organized by dictator Anastasio ('Tacho') Somoza García. Somoza García resented Figueres' association with the Caribbean Legion, and the Legion's activities against his dictatorship. Acting characteristically, Somoza García organized an ill-fated expedition of Costa Rican exiles to overthrow Costa Rican democratic government.

When young, Castro had been involved with a group of Cuban political activists in 1947 in the Cayo Confites expedition to overthrow the Dominican dictator, Rafael L. Trujillo. He was also allegedly involved in a 1948 demonstration in Bogota protesting the Ninth International Conference of American States that created the Organization of American States (OAS). The disturbances that resulted from the assassination of Colombian Liberal political leader J. E. Gaitán, caused so much urban destruction at the time that it came to be known as the *Bogotazo*.

Cuban support for Puerto Rico dates from the nineteenth century. For Martí the struggle for Cuban independence was also for Puerto Rico's. Puerto Ricans fought alongside Cubans for Cuba's independence. Puerto Rican poet Lola Rodríguez de Tió (1843–1924), who lived for many years in Cuba and died there, united both islands in her poem, 'Cuba and Puerto Rico':

> Cuba and Puerto Rico are
> The two wings of a bird
> They receive flowers and bullets
> On the very same heart.

When Pedro Albizu Campos (1891–1965), Harvard-educated lawyer and Puerto Rico's independence leader, was jailed for the Nationalist uprising of 30 October 1950, the then Cuban President Prío Socarrás intervened on his behalf. After having surrendered to the police, Albizu Campos was sentenced to several years' imprisonment for armed insurrection. He died shortly after he was set free. Support for Puerto Rico's independence has never been as strong in Cuba as under revolutionary rule, however.

Foreign Policy Principles

According to Carlos Rafael Rodríguez, Cuba's Vice President, the revolution's approach to foreign policy-making is based on the Marxist notion linking historical development to the ongoing national and international social-class struggle. Since 1917, when the Bolshevik revolution took place, such a struggle has symbolized a major world contradiction: the confrontation between socialism and capitalism. For the Cuban leaders, this means that the history of humanity inevitably leads to socialism. But this ultimate conclusion does not happen inexorably, or as a mechanical outcome all by itself. Men's struggle (subjective element) pursuing socialist goals is necessary in addition to the actual conditions (objective element) that make this development possible. A conscious action from revolutionaries, acting at the national and international level, is always necessary to advance the socialist struggle from being just a possibility to an actual reality (Rodríguez, 1981, pp. 10–11).

Marx stated, says Rodríguez, that man's social consciousness is not determined by his social conditions, but that his social conditions determine his social consciousness. Under Cuba's present system, its social and economic conditions determine the kind of social consciousness which provides collective support to the regime's foreign policy, and especially to proletarian internationalism. When properly conceived and implemented, such a world outlook is equally supported by the leadership and the masses. They are all motivated by equal social conditions, even if their level of revolutionary alertness and commitment differ from one another. After almost three decades of revolutionary rule, the leadership continues to play the vanguard role directing the course of the revolution and setting up its policy agenda.

Socialist solidarity from the Soviet Union and other socialist countries has helped to defend Cuba militarily and to sustain it economically. This is recognized in the Preamble to the 1976 Constitution, 'We, Cuban citizens . . .

basing ourselves on proletarian internationalism, on the fraternal friendship, help, and cooperation of the Soviet Union and other socialist countries, and on the solidarity of the workers and the peoples of Latin America and the world ... [have] decided to carry forward [our] triumphant Revolution' (Simons, 1980, pp. 100–1).

The regime's Marxist-Leninist ideology might explain some of the similarities between certain Cuban foreign-policy goals and those of the Soviet Union. It might explain, too, why Cuba has changed its strategy in Latin America—from supporting revolutionary movements to favoring establishing diplomatic relations with existent regimes. 'Cuba and the Soviet Union,' says Rodríguez, 'are socialist countries whose leaders follow the same Marxist-Leninist principles that guide them in their theoretical analyses.' Hence, it is logical that both nations, after having evaluated relevant issues from a common perspective, would arrive at similar conclusions. But it would be wrong, states the Cuban leader, to conclude because of this that their foreign policies are identical. Besides its own idiosyncratic characteristics, each regime operates within its own social context, which mirrors its own historical traditions. Also, their different stages of economic development determine the extent and nature of their own foreign policy initiatives, even if such actions still reflect common ideological commitments (Rodríguez, 1979, pp. 14–15).

According to Rodríguez, Cuba's policy strategy in Latin America in the 1960s, the 1970s, and now in the 1980s, has changed according to internal and external changes, but not because it has compromised its principles. Cuba's changing strategy reflects the changes in its own political and socioeconomic reality as well as Latin America's (Rodríguez, 1979, pp. 15–16). While Marxist-Leninist principles always play a central role in guiding the regime's foreign-policy analysis, it is the world's changing political reality that provides the catalyst for its international policy. Cuba's early support for revolutionary movements in Latin America was a principled defensive policy, born out of the 'hot war' conditions that Washington's anti-Cuba policies had created. The defeat of the counterrevolution in the 1960s, and the improving economic conditions of the 1970s, made possible a new hemispheric policy. The ensuing policy changes were based more then on the newly created hemispheric conditions than on ideology *per se*. Hence the exercise of revolutionary pragmatism. But in both cases, argues Rodríguez, policy strategies were arrived at after using Marxism–Leninism as a tool for guiding the theoretical and empirical study of existent international conditions.

Cuba's African policy since the 1970s was interpreted by its critics as an opportunistic change of scenery after Cuba had experienced several setbacks in Latin America. But this was a gross mistake, states Rodríguez,

It is a capricious interpretation from those who cannot understand the global coherence of Cuba's foreign policy, which is exercised when we speak at the United Nations in favor of disarmament, or when our military fight in Ethiopia or Angola, or when our diplomats defend the independence of Puerto Rico to the Yankees' chagrin.

And yet, he adds, Washington wanted later to single out Cuba for the Nicaraguan revolution. But it had to admit that there were several Latin American countries with different political and economic systems—i.e., Panama, Mexico, Venezuela, and Costa Rica—which had given support to the Nicaraguan revolutionaries, too.

Cuba could not be accused this time of subverting the order in Latin America. Nicaragua has been the Bay of Pigs' [Cuba] and Punta del Este's [Uruguay] counterpart, the revenge of the Dominicans suffocated by Yankee interventionism [in 1965], and the revindication of the principles defended by Cuba in Latin America. [Rodríguez, 1979, p. 17]

Another dimension of Cuba's strategic foreign policy vision is its relationship with capitalist nations, including highly industrialized ones. '[We] do not approach all capitalist regimes alike,' states Rodríguez, 'Even with those states that still are part of the imperialist system as a whole . . . [our] policy is the end product of a fluid evaluation differentiating among the diverse policies upheld by the different capitalist states.' Rodríguez adds that, 'this is [also] part of the irrefutable proof that we would like to have normal relations with all nations in the international community, including the United States' (Rodríguez, 1981, p. 31).

Revolution and Foreign Policy

One of the most important and constructive political aspects of the revolution is its foreign policy. The importance of the revolution itself, and the fact that Cuba has projected its own image world-wide since 1959, have given a geographically small country with a population that just recently reached ten million an international stature that only larger nations, or major powers enjoy. Paradoxically, the debate on the nature and objectives of Cuba's international relations, also increases the controversial nature of Cuban politics in some quarters.

Naturally, the immediate and major impact of the revolution and its foreign policy was in Latin America. Turning the South American Andes into a new Sierra Maestra, was the revolutionary cry in the western hemisphere after Castro's victory. The 1960s witnessed a revolutionary drive in the continent that led to Che Guevara's death in Bolivia in 1967. After the demise of the 'heroic guerrila,' Cuba's effort to export its revolution dwindled. Paradoxically, it was later in the 1970s when Cuba was deeply involved in Africa, that Central America's poverty, underdevelopment, and dependency syndrome finally burst into a revolutionary wave that provoked Washington's harsh response, leading to a new interventionist era under President Reagan.

Whether Cuba has a foreign policy of its own, the product of a truly independent polity, or not has been often debated. US officials and mass media commentators argue that it is not as much a Cuban foreign policy, as it is a Cuban–Soviet foreign policy—with Moscow dictating to Havana the course of action and defining political goals. Never mind that in almost three decades Cuba has proven itself as a highly nationalistic, independent country with a revolutionary leadership that has not hesitated to defy its major benefactor, the Soviet Union, on different occasions. Thus, for others, Havana is not doing the Soviet Union's bidding as its surrogate, but is acting on its own as an independent policy-maker. 'Cuba's public split with the Soviets in 1967 over the issue of armed struggle in Latin America is only the most dramatic example of numerous Cuban–Soviet disagreements over the past two decades of alliance' (Robbins, 1985, p. 280). In April 1982 a group of US foreign-policy specialists attended a Havana conference in which they were told by government officials that '[Cuba] disapproved of the Soviet invasion of Afghanistan . . . [and that] it would like the Soviet Union to stay out of Poland' (Azicri, 1985a, p. 186).

This long-debated issue is answered by most scholars confirming the independent nature of Cuba's foreign policy. And yet, a well-known Cubanologist raises a skeptical voice: 'I began by noting,' he writes in a review of scholarly works on Cuba, 'the debate over whether or not Cuba dictates its own foreign policy, with most scholars concluding that it does. In fact, no one really knows . . . A fair criticism of all of this scholarship (including my own) would be that authors often write with more confidence than the sources warrant' (Domínguez, 1988, p. 201).

But an insightful study of Cuban foreign policy after looking into its complex nature states that,

Any interpretation of Cuban foreign policy that focuses solely on Cuba's post-1959 ideological commitment to Marxism fails to understand the complex and subtle interplay of the currents that feed both this foreign policy and Cuba's ideological commitment to Communism. Such a narrow focus ignores Cuba's strong loyalties to the Soviet Union, Castro's own brand of Western defiance and nationalism, and the international visibility and leverage that a controversial foreign policy gives Cuba. *Washington too often forgets Cuban history*; Cuban–American writers and Cuban politicians both recall the legends of a vehemently nationalistic José Martí. [Falk, 1986, p. 151; emphasis added]

None the less, some individuals find it hard to accept that such a small country, with the need for economic support and aid, could be an independent international actor. On this, however, as on so many other subjects, Cuba has confounded its detractors. After all these years Castro and the Cuban revolution remain an incomprehensible mystery for many, including policy-makers and political analysts in the West, especially in the United States. It appears to be one more price that Cuba's socialist revolution pays for not fitting into a preconceived analytical mold, and, more importantly, for having changed the rules by which Caribbean and Central American countries conduct themselves, particularly regarding their relations with the United States.

Cuba's nationalism finds an important outlet in its foreign policy (Erisman, 1985). Rather than acting as a Soviet surrogate, Havana's globalist undertakings are an expression of its own world vision. This vision emanates from its own internal social order which is then projected on an international and global scale. Cuba's proletarian internationalism is then both a national duty (repaying the support received from socialist countries by helping other revolutionary regimes and national liberation movements) and the projection of its nationalist revolutionary will beyond its own borders.

In the time spanning from Martí's nationalism to Castro's Marxism–Leninism, an array of personalities, events, and diverse political forces have contributed to shape twentieth-century Cuba's world outlook. This outlook has provided a historic rationale for today's foreign policy.

Washington Versus Havana

Cuba's major foreign-policy problem is its relationship with the United States (or lack thereof). Since the triumph of the revolution this has been a central political concern for both Havana and Washington. Reflecting on the American perspective of this political problem, a scholar noted, 'Of the proverbial thorns in the side of the United States, none has irritated as long or sometimes as much as Cuba. A distinct Cuban policy and with it an identifiable "Cuban problem" has characterized official and private attitudes of Americans since the first years of the republic' (Langley, 1973, p. 1).

Under President Reagan, the antagonism of earlier days has returned with vengeance. For the United States, in addition to purely bilateral questions, Cuba's standing in regional (particularly Central American) and other Third World conflicts (particularly in Angola and Ethiopia), and its close ties (particularly military) with the Soviet Union and other socialist countries are among the outstanding issues awaiting a solution in Havana–Washington's conflictive agenda.

American and Cuban negotiating positions have changed on some issues over the years, while others have remained constant. For Cuba, the issues include: (1) ending the economic embargo and all other forms of commercial pressure; (2) ending all forms of subversive activities; (3) ending pirate attacks against Cuba from US bases in Florida and elsewhere; (4) ending all violations of Cuban air and naval space; and (5) returning the US Guantánamo Naval Base to the Cuban government. For the United States, the issues include: (1) financial compensation for confiscated American properties; (2) ensuring human rights; (3) ceasing participation in any kind of violence in the western hemisphere; (4) removing troops from Angola and Ethiopia; and (5) ending Cuba's close association with the Soviet Union, particularly militarily.

An important reason for Cuba to be so actively engaged in international politics has been to offset American emnity. Castro neutralized some of the negative impact of Washington's anti-Cuba policy by reaching out to other nations. Avoiding being isolated in the international arena became synonymous with survival. Havana's motivation to join the socialist bloc of nations in partnership and as the privileged recipient of assistance and protection could be partly explained by Cuba's 'American problem.'

A scholar and former American diplomat links Washington's Cuba policy to Havana's ties to Moscow explaining it as an action–reaction–response policy process:

The gulf between the United States and Castro's Cuba is not imaginary. Castro's early goals were nothing less than to extend revolution throughout Latin America and in the process to challenge US influence. In response to this out-thrusting on Castro's part, we felt we had to 'contain' Cuba. It was this mix of his goals and our reaction to them that led Castro to align with the Soviet Union . . . Hence, he turned to the Soviets for protection, eventually embracing Marxism–Leninism in an effort to assure that protection. [Smith, 1987, p. 278]

Havana–Washington's politics of hostility has managed to perpetuate itself. For Washington, if Cuba could only be 'immobilized' in international affairs, its socialist regime could become more palatable. It could even try to live with it. For Cuba, a real rapprochement with the 'colossus of the North' would mean that, in addition to accepting Cuba's socialist system, Washington had come to terms with Havana's global activism and commitment to proletarian internationalism, and had learned to deal with Cuba on equal terms and with mutual respect.

Cuba's support of wars of national liberation and anti-imperialist movements and regimes has been a major obstacle to a renewal of diplomatic relations between the countries. Washington has objected vigorously to what it considers unacceptable standards of international behavior by Castro in the Third World, especially in Latin America and Africa. In the summer of 1983, American diplomat John Ferch protested Cuba's proletarian internationalism at an international seminar held in Havana. Ferch, head of the US Interests Section in Havana (1982–5) until he became Ambassador to Honduras, was dismissed later as US envoy to Tegucigalpa by Assistant Secretary of State for Inter-American Affairs Elliott Abrams for not enforcing the Administration's Contra policy vigorously enough. Ferch asked the audience gathered at the seminar sponsored by Cuba's Centro de Estudios Sobre América (The American Study Center) if Havana's policy of interfering in other countries' internal affairs in pursuance of proletarian internationalism was lawful. He answered his own question by saying that it was not, and that it violated international law.

Paradoxically, the doctrine of low-intensity conflict practiced by the Reagan Administration has deprived Washington of a compelling argument against Castro's global activism. Support for the Contras in Nicaragua and 'freedom fighters' in other Third World countries is a violation of international law. But in this case the violator is the United States. It has reversed its traditional opposition to subversive revolutionary behavior, and modified its standing as a law-abiding nation.

On 27 June 1986, the International Court of Justice ruled that Washington was in violation of international law for its anti-Nicaragua policy which included supporting and aiding military and paramilitary forces by arming, training, financing, supplying, and directing them. It ordered the US government to cease supporting the Contras and to pay compensation to Nicaragua for the damages caused by its policy. The World Court's decision constituted a historic indictment of Reagan's subversive and unlawful actions against Nicaragua. US response, ignoring the World Court's ruling and continuing its Contra policy, made things worse. It undermined further the rule of law in international relations, and made US objections to Castro's support for revolutionary movements and regimes look at best hypocritical.

Cuba readjusted reluctantly to a new cycle of unproductive hostility with the Reagan Administration, fearing that the limited gains achieved under President Jimmy Carter might slip away. These included the opening of Interests Sections in each other's capitals in 1977; Washington's lifting of the ban on American citizens traveling to Cuba, and spending US dollars while visiting the island; and the visit by Cuban–Americans to their relatives back home, which had followed the Dialogue Conference held in Havana in November and December 1978, between representatives of the Cuban–American community and the Cuban government.

Castro attempted to aid Carter's re-election by calling off on 26 September 1980 the Mariel boatlift that had started on 21 April. Cuban refugees had been arriving in southern Florida throughout the summer following the events started at the Peruvian Embassy in Havana on 4 April. It had turned by September into a costly embarrassment to Carter. A year later, at the opening session of the Inter-Parliamentary Conference held in Havana on 15 September 1981, Castro showed his frustration by voicing his opinion of President Reagan and his Administration:

The US system is not fascist, but I am deeply convinced that the group which constitutes the main core of the current US administration is fascist; its thinking is fascist; its arrogant rejection of every human rights policy is fascist; its foreign policy is fascist; its contempt for world peace is fascist; its intransigent refusal to seek and find formulas for honorable coexistence among states is fascist. [*Granma Weekly Review*, 27 September 1981, pp. 2–4]

In 1987, well into the second Reagan Administration, Castro's opinion of Reagan and his policies had tempered, but he was still critical,

[Reagan] is skillful, he communicates well with the masses; . . . [He] has exercised great influence . . . [He] knew how to exploit US frustrations, its defeat in Viet Nam; . . . he extolled its chauvinism, its nationalism, and has imposed a costly arms race. Also, [Reagan] has established costly economic guidelines; [he] overvalued the dollar, raised interests, collected money from everybody, subsidized military expenditures, raised the national debt to two billion dollars in a few years . . . I believe that he will leave an ominous burden to the American people . . . [T]hat is what I think of his policies.

And regarding Reagan's persona,

I used to think that he was consistent, but I am disappointed. I used to say: he is reactionary but he believes in his policies, he is consistent. He likes to portray the image of a strong man, in one word, of a *cowboy*. But when the problems come, like the Iran–Contra scandal . . . he looks for scapegoats, lets others take the blame and denies that he knew what was going on, something that no one believes. [Miná, 1987, pp. 86–7]

Radio Martí and Human Rights

The Reagan Administration had come to office with several policy options towards Cuba: (1) military warfare (under Secretary of State Alexander Haig, 1981–2, the threat of military action looked not rhetorical but quite real); (2) psychological warfare (the threat of punitive action was also seen as mainly a war of nerves aimed at keeping Castro off balance to inhibit him from carrying out his policies); (3) economic warfare (tightening the US economic embargo originally imposed under President Kennedy); and (4) diplomatic and political warfare (reviving the Truman Doctrine used in Europe in the 1940s, but applying it this time to Nicaragua, Central American leftist guerrillas, Grenada, and Cuba, while the East–West conflict was blamed for the region's turmoil) (Azicri, 1983).

Other initiatives undertaken later by the Administration were to establish a radio station, Radio Martí, to broadcast news to Cuba in opposition to the Castro regime, and to launch a campaign in the United Nations charging Cuba with violating human rights. After effective lobbying by the Cuban American National Foundation, an association of wealthy Miami-based Cuban–Americans closely linked to the Reagan Administration, and its director, Jorge Más Canosa, Radio Martí was at last approved by the US Congress (Nichols, 1984). It finally went on the air on 20 May 1985. Radio Martí's immediate effect was to make Cuba cancel the immigration agreement Havana and Washington had reached in December 1984. When the agreement was finally reinstituted in late 1987 the Cuban inmates in federal prisons in Atlanta and Louisiana rioted in protest. They had been imprisoned since their arrival in the United States, in the Mariel boatlift under charges of having criminal records, but refused to return to Cuba.

Radio Martí ran into internal problems of its own under charges of censoring news, irregularities, and permitting Miami radio stations to broadcast some of its programs in violation of the statute that had placed Radio Martí under the administrative restrictions of the United States Information Agency, and the Voice of America. A subcommittee of the House of Representatives and the General Accounting Office have already begun an investigation. Nineteen employees signed a complaint alleging 'administrative irregularities.' Miami bureau chief, Hilda Inclán, resigned in September 1987 after accusing Radio Martí's director, Ernesto Betancourt, of censoring news coverage—Betancourt calls it 'selective coverage.' 'Inclán suspects that the station is engaged in "intelligence gathering". Betancourt says it isn't' (Zaldívar, 4 January 1988). And yet, there were plans in 1988 to expand Radio Martí into a television station, under the assumption that adding anti-Castro television programs to radio broadcasting would have a bigger impact on the Cuban population.

The United Nations Human Rights Commission has been the arena of heavy anti-Castro diplomatic maneuvering by the Reagan Administration since 1986. Washington has been proposing for two years that the Commission investigate Cuba's human rights record and has spared no efforts in its diplomatic campaign. The United States delegation is headed by a Cuban-born former political prisoner, Armando Valladares, who was granted American citizenship in record time. After having traveled there especially for the occasion, President Reagan's daughter, Maureen Reagan, was standing next to Valladares at the podium of the Commission in Geneva when the decision was announced. The Commission decided to approve by consensus a compromise resolution sponsored by Colombia and other Latin American countries. The resolution agreed that the chairman of the 43-nation Human Rights Commission and five other members would travel to Cuba and report their findings to the Commission in 1989. Initially proposed by Havana this resolution had had in it the provision that the United States should withdraw its initial condemnatory resolution.

The final resolution saved commission members from having to choose between Havana's or Washington's feuding positions. For Cuba's Deputy Foreign Minister, Raúl Roa Kourí, 'The outcome shows our continent's growing political unity . . . Cuba could not accept being put in the dark by a Government which has been trying to overthrow it for the last 25 years.' But the US delegation claimed victory, too. 'This was not a spontaneous and voluntary offer by Cuba,' said Valladares. 'The Cubans knew they would lose if we went to a vote' (*New York Times*, 11 March 1988).

After the decision was announced, the Reagan Administration continued its campaign by trying to influence the selection of the Commission members who would travel to Cuba to examine the country's human rights record. Evidently, there is considerable political capital at stake here. The Commission's report could answer the Cuban human rights controversy factually and definitely enough to prove that it has just been a scheme contrived by the Reagan Administration. Contrariwise, it could prove that there is substance in the charges brought against Cuba. But it could also be inconclusive enough for both sides to claim victory. Most likely, the issue will not be put to rest by the Commission's report alone.

Meanwhile, Cuba has responded with a national and international campaign of its own. Castro told Italian journalist Gianni Miná emphatically that,

This might be the only revolution in the world—and we know history very well—that has never used violence against a prisoner, or someone who has been arrested. In all these campaigns they are accusing us of torturing prisoners. I can say: not only after the triumph of the revolution, but not even in our war of liberation was one single prisoner ever tortured, not even when someone could have justified it as necessary to save our soldiers or win a battle. There was not a single case ... Our revolution took place because of certain ideas and values ... [which are] in opposition to crime and torture ... [*Granma Weekly Review*, 6 March 1988, p. 3]

Havana also exposed in its public campaign Washington's behind the scene maneuvers pressuring Commission members to vote against Cuba. As reported in the Cuban mass media:

We must not forget the shameless manner in which the head of the US delegation, the impostor Valladares, warned that India had not received 15 million dollars worth of US aid last year because it had sponsored a motion to block action on a similar US resolution at the Human Rights Commission session last year ... [*Granma Weekly Review*, 20 March 1988, p. 1]

After almost three decades of mutual animosity, the real challenge for Cuba and the United States is to learn how to move 'from confrontation to negotiation.' There are organized groups in the United States, however, that would rather see the politics of hostility between Havana and Washington continuing into the 1990s, and beyond (The Cuban American National Foundation, 1988). But in the eventuality that the road to normalizing relations is finally taken some ideas should still be kept in mind:

Two lessons stand out from prior efforts at accommodation. First, delay works against the process, because domestic political opposition builds as the process goes forward. Second, political leaders should not raise public expectations too high. The antagonisms and differences between the United States and Cuba have been built up over many years and run deep. Many of these are likely to remain, even after a normal relationship is established ... [Brenner, 1988, p. 89]

Many academics and laymen have been concerned with the issue of normalizing relations between the countries, and some have even labored to accomplish such an elusive goal. But as a student of Cuban affairs notes, 'Although scholars commonly have little impact on US policy toward Latin America, their inability to affect even the terms of discussion of Cuban issues surpasses their usual political irrelevance' (Domínguez, 1988, p. 196).

Cuba and the Soviet Union

Cuba's economy is integrated with socialist countries' economies through the Council of Mutual Economic Assistance (COMECON), and is politically aligned with the socialist bloc. According to some analysts, Cuba gains an economic payoff from the Soviet Union stemming from its activist brand of foreign policy. Hence, by increasing its leverage with Moscow, Havana is in a position to extract better trade agreements and wider support from its major partner. Without the Soviet Union's needed resources, Cuba could not afford to have this kind of foreign policy, especially engaging in such military undertakings as it has done in Angola and Ethiopia, where Cuban troops and major Soviet resources are being used.

After being disseminated in US official statements and through the media, the image of Cuba as a dependent Soviet surrogate lives on. The rationale behind the notion that Cuba acts as a Soviet surrogate is that Havana is paying back the Soviet Union for its largess in supporting its increasing economic needs by doing whatever demanding tasks are needed in the Third World. As a member of President Carter's National Security Council put it, 'The Soviet Union cannot undertake the kinds of activities and operations in the Third World that the Cubans do routinely without provoking global tensions and perhaps a response from the United States or the People's Republic of China' (Pastor, 1983, p. 207). Hence, the argument goes, Moscow relies on Havana to have such tasks accomplished using Soviet resources, rather than doing them itself. The commonsensical nature of this argument makes it hard for Western analysts to resist, even if it obscures reality instead of clarifying it: 'Of all the myths about Cuba, this one is the most prevalent . . . The logic of the "Cubans as pawns" argument is compelling' (Robbins, 1985, p. 280).

The nature of the Havana–Moscow relationship cannot be explained by simply applying dependency or surrogate concepts which stem from the market economies–Third World relationship: major powers *vis-à-vis* their dependent clients. The bedrock of the Cuba–Soviet relationship is their common socioeconomic objectives, ideological agreement, and the knowledge that they are both struggling, together with other nations, to change the present international order into one in which socialism will prevail. By sharing these objectives Cuba and the Soviet Union have gained an affinity that is not easily found elsewhere. Their political relationship is more subtle and complex than the dependency–surrogate syndrome explains.

Castro has said that the practice of mutual solidarity among socialist nations imposes no restrictions on a country's independence. 'It is impossible to question our country's independence, its own [independent] criteria, and its principled foreign policy,' he stated (Miná, 1987, p. 106). Thus the Havana–Moscow relationship is also seen as a mutually advantageous agreement from which a symbiotic interaction stems, with each side seeking to compensate for its own weaknesses or shortcomings by gaining from the other's strength or resources.

The Havana–Moscow connection has baffled political analysts for a long time. It was surmised in a study that 'Cuba is neither a "puppet," a nation whose policies are "prompted and controlled" by the Soviets, nor a "partner".' But neither is Cuba then a surrogate or proxy. This would also be inadequate, since 'it suggests that the Cubans are acting only in the Soviets' interests, whereas they are clearly acting in their own as well.' In this analysis, the Cubans appear motivated by three main interests: egoism, nationalism, and ideology (Pastor, 1983, p. 206).

Routinely, Cuban–Soviet relations are closely examined. They seem to fluctuate from agreement, to accommodation, and then to discord. As long as the outside world has no access to internal sources overt clues are used. Whether protocol is followed in formal ceremonies plays a major role in figuring the state of such relations. When Castro failed to attend the funeral of Konstantin Chernenko in 1985, Mikhail Gorbachëv's predecessor, it was undertood that the Soviets had been snubbed by him. But a warming trend was then noticed in 1986 at Cuba's Third Party Congress. Castro and Yegor Ligachev, the number two man in the Politburo at the time, who headed the Soviet delegation, had high praise for each other's countries using the occasion to its full potential. Then Castro attended the 27th Congress of the Communist Party of the Soviet Union, which was held just a few weeks after the Cuban Party Congress. The fact that Castro was awarded a place of honor among the visiting dignitaries, and that he paid tribute to Gorbachëv's report to the Congress, served to reinforce the warming trend notion (Duncan, 1986, p. 45).

But when Castro traveled to Moscow to participate in the celebration of the seventieth anniversary of the Soviet revolution in 1987, and upon returning to Havana gave a positive report of his visit, this was seen as him taking a 'defensive' public posture. The reason for this was that although relations are not really that good, the Cuban leader was pretending otherwise for state interests, and appearances' sake. A major clue behind this reasoning was Castro's late arrival in Moscow on 4 November, two days after the solemn ceremony opening the festivities. But fueling such speculations is the different direction taken by Moscow and Havana, and the effect that this might have on their relationship. While the Soviets are following

Gorbachëv's *perestroika* and *glasnost*, the Cubans are currently involved in the 'rectification process' announced in 1986 at the Third Party Congress.

As far as interpreting events by overt clues goes, for Western analysts the question is how much credence they are willing to give to Soviet and Cuban statements on the state of their relationship. Do they believe the assertion that every country has the right to follow its own path, and that socialism is not an ironclad formula applied equally and mechanically? The fact remains that Cuban–Soviet relations have had ups and downs since 1959, and might have more in the future. Once this fact is recognized and the reasons behind it understood, the question of whether Cuba has its own foreign policy independently from the Soviet Union is answered affirmatively.

The Revolution and Latin America

The triumph of Fidel Castro and his guerrillas on 1 January 1959 was a historic event not only for Cuba but for all Latin America. The first decade of revolutionary rule was marked by Havana's efforts to export its revolution to other countries in the western hemisphere. The attempt has been character-ized as 'romantic and relatively unsophisticated . . . [Cuba] endorsed virtually all . . . [guerrilla movements] and provided material assistance to most, regardless of how weak or miniscule they were' (LeoGrande, 1986, p. 230). Havana formalized this policy with such initiatives as the Tricontinental Conference (1966), and the foundation of the Organization of Latin American Solidarity, OLAS (1967).

Under US auspices, the Organization of American States's (OAS) foreign ministers voted 14 to 6 for Cuba's expulsion from the organization (Argentina, Bolivia, Brazil, Chile, Ecuador, and Mexico voted against the resolution), in a meeting held in Punta del Este, Uruguay (22–31 January 1962). On 26 July 1964, the OAS voted 15 to 4 to terminate all trade and diplomatic relations with Cuba (Bolivia, Chile, Mexico, and Uruguay voted against it, but only Mexico did not break relations with Havana). Cuba intensified its support for revolutionary movements in response to Washington's policy isolating the revolution from the rest of the hemisphere. But the effort was dampened after the death of Che Guevara in Bolivia in 1967. By the end of the decade Cuba had retreated from supporting revolutionary groups in Central America and South America; an introspec-tive mood had turned attention to internal matters.

Ricardo Alarcón, Deputy Foreign Minister, explains the reasons behind Havana's Latin American policy that dominated the 1970s: 'A serious foreign policy, like ours, must take into consideration the objective reality in which it takes place, as well as its evolution, and tendencies . . . We do not ignore those changes; that is a flaw of Yankee policy, not of ours.'

Havana's drive in the earlier part of the decade to re-establish relations with neighboring countries was implemented after weighing carefully how receptive they would be to such a policy: 'The main problem [was] to see if new conditions had been created allowing Cuba, with reasonable expectations of success, to pursue a policy aimed at reestablishing relations with other Latin American countries' (Alarcón, 1985, p. 316). It paid off handsomely. In 1972 Havana had relations with only two countries (Mexico and Chile), but in three years they had increased to eleven, and other nations had indicated that they were seriously considering normalizing relations.

Moreover, on 29 July 1975, the OAS by a vote of 16 to 3 (with 2 abstentions) voted to terminate diplomatic and trade sanctions. Each individual country was to re-establish relations 'at the level and in the form that each state deems convenient' (Franklin, 1984, p. 23: 1975). The US economic embargo continued, but Washington announced that it was granting licenses to foreign subsidiaries of American firms selling goods to Cuba. Despite these important political changes, Cuba's opposition to the OAS continued. It refused to even consider returning to it. Instead, Havana favored establishing the Organization of Revolutionary States of Latin America, or the Union of Peoples of Latin America.

The Reagan Administration encouraged Latin American countries to take anti-Cuban stands. Colombia in March 1981, and Jamaica in October of the same year, severed diplomatic relations with Havana. A conference held in Cancún, Mexico, in June 1981, to discuss relations between developed and underdeveloped countries, did not invite Cuba to participate despite the fact that President Castro was the Chairman of the Non-Aligned Movement at the time. President Reagan attended the meeting on condition that Castro not be invited. Washington's support for the regime in El Salvador fighting leftist guerrillas and the anti-Sandinista Contra war were also aimed against Cuba. The 1983 invasion of Grenada was directed against Castro even more. In 1987 Costa Rica voted in Geneva in support of the US resolution denouncing Cuba for human rights violations.

The 1982 Malvinas (Falkland) Islands war between Argentina and England was a turning point in Latin American relations with Washington, which had sided with London against Buenos Aires. The war put in motion a new phase of hemispheric unity that fostered warming relations with the Castro regime. An important outcome of this new phase of Latin American diplomatic activism was the Contadora diplomatic initiative. It brought together

Mexico, Venezuela, Colombia, and Panama in January 1983, seeking peaceful solutions to the Central American crisis. This ran contrary to Reagan's Contra war. Later, in August 1987, the Central American countries agreed on a peace plan proposed by the President of Costa Rica, Oscar Arias. This was another reversal for Washington's policies of rolling back by military means revolutionary regimes and movements in the hemisphere. Cuba endorsed both the Contadora process and the Arias Peace Plan.

By 1987 Cuba had diplomatic relations with twelve countries in Latin America and the English Caribbean: Mexico, Bolivia, Uruguay, Brazil, Ecuador, Peru, Argentina, Panama, Nicaragua, Guyana, Barbados, and Trinidad and Tobago. There were no diplomatic relations with the Dominican Republic, but lower level exchanges existed including sports and cultural programs (*Granma Weekly Review*, 31 May 1987, p. 9). The most northward country in the western hemisphere, Canada, always kept full diplomatic, trade, and cultural relations with Havana.

Nicaragua

The triumph of the Nicaraguan revolution on 19 July 1979 was the kind of victory that Cuba had been yearning for all along. Twenty years after Castro came to power, a new generation of revolutionaries had overthrown a corrupt, tyrannical, pro-US dictator, Anastasio Somoza Debayle. And this time it happened on Central American soil. Somoza Debayle was the heir of a dynasty established in 1934 by his father, Anastasio Somoza García. As head of the American-trained National Guard, Somoza García became Nicaragua's strongman after Washington withdrew its troops in 1933. Under Somoza García's orders, the National Guard assassinated Agusto César Sandino on 21 February 1934. Since 1927, Sandino had been fighting the American Marines occupying his country but had stopped fighting after their withdrawal. The assassination began a forty-five year dictatorship that lasted until the 1979 Sandinista victory.

The Sandinista National Liberation Front (FSLN) was founded in 1961 in Honduras by Carlos Fonseca Amador, Silvio Mayorga, and Tomás Borge. Cuba supported the FSLN throughout the 1960s providing it with arms and training. But under the Latin American policy of the 1970s, material support for revolutionary groups had stopped, including that for the FSLN. However, political support and moral solidarity never ceased. Cuba also provided sanctuary to Nicaraguan revolutionaries; a place where they could travel to rest, reorganize themselves, and plan new strategies. Castro 'urged the Sandinistas to play down the Marxist nature of their programs and to form a broad united front with members of the Nicaraguan business, professional, and landowning communities that opposed Somoza' (Robbins, 1985, p. 248). Not until 1978 did Cuba reverse itself and begin again to provide material support to the FSLN. Havana realized then that it had underestimated the depth of the Nicaraguan struggle and the extent of revolutionary conditions in Central America (LeoGrande, 1986, pp. 232–3).

Only a week after their victory, a delegation of Nicaraguan revolutionaries joined Castro in Holguín, Cuba, during the celebration of the 26 July anniversary. Three FSLN commanders, Humberto Ortega, Bayardo Arce, and Carlos Nuñez; two members of the Nicaraguan Government of National Reconstruction, Moisés Hassán and Alfonso Robelo; and twenty-six Sandinista commandos, had come to Cuba to rejoice in their triumph. It was a moment of unity for Latin American revolutionaries. But it was not long before one of the Nicaraguan leaders, Robelo, would join the Contras in their war against the FSLN. On 19 July 1980, Castro traveled to Managua to celebrate the first anniversary of the Sandinista victory.

Cuba provided massive support to Nicaragua in the form of teachers, medical doctors, technicians in different fields, and material resources. Havana's expertise played an important role in carrying out the literacy campaign launched in 1980. Thousands of urban and rural Nicaraguans learned to read and write. The Reagan Administration's Contra policy made military assistance to the Sandinista regime an urgent matter. Havana played a central role in helping Managua defend itself from Reagan's Contra war. Cuba's experience in combating CIA schemes for over two decades proved to be a valuable asset to the Sandinistas. Two Latin American revolutionary regimes found themselves fighting side by side against a common enemy. The significance of this historic development was not lost in Latin America, or elsewhere.

Defeat in Grenada

After Che Guevara was killed in Bolivia in 1967 and Chilean President Salvador Allende in 1973, the worst setback Cuba suffered in its international relations was the US invasion of Grenada on 25 October 1983. Maurice Bishop and his New Jewel Movement had overthrown Eric Gairy's corrupt dictatorial regime on 13 March 1979. As Prime Minister of the newly established People's Revolutionary Government (PRG), Bishop established relations with Cuba on 14 April and presided over the ceremony to signify the special relationship between both countries.

Grenada was the fifth member of the Caribbean Community

(CARICOM) to establish diplomatic relations with Havana, but this time it was different. While Bishop denounced US policies in the region, Cuba sent aid missions to Grenada. The two countries developed very close ties rapidly. 'Cuba's presence in Grenada was limited but real ... Grenada's militia followed Cuba's line of domestic surveillance similar to that of the Committee for the Defense of the Revolution (CDR)' (Falk, 1986, p. 47).

Cuba provided military assistance to Grenada. But it also provided assistance to build a new airport near St George's, Grenada's capital. Cuba sent over six hundred workers to build the airport at Point Salines, and offered to cover part of the estimated $50 million cost. The United States objected to Grenada's new airport, and especially to the role Cuba was playing in its construction. Bishop's assurances that it was necessary to develop a tourist industry, and that England had a direct part in the construction and future management of the airport did not assuage Washington.

President Reagan, addressing the nation on national television, pointed out the threat posed to the security of the United States by an airport with a 10,000 foot runway on an island with little more than 100,000 inhabitants. However, 'Testifying before the Subcommittee on Inter-American Affairs of the House Committee on Foreign Affairs in the spring of 1980, Martin Scheina and Colonel Ralph Martinez-Boucher of the Defense Intelligence Agency both denied that the Cuban-built airport in Grenada would constitute a security threat to the United States' (Robbins, 1985, p. 243).

Bishop was placed under house arrest on 13 October 1983 by General Hudson Austin, the Commander of Grenada's People's Revolutionary Army. In the previous month Bishop and Deputy Prime Minister Bernard Coard had had a disagreement. Coard, following a harder line than Bishop, favored a political system organized along more strict Marxist-Leninist lines, and closer ties with the Soviet Union. On 19 October, after having momentarily been freed by supporters, Bishop was recaptured and executed. General Austin had been installed as head of a sixteen-member Military Revolutionary Council, which had taken over power. Six days later, President Reagan ordered the invasion. Over fifty Cubans and more than a hundred Grenadians died fighting the invasion, and over a hundred American troops were killed or wounded.

Larry Speaks, President Reagan's spokesman for six years (1981–7), asked rhetorically whether the invasion of Grenada was necessary: 'Did we need to invade Grenada? I'm not so sure we did.' He added:

We were claiming ... that the OECS [Organization of Eastern Caribbean States] had invited us to participate in the invasion. The truth of the matter is that on Sunday, October 23, the day the 'invitation' was issued, a representative of President Reagan

. . . was on hand at the OECS meeting in Bridgetown, Barbados—just to make sure that when the invitation was issued, it was sent to the right address. You might also say that we RSVP'ed in advance.

Regarding the safety of the American medical students, a prime justification by the Administration for the invasion: 'President Reagan himself admitted to the press that the Americans on the island "were in no danger in the sense of that, right now, anything was being done to them . . . This was a case of not waiting until something actually happended to them"' (Speaks, 1988, pp. 160–1). Paradoxically, one of the inspirations in Bishop's life had been Martin Luther King and the US civil rights movement.

(Thomas) Tip O'Neill, Speaker of the US House of Representatives for ten years (1977–87), has also given his recollection of the events preceding the invasion, and how he learned about it from President Reagan in a meeting at the White House,

[Jim] Baker [then White House Chief of Staff] told me to report to the side door of the Executive Office Building at ten minutes to eight. On the way over, I said to Kirk [O'Donnell; O'Neill's general consul and advisor] 'I don't know what this is about, but I bet we're invading Grenada'.
[O'Donnell:] 'Grenada? You can't be serious'.
[O'Neill:] 'I am' . . . 'I just have a feeling about it. The administration has been wanting to go in there for a long time. . . .'
[O'Donnell:] 'Then you don't think the meeting is about Lebanon?'
[O'Neill:] 'Sure I do' . . . 'They're invading Grenada so people will forget what happened yesterday in Beirut'. [241 U.S. Marines were killed in Beirut on 23 October 1983, when a truck full of explosives was driven into their compound.] As far as I can see, it was all because the White House wanted the country to forget about the tragedy in Beirut. [O'Neill, 1987, pp. 364–7]

Cuba felt deeply the bitterness and humiliation of the Grenada defeat. 'According to one Cuban diplomat: "We were badly shaken by what happened in Grenada. It was the first time since 1961 that we fought the US directly and we lost. We know that we can't defend other countries against direct US aggression"' (Robbins, 1985, pp. 353–4). But Grenada was more than a political setback for Cuba. Bishop and Castro were very close friends. The death of the Grenadian Prime Minister was a personal loss for the Cuban President, and to a large extent, for the Cuban people as well. Recognizing that the events leading to Bishop's arrest, his tragic and untimely death, and what happened afterwards had been played out under circumstances that Cuba would have opposed and would have tried to stop at all costs, Castro was reported saying later: 'The revolution had committed suicide . . . We would have reduced our cooperation' (Falk, 1986, p. 47).

Crafting a Central American Policy

The Sandinista victory in Nicaragua had a major impact in Latin America, but particularly in Central America. The winds of revolution were blowing strong in the region. El Salvador was reaching a point close to Nicaragua's in the last year of Somoza, and Guatemala was going through a renewal of a guerrilla struggle that had ravaged the country for years. For Cuba it was a momentous occasion with a potential for great happenings but serious danger as well. Returning to the detached policy of the early 1970s was out of the question in the face of current events. Moving into an all-out support for the guerrillas in Central America could have the effect of provoking Washington into a repressive response that could put in danger the revolutionary struggle in El Salvador and Guatemala, and even the revolutionary government in Nicaragua. A policy of cautious support for the Central American guerrillas and vigorous support for Nicaragua was followed. The Carter Administration understood this, and did not appear to be overtly concerned about Cuban activism in Central America at the time (LeoGrande, 1986, pp. 236–7).

The tenuous balance between the different actors in the region in 1979 and 1980 was broken with the election of Ronald Reagan as President of the United States in November 1980. Knowing of his conservative and anti-revolutionary ideological and policy commitments, the Salvadorean guerrillas wanted to present the new American president with a *fait accompli*: a revolutionary victory in El Salvador, similar to Nicaragua's, before he entered office in January 1981.

The Salvadorean 'final offensive' was born, and Nicaragua and Cuba agreed to help. Military hardware moved into El Salvador at a lower level than the Reagan Administration claimed afterwards to justify its massive support for the military regime's repressive anti-insurgency campaign, but the guerrillas received military aid from Managua and Havana. Cuba and Nicaragua later acknowledged having sent aid. But the revolutionary offensive failed. Before leaving office, Carter renewed military aid to El Salvador, which was escalated to unprecedented heights under Reagan. The new US President wanted to abort a revolutionary victory in El Salvador and in the region at large, and to punish Nicaragua and Cuba for having given aid to the Salvadorean guerrillas. The Cuban Central American policy of cautious involvement seemed to be in disarray. But Havana kept its priorities straight: a comprehensive support for Nicaragua, and political and moral support for the Salvadorean guerrillas. In Central America in the 1980s, a return to the policy of the 1960s, with total involvement and romantic expectations of a successful outcome in the near future, was a total impossibility. In the context of prevailing political realities, the support given to the guerrillas' 'final offensive' in El Salvador had to be an aberration, and nothing more.

Washington's charges of Cuba's involvement in Costa Rica and Honduras lacked evidence and credibility. There was no guerrilla insurgency in either country. Honduras was being used by the Reagan Administration as a military enclave for its Contra policy which created increasing resentment by the population. Anti-American sentiment was on the rise. But a broadly based support for guerrilla warfare was not there, despite the interventionist policy of the Reagan Administration and the inimical effect it had on the country's transition to civil rule. Behind poorly kept appearances, in Honduras the military continued ruling under the advice of the US ambassador, perhaps more than before.

Costa Rica had exercised regional leadership seeking a peaceful solution to the Central American crisis under President Arias. The terrorist incidents of 1984 were attributable to the Contra presence in Costa Rica. President Luis Alberto Monge (Arias' predecessor) had allowed the country to be used by the United States as the southern flank of its Contra policy. This created a deep turmoil in Costa Rican social and political life. Contrary to political tradition, terrorist incidents took place in opposition to the Contra policy and Costa Rica's backhanded involvement with it. But this was ended under President Arias. He had even neutralized the internal opposition to his brand of diplomatic activism after having received the Nobel Peace Prize in 1987.

Castro was on record in support of the Arias plan. Cuba's Central American policy supported a peaceful solution to the regional crisis. Its rationale was that 1987–8 was a time to consolidate the Nicaraguan revolution, while the progressive forces in the region could advance politically if a window was opened for them. Although Washington and its Central American political and military allies did not see it this way, this was a moment for creative diplomacy, when non-violent political solutions could have been reached for the benefit of the Central American people.

Cuba in Africa

While Cuba was less involved in Central America in the early 1970s, it was then that it became heavily involved in Africa—or when its involvement seemed to matter most. This was not the first time Cuba had become entangled in African affairs. While Che Guevara's historic African tour in

1964–5 laid the foundation for an internationalist policy in the continent, Cuba's involvement had preceded it. In the second year of revolutionary rule, Cuba was already supporting the Algerian Liberation Front (FLN) with military and medical supplies. It established a military mission in Ghana from 1961 to 1965, and another in Algeria under Ben Bella, from its independence until 1965. The first time Cuban troops were deployed overseas was during the Algerian–Moroccan border war in 1963, in which a Cuban batallion participated in support of Algeria (LeoGrande, 1982, p. 18).

Even though it failed to draw much attention at the time, Cuba's involvement in Africa in the 1960s was significant. In retrospect, it seems 'particularly ironic in the case of Cuba's African involvements, which were substantially greater than any of its involvements in Latin America. Over a thousand Cuban advisers were sent to Africa during the 1960s, as compared to several hundred to Latin America for the same period' (Robbins, 1985, p. 58).

In October–November 1975 Cuba started sending troops to Angola in support of Dr Antonio Agostinho Neto's Popular Movement for the Liberation of Angola (MPLA). Its earlier military involvement was limited to some advisers and training personnel. But Neto requested Cuban troops in desperation: forces of the rival National Front for the Liberation of Angola (FNLA) led by Holden Roberto were advancing and challenging Neto's. Roberto was backed strongly by Peking, Zaïre, and the United States. Also, another group, Jonas Savimbi's National Union for the Total Independence of Angola (UNITA), was operating in the Western part of the country, and Savimbi was supported by South Africa and Peking (and after 1975 by the United States).

The deployment of Cuban troops in Angola was incremental, and it followed a fast pace: from eighty-two men departing from Cuba to Angola on 7 November, the numbers increased rapidly to 4,000. Later, 5,000 to 7,000 additional troops were flown in using Soviet transport, increasing to approximately 18,000 strong, their numbers varying as some returned home and others were replaced. Cuba stated repeatedly that it was its own decision to support Neto with troops in the face of an invasion of South African troops launched from Namibia on 23 October and of mounting attacks by the externally supported Roberto's FNLA and Savimbi's UNITA. Hence, seemingly the Soviet Union's involvement in Angola followed the Cuban initiative. For Havana, Angola represented a major victory for its African policy, enhancing its Third World leadership aspirations.

The United States accused Cuba of having violated the agreement announced in Alvor, Portugal, on 15 January 1974, which had been signed by the three contending groups. According to the Alvor Agreement, the three groups would determine in negotiations with the Portuguese the terms of Angolan independence. Also, it was agreed that a provisional government representing the three groups would hold power until elections were held. Responding to Castro's successful intervention supporting Neto's MPLA, President G. Ford called the Cuban government a 'regime of aggression,' and referred more specifically to Castro as 'an international outlaw.'

But the recollection of events by former US diplomat Wayne S. Smith does not agree with the Ford Administration's charges. According to Smith,

One would have expected the US to back [the Alvor Agreement] to the full and to urge other interested parties—such as Moscow, Havana, and Pretoria—to respect it also and keep hands off. Instead, incredibly, the Ford Administration moved to do the exact opposite, to shred the Alvor Agreement. It did not even wait a decent interval to see if the agreement might work; only days after the Alvor Agreement had been signed, the National Security Council's 40 Committee (which oversees clandestine CIA operations) authorized some $300,000 in covert aid to Holden Roberto. (The CIA had earlier supported Roberto without the committee's authorization.) Kissinger later insisted that the money was given for political purposes only, but such an assertion is hardly credible. Certainly Holden Roberto did not use it for political purposes. . . . The US, then, was instrumental in shattering the Alvor Agreement and starting the bloody civil war that was to rage in Angola well into 1976 . . . [It] bothered me deeply . . . the obvious willingness of senior levels of the US government to lie to the American people. And this soon after Watergate . . . [Smith, 1987, pp. 95–8]

The Clark Amendment banning aid to insurgent forces in Angola was repealed in 1986 at the request of the White House. Savimbi's UNITA had been fighting the Luanda regime with South African support; now it would receive US military support. While visiting Washington in 1986 Savimbi was received in the White House by Reagan. Conservative groups gave him a hero's welcome and praised him as a Third World liberator.

The question of Namibia has been linked to the presence of Cuban troops in Angola. In violation of United States Resolution 435, South Africa continues occupying Namibia. Although Pretoria accepted Resolution 435 in principle, it has refused to implement it while Cuban troops remain in Angola. But in May 1988, representatives of Angola, South Africa, and Cuba met in London in the presence of US Assistant Secretary of State for African Affairs, Chester A. Crocker. After two days of negotiations it was announced that progress had been made, and that more meetings would be held (Lewis, 1988, p. 29). If the talks are successful, an agreement would bring a final resolution to the Angola–Namibia problem. Namibia could become an independent nation after the South African occupation ends, the Cuban troops could finally withdraw, and the civil war that has been ravaging Angola for almost fifteen years could come to an end.

Another major Cuban military intervention in Africa took place in Ethiopia. In January–March 1978, during the Carter Administration, fighting side by side with Soviet and Ethiopian armed forces, Cuban troops became involved in the Ogaden desert war. They had been sent to Ethiopia to support the revolutionary government headed by Lieutenant Colonel Mengistu Haile Marian. In a five-month period, from December 1977 to April 1978, Cuban troops increased forty times, from 400 to approximately 16,000. The war had been started by Somalia, which sent troops to the Ogaden to validate its claim for the region, based on the fact that its population was mostly of Somali ancestry.

Havana had been reluctant to enter this conflict. Somalia was a fellow Third World country, and a former Cuban and Soviet ally, although by the time of the war it had changed sides, asking and receiving support from the United States. On 15 March 1978, Castro stated his government position: 'we deeply regret the conflict between Somalia and Ethiopia; we did all we could to avoid it ... to prevent the leadership of Somalia, with its territorial ambitions and aggressive attitude, from going over to imperialism. We were not able to prevent it' (Azicri, 1980c, p. 50).

Later, however, the Cuban support for Mengistu's campaign against Ethiopia's rebellious northern province of Eritrea contradicted Havana's self-imposed limited role in Ethiopia. Furthermore, Cuba had supported the Eritrean separatist movement, which protested the annexation of the province in 1962 by Ethiopia, after Eritrea had been federated in 1952.

The Cuban military fought well; the 'required time to turn the war around was just seven weeks in Ethiopia, but seventeen in Angola' (Valdés, 1982, p. 76). Even though the Cuban, Soviet, and Ethiopian troops prevailed in the Ogaden war with Somalia, Ethiopia did not represent the same kind of victory that Cuba had achieved in Angola. In the latter, Cuba had acted as a Third World champion fighting against imperialist forces, but in Ethiopia the conflict was between two Third World nations, and the Soviet Union had been involved militarily in the conflict even before Cuba was. Hence Ethiopia lacked the luster of the Angolan victory. The Angolan and Ethiopian conflicts marked the highest point of Cuban military involvement in Africa in the 1970s, and since. Reportedly, Cuban military personnel was close in number in both countries (somewhat higher in Angola), but the civilian personnel was seventeen times higher in Angola than in Ethiopia (Domínguez, 1982b, p. 123).

There were other military involvements in Africa, such as support for the Patriotic Front in Zimbabwe and the South West African People's Organization (SWAPO) in Namibia. By the late 1970s, Cuban 'military and foreign-aid personnel were posted in over two dozen countries in Africa, Asia, and the Americas' (Domínguez, 1982b, p. 107).

Castro's Third World Leadership

Cuba is a founding member of the Nonaligned Movement, and in 1979 hosted its Sixth Summit Meeting in Havana. For the following three years and some months, until the Seventh Summit was held in India in 1983, President Castro presided over the Nonaligned Movement and spoke on its behalf on several occasions, including a major speech delivered before the United Nations in October 1979. At the Seventh Summit Meeting in New Dehli, presided over by Indira Gandhi, Castro offered a written report as outgoing chairman of the Nonaligned Movement (Castro, 1983).

The report had been written under Castro's direction by a staff of social scientists from Cuba and other countries, and it detailed in scholarly fashion the main socioeconomic problems affecting the developing nations, especially in their exchanges with industrialized nations (i.e., external debt, commodity trade problems, food production, health and education, military expenditures, and others). The study examined the plight of the Third World and the facts behind the nonaligned campaign calling for a new international economic order.

While the United States and other Western nations and some conservative members of the Nonaligned Movement have taken issue with Cuba's close association with socialist nations while continuing its nonaligned status, for Cuba this is a spurious issue. Havana claims that socialist countries, particularly the Soviet Union, are the natural allies of the Third World—especially when developing nations face an economic and political confrontation with market economy nations, as they do today. Cuba's position on this issue was not fully accepted by nonaligned countries. It caused disagreement among the delegates attending the Havana Summit, but it has gained credibility among some Third World nations since. The Reagan Administration's interventionism in Central America and in other areas has prompted some Third World nations to reexamine Cuba's position. The issue might be brought up again at future nonaligned meetings.

Cuba's role as a leader of the Third World and the champion of the radical version of nonalignment actually started in 1959. Attending the First

Nonaligned Conference in Belgrade in 1961 was the natural thing for the revolutionary government to do. Cuba's revolution without frontiers and globalist politics, according to political scientist H. Michael Erisman, has followed a series of four consecutive phases. The early phase ran from 1959 to 1972 and included a stage of romantic radicalism followed by retrenchment and reconciliation. A second phase, of incipient globalism, ran from 1972 to 1975. At this stage Cuba increasingly dedicated itself to Third World and nonaligned issues. The North–South question was more pressing than the ongoing East–West conflict. A maturation stage started the third phase, from 1975 to 1979. Cuban globalism went into high gear during this period, particularly in Africa.

Cuba's assistance to developing nations was technical (teachers, medical doctors, engineers), as well as military. A final phase of contemporary globalism started in 1979 and continued into the 1980s. Castro could boast in his 1980 May Day speech that at that very moment 50,000 Cubans were fulfilling internationalist missions in thirty-five countries (Erisman, 1985). Two thousand Cuban medical doctors and public health workers were stationed in twenty-five Third World countries, said Castro in 1985 (Cebrián, 1985, p. 6). While the focus of attention had moved from Africa and the Middle East to Central America and the Caribbean, and there was an interventionist administration in Washington ready to accept that a military solution to many Third World problems was a desirable option, Cuban globalism continued as strong as ever.

But Cuba suffered setbacks as well. The 1979 Soviet invasion of Afghanistan was a costly experience for its leadership ambitions in the Third World. It lost an opportunity to gain a seat at the influential United Nations Security Council because of it. Paradoxically, this happened at the moment when Castro was the Chairman of the Nonaligned Movement and his personal standing in the Third World was at a peak. A Cuban military defector, General Rafael del Pino, has called Cuba's prolonged military presence in Angola 'a Cuban Vietnam' (*Cambio 16*, 13 July 1987, pp. 84–5). Although hyperbolic, del Pino's statement serves to underscore the fact that foreign interventions tend to reach a point of diminishing returns. The aura of victory is replaced by the daily administrative tasks of managing the technical and military programs to prop up a troubled ally. Also, the human cost of a protracted war wears thin the initial fervor that follows the decision to get involved in the first place. On the other hand, Cuba's commitment to proletarian internationalism proves itself not so much in the euphoria of the initial victory, but in the arduous and tedious sacrifices that come later.

Cuba's Third World advocacy has been effective in the 1980s on the external debt issue. The radical solutions advocated by President Castro (i.e., asking for a moratorium in servicing the debt, or, better, its entire cancellation, and that private banks be paid from the defense budget of the two superpowers) have not been followed as such by any debtor country so far (the fear of retaliation from lending institutions is too strong, among other reasons), or by the superpowers themselves. However, Cuba has contributed more than any other developing nation in calling world attention to this critical problem. And even if they seemed initially too radical, the ideas built into Castro's proposed solutions have been used with important modifications by such debtor nations as Brazil, Argentina, and Peru. A growing consensus that the external debt cannot be paid as it stands today validates Cuba's standing on this issue. In addition to the international external debt conference held in Havana in the summer of 1985, Castro has spoken in more press conferences and given more talks on the subject than any other world leader. Without a doubt he is a major authority on the external debt problem, including its causes and its political and socioeconomic consequences.

What Castro has been warning the world community about is that, if this problem is not dealt with properly, social turmoil in the Third World, which might easily involve the industrialized nations as well, is in store. Asked by a journalist from EFE, the Spanish news agency, 'If the flames go up, [will it] really burn[?]', Castro said: 'I simply analyze the problem and say with absolute conviction what will happen if this situation continues. I think the explosive situation can ease if the debt is canceled in one way or another, by agreement between the parties or by a decision of the debtors' (Castro, 1985, p. 49). And as he told a leading Spanish journalist on another occasion,

The only alternative for Latin America is not paying the debt. I am not talking about Cuba; its convertible currency debt is relatively small, and it is one of the few countries that wants to, and can afford to pay it without major sacrifices. I am not saying that not paying the debt is the solution to the problems of Latin America, but it is a beginning. As far as the private banks are concerned, the industrialized nations can absorb the debt, which is not as large as the moneys used for military expenses. In one single year they spend more money for defense than the entire debt accumulated by the Third World. [Cebrián, 1985, pp. 6–7]

The Soviets started withdrawing troops from Afghanistan on 15 May 1988, and planned to have it completed in nine months. They left behind more than 10,000 Soviet casualties; a weak regime in Kabul by most accounts; and a diplomatically and politically costly venture that provoked a United Nations resolution, overwhelmingly supported by Third World nations, condemning the Soviet military incursion into Afghanistan in December

1979. Without any new hurdles coming from the socialist camp (like the Soviet military intervention in Afghanistan), Cuba's prospects as a Third World leader are promising. Today the developing nations need a champion more than ever, and Castro seems to fit the part.

10 Conclusions

Cuba's social, economic, and political changes will be discussed in this chapter based on the material presented in earlier chapters. Following a brief discussion of the colonial and the early republican experience (1902–58), the changes that have taken place in society, the political system, the economic system, and in foreign policy under revolutionary rule will be evaluated. The three decades of revolutionary government, the 1960s, the 1970s, and the present decade of the 1980s, will be examined according to the four change areas.

Cuba's strategic geographical location has been central to its historical development. It is surrounded by, or close to, the Caribbean Sea, the Gulf of Mexico, the Atlantic, and the Panama Canal. Mexico, the United States, and Haiti are close neighbors. Given the relatively short distance separating Cuba from Florida, eventually their histories were bound to become closely connected, as they are today. Florida has been home for Cuban *émigrés* in colonial and republican periods, and expeditions and attacks against Cuba have been launched from it. The Cuban–American community in southern Florida represents a population of Cuban stock that is larger than the population of many Cuban cities.

Its people and culture are influenced by and have influenced the colorful traditions and culture that together make up the mosaic of Caribbean islands. Cuba's insularity has both protected and isolated it. And this has also forced Cuba to reach out to its immediate neighbors, and beyond. Havana is Cuban, Caribbean, African, Spanish, and, as a result, very cosmopolitan. Visiting Cuba while *en route* to Europe from Mexico or the United States, or vice versa, was an attractive idea for the traveler. It was always a worthwhile addition to his itinerary. And, in return, the visitor would enrich the local culture, making it less parochial, more worldly. But only a few visitors would take the time to learn about the real Cuba, looking under the glossy façade of postcard appearances and learning about its culture and national ethos, and of its yearning to achieve mature nationhood and true independence. Nor would most visitors learn of its desire to escape from being a major power's colonial or semicolonial enclave, thus to gain the respect of others and its own sense of dignity.

The answer to the intriguing question of why this island, no bigger than the US state of Pennsylvania, has always had such an international profile, lies in the diverse ingredients that together have historically shared in forming Cuba's culture and nationality. And it lies mostly in the Cuban revolution, the most important event in the island's contemporary history. Cuba's twentieth century is divided into two epochs: before and after 1959. It is not an exaggeration to say that to some extent this is also true of Latin America. Even though Cuba's stature in the world today is largely due to its revolution and the fact that it is the first socialist state in the western hemisphere, it appears that the island spent most of its history preparing itself for the role it is playing on the world scene today.

The Ever-faithful Island of Cuba

When the British captured Havana militarily in 1762, the population fought against the English-speaking occupying army. However, Havana learned to trade freely for a year under British rule. When Spain re-established its old trade restrictions, the population could compare notes on colonial abuse, and some Cubans started to realize that their allegiance to Spain was misplaced; the metropolis did not deserve their loyalty. But during the next century, Cuba's loyalty to Spain was never questioned: it always was, and would always be, the 'ever-faithful island of Cuba' to Madrid.

The Spanish colonial experience of Cuba was complex and contradictory. It meant economic exploitation, social prejudice, racism and slavery, religious bigotry, and lack of political rights for the Cuban-born population. But besides its poor record as a colonial power, Spain also provided the foundation of the emerging Cuban nationality. Spanish culture and values and love for the humanities were brought to, and planted in, the island. And they flourished while creating a new culture. Not surprisingly, after an initial hesitation, writers, poets, teachers, and even scientists emerged and helped in the formation of the new nation in the eighteenth and nineteenth centuries. They provided the foundation for the nation's twentieth-century culture.

Cuba's cultural traits, values, and behavioral patterns—both conscious and subliminal—are traceable to its Spanish heritage and to the mix that emerged from the influx of Africans brought into the country, who enriched the island's ethnic and cultural mixture. Both ethnicity and color were central factors in allocating roles in a highly stratified and racist society. Racial prejudice became institutionalized. It added another layer to the discrimination already practiced against those born in Cuba, while the Spanish born enjoyed all sorts of privileges. Racial prejudice survived the colonial period, living well into the twentieth century. Politically, the colonial years were an exercise in authoritarian rule and abuse of power. They left ingrained in the collective psyche a desideratum for *caudillo* worship that undermined representative democratic government.

As early as 1515 the Spanish authorities were petitioning the Crown to import African slaves to Cuba. A sugar-plantation economy using slave labor became the economic mainstay of the island. But slavery was not limited to sugar production. Agriculture, mining, and construction used slave labor too. By the mid-nineteenth century over half a million slaves had been brought to the island. Runaway slaves, *cimarrones*, lived in their own settlements, *palenques*, while hiding from the authorities.

The Independence Movement

Even though conspiracies against Spanish rule started as early as 1810 (e.g., José Aponte was executed for leading a rebellion by slaves to gain their freedom; Narciso López was executed for leading two expeditions that landed in the northern coast in the 1850s), Cuba had no part in the wars that brought independence to South and Central America in the early part of the nineteenth century. The anti-Spanish political sentiment found expression in three different movements: autonomism, annexationism, and independentism.

The autonomists wanted home rule while continuing colonial ties with Spain. The annexationists wanted to replace links with the United States for those with Spain. The independentists fought for a free Cuba with no colonial ties to either Spain or the United States. In the end, independence prevailed, but at a cost. The United States intervened in 1898 in the war of independence that had started in 1895, becoming the new major power determining Cuban affairs.

Three wars were fought for Cuba's independence. The first was the Ten Year War (1868-78). After freeing his slaves on 10 October 1868 in his sugarmill, La Demajagua, Carlos Manuel de Céspedes started the war. It was a patrician-led war fought in the eastern half of the island, but the ruling class opposed it bitterly. The *criollos* who burned down their sugarmills following Céspedes' orders were ruined by the end of the war. American investment in the sugar industry increased during the period.

Leaders like António Maceo, and his brother José, Calixto García, and others, refused to accept the Zanjón Pact putting an end to the war. The so-called Little War (Guerra Chiquita), 1879-80, was launched, but was soon over. The Ten Year War had sapped the revolutionary spirit; there had been too much death and destruction.

New leadership was needed, and it would come in José Martí (1853-95).

He was probably the most remarkable man in Cuban history. He was sentenced to forced labor in prison when he was only sixteen. The charges of subversive activities against Martí were based on a letter critical of Spain, which it was alleged that he wrote and which the police intercepted. Martí was later freed and exiled to Spain where he pursued his studies. From Spain he moved to Latin America, and finally to New York City. His literary and journalistic work was paired by his dedication to Cuba's independence. He became the new force that was needed to resurrect the movement.

The War of Independence started with an uprising in the village of Baire, on 24 February 1895. Martí landed in Cuba two months later, on 11 April, and was killed in action in Dos Ríos the following month, on 19 May. The war continued under the leadership of António Maceo, Calixto García, and other Cuban patriots, but the death of Martí had already changed Cuban history. Neither the way independence was finally attained, nor the direction that the new republic would follow did justice to all the sacrifices thousands of Cubans endured and the long years spent struggling to liberate the island from Spain. The War of Independence turned into the American–Cuban–Spanish War of 1898. It was followed by the first American intervention, which lasted four years (1898–1902). There would be other American interventions later, in 1906–9, and in 1912 and 1917. After the 1901 Constitution was approved, the Cuban Republic was inaugurated on 20 May 1902.

The Cuban Republic (1902–58)

The Cuban Republic started in a manner contrary to Martí's vision of a politically and economically independent nation. It was compromised (*mediatizada*) from its creation. The real power was the United States. The Platt Amendment was added to the 1901 Constitution; it allowed Washington to intervene in Cuba 'for the preservation of life, property, and individual liberty'. A commercial reciprocity treaty signed between Washington and Havana in 1903 decided the economic future of the newly born republic (it was replaced by a new similar treaty in 1934). A tariff preference for Cuban sugar entering the American market perpetuated a single-crop economy, and the Cuban market was opened for many American products. One Cuban president after another behaved according to the rules of political dependency: it was understood that the final arbiter of major internal disputes was the US ambassador, who would decide or ask Washington what the position was on a given issue. The political system was soon corrupt. The government bureaucracy was in the hands of the politicians, and they used it for their own benefit.

The period from the inauguration of the republic to the coming to power of the Castro regime is subdivided here into two distinct political systems, or periods of political development. The first system extends from 1902 to 1933, and the second from 1934 to 1958. The first system was marked by direct US control of the polity, with new military interventions legalized by the Platt Amendment. The control of the central government exercised by Washington precluded Havana from developing a stronger central government, while different political, economic, and social power centers proliferated in the country. But the republic became a political caricature of what an independent polity could, and should, be. A national propertied class emerged lacking any sense of economic nationalism. Their economic and political allegiance was given to conservative administrations that relied on Washington's approval to stay in power.

The transition from the first to the second political system took place under the brutal dictatorial regime of Gerardo Machado. The aborted 1933 revolution that brought his regime down also meant the coming of age of the Cuban Republic. Its political development advanced in the 1930s and 1940s, even if its full potential did not reach fruition. New political and interest groups emerged. They were more directly involved in the political process, forcing it to become more accountable to popular needs. This political activism was true for both labor and the Havana University student movement. Trade unions were organized and became a political force. The Cuban Communist party was also active after being founded in 1925, particularly among trade unions, although it never had a large membership. More importantly, after having ignored Cuban demands, Washington finally abrogated the Platt Amendment in 1934.

Even though Washington's grip over Cuban life lessened after 1934, the dependent political and economic structure that had been built since 1902 made possible a more subtle form of interventionism and control. The short-lived first Ramón Grau San Martín administration (10 September 1933–15 January 1934) could not survive because it lacked US diplomatic recognition. A new 'strong man' emerged dominating Cuban political life, General Fulgencio Batista, who controlled the political system on and off until 1958. He offered law and order at any cost to the propertied classes and US interests, two commodities highly regarded by them, especially at a time of unrest. During the second political system the central government grew stronger, improving its administrative control of the country.

In the aftermath of the inconclusive 1933 revolution a cynical attitude developed, even among those groups born during the anti-Machado struggle. Grau San Martín's return to power in 1944 in a great political victory was a leading example. His administration would prove to be another major disappointment. A second Auténtico administration, that of Carlos Prío Socarrás, continued the same corruption practiced by Batista and Grau. Batista's *coup d'état* on 10 March 1952 was facilitated by the destructive effect that unchecked public dishonesty had on political institutions that already had poor legitimacy. Under Batista, during the next seven years, a new generation moved into the political arena. After some peaceful attempts had failed, revolutionary action proved to be the only viable way to remove Batista from power. When the old political leaders proved ineffective, Fidel Castro gained stature as a major political actor. By becoming the main revolutionary leader when revolutionary politics prevailed, Castro came to control the anti-Batista struggle, earning the right to determine who would be Batista's successor. But the direction followed by Castro once in power was a surprise to many Cubans. Although some reforms were wanted and expected, very few anticipated the radical transformation of Cuban society that ensued. And when such a radical system was initially instituted, many Cubans thought that it would never survive the kind of attack Washington had unleashed against it in alliance with the national bourgeoisie.

Pre-1959 Cuba appeared the least possible candidate for a radical revolution. By most Latin American standards, the country seemed affluent and developed. Major cities, particularly Havana, were modern. But the country's development was asymmetrical; most notably there was an abysmal difference between urban and rural areas. And while the political system's endemic violence permitted a revolutionary government to come to power, the society's structural characteristics facilitated radical social transformation.

There was no patrician system established after 1902. No *criollo* aristocracy became entrenched as such at the top of the social pyramid. The social system was fluid, lacking a permanent stratification system. The class system was mostly based on wealth: if a person acquired it, he could then experience upward social mobility. One pervasive obstacle to this was racial prejudice. Membership in upper strata associational groups was restrictive; it was based on race in addition to wealth, hence blacks were kept out. The middle sectors had an urban orientation, and labor was imbued with modern social and political doctrines. The peasants' living standards were not as bad as found elsewhere in Latin America, but in comparison with urban centers the rural areas were always neglected. The sugar industry had also created an urban and rural working class, which had gained trade-union experience and militancy. By being more modern and politicized, the popular sector was positively predisposed for the kind of political mobilization practiced later under the revolutionary government.

The Revolutionary System After 1959

The third political system in the history of the Cuban Republic started in 1959. In less than two years, the revolutionary government moved from an initial bourgeois–democratic phase to a socialist one, defined by Castro as Marxist–Leninist at the end of 1961. The revolutionary process had an internal dynamic of its own, advancing to a higher level of radicalization at every step. The regime's policies put the process in motion in the first place. However, the negative response from domestic and foreign economic interests, affected by policies redistributing wealth and providing social services to low-income population sectors, caused the regime to take another step along the radicalization process. Also, the unwavering support given by the lower income groups (the majority of the population) to the revolutionary government reinforced the regime's drive for radical social change.

The Mobilization Politics of the 1960s

Under revoutionary rule the central government grew further, to a level not envisioned in earlier periods. The degree of social penetration attained allowed the regime to mobilize the population, bypassing old and new social cleavages. A positive by-product of the mobilization politics practiced by the revolution was the additional capacity the government gained to pursue developmental programs. The country's limited resources and lack of technical know-how almost pre-determined the mobilization approach the regime favored. Mobilizing the population to its highest potential adroitly compensated for these shortages.

When the revolutionary government came to power, the country moved into a totally different political system. The revolutionary government could not operate in a sociopolitical vacuum. Neither the regime nor its policies could do without the enthusiastic support of the populace, so the population had to be integrated into the revolutionary process, and its revolutionary commitment kept alive through mobilization campaigns. The revolutionary political culture that emerged in the 1960s was highly supportive of the revolution's developmental programs. Mobilization, participation, and revolutionary praxis became known as expressions of *conciencia* (consciousness)— indicating an individual's higher level of revolutionary integration.

A network of mass organizations provided conduits through which the people could be integrated into the revolution and be politically active. To the Confederation of Cuban Workers (CTC) new mass and social organizations were added: the Committees for Defense of the Revolution (CDRs), the Federation of Cuban Women (FMC), the Union of Communist Youth (UJC) (which replaced the early Rebel Youth), the National Association of Small Farmers (ANAP), the Union of Pioneers of Cuba and others.

Social change.   The first decade of revolutionary rule experienced the highest degree of social transformation. The government sought to eradicate the *ancien régime*'s social institutions and cultural system. The traditional value system was replaced with a revolutionary one. Values sanctioning hierarchical elitism were substituted by support for an egalitarian society. Also, collectivism replaced subjectivism. Unselfishness and mass mobilization were central values defining new forms of political and social relations. The elimination of racism as both an institutionalized practice and a cultural value was of primary concern. Women's integration into the revolutionary political process and the labor force modified long-established practices that treated women as inferior. New educational opportunities made possible an unprecedented degree of social mobility among lower income groups and those traditionally discriminated against.

Marxism–Leninism as an official revolutionary ideology complemented the ongoing cultural transformation process. The new values gained legitimacy as a cultural expression of Marxism-Leninism. The rejection of the revolutionary process by disaffected groups was based as much on their disapproval of the cultural transformation that had taken place as on their refusal to accept a Marxist-Leninist ideology.

Political changes.   The revolutionary political system was organized with a Council of Ministers with executive and legislative powers, and a supervisory function over the court system. The Council of Ministers was headed by a President, but the government functioned under a Prime Minister. From February 1959 to December 1976 Fidel Castro was Prime Minister.

Castro's charismatic leadership has been a main source of legitimacy for the revolution. His personal appeal has received wide support from the people. A symbiotic relationship developed between leader and populace, both seeking and supporting one another. It happened outside whatever formal institutions of government had been established, but it became an important feature of the new political system. Direct communication between Castro and the people at mass gatherings became an invaluable exercise of revolutionary democracy. It also worked as a major springboard for mobilization campaigns, with the masses being energized to become involved in voluntary work and in a myriad of developmental programs. This type of political modality was particularly important given the existent centralization of power under Castro's leadership, which created a vertical decision-making structure usually closed to meaningful input from below.

A new revolutionary political party, the Integrated Revolutionary Organizations (ORI) (1961-3) was formed with three revolutionary organizations—the 26 July Movement, the (Havana University) Student's Revolutionary Directorate, and the Popular Socialist Party (the old communist party). It was replaced by the United Party of the Socialist Revolution (PURS) (1963-5). This gave way in 1965 to the Cuban Communist Party (PCC), the present and only political party in the political system. The amalgamation of the three revolutionary groups into a well-organized communist party was a stormy and protracted process. The PCC did not hold its first congress until 1975. In the 1960s the political party structure was rather weak, as were most institutions, including such mass organizations as the trade unions.

Changes in the economy. The rationale behind transforming the economy was based on the conditions inherited by the revolution. The nation's economy before 1959 was characterized by a high level of unemployment, marginality, a vulnerable external sector, and poor economic dynamism. It had created a low national income level and insufficient social services. Also, the amount of US interests in the Cuban economy had had the effect of distorting its growth and development.

The regime sought structural changes, including agricultural diversification, industrialization, reduction of the historical dependence on sugar, and an increase in the rate of economic growth. It also sought full employment and a general improvement in the living conditions of the rural population and low income groups, and economic independence from the United States. But the economic embargo imposed under the Kennedy administration was highly disruptive of Cuba's economic program—the embargo is called the 'economic blockade' in Cuba. Havana had to learn to live with it as an additional, even if unfair, economic burden; a burden that has become heavier under Reagan, who has imposed it more strictly.

The initial drive for rapid industrialization was halted later when agricultural policy was again given a higher priority. This period was marked by the controversy over moral and material incentives, with a preference for the former leading to the creation of a 'moral economy.' This meant that socialist values were thought to be served better by moral incentives, while material ones would perpetuate a capitalist mentality in the population. In retrospect this proess is seen to be characterized by idealism and romantic notions of how to build socialism. Moral and material incentives were later integrated into a single approach combining elements of both. Under this system rewards were allocated through a collective process—i.e., a committee of workers at a work center would decide who among the workers should receive a moral/material reward allocated to them. The decade ended with the 1970 Ten Million Tons campaign. The failure to achieve the officially set production goal prompted the institutionalization campaign that dominated the 1970s.

Foreign policy.   The regime moved forcefully into the international arena. An aggressive foreign policy was seen as a proper defense for the revolution. In the face of Washington's campaign to isolate it, Havana responded with several attempts to export its revolution to Latin America. Cuba was integrated into the socialist bloc and diplomatic and trade relations with the Soviet Union and other socialist countries were established. Havana also became a founding member of the Nonaligned Movement. International relations were expanded, and policy positions were taken on most important issues. The Cuban ambassador at the United Nations voiced the revolution's position on major international questions.

The death of Che Guevara in Bolivia in 1967 was a major setback for the revolution. It slowed down Cuba's support of revolutionary movements in Latin America, leading later to a radical decrease in its involvements. By the end of the decade, Cuba was in an introspective mood, far from the revolutionary international activism of the early 1960s.

The Institutionalization of the 1970s

By the end of the 1960s the regime had modified many of the policies it had promoted earlier. Changes in economic policy and international relations were coupled with a more pragmatic approach to moral and material incentives. But the major change came as a result of the problems created by the Ten Million Tons campaign. Castro had put much political capital on the assertion that any amount below the target level would be a failure. Even though the final amount of sugar produced was short by only 1.465 million tons (14.65 percent), the political fallout was of major proportions.

The problem was properly understood as an institutional one. The structures and mechanisms of decision-making that had been used all along had to be modified; an orderly process had to be established. The process of change gained momentum and dominated the second decade of revolutionary rule. The institutionalization of the political system was finally going to take place.

Social change. After two years of intense mobilization and voluntary work, the immediate effect of the arduous Ten Million Tons campaign was to leave the population in a state of near exhaustion. Consequently, the voluntary work campaigns of the 1960s decreased in number and intensity. A more rational approach to problem solving, recognizing objective conditions and relying less on subjective commitment, was progressively instituted. This had a beneficial effect on social relations, making personal dedication to revolutionary tasks less demanding. Also, exercising *conciencia* (acting according to revolutionary values), while violating established procedures (ignoring rules and certain formalities), was not seen lightly, nor condoned as before. A campaign emphasizing the need to respect socialist legality was instituted later in the decade.

The transition from experimentation to more clearly defined administrative procedures that was taking place at higher levels of government affected society as well, improving some of the more demanding aspects of people's lives. The improved economic conditions of the mid-1970s also benefited the population, particularly as consumers.

Family relations had been transformed by many of the social changes of the 1960s. The FMC had been an advocate for the improvement of women's education and their integration into the labor force, as well as their full participation in political, social, and cultural life under the revolution. The enactment on 14 February 1975 of the Family Code (Law 1289) was an important recognition of those rights. The new family that had developed under the revolution was expected to possess the features of a socialist society, 'in which private property and man's exploitation by man have been abolished.' By eliminating what it saw as the pernicious influence of private property in family relations, Cuba claimed that under socialism love and sexual relations would not take second place.

Political changes. The decade of the 1970s was a most important state-building period for the regime. The revolution finally built permanent institutions. The constitutional and political structure was institutionalized. The First Congress of the Communist Party (PCC) was held in December 1975. The party had to institutionalize itself first, and then proceed to discuss and approve the new Constitution and the institutions that would give a permanent character to the sociopolitical and economic changes achieved in the 1960s. Henceforth, ideologically as well as institutionally, Cuba was, in its structural and political setting, a Marxist–Leninist state.

The new institutions had a trial period in the province of Matanzas in 1974–5. After the experimental phase, the Organs of People's Power (OPPs) became the new politico–administrative organs of the state. The 1976 Constitution created a permanent legal order for the system. It also recognized the Marxist–Leninist nature of the Cuban Republic, and the place the Communist Party, the mass organizations, and other state organs would occupy in the political system. But new political roles had to be learned. The entire population needed training in how to use revolutionary power as an effective instrument of socialist democracy.

There were important questions regarding the nature and long-term effect of the new political modalities. Were the Organs of People's Power at the national, provincial, and municipal level effective democratic bodies expressing the people's wishes and aspirations, or were they merely ratifying what had been approved by the PCC's top leadership? It could be argued that this is the wrong question, as long as it assumes that there is a difference between what the PCC decides and what the people want. But it is difficult to assume that the PCC would always know what the people wanted and decide accordingly. Whether the internal structure of the PCC fosters democratic centralism, operating as both an upward and a downward communication conduit in the decision–making process, and whether the organic insulation of the OPPs allows them to make decisions as the sovereign representative of the people, are central questions to a truly democratic socialist system.

It is not easy to practice effectively the dictatorship of the proletariat or socialist democracy. Built-in mechanisms, however, are helpful in the accountability of the new system. The rendition of accounts (*rendición de cuentas*) procedure keeps OPPs delegates accountable to their constituencies, making them responsible for their performance as the people's representatives. Recall procedures are available if OPPs delegates fail in performing their jobs. But the recall procedure has been modestly used so far.

Changes in the economy.   The institutionalization of the system spread into the economy, too. It was precisely the need for orderly decision–making procedures in the economy and other areas of the system that made the need for the institutionalization of the state such a pressing matter. In the mid-1970s the New System of Economic Management and Planning (SDPE) was introduced and expected to be fully operational by the early 1980s. It recommended using monetary controls, prices, budgets, credit, and interests. This was a departure from the centralized economic system practiced before, when state enterprises functioned as non-autonomous economic units. Cuban planning was seen as similar in form to that of the Soviet system, but not in terms of its content. Similarly to the 1965 Soviet reforms, it puts the enterprises on a self-financing basis, introducing profitability as a concept in enterprise management which includes decentralization and efficiency.

Parallel markets were established, which improved the choices available to consumers under a dual price system. While ration cards with subsidized prices were still used, 'free' floating prices were applied to many products. The consumer had a choice, even if still a limited one. Compared to the standards of the 1960s, however, this was a remarkable improvement.

Some problems stemmed from the tension between a central planning system and the use of material incentives to stimulate an increase in production. Prices were centrally administered, so market mechanisms were not used to determine them. This resulted in shortages of products even if the person had the money to buy them. Using material incentives as a mechanism to increase production seemed deceptive under those conditions. Notwithstanding the many problems and shortcomings created by using the SDPE, Cuban authorities seemed cautiously satisfied with the results obtained with it. Overall, the economy performed at a higher level of productivity and efficiency in the 1970s than in the 1960s. The higher price of sugar during the early part of the decade improved economic conditions, although economic growth declined toward the end of the decade.

Foreign policy. The 1970s was a period of retrenchment in Latin America, and increased involvement in Africa. Cuba intervened in support of two African allies, Angola and Ethiopia. Havana found itself involved in two different wars, fighting different alignments of forces, all in the name of proletarian internationalism. While some observers were surprised that Cuba went as far as it did in defense of its internationalist commitments, Havana saw the matter differently. Castro claimed that Cuba is as African as it is Spanish. Hence his support for the Angolan Agostinho Neto's MPLA forces fighting imperialist surrogates was a proper decision to make. But his involvement in Ethiopia was more difficult to explain. Cuba had been an ally of Somalia, a fellow Third World country. Territorial ambitions on the part of Somalia, and its incursion into Ethiopia's Ogaden desert region, were sufficient reasons for Castro to come out in support of Mengistu's regime. However, fighting side by side with Soviet military forces in Ethiopia against Somalia did not enhance Cuba's image as a truly Third World champion.

But the 1970s were successful years in international relations for Cuba. Its major feats in Africa caused admiration in the Third World and the socialist bloc, and bewilderment among many Western countries. Also, there were two revolutions in the western hemisphere in 1979. Grenada and Nicaragua became Cuban allies in the region. The 1983 US invasion of Grenada put an end to Cuba's presence in the island, but its close association with Nicaragua continued. Given the Reagan administration's support for the Contra war, Havana found itself performing a difficult balancing act in its Central American policy: support for Nicaragua and the Arias plan (and Contadora before it), and political and moral support for guerrillas in El Salvador and elsewhere.

Washington's policy of isolating Havana came to an end in 1975 when the OAS voted to terminate the diplomatic and trade sanctions imposed in 1964. Diplomatic ties were restored with several countries, and new relations established with the English-speaking Caribbean island-nations.

The Rectification Process of the 1980s

Despite the Mariel boatlift (April–September 1980), when thousands of Cubans left for the United States and other countries, the third decade of revolutionary rule started under good auspices. The institutionalization of the state had been completed in the mid-1970s, and some routinization had taken place in the intervening years. People were already familiar with the new political roles and institutions. The economic measures applied in the 1970s had brought benefits for the population. The free farmers' markets were thriving; people were taking advantage of the new opportunities offered to consumers.

But difficult economic years lay ahead. The economic recession started in 1982–3 in the United States and other industrialized nations. It hit the developing nations hard, and socialist countries did not escape its negative effects. The Reagan administration's tax-cut policies created a national deficit in the United States that resulted in an overvalued US dollar. This meant disaster to debtor countries, which had to service their external debt in free floating dollars. For every decimal point upward in the price of the US dollar, the interest payments escalated accordingly. Even though Cuba was fairly insulated by having approximately four-fifths of its external commerce with socialist countries, it was adversely affected by the world economic crisis, too. What had started as good years turned half way in the decade into the rectification process announced at the Third Party Congress in 1986. Painful changes had to be made affecting the country as a whole.

Social change.   With better salaries, more products available in stores and markets, and production bonuses paid in many work centers, the lives of most Cubans had improved noticeably. Even though the farmers' markets put an inordinate amount of money in the hands of a small population sector, its benefits seemed to override its negative potential. At least, many people thought so, being better satisfied consumers. When the government announced in May 1986 that it was closing down the farmers' markets, many people thought immediately that the relative abundance they had enjoyed was over. However, it was reported later that the situation was not really that bad; the state markets were themselves able to satisfy the consumer's needs.

But the measures established under the rectification process had a taste of *déjà vu*. Some of the themes belonged to the 1960s. The greed heightened by material incentives was denounced as a reprehensible deviation from socialist ethics. Public fairs where artisans sold hand-made products with prices freely determined by supply and demand were closed down. Classified advertisements were not published any more, and the private businesses they publicized were discontinued.

Surprisingly enough for the outside observer, the people's morale improved under the rectification proess. The measures established under the program were received favorably. Apparently, the people understood that some of the policies of the late 1970s and early 1980s were having a pernicious effect on society. Moreover, the people agreed that it had to stop. Cuban society in the 1980s was in a state of change, but its direction was not as clear as in earlier periods.

Political changes. Two party Congresses took place in the 1980s, the Second Congress (1980), and the Third Congress (1986). There was a striking difference between the two, however. The themes, direction, and general mood had changed substantially from the beginning of the decade to the middle of it. As customary in party congresses, past and current issues were examined, and policies dealing with major problems were discussed and approved. The rectification process emerged from the two-session (February and November-December) Third Party Congress.

There were two sides to Castro's report to the Third Party Congress. A woman and a black man were elevated to the Politburo, the highest rank of the PCC next to its Secretariat, as part of an affirmative action policy within the party (youth was also singled out as a criterion for higher positions). Highly positioned leaders in the party and government (including two Commanders of the Revolution, Ramiro Valdés and Guillermo García Frías) were replaced for ineptness or behavior considered improper for a person of such standing. The message that everybody was accountable for his performance was loud and clear. And it was a needed message. In a one-party system that party must police itself effectively if it means to perform its assigned tasks (which are formidable) properly. To a large extent the PCC was doing just that in 1986.

But there was a negative side to Castro's report, too. Almost everyone was surprised by the extent of the negative evaluation which included practically every policy area. Too many mistakes were made in administration and production and they had to be rectified. A dangerous complacency coupled with creeping corruption had settled on enterprise managers. The nature and level of corruption might look almost negligible in a capitalist society, but for a developing nation like Cuba, in the process of building socialism, such misbehavior was unacceptable. But no purge of party membership took place, and the new appointments were based on competence and efficiency.

Nine months after its first session, the Third Party Congress approved its program for the next five years. How much Cuba is moving away from pragmatism and decentralization in decision-making, and bringing back moral incentives at the expense of material ones under the rectification process is a matter of speculation. Is Castro's support for 'awareness and educating the people' signaling a return to *conciencia* (revolutionary consciousness) at the expense of formal channels of decision-making, as implied when he derided the place of 'mechanisms' in the construction of socialism? Also, is this an aberration, given the difficult economic conditions in the world economy, or a more permanent trend in party policy? And if it is not a policy hiatus, in what direction is Cuba embarking now? For these and other questions, time will bring new answers, and some new questions.

Changes in the economy. The problems facing the Cuban economy in the late 1980s are rather serious. While some are internal and structural, others depend on external circumstances. The latter include the conditions of the world economy; the price of sugar in the world market; whether the external debt with market economies can be renegotiated under favorable conditions or not; and the nature of future commercial relations with socialist nations, which so far have been favorable to Cuba.

Cuba's economic growth in 1981–2 had been respectable, and its GSP average growth for five years (1980–4) was 7.2 percent. But it decreased to 1.4 percent by 1986. A cluster of adverse circumstances accounted for the latest trend, but they were real nevertheless. Among the most serious ones, which are internal and deal with Cuba's economic infrastructure and personnel, are mistakes made by economic planners and enterprise managers, and the low level of labor productivity and efficiency. The problems with JUCEPLAN, the Central Planning Board, started in 1984, when its director,

Humberto Pérez, was demoted. Pérez had a solid reputation as an economist and able administrator, so questions were raised as to whether he had paid personally for problems which were not his responsibility, and beyond JUCEPLAN's capacity to solve.

At the heart of Cuba's economic problems is whether a socialist nation can forget that its economy must remain a moral economy. Evidently, Castro refuses to do so. Besides the immediate benefits provided by the farmers' markets to the consumer is the problem of the social dislocation that accumulation of monetary and material resources in a few hands could mean for Cuba. But Havana cannot afford to dismiss the economic mechanisms built into the system in the late 1970s either. So the dilemma is how to keep *conciencia* and still have the economy functioning with the attributes of central planning. Such economic mechanisms and objectives as efficiency, enterprise profitability, self-financing, decentralization, and higher productivity rates cannot be dismissed or ignored. So they have to be mixed with moral economy features in a workable formula. The rectification process seeks to achieve such a goal in the economy, as well as in the rest of the polity.

Foreign policy.   Cuba's foreign policy glass in the 1980s was half-full or half-empty, depending from what side one is looking at it. On the minus side is the US invasion of Grenada in 1983, the seat lost in the United Nations Security Council because of the fallout from the Soviet invasion of Afghanistan in 1979, and the challenges and conflicts caused by Reagan's policies in Nicaragua, Angola, and elsewhere.

On the plus side, many accomplishments in the 1980s have been carried over from the 1970s. For one, the problems facing Cuba are not Cuban in a strict sense. They are Third World problems, too, problems that national liberation movements face today. Inasmuch as Cuba defends and represents the aspirations of developing countries—and it has been closely involved in them—they have become Cuba's problems and setbacks. By the same token, Washington's selective application of the low intensity conflict policy has strengthened Cuba's role as a Third World leader. But it is not easy for either Cuba or the Third World. Havana's radical standing in the Nonaligned Movement is more compelling today, after Washington's attacks against leftist regimes and national liberation movements in the 1980s, than it seemed at the Sixth Summit Meeting in 1979.

Also on the plus side of Cuba's foreign policy, is the fact that the Sandinistas are in power while the Contras are in disarray; the MPLA regime headed by President José Eduardo dos Santos is in office; Mengistu's regime is in power; the guerrilla movement in El Salvador is strong and viable, while the Napoleón Duarte Administration has suffered sensitive political losses to the extreme right; the Arias peace plan, supported by Cuba, has received world support and acclaim; and many Latin American nations have either re-established relations with Cuba or are considering doing so. Paradoxically, the Soviet withdrawal from Afghanistan is a plus for Havana, as long as it eliminates an irritant in its relations with the Third World.

Central as relations with the Third World are for Havana, its international relations are not limited only to them. Cuba has interests to protect with the Soviet Union and other socialist countries and with industrialized market economies. Balancing all of them has not been an easy task.

For Cuba, having to admit that it could not defend Grenada when it was invaded, or Nicaragua if it is ever invaded by Washington, is a recognition of its own limits. This could have a detrimental effect on its foreign relations. Any Third World nation could now wonder how desirable it is to have a close association with Havana if Cuba cannot save it from Washington's aggressive actions. The stakes in international relations are unusually high and Havana–Third World relations are no exception. But Cuba has learned to cope with these problems for almost three decades. After having paid the price of its revolutionary brand of leadership, Havana seems to be looking forward to more foreign policy involvements in the 1990s, and beyond.

Notes

Chapter 1

1. Admitting being emotionally and intellectually involved with Cuba's past, President Castro stated candidly, 'As I grew, I developed a deep admiration for the men in our history . . . [Cuba] was the last colony to gain its independence from Spain—it fought Spain for thirty years. *We can call Cuba the Vietnam of the nineteenth century because we barely had a population of one million and we had to fight nearly three hundred thousand Spanish soldiers.* This gives an idea of the magnitude of our fight without logistics, without a supply of arms, without help of any class. *Extraordinary pages of heroism were written. Ours is a beautiful history*' (Mankiewicz & Jones, 1975, p. 51; emphasis added. Also, see Betto, 1985, p. 93).

2. Under the new politico-administrative provincial division established by the 1976 Constitution the country is currently divided in fourteen provinces: (from west to east) Pinar del Río, Havana, City of Havana, Mantanzas, Cienfuegos, Villa Clara, Sancti Spíritus, Ciego de Ávila, Camagüey, Las Tunas, Granma, Holguín, Santiago de Cuba, and Guantánamo. Formerly, there were only six provinces: (from west to east) Pinar del Río, Havana, Matanzas, Santa Clara, Camagüey, and Oriente.

3. *Agricultural and Industrial Evolution from the Seventeenth to Nineteenth Centuries*
   The Sugar Industry: After 1765, but especially since 1778, there was a significant increase in sugar production. This period of economic prosperity lasted until the early 1800s. It was followed by the expansion of the sugar industry as the basis of a growing system of capital colonialism—always at the expense of the rest of the economy, which was more vulnerable. This type of unbalanced economic cycle marked later the fluctuations of the sugar-based Cuban economy.
   The Tobacco Industry: Tobacco plantations (*vegas*) dated back to the early 1700s, but their growth was deterred by trade restrictions imposed by the Spanish. Once the tobacco monopoly was lifted in 1817 there was an expansion of the industry by cigar makers, who could sell and export their product freely. Attracted by the fame of Cuban cigars (*puros*, or *habanos*), foreign merchants increasingly purchased the product. In 1850 there were approximately 15,000 cigar workers in Havana alone.
   Coffee: Cuban *cafetales* (coffee plantations) initially rivaled the attention of great planters, whose land was sown with sugar or coffee according to local conditions. Initially, a coffee plantation needed less capital to start than a sugar plantation but it would follow a rapid incremental growth by the second and third year. The average *cafetal* had between fifty and sixty slaves; its slaves would double by its second year. A well-established *cafetal* had 200,000 coffee trees,

approximately a hundred slaves, and produced around sixty tons of coffee a year (it was not until the fourth year that coffee trees could be harvested). The capital invested in coffee in 1829 was slightly higher than in sugar—85 to 84 milion pesos (dollars), respectively. The coffee crop value, however, was only half of the sugar crop value, $4.3 million of the former (a return of nearly 5 percent) for $8 million of the latter (a return of about 10 percent). Only seventeen years later, in 1846, the number of *cafetales* had dropped considerably, to 1,670. In a period of thirty years, from 1829 to 1859, the total coffee investment was reduced to half of what it used to be—to around $40 million.

Cattle-raising: Looking for natural pasture lands in the 1600s for cattle-raising was a process that marked the penetration of the island from the coastline to the interior. It spread in the form of *sitios* within the latifundia (large land holdings), but keeping it undivided in what was called *hacienda comunal* (communal ranch). While contributing to colonization, cattle-raising dispersed the population into small groups (the opposite of agriculture which concentrated it). This process was started early in the western provinces, but in the central and eastern areas it did not begin until rather late, sometimes not even until the nineteenth century.

Other important economic activities included:

(1) *Mining*: exportation of copper ceased after 1610, but mining continued. After several attempts to revive copper mining had failed, an English company, Consolidated Copper, obtained a concession to work the mines of Cobre. Its production averaged approximately fifty tons a day. Beginning in the 1830s, for approximately thirty years, Cuba became the main supplier of copper to England; it was shipped abroad in an unrefined state. United States monopolies started to work iron deposits in Oriente province in the 1880s.

(2) *Other industries*: The fishing industry was organized as a private enterprise in the nineteenth century. There were serious charges, however, that in many cases it served as a cover for smuggling operations. Several foundries were operated with some success in the 1800s, supplying sugarmills with spare parts, most notably in Jovellanos and other towns in Matanzas province.

(3) *Railroads*: The first railroad built in Cuba was inaugurated on 19 April 1837, and it ran for 27 kilometers from Havana to the town of Bejucal. By December 1838, a second section was opened running from Bejucal to Güines. The entire line, Havana–Güines, was sold to a private company in 1842 for three million pesos. Railroads were built in the nineteenth century in response to the demands of the sugar industry. Following Havana, the movement for railroad building in the province of Matanzas developed rapidly in the 1860s, given its importance as a sugar center. (Le Riverend, 1967, pp. 87–94, 160–73; Thomas, 1971, pp. 97–8, 128–35.)

4. In his insightful study of Martí, Kirk says: 'That José Martí has been utilized as a source of inspiration by the many different regimes of independent Cuba demonstrates his fundamental importance as a symbol of *cubania* (the essence of Cuban identity), as the exemplary Cuban whom all citizens of the Republic should emulate.' Moreover: 'Because of the unfortunate (though understandable

considering Martí's importance for all Cubans) polarization of views on José Martí, any study of his sociopolitical thought is bound to invite criticisms from *martianos* (Martí specialists) of differing political opinions' (Kirk, 1983, pp. 153, x).

As seen by a Cuban-American historian, '[Martí] believed in nineteenth-century classical liberalism, but maintained that national wealth should flow from agriculture more than industry.' Also, Martí's writings have 'been taken out of context to show him as being strongly anti-Yankee, or to portray him as the advocate of a Latin America in the image of the United States' (Suchliki, 1974, pp. 86–7). None the less, according to Foner, '[Upon reading Martí's writings on North America] one will clearly discern the reasons that led Martí to refer to the United States as the "Other America", in contradistinction to Latin America—"Our America"' (Foner, 1975, p. 11).

Upon reporting on the first Inter-American Conference held in Washington in 1889 and 1890, Martí expressed clearly his concern about US intentions for Latin America:

> For all of Latin America, from independence to the present, there was never any matter that required as much good sense, and vigilance, or ... thorough examination, than this invitation of the United States ... Now, after seeing with judicial eyes the antecedents, causes, and purpose of this invitation, it is necessary to say—because it is the truth—that the time has arrived for Spanish America to declare her second independence.

As for Cuba, Martí 'realized that in order to win political independence for the *patria* [Cuba] not only did he have to defeat the Spanish forces but also to keep the United States firmly at bay' (Kirk, 1983, pp. 57, 55).

5. The island's pre-revolutionary experience as a dependent underdeveloped polity has been studied by Cuban social scientists with remarkable scholarly results. For a comprehensive study looking at the sociopolitical and economic developmental process in its colonial and pre-1959 republican period, see López Segrera, 1972. More specifically, the American takeover of the Cuban economy through a selective control of the country's natural resources, is studied in Pino-Santos, 1973. Joint research by social scientists from Cuba and the German Democratic Republic produced an invaluable study documenting the operational practices of American monopolies in Cuba, see *Monopolios Norte-americanos en Cuba*, 1973. A uniquely comprehensive analysis of the central role played by its sugar-based economy in the country's overall development during the eighteenth and nineteenth centuries is included in the three volume study by Moreno Fraginals, 1977.

6. Putting this period and his own experience in historical perspective, Castro stated that: 'During that period the [Batista's] repression did not have the refinement that it would acquire later in other Latin American countries, like in Chile, Argentina, Uruguay ... Because [in Cuba] it happened in the fifties, and in these other cases it took place almost twenty years later, when the Americans

had gone through the Vietnam experience, and when the CIA had acquired greater repression and torture technology, and had transmitted it to Latin American repressive bodies, to the police and the military ... Those [Latin American] countries in the seventies had then more refined repressive forces, with more advanced technology' (Betto, 1985, p. 196).

Chapter 2

1. Article 7 of the 1976 Cuban Constitution lists the social and mass organizations including the Cuban Trade Unions (CTC), the Committees for the Defense of the Revolution (CDRs), the Federation of Cuban Women (FMC), and the National Association of Small Farmers (ANAP). Also, the Federation of University Students, the Federation of Secondary Education Students, and the Pioneers of Cuba (Simons, 1980, pp. 102, 100–34).
2. Domínguez offers a different view: 'After 1959, the ability of political and governmental organizations to operate without central direction, especially from Fidel Castro, declined drastically; in fact, a distinctive feature of Cuban politics today is the lack of autonomy for organizations, including government agencies' (1978, p. 6).
3. Nevertheless, a remarkable aspect of the mutations undergone by the Cuban revolution is that when its early reformism developed into Marxism–Leninism by 1961, this change did not produce a substantive dissension among either the majority of the population or the core of revolutionary leaders surrounding Castro. The massive exodus of disaffected Cubans to the United States and other countries was basically reinforced by these ideological changes in the revolution, although the earlier radicalization of 1959 and 1960 was already sufficient to alienate sectors of the population whose interests were affected by some revolutionary laws aimed at the redistribution of Cuba's wealth, or for some other reasons. Fidel Castro, however, offers a different explanation whereby the changes in the revolution's ideology and approach are seen in a sequential organic growth and development: '*Today*,' said Castro, '*I am making the same revolution that I promised from the beginning—But I have had to make it in different ways than I foresaw*. The realities of economics, politics, foreign relations and social aims were in contrast with the liberal ideas' (Matthews, 1967, pp. 4–5; emphasis added). For an interesting discussion of this subject by Castro, see Betto, 1985, pp. 131–72, *passim*.
4. The announcement in the 26 July official newspaper, *Revolución*, that Castro had become Prime Minister, included a list of twenty policies planned to be carried out: (1) agrarian reform; (2) import tax reform; (3) industrialization (50,000 new jobs in three months); (4) housing programs for the people; (5) special attention to the needs of the provinces; (6) salary increments; (7) salary reductions to government ministers; (8) a solution to the problem of gambling casinos; (9) reduction of rents (housing); (10) reduction in rates for utilities; (11) a

new metropolitan area for Havana; (12) creation of a merchant fleet; (13) promoting a national film industry; (14) planning an integrated educational system; (15) creation of a Sub-secretary for Latin American Affairs in the Foreign Affairs Ministry; (16) a fast ending, in fifteen days, of the trials of those accused of war crimes; (17) a campaign supporting the use of goods produced in Cuba; (18) a campaign against traffic accidents; (19) a campaign to increase the sales of bonds of the House and Savings Institute; and (20) celebrating a World Fair in Cuba (*Revolución*, 16 February 1959, p. 1).

5. The scholarly literature on the Bay of Pigs and the 1962 missile crisis is ample and varied. For the former, see Meyer & Szulc, 1962; Johnson, 1964; and Wyden, 1979. For a discussion of counterrevolutionary actions by the CIA and Cuban exiles, see Ayers, 1976; and Rivero Collado, 1976. For the missile crisis, see Allison, 1971; Chayes, 1974; Divine, 1971; Kennedy, 1971, Larson, (ed.), 1963.

6. The transformation of the educational system was massive and thorough: 'A significant innovation at the university level ... [was] the Facultad Preparatoria Obrero-Campesina ("Preparatory School for Peasants and Workers") which attempts to link farming, industry, and higher education more closely. The program seeks to prepare industrial workers and peasants aged eighteen through forty for university study' (Paulston, 1971, p. 389).

7. There have been six stages of Cuban migration from 1959 to 1980. During this period the number of Cuban arrivals to the United States was estimated at approximately 611,339 but it is known to be much higher than that. The Cuban-American population in the 1980s is considered already to be above one million. After the 1980 Mariel boatlift an Immigration Agreement was signed by the United States and Cuba in December 1984. When the Reagan Administration's Radio Martí went on the air on 20 May 1985, however, Cuba cancelled the agreement in protest for what it considered 'an unfriendly act' from the United States. From a Cuban standpoint, Radio Martí is considered to be dedicated to subvert the revolutionary government. For a discussion of Cuban migration to the United States since 1959, see 'The Cuban Exodus: A Symposium,' 1981–2.

8. In agreement with Cuba's official position on this matter, an American economist says that, 'Cuban socialism was inevitable in the sense that it was necessary if the island was to be rescued from permanent economic stagnation, social backwardness and degradation, and political do-nothingism and corruption' (O'Connor, 1970, p. 6).

9. 'Cuba's relations with the USSR do not correspond to "dependency relations" as most dependency theorists have elaborated them, particularly with regard to their effects on Cuba's domestic economy, e.g., on accumulation, income distribution, and sectoral investment. The inequality of the Cuban-Soviet relationship, i.e., Cuba's vulnerability, certainly results from the asymmetrical economic development of the two nations' (Leogrande, 1979, p. 28).

10. 'The discussion of incentives is often approached in relatively moralistic terms and focuses on a dichotomy between "material" and "moral" incentives. The terminology is, however, rather misleading ... The incentives discussion

revolves around the alternatives of motivating individuals through their desire for *personal* gain or of motivating individuals through their concern for the *collective* ... It would seem appropriate to speak of "personal incentives" and "collective incentives". This terminology ... is useful in bringing out the relationship between power and incentives' (MacEwan, 1976, pp. 81–2). Also, see Bernardo, 1971.

11. There is an extensive literature on this subject. For example, see 'The Cuban Exodus: A Symposium,' 1981–1982.

Chapter 3

1. For a discussion of the revolutionary government's social projects addressing the needs of slum dwellers, see Butterworth, 1980. This work covers 'social, economic, and political aspects of the lives of the residents of the [Buena Ventura] housing project'. It also presents a 'portrait of Las Yaguas (its real name), the slum from which most of the families in Buena Ventura were resettled.'

2. 'In absolute numbers, Cuba's union membership—including white-collar and blue-collar workers—was surpassed in Latin America in the 1950s only in Brazil, Argentina, and Mexico, all countries with exceedingly larger populations than in Cuba' (Manitzas, 1973a, p. M260–10). Also, see *Las Clases y la Lucha de Clases en la Sociedad Neocolonial Cubana*, 1981, Vol. 1, pp. 43–110.

3. Carlos More, a political ethnologist, is a lecturer at the University of the French West Indies. His forthcoming two-volume work, *Cuban Race Politics*, will be published by UCLA Press.

4. Vilma Espín, president of the Cuban Federation of Women (FMC) and member of the Politburo and the Central Committee of the Cuban Communist Party, told an American delegation visiting the FMC's Havana headquarters in 1981 that in Cuba almost everyone has some kind of racial mix. As she put it, 'In the background of almost every Cuban there is a "Congo" or "Carbalí" ancestor.' (In reference to many black Cubans' ancestry.) Espín answered in the vernacular questions from some American delegates imbued with black nationalist concerns. She articulated, however, a popular view of how most Cubans see the question of racial relations: 'in the end we are all very much the same'.

5. The foremost exponent of the desirability of aiming towards the creation of a 'socialist man' in Cuba was the Argentine born Cuban revolutionary, Ernesto Che Guevara. He held several important posts in the revolutionary government, including Minister of Industry and President of the National Bank (see Guevara, 1974, pp. 627–39).

6. Cuba's population censuses correspond to three historical periods: first, the colonial period, extending until the proclamation of the republic in 1902; second, the first republican period, from 1902 to 1958; the third, under the revolutionary regime, from 1959 to today. In the first period, nine censuses were

conducted with considerable mistakes (including underestimating the number of slaves to avoid paying taxes), in 1774, 1792, 1817, 1827, 1841, 1861, 1877, 1887, and 1899. The 1899 census, under the US military administration, was the first technically sound census conducted in Cuba. It was used by the American military government as a pilot project testing new census techniques in preparation for the forthcoming census in the United States the following year. During the second period, 1902–58, there were five population censuses, in 1907, 1919, 1931, 1943, and 1953. Under the revolutionary government, two censuses have been conducted, in 1970 and 1981 (*La Población de Cuba*, 1976, Chapter 2; *Anuario Estadístico de Cuba 1982*, n.d., pp. 55–87).

7. The population forecast for the 1990–2000 decade confirms some demographic trends. From 1970 to 1981 the male population had increased 11.7 percent, and the female 14.8 percent. The former constituted 50.5 percent of the total population, and the latter 49.4 percent. The population under 30 years old decreased from 62.1 percent (1970) to 58.3 percent (1980). In the 30–60 years old category, it increased from 28.9 percent (1970) to 31.1 percent (1980), and from 9 percent (1970) to 10.6 (1980) among those over 60 years (*Anuario Estadístico de Cuba 1975*, 1976, p. 32; MINSAP, *Anuario Estadístico 1973*, p. 106, *passim*; United Nations, 1960, *passim*).

8. 'Miami . . . is the only large city where the biggest and most vocal political bloc is represented by exiles from a communist regime, with Hispanics—mostly those of Cuban descent—making up 60% of the population and more than 40% of the registered votes'. 'When a group called the Coalition for Non-Intervention in Central America scheduled a slide show on Nicaragua . . ., it had to hire security officers after organizers said they got 28 threatening calls'. ' "Miami is threatening to become another country," contends Ray Fauntroy, the president of the local chapter of the Southern Christian Leadership Conference, which sponsored a rally in April to support free speech. "People have come here in great numbers who haven't been taught the American way, resulting in a contempt for the Constitution and the Bill of Rights" ' (Nazario, 1986).

9. When President Reagan's popularity polls were at an all time low after the Iran–Contra affair became public in November–December 1986, Patrick Buchanan, the White House communications director, spoke to approximately 3,000 Cuban-Americans in Miami. It was the opening of a pro-Reagan public opinion campaign. As expected, the audience supported Reagan enthusiastically. Cuban-Americans attending the rally seemed to agree with Buchanan that, by denouncing President Reagan, the media (particularly the *Washington Post*) provided a ' "windfall" for the Soviet Union. "Traitors!" the crowd screamed' (*Newsweek*, 22 December 1986, p. 21; also, see Toner, 1986, p. 16; and de Córdoba and Ricks, 1987, pp. 1, 11).

Chapter 4

1. 'The present power structure under Castro and the relative importance of the figures in it are generally little known and understood, even in Cuba. First come the old companions. Among them, Raúl Castro is number one, having been at his older brother's side since before Moncada. He is general of the army and defense minister in addition to all his titles as Fidel's deputy for everything—and he is his designated successor and second secretary of the Communist party. He conducts much of the day-to-day business of governing Cuba as his brother devotes more time to his global and ideological concerns . . . The few foreigners from the non-Communist world who meet Raúl generally find him quite charming and interesting' (Szulc, 1986, p. 58).

   Che Guevara's speeches, writings, and press conferences are highly regarded by Cubans as well as outsiders. They are significant because of his penetrating and intelligent mind (i.e., his theoretical contribution to revolutionary guerrilla warfare), but also because as a leader he spoke clearly about the problems confronting the revolution during his tenure in different leading posts—head of the National Bank, Minister of Industry, and others—until he left Cuba to meet his untimely death in Bolivia in 1967. (For a collection of his works, see Guevara, 1977.)

2. 'Unlike most top Cuban Communists, Rodríguez thrives on good conversation and every form of art and literature, being himself the author of remarkably readable books of essays and memoirs. A onetime Havana University professor and newspaper editor, he enjoys attending art gallery openings, interesting social and diplomatic occasions, and intellectually satisfying small dinners—always shining with wit and courtesy. But sad to say, Carlos Rafael Rodríguez seems to be the last of his breed: They no longer make politicians of his brain and charm, Communist or not, in Cuba' (Szulc, 1986, pp. 62-3).

3. 'GSP (global social product) differs from gross national product (GNP) and gross domestic product (GDP)—macroeconomic indicators commonly used in Western economies to measure economic growth. The differences go beyond which sectors of the economy are covered (GSP excludes so-called non-productive services sectors, such as education and housing, which are included in both GNP and GDP) to the very concept of the economic activity being measured (GSP includes the value of intermediate outputs, while GNP and GDP measure value added)' (Pérez-López, 1986, pp. 17-18). Also, 'Cuba's national accounts . . . correspond to the Soviet concepts of global social product (GSP) and gross material product (GMP). Both GSP and GMP include the production of "material goods" in agriculture, fishing, mining, industry and construction. In addition, GSP includes the value of such "material services" as transportation, trade and communication that are directly connected with the production of material goods. Conversely, GMP excludes the value of material services' (Mesa-Lago, 1981, p. 33).

Chapter 5

1. The definitive work on Fidel Castro has not been written yet. There are long interviews with Castro, personal accounts relating direct knowledge of him (some of them by political opponents who are usually eager to tell their own stories), and some biographies. The quality is uneven, but altogether they contribute to the literature on contemporary Cuba. (See Casuso, 1964; Urrutia Lleó, 1964; López Fresquet, 1966; Lockwood, 1969; Matthews, 1970; Gerassi, 1973; Mankiewicz & Jones, 1975; and Szulc, 1986).

   'Fidel Castro is a fascinating phenomenon in our century's politics: to the increasingly gray and dull Western world, a man of panache, a romantic figure, an ever-defiant, dizzyingly imaginative, and unpredictable rebel, a marvelous actor, a spectacular teacher and preacher of the many credos he says he embraces. But Castro makes other impressions as well. Though his personal popularity in Cuba is immense, there is a segment of Cubans [mostly exiles, but some still living in Cuba] to whom Castro looms as a ruthless and cunning dictator, a cynical betrayer of liberal democracy in whose name he first rallied millions of Cubans to his cause and banner, a servile satellite of the Soviet Union . . .' (Szulc, 1986, p. 38).

   'It would be difficult to imagine genuine indifference toward Fidel Castro— in Cuba or abroad. He may be loved or he may be hated, but there are no neutral sentiments about him, only strong emotions. That is why Castro seems to attract so magnetically every kind of admiring or pejorative adjective to his name' (Szulc, 1986, p. 41).

Bibliography

Aguilar, L. E. 1971. *Cuba 1933: Prologue to Revolution*. Ithaca, NY, Cornell University Press.

Aguirre, B. E. 1984. 'The conventionalization of collective behavior in Cuba.' *American Journal of Sociology*, vol. 90, no. 3.

Alarcón, R. 1985. 'Entrevista a Ricardo Alarcón.' *Cuadernos de Nuestra América*. Vol. 2, no. 4.

Allison, G. T. 1971. *Essence of Decision*. Boston, Little Brown.

Álvarez Tabío, F. 1981. *Comentarios a la Constitución Socialista*. Havana, Editorial de Ciencias Sociales.

Anuario Demográfico de Cuba 1979 1981. Havana, Dirección de Demografía, Comité Estatal de Estadísticas.

Anuario Estadístico de Cuba 1972 1974. Havana, Junta Central de Planificación, Dirección Central de Estadística.

Anuario Estadístico de Cuba 1975 1976. Havana, Comité Estatal de Estadísticas.

Anuario Estadístico de Cuba 1980 1981. Havana, Comité Estatal de Estadísticas.

Anuario Estadístico de Cuba 1982 n.d. Havana, Comité Estatal de Estadísticas.

20 Años de Matrimonios en Cuba 1977. Havana, Editorial de Ciencias Sociales.

Arañaburo, J. 1979. Report given at the panel on 'Decentralizing Decision-Making: the Role of Popular Power.' New York, National Conference on Cuba, Center for Cuban Studies.

Aranda, S. 1980. *La Revolución Agraria en Cuba*. Mexico, Siglo Veintiuno.

Atlas de Cuba, 1978. Havana, Instituto Cubano de Geodesia y Cartografía.

Ayers, B. E. 1976. *The War that Never Was*. New York, Bobbs-Merrill.

Azicri, M. 1977. 'The governing strategies of mass mobilization: the foundations of Cuban revolutionary politics.' *Latin American Monographs Series*, no. 2, Erie, Pennsylvania, Northwestern Institute for Latin American Studies.

— 1979. 'Women's development through revolutionary mobilization: a study of the Federation of Cuban Women.' *International Journal of Women's Studies*, vol. 2, no. 1.

— 1980a. 'The Cuban Family Code: some observations on its innovations and continuities.' *Review of Socialist Law*, vol. 6, no. 2.

— 1980b. 'The institutionalization of the Cuban state: a political perspective.' *Journal of Interamerican Studies and World Affairs*, vol. 22, no. 3.

— 1980c. 'Cuba and the US, on the possibilities of rapprochement.' *Caribbean Review*, vol. 9, no. 1.

— 1982a. 'The politics of exile: trends and dynamics of political change among Cuban-Americans.' *Cuban Studies/Estudios Cubanos*, vol. 11, no. 2 and vol. 12, no. 1.

—— 1982b. 'Cultural and political change among Cuban-Americans (1959-1982).' *Revista/Review Interamericana*, vol. 12, no. 2.

—— 1983. 'Cuba and the United States: what happened to rapprochment.' In Barry B. Levine (ed.), *The New Cuban Presence in the Caribbean*. Boulder, Colorado, Westview Press.

—— 1985a. 'Socialist legality and practice: the Cuban experience.' In Halebsky, S., & Kirk, J. M. (eds), 1985.

—— 1985b. 'Crime, penal law, and the Cuban revolutionary process.' *Crime and Social Justice*, no. 23.

—— 1986. 'Twenty-six years of Cuban revolutionary politics: an appraisal.' *Contemporary Marxism*, no. 14.

—— & Moreno, J. M. 1981. 'Cultura, política, movilización indirecta y modernización. Un análisis contextual del cambio revolucionario en Cuba: 1959-1968.' *Revista Mexicana de Sociología*, vol. 43, no. 3.

Balari, E. R. 1979. 'Cinco años de trabajo del Instituto Cubano de Investigaciones y Orientación de la Demanda.' In *Investigaciones Científicas de la Demanda en Cuba*. Havana, Editorial Orbe.

—— 1985. *Cuba-USA Palabras Cruzadas*. Havana, Editorial de Ciencias Sociales.

Banco Nacional de Cuba. 1982. August. *Informe Económico*. Havana.

—— 1985. February. *Economic Report*. Havana.

—— 1987. May. *Informe Económico*. Havana.

—— 1987. June. *Cuba: Informe Económico Trimestral*. Havana.

Banks, A. S. (ed.), 1986. *Political Handbook of the World: 1986*. Binghamton, New York, CSA Publications.

—— 1987. *Political Handbook of the World: 1987*. Binghamton, NY, CSA Publications.

Behm, H. 1980. 'La mortalidad actual en paises desarrollados y en el Tercer Mundo.' CELADE, San José, Costa Rica.

Bernardo, R. M. 1971. *The Theory of Moral Incentives in Cuba*. University, University of Alabama Press.

Bengelsdorf, C. 1979. 'A large school of government.' *Cuba Review*, no. 6, September.

Beretta, G. 1987. 'III Congreso del PCC: firmeza revolucionaria frente a crisis económica.' *Pensamiento Propio*, vol. 5, no. 39.

Betto, F. 1985. *Fidel y la Religión: Conversaciones con Fidel Castro*. Havana, Cuba, Oficinas de Publicaciones del Consejo de Estado.

Black, J. K., Blutstein, H. I., Edwards, J. D., Johnston, K. T. & McMorris, D. S. 1976. *Area Handbook for Cuba*. Washington, DC, Government Printing Office.

Blasier, C. 1979. 'COMECON in Cuban development.' In Blasier, C. & Mesa-Lago, C. (eds), *Cuba in the World*, Pittsburgh, University of Pittsburgh Press.

Bonachea, R. L. & San Martín, M. 1974. *The Cuban Insurrection, 1952-1959*. New Brunswick, Transaction Books.

Boorstein, E. 1968. *The Economic Transformation of Cuba*. New York, Modern Reader Paperbacks.

Brenner, P. 1988. *From Confrontation to Negotiation: US Relations With Cuba*. PACCA, Westview Press, Boulder, Colorado.

Brundenius, C. 1985. 'Cuba: redistribution and growth with equity.' In Halebsky, S., & Kirk, J. M. (eds), 1985.

Burton, J. 1985. 'Film and revolution in Cuba: the first twenty-five years.' In Halebsky, S., & Kirk, J. M. (eds), 1985.

Butterworth, D. S. 1980. *The People of Buenaventura: Relocation of Slum Dwellers in Postrevolutionary Cuba*. Urbana, University of Illinois Press.

Cambio 16 1987. 'General del Pino: "Angola es el Vietnam de Cuba"'. No. 815, 13 July.

Cañizares, F. D. 1979. *Teoría del Estado*. Havana, Editorial Pueblo y Educación.

Características de la Divorcialidad Cubana. 1976. Havana, Editorial de Ciencias Sociales.

Casal, L. 1971. 'Literature and society.' In Mesa-Lago, C. (ed.) *Revolutionary Change in Cuba*. Pittsburgh, University of Pittsburgh Pres.

Castro, F. (n.d.). *History Will Absolve Me*. New York, Center for Cuban Studies.

—— 1976. 'Main report presented to the 1st Congress of the Communist Party of Cuba.' *Granma Weekly Review*, 4 January.

—— 1977. 'Palabras a los intelectuales.' In *Política Cultural de la Revolución Cubana: Documentos*. Havana, Editorial de Ciencias Sociales.

—— 1980. *Main Report Presented to the 2nd Congress of the Communist Party of Cuba*. Havana, Political Publishers.

Castro, F. 1983. *The World Economic and Social Crisis: Its Impact on the Underdeveloped Countries, Its Somber Prospects and the Need to Struggle if We Are to Survive*. Havana, Cuba, Editora Politica.

—— 1985. *On Latin America's Unpayable Debt, Its Unforeseeable Consequences and Other Topics of Political and Historical Interest: Interview Granted to EFE News Agency*. Havana, Cuba, Editora Politica.

—— 1986. 'Fidel's main report to the 3rd Congress.' *Granma Weekly Review*, 16 February.

—— & Castro, R. 1975. *Selección de Discursos Acerca del Partido*. Havana, Editorial Ciencias Sociales.

Casuso, T. 1964. *Cuba and Castro*. New York, Random House.

Cavallini, M. 1986. 'La revolución es una obra de arte que debe perfeccionarse.' *Pensamiento Propio*, vol. 4, no. 33.

Cebrián, J. L. 1985. 'Entrevista con Fidel Castro: "America Latina Está en una Situación Explosiva."' *El País*, 21 January.

CEPAL 1980. *Cuba: Estilo de Desarrollo y Políticas Sociales*. Mexico, Siglo Veintiuno.

Charadán López, F. 1982. *La Industria Azucarera en Cuba*. Havana, Editorial de Ciencias Sociales.

Chayes, A. 1974. *The Cuban Missile Crisis*. London, Oxford University Press.

Comunicado—La Población de Cuba Alcanza los Diez Millones 1984. Havana, Comité Estatal de Estadísticas.

Crahan, M. 1979. 'Salvation through Christ or Marx: religion in revolutionary Cuba.' *Journal of Interamerican Studies and World Affairs*, vol. 21, no. 1.

Cuadra, A. 1986. *Escritores en Cuba Socialista*. Washington, DC, La Fundación Nacional Cubano-Americana.

Cuba: Territorio Libre de Analfabetismo 1981. Havana, Editorial de Ciencias Sociales.

'Cuba' 1986. In Banks, A. S. (ed.), *Political Handbook of the World: 1986*. Binghamton, NY, CSA Publications.

de Córdoba, J. & Ricks, T. E. 1987. 'Cuban connection: Bay of Pigs Veterans Find in Nicaragua a New War to Fight.' *Wall Street Journal*, 16 January.

de la Cuesta, L. 1976. 'The Cuban socialist constitution: its originality and role in institutionalization.' *Cuban Studies/Estudios Cubanos*, vol. 6, July.

Díaz-Briquets, S. 1983. Review of *La Fecundidad Retrospectiva y el Deseo de Tener Hijos de las Mujeres en Union Matrimonial*. Havana, Cuba, Comité Estatal de Estadísticas, 1981, and other works. *Cuban Studies/Estudios Cubanos*, vol. 13, no. 1.

Directory of Officials of the Government of Cuba. 1985. Government of the United States, Directorate of Intelligence, CR 85–13573, Washington, DC.

Divine, R. A. 1971. *The Cuban Missile Crisis*. Chicago, Quadrangle.

Domínguez, J. 1974. 'The civic soldier in Cuba.' In C. McArdele Kelleher (ed.), *Political-Military Systems: Comparative Perspectives*. Beverly Hills, Calif., Sage.

—— 1978. *Cuba: Order and Revolution*. Cambridge, Mass., The Belknap Press.

—— 1982a. 'Revolutionary politics: the new demands for orderliness.' In J. Domínguez (ed.), *Cuba: Internal and International Affairs*. Beverly Hills, Calif. Sage Publications.

—— 1982b. 'Political and military limitations and consequences of Cuban policies in Africa.' In Mesa-Lago, C. & Belkin, J. S. (eds) 1982.

—— 1986. 'Cuba in the 1980s.' *Foreign Affairs*.

—— 1988. 'Cuba in the international arena.' *Latin American Research Review*, vol. 22, no. 1.

Duncan, R. W. 1986. 'Castro and Gorbachëv: politics of accommodation.' *Problems of Communism*, vol. 25, March–April.

Edelstein, J. C. 1985. 'Economic policies and development models.' In Halebsky, S., & Kirk, J. M. (eds), 1985.

Elder, B. 1985. 'Report on Cuba's First Symposium on Politics, Ideology, and Law.' *Crime and Social Justice*, vol. 23.

Erisman, H. M. 1985. *Cuba's International Relations: The Anatomy of a Nationalistic Foreign Policy*. Boulder, Colorado, Westview Press.

Espín, V. 1986. 'La batalla por el ejercicio pleno de la igualdad de la mujer: acción de los comunistas.' *Cuba Socialista*, no. 20.

Estadísticas de Migraciones Externas y Turismo. 1982. Havana, Dirección de Demografía, Comité Estatal de Estadísticas.

Estatutos del Partido Comunista de Cuba Aprobados por el I Congreso, con las Modificaciones Acordadas por el II Congreso. 1981. Havana, Editora Política.

Evenson, D. 1986. 'Cuba's Prisons.' *CUBA Update*. Center for Cuban Studies.

Fagen, R. R. 1968. *Cubans in Exile*. Stanford, Calif., Stanford University Press.

Falk, P. S. 1986. *Cuba Foreign Policy: Caribbean Tempest*. Lexington, Mass., Lexington Books.

Feuer, C. H. 1987. 'Agricultural policy and development in Cuba.' In Zimbalist, A. (ed.), 1987.

Foner, P. S. (ed.), 1975. *Inside the Monster: Writings on the United States and American Imperialism by José Martí*. New York, Monthly Review Press.

Fox, G. E. 1971. 'Cuban Workers in Exile.' *Transaction*, vol. 8, no. 11.

Franklin, J. 1984. *Cuban Foreign Relations: A Chronology, 1959–1982*. New York, Center for Cuban Studies.

Freeman Smith, R. 1966. *Background to Revolution: The Development of Modern Cuba*. New York, Alfred A. Knopf.

Georgakas, D. 1986. 'Armando Valladares: pious poet or counterrevolutionary?' *The Guardian*, 24 September.

Gerassi, J. 1973. *Fidel Castro: A Biography*. New York, Doubleday.

González, E. 1976. 'Castro and Cuba's new orthodoxy.' *Problems of Communism*, vol. 25, January–February.

Greenberg, R. 1982. 'Cuba's Jews speak.' *Cubatimes*, vol. 2, no. 4.

Grobart, F. 1981. 'El proceso de formación del Partido Comunista de Cuba.' *Cuba Socialista*, vol. 1, no. 1.

Gorbachëv, M. 1987. *Perestroika: New Thinking for Our Country and the World*. New York, Harper & Row.

Guevara, E. Ché. 1974. 'El socialismo y el hombre en Cuba.' In his *Obra Revolucionaria*. Mexico, D.F., Ediciones Era.

—— 1977. *Escritos y Discursos*. Nine Volumes. Havana, Ministerio de Cultura.

Halebsky, S. & Kirk, J. M. (eds), 1985. *Cuba: Twenty-Five Years of Revolution, 1959–1984*. New York, Praeger.

Hamberg, J. 1986. *Under Construction, Housing Policy in Revolutionary Cuba*. New York, Center for Cuban Studies.

Hart, A. 1978. *Del Trabajo Cultural*. Havana, Editorial de Ciencias Sociales.

Hernández del Campo, A. 1975. *Principios de Investigaciones de la Demanda*. Havana, Editorial Científico-Técnica.

Hicks, N. 1979. 'Growth vs. basic needs: is there a trade-off?' *World Development*, vol. 7.

Hinkle, W. 1986. 'Cuba bashing.' *San Francisco Examiner*, 3 August.

Hitchens, C. 1988. 'Minority report.' *The Nation*, 23 January.

Johnson, H. 1964. *The Bay of Pigs*. New York, W. W. Norton.

Jover Marimón, M. 1971. 'The Church.' In Mesa-Lago, C. (ed.), *Revolutionary Change in Cuba*. Pittsburgh, University of Pittsburgh Press.

Judson, C. F. 1985. 'Continuity and evolution of revolutionary symbolism in *Verde Olivo*.' In Halebsky, S., & Kirk, J. M. (eds), 1985.

Karol, K. S. 1970. *Guerrillas in Power*. New York, Hill & Wang.

Kennedy, R. F. 1971. *Thirteen Days*. New York, W. W. Norton.

Kirk, J. M. 1983. *José Martí: Mentor of the Cuban Nation*. Tampa, University Presses of Florida.

—— 1985. 'From counterrevolution to modus vivendi: the Church in Cuba, 1959–1984.' In Halebsky, S., & Kirk, J. M. (eds.), 1985.

Knight, F. W. 1970. *Slave Society in Cuba During the Nineteenth Century*. Madison, University of Wisconsin Press.

Langley, L. D. 1973. 'Cuba: a perennial problem in American foreign policy.' *Forums in History*, St. Charles, Missouri, Forum Press.

La Población de Cuba 1976. Havana, Editorial de Ciencias Sociales.

Larson, D. L. 1963. *The 'Cuban Crisis' of 1962*. Boston, Mass., Houghton Mifflin.

Las Clases y la Lucha de Clases en la Sociedad Neocolonial Cubana. 1981. Five Volumes. Havana, Editorial de Ciencias Sociales.

Le Riverend, J. 1967. *Economic History of Cuba*. Havana, Book Institute.

— 1978. *Breve Historia de Cuba*. Havana, Editorial Ciencias Sociales.

LeoGrande, W. M. 1979. 'Cuban dependency: a comparison of pre-revolutionary and post-revolutionary international economic relations.' *Cuban Studies/Estudios Cubanos*, vol. 9, no. 2.

— 1979. 'Arms and politics: new trends in Cuban civil–military relations.' Paper presented at the Latin American Studies Association Meeting, Pittsburgh, Pennsylvania.

— 1982. 'Cuban–Soviet relations and Cuban policy in Africa.' In Mesa-Lago, C. & Belkin, J. S. (eds) 1982.

— 1986. 'Cuba.' In Blachman, M. J., Leogrande, W. M., & Sharpe, F. (eds), *Confronting Revolution: Security Through Diplomacy in Central America*. New York, Pantheon Books.

Lewis, A. 1988. 'A glimmer of hope.' *New York Times*, 8 May.

Lewis, F. 1987. 'Reverse gear in Cuba.' *New York Times*, 23 February.

Leiner, M. 1985. 'Cuba's schools: 25 years later.' In Halebski, S., & Kirk, J. M. (eds), 1985.

Littler, W. n.d. *The Metropolitan Opera and the Kennedy Center Present: Ballet Nacional de Cuba*. Washington, DC, Atelier leBas.

Lockwood, L. 1969. *Castro's Cuba, Cuba's Fidel*. New York, Random House.

López Fresquet, R. 1966. *My 14 Months With Castro*. Cleveland, Ohio, World Publishing Co.

López Segrera, F. 1972. *Cuba: Capitalismo Dependiente y Subdesarrollo (1510–1959)*. Havana, Casa de las Américas.

MacEwan, A. 1976. 'Incentives, equality, and power in revolutionary Cuba.' In Radosh, E. (ed.), *The New Cuba: Paradoxes and Potentials*. New York, William Morrow.

Malloy, J. M. 1971. 'Generation of political support and allocation of costs.' In Mesa-Lago, C. (ed.), *Revolutionary Change in Cuba*. Pittsburgh, University of Pittsburgh Press.

Mañach, J. 1975. *Martí, El Apóstol*. Madrid, Espasa-Calpe.

Manitzas, N. R. 1973a. 'The setting of the Cuban revolution.' In Barkin, D. P. & Manitzas, N. R. (eds), *Cuba: The Logic of the Revolution*. Andover, Mass., Warner Modular.

— 1973b. 'Social class and the definition of the Cuban nation.' In Barkin, D. P. & Manitzas, N. R. (eds), *Cuba: The Logic of the Revolution*. Andover, Mass., Warner Modular.

Mankiewicz, F., & Jones, K. 1975. *With Fidel: A Portrait of Castro and Cuba*. New York, Ballatine Books.

Martí, J. 1953. *Páginas Escogidas*. Madrid, Espasa-Calpe.

Martínez-Alier, V. 1974. *Marriage, Class, and Colour in Nineteenth Century Cuba*. Cambridge, Cambridge University Press.

Martínez Fagundo, C. 1986. 'El Perfeccionamiento del Mecanismo de Estimulación Material en Cuba.' *Cuba: Economía Planificada*, vol. 1, no. 1.

Masó, C. C. 1976. *Historia de Cuba*. Miami, Florida, Ediciones Universal.

Matas, J. 1971. 'Theater and cinematography.' In Mesa-Lago, C. (ed.), *Revolutionary Change in Cuba*. Pittsburgh, University of Pittsburgh Press.

— 1983. 'Revolución, literatura, y religión Afrocubana.' *Cuban Studies/Estudios Cubanos*, vol. 13, no. 1.

Matthews, H. L. 1967. 'Fidel Castro revisited.' *War/Peace Report*.

— 1970. *Fidel Castro*. New York, Simon and Schuster.

Mellanby, J. 1987. 'The death of the soul in Cuba and Communist China.' *International Journal on World Peace*, vol. 4, no. 1.

Memorias 1984. *I seminario sobre la situación de las comunidades Negra, Chicana, Cubana, India, y Puertorriqueña en Estados Unidos*. Havana, Editora Política.

Mesa-Lago, C. 1971. 'Economic policies and growth.' In Mesa-Lago, C. (ed.), *Revolutionary Change in Cuba*. Pittsburgh, University of Pittsburgh Press.

— 1978. *Cuba in the 1970s: Pragmatism and Institutionalization*. Albuquerque, University of New Mexico Press.

— 1981. *The Economy of Socialist Cuba*. Albuquerque, University of New Mexico Press.

— & Belkin, J. S. (eds) 1982. *Cuba in Africa*. Latin American Monograph and Document Series 3, Pittsburgh, University of Pittsburgh.

Meyer, K. E. & Szulc, T. 1962. *The Cuban Invasion*. New York, Praeger.

Meyer Rogg, E. 1980. 'Adaptation and adjustment of Cubans: West New York, New Jersey.' *Hispanic Research Center*, Fordham University.

Miná, G. 1987. *Un Encuentro con Fidel*. Havana, Oficinas de Publicaciones del Consejo de Estado.

MINSAP 1975. *Anuario Estadístico 1973*. Havana, Editorial Orbe.

Monopolios Norteamericanos en Cuba: Contribución al Estudio de la Penetración Imperialista 1973. Havana, Editorial de Ciencias Sociales.

Moreno, J. A. 1971. 'From traditional to modern values.' In Mesa-Lago (ed.), 1971.

Moreno Fraginals, M. 1977. *El Ingenio*. Havana, Editorial de Ciencias Sociales.

Nazario, S. L. 1986. 'Freedom of speech is a debatable issue for many in Miami: some say Cuban community muzzles dissent in its zeal to confront Communism.' *Wall Street Journal*, 2 June.

Nichols, J. S. 1984. 'When nobody listens: assessing the political success of Radio Martí.' *Communication Research*, vol. II, no. 2.

O'Connor, J. O. 1970. *The Origins of Socialism in Cuba*. Ithaca, NY, Cornell University Press.

O'Neill, T. 1987. *Man of the House*. New York, Random House.

Organization of American States, 1983. *The Situation of Human Rights in Cuba. Seventh Report*. Washington, DC, General Secretariat, Organization of American States.

Otero, L. 1987. 'Interview: Lisandro Otero.' *Cuba Update*, Center for Cuban Studies, vol. 8, nos 5–6.

Padrón Larrazábal, R. 1975. *Manifiestos de Cuba*. Seville, Universidad de Sevilla Press.

Pastor, R. A. 1983. 'Cuba and the Soviet Union: does Cuba act alone.' In Barry B. Levine (ed.), *The New Cuban Presence in the Caribbean*, Boulder, Colorado, Westview Press.

Paulston, R. G. 1971. 'Education.' In Mesa-Lago, C. (ed.), *Revolutionary Change in Cuba*. Pittsburgh, University of Pittsburgh Press.

Pedraza-Bailey, S. 1985. 'Cuba's exiles: portrait of a refugee migration.' *International Migration Review*, vol. 19, no. 1.

Peral Collado, D. 1980. *Derecho de Familia*. Havana, Editorial Pueblo y Educación.

Pérez, H. 1985. Address on Behalf of the Council of Ministers Presenting the Draft Law on the Integral Plan for Economic and Social Development. *Granma Weekly Review*.

Pérez, L. 1983. 'The holdings of the Library of Congress on the population of Cuba.' *Cuban Studies/Estudios Cubanos*, vol. 13, no. 1.

Pérez González, H. 1982. 'La plataforma programática y el desarrollo económico de Cuba.' *Cuba Socialista*, no. 3 (June).

—— 1986. 'Cubans in the United States.' *The Annals*, no. 487.

Pérez-López, J. 1986. 'Cuban Economy in the 1980s.' *Problems of Communism*, vol. 35.

Pérez-Rojas, N. 1979. *Características Sociodemográficas de la Familia Cuban, 1953–1970*. Havana, Editorial de Ciencias Sociales.

Pérez-Stable, M. 1985. 'Class organization, and conciencia: The Cuban working class after 1970.' In Halebsky, S., & Kirk, J. M. (eds), 1985.

—— 1987. 'Charisma and conciencia: Castro takes the economy in hand.' *The Nation*, 26 September.

Pino-Santos, O. 1973. *El Asalto a Cuba por la Oligarguía Financiera Yanqui*. Havana, Casa de las Américas.

Programatic Platform of the Communist Party of Cuba 1976. Havana, Cuba, Department of Revolutionary Orientation of the Central Committee of the Communist Party of Cuba.

Quinn, S. 1977. 'Wilma Espín: First Lady of the Revolution.' *The Washington Post*, 26 March.

Radosh, R. 1986. 'Review of Armando Valladares, *Against All Hope*, New York: Alfred A. Knopf, 1986'. *New York Times Book Review*.

Rabkin, R. P. 1985. 'Cuban political structure: vanguard party masses.' In Halebsky, S., & Kirk, J. M. (eds), 1985.

Ritter, A. R. M. 1985. 'The Organs of People's Power and the Communist Party.' In Halebsky, S., & J. M. Kirk (eds), 1985.

Rivero Collado, C. 1976. *La Contrarrevolución Cubana*. Madrid, Akal Editor.

Robbins, C. A. 1985. *The Cuban Threat*. Philadelphia, ISHI Publications.

Roca, S. 1976. *Cuban Economic Policy and Ideology: The Ten Million Ton Sugar Harvest*. Beverly Hills, Calif., Sage.

Rodríguez, C. R. 1979. 'Entrevista con Carlos Rafael Rodríguez.' *Areíto*, vol. 6, no. 21.

—— 1981. 'Fundamentos estratégicos de la política exterior de Cuba.' *Cuba Socialista*, December.

Rodríguez, G. M. 1980. *El Proceso de Industrialización de la Economía Cubana*. Havana, Editorial de Ciencias Sociales.

Rodríguez, J. L. 1987a. 'El desarrollo de Cuba en el contexto de la crisis económica Latinoamericana.' *Temas de Economía Mundial* (Revista del CIEM), no. 19.

—— 1987b. 'Agricultural policy and development in Cuba.' In Zimbalist, A. (ed.), 1987.

Salas, L. 1979. *Social Control and Deviance in Cuba*. New York, Praeger.

Shaw, T. 1986. 'US Exclusion of Cubans draws criticism from academics, Special Olympics affected as visa policy is used to press Castro.' *Washington Post*, 12 December.

Simons, W. B. (ed.), 1980. *The Constitutions of the Communist World*. Alphen ann den Rijn, Sijtoff and Noordhoff.

Smith, W. S. 1985. 'US–Cuba relations: twenty-five years of hostility.' In Halebsky, S., & Kirk, J. M. (eds), 1985.

—— 1987. *The Closest of Enemies*. New York, W. W. Norton.

Sobre las Dificultades Objetivas de la Revolución 1979. Havana, Editora Política.

Speaks, L. 1988. *Speaking Out: The Reagan Presidency From Inside The White House*. New York, Charles Scribner's Sons.

Statutes of the Communist Party of Cuba 1976. Havana, Cuba, Department of Revolutionary Orientation of the Central Committee of the Communist Party of Cuba.

Suchlicki, J. 1969. *University Students and Revolution in Cuba: 1920-1968*. Coral Gables, Florida, University of Miami Press.

—— 1974. *Cuba: From Columbus to Castro*. New York, Charles Scribner's.

Sweet, D. R. 1980. 'Expenditures for Cuba's military and internal security forces.' Paper presented at the Latin American Studies Association Meeting, Bloomington, Indiana.

Szulc, T. 1986. *Fidel: A Critical Portrait*. New York, William Morrow.

Talmon, J. L. 1961. *The Origins of Totalitarian Democracy*. New York, Praeger.

The Cuban American National Foundation 1988. *Towards A New US-Cuba Policy*, Washington, D.C.

'The Cuban Exodus: A Symposium' 1981-1982. *Cuban Studies/Estudios Cubanos*, vol. 11, no. 2.

Theriot, L. H. 1982. *Cuba Faces the Economic Realities of the 1980s*. Joint Economic Committee, Congress of the United States. Washington, DC, US Government Printing Office.

Thomas, H. 1971. *Cuba: The Pursuit of Freedom*. New York, Harper & Row.

Toner, R. 1986. 'The President's allies are rallying round . . .'. *New York Times*, 19 December.

Turits, R. 1987. 'Trade, debt, and the Cuban economy.' In Zimbalist, A. (ed.), 1987.

United Nations 1960. *Estudios Demográficos*. As cited in Behm, H. 1980.

—— 1983. *World Statistics in Brief*. New York, United Nations.

Urrutia Lleó, M. 1964. *Fidel Castro and Company, Inc*. New York, Praeger.

US Arms Control and Disarmament Agency. 1987. *World Military Expenditures and Arms Transfers, 1986*. Washington, DC, Defense Program and Analysis Division.

Valdés, N. 1982. 'Cuba's involvement in the Horn of Africa: the Ethiopian–Somali war and the Eritrean conflict.' In Mesa-Lago, C. & Belkin, J. S. (eds), 1982.

Weiss, J. A. 1985. 'The emergence of popular culture.' In Halebski, S., & Kirk, J. M. (eds), 1985.

Wilkerson, L. 1965. *Fidel Castro's Political Programs, From Reformism to 'Marxism-Leninism.'* Latin American Monographs, Center for Latin American Studies, Gainesville, University of Florida.

Wyden, P. 1979. *Bay of Pigs*. New York, Simon and Schuster.

Zaldívar, R. A. 1988. 'Radio Martí: internal static.' *Miami Herald*, 4 January.

Zimbalist, A. 1985. 'Cuban economic planning: organization and performance.' In Halebsky, S., & Kirk, J. M. (eds), 1985.

—— (ed.) 1987. *Cuba's Socialist Economy Toward the 1990s*. Boulder, Colorado, Lynne Rienner Publishers ('Introduction: Cuba's socialist economy toward the 1990s' by A. Zimbalist).

—— & Eckstein, S. 1987. 'Patterns of Cuban development: the first twenty-five years.' In Zimbalist, A. (ed.), 1987.

Newspapers and Periodicals

Granma
Granma Weekly Review
Newsweek
New York Times
Revolución
Time
Washington Post Weekly Edition

Index